Coronado Cuarto Centennial
Publications, 1540 - 1940

Edited by

GEORGE P. HAMMOND

The University of California

Volume III

PUBLISHED UNDER THE
CORONADO HISTORICAL FUND

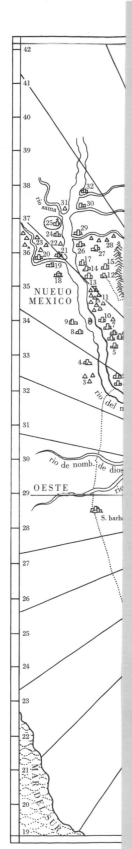

Castaño de Sosa was the next to leave for the north. He uprooted his entire colony of one-hundred-seventy people, and without authorization, and against specific orders to the contrary, embarked upon a venture of colonization.

Morlete, who had delivered the original orders forbidding Castaño to depart, set off in pursuit. Arriving at the pueblo of Santo Domingo, Morlete embraced Castaño, read him the viceroy's orders, and promptly had Castaño put in chains. In no hurry to return, Morlete explored the territory for about thirty days with his shackled captive. On returning to Mexico, Castaño was found guilty of disobeying the orders of the viceroyalty. He was exiled to the Philippines and died at the hands of mutinous Chinese galley slaves. His name was cleared after his death.

The last expedition was that of Leyva and Humaña. This was a punitive expedition to put down an Indian revolt. But Leyva decided to launch a full-scale invasion of New Mexico. When a disagreement arose between the two men, Humaña called Leyva to the camp and murdered him with a butcher knife, thereafter rallying the men around himself. This party journeyed to the Buffalo Plains, the same Quivira that Oñate later traveled to, believed to be located somewhere in southern Kansas.

GEORGE P. HAMMOND, noted Spanish scholar, was director of the famous Bancroft Library and Professor of History at the University of California, Berkeley. He is also general editor of the Coronado Historical Series, and has made many significant contributions to the history of New Mexico and the Southwest.

AGAPITO REY, formerly Professor of Spanish at Indiana University, has translated many works from the Spanish. This volume marks the third time that he and Dr. Hammond have collaborated on a volume of the Coronado Historical Series.

CORONADO CUARTO CENTENNIAL
PUBLICATIONS

THE REDISCOVERY OF NEW MEXICO, 1580-1594

THE MARTÍNEZ MAP OF 1602

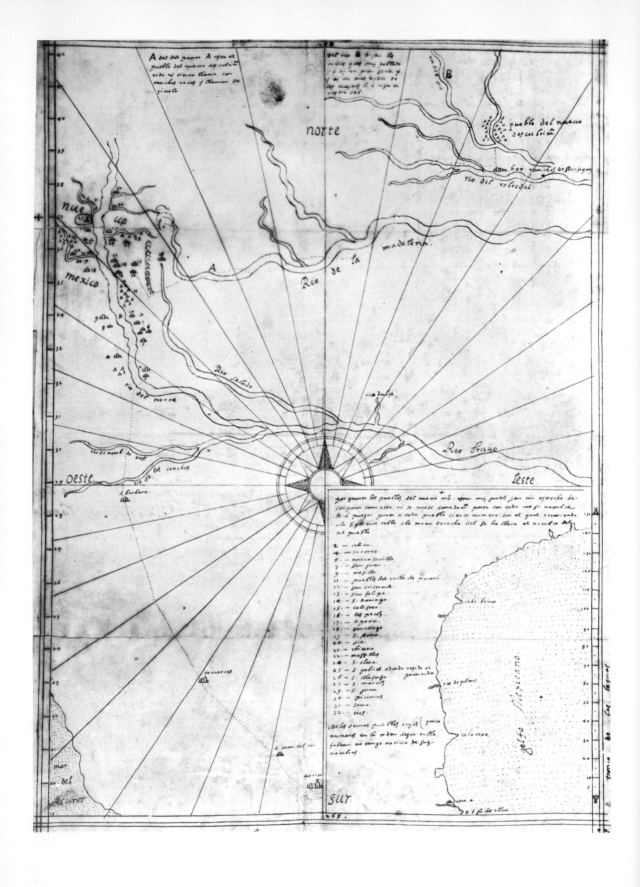

norte

A des del punto A esso el
pueblo del nueuo descubrim[to]
toda es tierra clara con
muchas vacas y llaman de
siuola

del rio B dize la
india y que muy poblado
y que ay vn gran gente y
y ay vn mas noble de
los mayores y digo m[as]
negros del

B

pueblo del nueuo
descubrim[to]

ay 600 ranchos de Santiago
rio del robredal.

Rio de la madalena.

A

mexico

nue   uo

Oeste.   Teste.

Rio salado

rio del norte

rio de nomb de dios

rio de los conchos

S. Barbara

rio dulce

Rio Brauo

por quanto los pueblos del nueuo m[e]x[ico] segun muy puntos son sin estrecha des-
cripcion como esta ni se puede como dem[as] poner con cada vno su nombre
se ha puesto junto a cada pueblo cierto numero con el qual ocurriendo
a la figa con esta tabla a la mano derecha del se ha clara el nombre del
tal pueblo

2 — caloca.
4 — socorro
6 — nueua seuilla
7 — San Juan.
9 — mesilla
11 — pueblo del valle de picara
12 — san cristoual.
13 — San felipe.
14 — S. Domingo.
15 — calispeo.
16 — los peces.
17 — lipoim.
18 — Santiago
19 — S. Anna.
20 — sia.
21 — chicaui
22 — mess.eloz
24 — S. clara.
26 — S. gabriel adonde reside el   gouernador
26 — S. illefonso
27 — S. marcos.
29 — S. Juan.
30 — picurina
31 — sama.
32 — taos.

Selos demas que llos cuys[?] puice
numeros en la orden dizen en lla
faltan no tengo noticia de sus
nombres

cabo brauo

golfo Mexicano

rio de palmos

cabo roxo

cacaxecas

S. Juan del rio

mexico

SUR.

268.

mar
del
Sur

tierra de los caguas

los 5 fte de villa

THE REDISCOVERY OF NEW MEXICO

1580 - 1594

The Explorations of Chamuscado, Espejo,
Castaño de Sosa, Morlete,
and Leyva de Bonilla and Humaña

GEORGE P. HAMMOND, *University of California*

AGAPITO REY, *Indiana University*

THE UNIVERSITY OF NEW MEXICO PRESS

ALBUQUERQUE

1966

F
799
.H33

Manufactured in the United States of America
by the University of New Mexico Printing Plant
Library of Congress Catalog Card No. 66-14778
First edition

And above all, when Espejo's little party of fourteen men and one friar had explored nearly the entire Southwest, from Arizona to Texas, and had returned with the kind of tales every sourdough lives by, what led Castaño de Sosa to uproot his entire colony of some 170 people, in the province of New León, and to lead them to the Pueblo country? He left not only without authorization, but against the express orders of the viceroy, delivered to him personally by Captain Juan Morlete. Or why did Captains Leyva and Humaña, of whose exploits we have no detailed diary, try to do the same, in the face of what had happened to their fellow frontiersmen in this area?

This book, long in preparation, records in diaries and reminiscences what happened during the end of the sixteenth century in the Pueblo country. Some parts of this study were published at the time when the New Mexico Historical Society, under its capable editor, Lansing B. Bloom, launched its famous *Review* in 1926—and was avidly seeking contributions. Some of our earlier works have now been reviewed, re-translated, new notes and annotations provided, to form Volume III of the Coronado Historical Series, launched in 1940 as part of the Coronado Cuarto Centennial celebration. Among the leaders in that regional achievement were our friend, now the distinguished senior senator from New Mexico, Clinton P. Anderson; the late president of the University of New Mexico, James F. Zimmerman; and many well-known leaders of New Mexico and the Southwest.

We regret the delay in publication of this volume, especially since so many subscribers to the Coronado Historical Series have been disappointed in not being able to complete their sets. With the publication of this book, only one remains to finish the series, and that is in the capable hands of an able scholar, France V. Scholes.

GEORGE P. HAMMOND
AGAPITO REY

Madrid, Spain
June 1966

FOREWORD

THE FASCINATION of history is timeless—endless. Man has never ceased to wonder where he came from, how he developed his present characteristics, or the process by which they evolved.

In the early history of America, the origin of its first occupants is still interesting and perplexing. Ethnologists are pretty well agreed on the theory that man, after an origin somewhere in central Asia, made his way via Bering Straits, or possibly the Aleutian Islands, into North America, and thereupon scattered over the land mass of the New World. But there are those who differ, who dream, for example, that man was wafted, perhaps accidentally, by primitive boat, over the vast stretches of the Pacific Ocean, and so reached the shores of the land we know as America.

The Spaniards who trod in the footsteps of Columbus and the first generation of explorers and settlers were filled with this sense of wonder. This was especially true after the discovery of such fabulous cultural centers as Mexico, Yucatan, Guatemala, and Peru. What would they find next? The spirit of adventure applied with equal force to the region we know as northern Mexico and the southern United States. The discovery of silver and gold in present-day Mexico fed their hopes and expectations. One must understand this essential fact to realize why New Mexico was so important, why every expedition of discovery, whether one thinks of Guzmán, Coronado, Ibarra, or Río de Losa, assumed the significance that it did, why expeditions such as those discussed in this volume have stimulated the imaginations of later generations.

After the disappointing reports of the Coronado expedition forty years earlier, what induced eight lonely soldiers to accompany Francisco Sánchez Chamuscado and Fray Agustín Rodríguez to prospect the rumors of a better people, a better land somewhere in the distant north? What led Espejo to spend the fortune he had accumulated in Mexico to lead an expedition the very next year to this same land? The answer lies in the endless curiosity of man, and the expectation of earthly reward and glory.

TO CARRIE AND DOROTHY

CONTENTS

INTRODUCTION

INTRODUCTION

WHEN COLUMBUS discovered America in 1492, he thought he had found a shorter, magic route to India and the treasure-laden Spice Islands of the Orient. Even more significant, that a *mundus novus* lay between Europe and these Eastern lands was left for others to establish. Indeed, explorers who came after him, less inhibited by preconceived ideas of geography, soon recognized that "the Indies" discovered by Columbus were in fact stepping-stones to a new continent, inhabited by strange and different peoples and by plants and animals unknown in Europe. Bit by bit they learned the nature and extent of the Caribbean islands— Santo Domingo, Puerto Rico, Cuba, and Jamaica—conquered their people, and within twenty-five years of Columbus' first voyage began to explore the waters north and west of Cuba and to map in a superficial way the coastline and the character and tremendous resources of the land beyond.

A young man, Hernando Cortés, who already had given evidence of courage, judgment, and skill in handling men and arms, was one of the first to sense the significance of the reports brought back to Cuba from the waters to the west. The fact that he was a favorite of the governor of Cuba naturally aided him in his schemes for advancement. In 1519, encouraged by the accounts of two voyages to the coasts of Yucatán and Tabasco, Cortés obtained permission to follow up these meager discoveries with a new expedition. This was the legendary one that included his famous "army" of about five hundred or five hundred and fifty men equipped with sixteen "noble" horses. This expedition carried out the incredible conquest of Mexico, subjugated its ancient civilization, and brought new honors and wealth to Spain and Spanish arms such as Columbus had never dreamed of. It not only made Cortés a glamorous name among the Spanish conquistadors of the sixteenth century but made the term Mexico synonymous with success, wealth, and glory for God and king. In fact, Cortés's achievement in conquering the Mexican nation and making it pay tribute helped to launch Spain's *Siglo de Oro* and to glorify the kingdom of Charles V, just inherited from Ferdinand and Isabella, as the greatest on earth.[1]

From the time of Cortés, thousands of Spaniards left home to find

---

1. The books on Cortés and the Conquest of Mexico are many. Especially significant among recent studies are Salvador de Madariaga, *Hernán Cortés, Conqueror of Mexico* (1941); and Henry R. Wagner, *The Rise of Fernando Cortés* (1944).

fortune in the New World, with the hope of emulating his achievement. In Peru, Francisco Pizarro proved it could be done when he discovered and took possession of the fabulous Inca empire and seized the gold of the Inca Atahualpa. This was in the early 1530's when the Spanish conquistadors were still at the height of their fame, and when the impossible was always possible.

In Mexico, the border of the conquered area edged steadily northward until, by the end of the sixteenth century, it reached the gulf of California and the present state of Chihuahua. The progress of this conquest, marked by occasional setbacks like the Mixtón war of 1540 in New Galicia, continued without major interruption. If one adventurer failed to find the treasure of his dreams and was struck down, there was always another ready to take his place. All fought with great valor. The native tribes, who clung to their homes and lands and defended them with great courage, yielded or were pushed out of their own country. Usually they remained and became a part of the conquered territory, and saw Spanish posts, presidios, and missions planted in their midst. With new discoveries of gold elsewhere, or of native tribes that could be exploited, the process would be repeated, and the line separating the conquered or "pacified" area from the unknown frontier would advance still further. In this way, one arm of Spain's invading forces struck northward up the Pacific coastal plain; another, separated from the western dagger by the rugged and impenetrable mountain barrier, the Sierra Madre Occidental, pushed up the central plateau. Now and then these pioneer soldier-settlers found traces of the endlessly rumored gold or silver, especially in the area which is now southern Chihuahua.[2]

Led by men like Francisco de Ibarra and Rodrigo del Río de Losa, veterans of exploration and fighting on this frontier, some mining settlements were founded in the wake of the spreading conquest. One of these was Indé, midway between Durango and Santa Bárbara, established in 1567 by Rodrigo del Río, who conquered the Indians in the vicinity and subjected them to Spanish rule at the request of New Vizcaya's governor, Francisco de Ibarra. Later in the same year, in pursuance of similar orders to found settlements on the Conchos river, Rodrigo del Río founded the mining settlement of Santa Bárbara, in the present state of Chihuahua, destined to become one of the richest in northern Mexico. Santa Bárbara lay in the San Bartolomé valley, on the Florido

2. Philip W. Powell in *Soldiers, Indians & Silver, the Northward Advance of New Spain, 1550-1600* (1952), gives an excellent account of the Spanish advance into the regions north of Mexico city. See also J. Lloyd Mecham, *Francisco de Ibarra and Nueva Vizcaya* (1927); and Edward H. Spicer, *Cycles of Conquest; the Impact of Spain, Mexico, and the United States on the Indians of the Southwest, 1533-1960* (1962).

river, a northern branch of the Conchos, seventy-five miles beyond Indé.[3]

The people here belonged to the Conchos nation, occupying a large part of the Conchos valley. Culturally underdeveloped, they wore no clothes and had no permanent habitations, according to Hernán Gallegos, chronicler of the Chamuscado-Rodríguez expedition. They knew nothing of agriculture, lived on ground mesquite, prickly pears, calabashes, roots of various kinds, and on such wild animals as they could capture. Presumably they were useful laborers in the mines of Santa Bárbara, which were rich in ore and prospered miraculously, especially after 1631 and 1632, when the richest strikes were made. Whereas this village numbered but thirty inhabitants in 1575, by 1600 it had increased to seven thousand and had become the largest settlement in New Vizcaya, even larger than the capital city of Durango.[4] The mine of San Francisco del Oro, opened in the 1650's and others still in operation, accounted largely for the growth of the area.

This settlement of Santa Bárbara, or Santa Bárbola, as it was often written in the documents of the sixteenth century, was at that time probably the most renowned spot on the northern prong of Spanish advance in Mexico. It was the magnet that attracted a swarm of frontiersmen—miners, farmers, cattle raisers, priests, and adventurers—and it became the most civilized center of the north. Fabulously wealthy, it beckoned men northward and served as a guidepost for future explorers and conquerors ambitious to discover and subjugate new kingdoms, like legendary Quivira, with its golden palaces and scintillating jewels. Dreams? Of course they were figments of the imagination! But when if ever has man not been lured by such visions, and then watched them come true?

Santa Bárbara was, in short, the focus of sixteenth-century adventurers in northern Mexico, the "end of the line" for layman, soldier, or priest, and the home base or point of concentration for fitting out new prospecting ventures. Here the expeditions of Chamuscado and Espejo, hopeful of finding "another Mexico," were conceived and launched. Probably no other center on Mexico's northern frontier so completely nourished and fed the little groups that were to go still farther into the unknown interior. Nearly four centuries later this city of Santa Bárbara

3. José G. Rocha, "La Primera Fundación Española en Territorio Chihuahuense," in Sociedad Chihuahuense de Estudios Históricos, *Boletín*, July and September, 1938, pp. 67-71, 152-158.

4. Rocha, *op. cit.*, pp. 70-71; Mecham, *Francisco de Ibarra*, p. 230 ff. See also Robert C. West, "The Mining Community in Northern New Spain: The Parral Mining District," *Ibero-Americana*, No. 30 (1949), especially pp. 47-53.

in Chihuahua is still a mining center, but it is a somnolent village of only fifteen thousand inhabitants. Today it is overshadowed by Parral, the city of Chihuahua, and others, but its vast ore dumps give evidence of its ancient pre-eminence.

THE CHAMUSCADO-RODRÍGUEZ EXPEDITION

IN THESE SURROUNDINGS, at San Bartolomé, now Allende, a Franciscan convent was established about the year 1570 on the banks of a tree-lined river. One of the friars in this convent, a lay brother dedicated to the teaching and conversion of the lowly Conchos Indians, was Agustín Rodríguez (or Ruíz, in some accounts), who had shown much skill in dealing with the natives. From them, or perhaps from slave-raiding expeditions, he had learned that farther north there were other nations of idolatrous Indians, hitherto unknown and without the blessings of salvation. Moved by a spirit of charity and the hope of salvation for so many souls, he asked the viceroy, Don Lorenzo Suárez de Mendoza, Marqués de la Coruña, for permission to undertake an expedition to visit these distant peoples. Indeed, in 1580 he went to Mexico city to plead his case before the proper officials of the viceroy's court.[1]

This is one version of the story, and it may be correct, for there was no other practical way to obtain permission for such a project. The alternative was to leave without official approval, as slave-raiding parties were accustomed to do until the late sixteenth century. This was changed by the Laws of 1573, when the Council of the Indies established a new procedure for extending the royal domains. The New Laws of 1542-1543, the first great code for regulating the relations of Spanish conquerors with the Indians, had been only partially successful, and much disorder continued to prevail. Viceroys and audiencias contracted with individuals to lead expeditions of conquest, or permitted governors and adelantados great liberty in doing so, a policy that often led to extreme cruelty and oppression of the natives.

Since it had proved impossible fully to implement the laws of 1542, the legislation of 1573 was enacted. This code was designed to overcome the deficiencies of the earlier regulations respecting exploration and settlement. No longer would "conquests" be permitted; in fact, the use of that word was specifically forbidden. Discoveries were to be undertaken "with peace and mercy," and there would be no excuse for

1. Rocha, *op. cit.*, pp. 154-155; viceroy to the king, November 1, 1582; and also the testimony of Bustamante, Gallegos, and Barrado.

any action that might injure the Indians. Viceroys and governors were still to be alert to new discoveries, to inform themselves fully about them, but they and their agents must use peaceful means in making such investigations.[2]

Similarly, great care was to be exercised in the selection of the persons entrusted with new discoveries. They must be men of approved Christianity, of good conscience, lovers of peace who desired the conversion of the natives; they had to be of the kind that could give absolute assurance that no harm would be done to the Indians. They must do them no wrong, must not take them away from their homes (except for three or four interpreters, who had to be paid for their services), and of course they must not become involved in war or conquest or render aid to one tribe against another.

In the light of the above, priests and friars were to be favored in efforts to discover new lands and to spread the gospel, and they were to be provided with all necessities for such undertakings. No one, not even the religious, would be permitted to explore or settle new regions without a license from the king, or from the viceroy in his name, under pain of death and loss of property. To protect these holy men from hostile or warlike tribes, the missionaries were permitted a soldier escort, which, though small, made possible the continuation of explorations into unknown territory. In this practical manner, the king's conscience was relieved of the accusation of destroying the Indians, an accusation which Fray Bartolomé de las Casas, the famous Protector of the Indians, and others had made much of.[3]

Fray Agustín Rodríguez appears to have been the religious head of the little expedition of 1581 and Captain Francisco Sánchez Chamuscado its military and de facto leader. In a lengthy testimonial of the *méritos y servicios* of Gallegos, notary and chronicler of this expedition, who was then in Spain (1584) seeking to gain some office or reward for his pioneering journey, it is acknowledged that Chamuscado held a commission from the viceroy, authorizing him to make the discovery and to command the soldiers in the party. But he was probably nominated by Fray Agustín, as suggested by the viceroy in his letter of November 1, 1582, to the king. By virtue of this commission, Chamuscado en-

2. These laws are printed in the *Colección de Documentos Inéditos de Indias. . . .* (1864-1884), vol XVI, pp. 143-187. A full discussion of their significance is given by Juan Manzano Manzano, *La Incorporación de las Indias a la Corona de Castilla* (Madrid, 1948), pp. 207-217. Clarence H. Haring, *The Spanish Empire in America* (1947), pp. 111-112, merely notes that these laws crystalized preceding legislation relating to discovery, conquest, and settlement.

3. The latest study of the great friar is Henry R. Wagner's *Bartolomé de las Casas, Protector of the Indians,* now in press.

listed eight additional soldiers, mostly from Santa Bárbara, though twenty had been authorized by the viceroy.[4]

Baltasar Obregón, one of the principal chroniclers of northern Mexico in the late sixteenth century, has preserved the names of the soldiers, as has Gallegos, though the latter mentions them but casually in the pages of his "Relation." They were Hernando Barrado, Pedro de Bustamante, Hernán Gallegos, Pedro Sánchez de Chávez, Felipe de Escalante, Pedro de Herrera, Pedro Sánchez de Fuensalida and his brother Juan, together with Captain Francisco Sánchez Chamuscado.[5]

Accompanying Fray Agustín were two other friars, Francisco López, who went as guardian or superior, and Juan de Santa María; so the entire party consisted of three friars and nine soldiers, nineteen Indian servants, six hundred head of stock, and ninety horses, in addition to provisions and articles for barter, as permitted by law.

These servants of King Philip, soldiers and friars, motivated by different forces, were destined to become the real discoverers of New Mexico. Completely unaware, apparently, of Coronado's exploration of 1540-1542, which was not strange in an era when there were almost no printed books except for religious tracts, these men set out on their mission into the unknown wilderness. They were moved by a spirit of Christian idealism and sacrifice in bringing the light of civilization to new lands and peoples, a desire to serve both God and king, and the hope of bettering their own fortunes.

There has been some question among students of southwestern history as to who should receive credit as the promoter or chief spirit in the organization of this expedition, Fray Agustín Rodríguez or Captain Francisco Sánchez Chamuscado.[6] Though this is a question of some delicacy since it involves the primacy of church and state, it is never-

4. The viceroy's letter is given on p. 123. For the Gallegos document, see "El Capitán Hernán Gallegos sobre que se le encomiende el descubrimiento de la Nueva México." Also cited as "Información de los méritos y servicios del capitán Hernán Gallegos." Archivo General de Indias (hereafter cited as A.G.I.), Patronato, legajo 77. Most of this record was made in Mexico city in October 1582, and the latter part in Seville in September 1584.

5. Obregón's History of 16th Century Explorations in Western America, tr. and ed. by George P. Hammond and Agapito Rey (1928), p. 269.

6. Cf. J. Lloyd Mecham, "The Second Spanish Expedition to New Mexico," in New Mex. Hist. Rev., vol. I (1926), pp. 266-267; and also his "Supplementary Documents relating to the Chamuscado-Rodríguez Expedition," in Southwestern Hist. Quar., vol. xxix (1926), pp. 224-231.

Father Zephyrin Engelhardt in his study of the expedition held that Chamuscado and the soldiers had come merely to escort the missionaries so that they might begin the conversion of the Indians, and that Chamuscado had exceeded his authority in exploring the country and opposing the determination of the friars to remain in New Mexico. See "El Yllustre Señor Xamuscado," in Southwestern Hist. Quar., vol. xxix (1926), pp. 296-300; and a review of Mecham's article, cited above, in The Southwestern Catholic, January 6 and 13, 1922, published at Santa Fé, New Mexico.

theless largely of academic interest and import. Both elements, the priestly and the military, it is recognized, were indispensable to the success of the expedition—the friars to convert the natives and the soldiers to protect the friars from Indian hostility, as well as to explore the land. In the final analysis, it was the king, as the practical head of both entities, who authorized the enterprise, and both groups had to answer to him for their accomplishments, and to appeal to him for the means and resources to continue their functions.

Hernán Gallegos has left the best account of the Chamuscado-Rodríguez exploration that has been preserved (presented herewith in translation), although Baltasar Obregón adds some details in his chronicle which are very good for both expeditions. Though brief, they are specific, and either confirm other reports of these explorations or add details not mentioned in them. Among modern students, J. Charles Kelley has made an archaeological-historical study of the Conchos area, based on field excavations, covering the first portion of the route, extending along the Conchos river and its junction with the Río Grande, an excellent contribution to the literature of northern Mexico.[7] Earlier studies of special significance for the pueblos of the Río Grande include Adolph F. Bandelier's *Final Report of Investigations among the Indians ofthe Southwestern United States* (2 vols. 1890-1892) . This was a pioneer work of great value, but it should be used in conjunction with later studies such as Reginald G. Fisher's "Archaeological Survey of the Pueblo Plateau" (1931), and H. P. Mera's "Population Changes in the Río Grande Glaze-Paint Area" (1940).

The Chamuscado-Rodríguez party set out from Santa Bárbara June 5, 1581, descended the Río Florido a dozen leagues to the Conchos, thence followed its course for another fifty, most of the way through the lands of the lowly Conchos Indians. At the modern Cuchillo Parado, a ridge called the Sierra Grande separated these Indians from other tribes down the river. These were the Cabris of Gallegos, called Passaguates by Luxán of the Espejo party a year later, and now known as Julimes. At Cuchillo Parado the party crossed this ridge, then again followed generally the Conchos to San Juan Bautista, a few leagues from its junction with the Río Grande, where the soldiers struck northward to that river at the pueblo of San Bernardino near the modern Porvenir, about twelve miles above the junction, generally called La Junta. It is not clear how much exploration Chamuscado's men engaged in before leaving the densely populated Conchos-Río Grande area, for they soon

7. J. Charles Kelley, "The Historic Indian Pueblos of La Junta de los Ríos," in *New Mex. Hist. Rev.*, vol. XXVII (1952), pp. 257-295; and vol. XXVIII (1953), pp. 21-51.

continued upstream in the direction of their real objective—the settled regions of which they had heard rumors while in Santa Bárbara.

The people at the junction (variously called Patarabueyes, Passaguates, and Jumanos) had a culture superior to that of the Conchos, lived in permanent dwellings, and though afraid of the Spaniards whose appearance in the past had invariably meant a slave-raiding party, were soon persuaded of the friendly intentions of the newcomers.

The interrelationships of these tribes at La Junta, usually called Jumanos, have long puzzled scholars. Carl O. Sauer (1934) stated that the Jumanos inhabited not only the area about La Junta but extended up both sides of the Río Grande about halfway to El Paso and eastward into the Texas plains. In his opinion these La Junta tribes had ranged eastward into the Buffalo Plains from the earliest Spanish times. Then, as the Apaches farther north began to expand and exert pressure toward the south, the Jumanos drifted away from the settlements along the Río Grande, generally toward the east, and some of them were absorbed by the Apache and Caddoan tribes, while others were absorbed among the Conchos where Chamuscado, Espejo, and other early Spanish explorers found them.[8]

France Scholes (1940), in a discerning analysis of the Jumano puzzle, i.e., the relationship of the various tribes at La Junta with the Jumanos of New Mexico and Texas, conjectured that the Spaniards applied the name Jumano to all *indios rayados,* whether they were tattooed, painted, smeared, striped, or dyed, irrespective of where they lived.[9] Body decoration was of course a widespread trait among the Indians of the Southwest. He points out that Gallegos did not use the term Jumano in speaking of the tribes at La Junta, nor did Luxán, but only Espejo, and he applied it only to the natives he met on his return from New Mexico between the Pecos river and the Río Grande in 1583. Scholes is not convinced, therefore, of the soundness of using the name Jumano as an alternative for Patarabueyes at La Junta.

More recently, J. Charles Kelley in his archaeological investigations in the Conchos-La Junta region (1948-1951) came to the conclusion that the Patarabueyes were a fairly homogeneous cultural unit, but distinct from the Jumanos, and that they were a linguistic rather than an ethnic group. In this reasoning he finds some support in Bandelier's

8. Carl O. Sauer, "Distribution of Original Tribes and Languages in Northwestern Mexico," *Ibero-Americana,* No. 5 (1934).

9. France V. Scholes and H. P. Mera, "Some Aspects of the Jumano Problem," in *Contributions to American Anthropology and History,* No. 34, Carnegie Institution of Washington, Publication 523 (1940).

work, which suggested that the Patarabueyes and Jumanos, though living together at La Junta, were in reality two separate groups.[10]

Jack D. Forbes, in his review of the Southwestern tribes, accepts Scholes's account of the origin of the term Jumano, namely that it was used for widely dispersed groups of painted or striped Indians, but points out that according to our best historical account, that of Luxán, the Jumanos in the 1580's were a group of Indians living between La Junta and the Pecos river. As for the people at La Junta, called Pata-rabueyes at this time, he believes that the Otomoacos were identical with the Cholomes, and the Abriaches with the Julimes. By the 1620's, usage of the term Jumanos for the La Junta people had disappeared and it belonged properly only to the Jumanos of southwestern Texas. That is, down to 1700, they were the Plains people, living between La Junta and the Colorado river of Texas, and the Tompiros of Jumano pueblo, New Mexico.[11]

About 1700, continues Forbes, a new group of Jumanos located in present Oklahoma entered into history. They were Tawehash and other Wichitan groups of Caddoans. Indeed, to the Spaniards of New Mexico they were the only Jumanos after that date, though in the south the old Jumanos of the La Junta-San Antonio region continued to exist.

Leaving La Junta and proceeding up the Río Grande, Chamuscado's party met different tribes, but our chronicler, Gallegos, is often vague and indefinite in his descriptions, particularly after he reached the first pueblos of present New Mexico. This was a few miles south of the modern San Marcial, about thirty miles below Socorro. Obviously warned of the approach of these strangers with their terrible horses, the inhabitants, now known as Piros, had fled their homes.

Thus far, the explorers had traveled on the west side of the Río Grande, so far as can be determined from the sources, though it does not seem plausible that Gallegos, the diarist, could describe the pueblos on both sides of the river, and give the number of houses and population in each, without crossing the stream from time to time. He makes no mention of such crossings, however, though they would have been quite feasible at that time of the year, when the river would be very

10. Adolph F. A. Bandelier, *Final Report of Investigations among the Indians of the Southwestern United States* . . . Part I (1890), pp. 80-81, 84-85; and J. Charles Kelley, *Jumano and Patarabueye: Relations at La Junta de los Ríos*. Ph.D. thesis. Cambridge, 1947.

11. Jack D. Forbes, "Unknown Athapaskans: The Identification of the Jano, Jocome, Jumano, Manso, Suma, and other Indian Tribes of the Southwest," in *Ethnohistory* (1959), pp. 97-159; and also his *Apache, Navaho, and Spaniard* (Norman, Okla, 1960), pp. 47-56.

low. Harrington in about 1910, observed that its waters frequently
sank into the sand a short distance above Bernalillo.[12]

When Chamuscado and party reached the first pueblo of New Mexico, they found it abandoned and in ruins. They were pleased to note
that the walls had apparently been three stories high, an indication of
an opulent and substantial society. The next day, at a distance of two
leagues, they found a living pueblo, though the occupants had fled in
fear. Soon, however, a few Indians, bolder than the rest, came back, en-
ticed by friendly gestures, and when they realized that the visitors meant
them no harm, more of their people returned. "There was not a day
when we were not surrounded and accompanied by more than 12,000
people," wrote Gallegos in his enthusiasm. To the nine soldiers and
three friars, with their nineteen servants, the number of their hosts
might indeed have seemed to multiply into the thousands.

At the first uninhabited pueblo, Captain Chamuscado and his men,
as agents of the king, took possession of the land on August 21, 1581.
They named the pueblo where the act was performed San Felipe, and
also gave that name to the entire province.[13] The river they called
Guadalquivir, in memory of the largest river in southern Spain. The
name San Felipe, as applied to the Pueblo country, did not long sur-
vive. At first the province was called San Felipe or San Felipe del Nuevo
México. Gallegos generally used the term San Felipe, but this seems
not to have been used when Espejo and his party started north in the
autumn of 1582. Obregón in his *Historia,* written in 1584, almost invariably wrote San Felipe del Nuevo México. In the Espejo documents,
1582-1583, the term was shortened to New Mexico, by which it has been
known ever since.[14]

Up to the point where the pueblos of New Mexico begin, about
thirty miles south of Socorro, Gallegos' narrative follows a chronological sequence, enabling us to follow his trail very well. This is not so
thereafter, when his description takes on a more general or topical
nature. The only specific dates he gives after August 21, when the party
reached San Felipe, are September 2, when Chamuscado took possession
of the pueblo of Cáceres, located in the Bernalillo area; September 6,
when the same ceremony was performed at Valladolid, which may have

12. John P. Harrington, "The Ethnogeography of the Tewa," in *29th Annual Report,*
Bureau of Ethnology (1916), p. 101.
13. See the Gallegos and Pedrosa lists of pueblos, and also Gallegos' chapter 8.
14. Cf. Lansing B. Bloom, "Who Discovered New Mexico," in *New Mex. Hist. Rev.,* vol.
xv, pp. 101-132. In the chapter on the Espejo expedition in Juan González de Mendoza's
History of China, there is the statement that they called the province "New Mexico because of its many likenesses to the old Mexico."

been Zía; September 10, when Gallegos as notary drew up an official protest against the departure of Fray Juan de Santa María for Mexico, while they were in the Galisteo valley, although he does not record the name of the pueblo where this happened; September 28, when the party set out from the pueblo of Malpartida (San Marcos) for the buffalo country; October 9 and 19, while on the buffalo trip to the plains of eastern New Mexico, where they found great herds of these monstrous animals; January 31, 1582, when the party left Puaray and started the return journey to Mexico; and February 13, 1582, when an affidavit was drawn up, protesting the decision of Friars López and Rodríguez to remain at Puaray. The document does not name the place where this act was performed, so it may have been drawn up later (or they may have dallied awhile among the pueblos before actually setting out for home).

While Gallegos does not describe the explorations of the Chamuscado party to our satisfaction, he does make it clear that they covered a wide area, probably visiting most of the present-day pueblos except those about Taos and those in Arizona. Indeed, there is included in his narrative not only his own "Account of the Pueblos Visited," but also a second list, only slightly different, which was drawn up by a notary, Martín de Pedrosa, probably in the office of the viceroy and at his order.[15] This Pedrosa list was evidently based on documents of the expedition that no longer exist, and perhaps on oral testimony of the returning soldiers. Both accounts of these pueblos name San Felipe as the first one the Spaniards found, and then continue by naming or describing some sixty-odd towns that they saw or heard of. The Pedrosa document is therefore of the greatest importance in New Mexico history, even though neither of these lists of pueblos gives the native names of towns visited, to the confusion of modern archaeologists, ethnologists, and historians. These accounts of the pueblos do, however, tell a little about each one—the number of houses, how many stories high, and the name applied to each. As the names given were, in the main, Spanish— the explorers were ignorant of the native languages—they are, unfortunately, of little value in identifying them with modern geography and place names. Occasionally, however, the chroniclers used the native name for a pueblo, as in the case of Acoma and Zuñi, which helps in some measure to pinpoint the expedition's itinerary. We present a more detailed analysis of the conjectural location of these pueblos at the end of this Introduction.

15. See pp. 115-120.

Study of the Gallegos "Relation" and allied documents, with some help from the Luxán and Espejo accounts of their trip the next year, shows that the small Chamuscado party explored the Río Grande valley as far north as the Queres towns, reconnoitered the Galisteo basin and the Jémez valley, and then visited the classic pueblos of Acoma and Zuñi, so outstanding they could not be missed. The Spaniards also heard of the Hopi pueblos in Arizona—the Hopis were called Moqui at that time—but did not venture to go that far. They did, however, on their return trip, visit the Saline towns back of the Manzano mountains in the vicinity of Estancia and Willard, New Mexico, where the salt marshes still exist, much as in the sixteenth century. They also went to investigate the reports of that strange animal, the buffalo, going as far as the Canadian river. To these extensive plains they gave the name of "Plains of the Cattle," or Buffalo Plains.

While returning to Mexico, Gallegos reports that Chamuscado fell ill and died when only thirty leagues from Santa Bárbara. Luxán, who accompanied Espejo over this same route the next year, was more specific and noted that Chamuscado was buried at a spot called El Xacal—the hut—two leagues down the Conchos from the San Pedro river. This was near modern Julimes, Chihuahua.

The return of the Chamuscado party to Santa Bárbara on April 15, 1582, with stories of the discovery of a vast new country, heavily populated, the people living in large houses and having cotton clothing, created great excitement on the frontier, but also some consternation. Fray Bernardino Beltrán at Santa Bárbara, saddened that his co-workers, Friars López and Rodríguez, had remained in Puaray to begin the conversion of the Indians among strange and possibly dangerous heathens, set about finding means to succor them. Anxiety for their safety increased when it became known that Fray Juan de Santa María, who had left New Mexico on September 7, 1581, unaccompanied by any escort, much against the wishes of the soldiers and the other friars, had been killed three days later, probably by the eastern Tigua (Tiwa). The Chamuscado party, which had learned of this murder from the Indians in the Galisteo valley on their return from the trip to the Buffalo Plains, feigned ignorance of it, while they continued their exploration of the Pueblo area. On their return to Santa Bárbara, however, they told of their adventures, and also of the martyrdom of Father Santa María, and many feared that the same fate might befall his brother friars at Puaray.[16]

16. Cf. pp. 127-144; and J. Lloyd Mecham, "The Martyrdom of Father Juan de Santa María," in *The Catholic Hist. Rev.*, vol. VI (1920), pp. 308-321.

Frontier entrepreneurs, always alert for fresh enterprises, were excited by the prospects of wealth in the newly discovered region. Naturally, the returning soldiers could not keep the good news of their discovery to themselves. In fact, they had fired their harquebuses in salute on their arrival at Santa Bárbara to let the people know they were safe. Within a few days, when it became clear that a great new kingdom had been found, a move got under way at Santa Bárbara to arrest Gallegos, seize his papers as notary, and "to place the new land under the jurisdiction of Diego de Ibarra." This was evidently a maneuver of the old-timers of the region, who had no intention of allowing Gallegos and his few companions to take this bonanza for themselves—only eight of them, now that Chamuscado was dead. Gallegos and Bustamante managed to escape their clutches, however, and reached Mexico City on May 8, 1582, with their papers, and reported on their adventures to the viceroy and audiencia a week later. We give their testimony in the documents of this volume.[17]

In the months that followed, Gallegos became one of the contenders for the honor and reward of "pacifying" New Mexico, that is, settling it with Spaniards, and went to Spain to carry on his campaign. There he submitted the appropriate petitions to king and council, but though he was described as a man of ability, both with pen and sword, he was not successful in his quest.[18]

Meanwhile, one can imagine how the frontier must have buzzed with excitement at the news brought back about the pueblos of New Mexico. In contrast with the impoverished or roving tribes of Chihuahua and neighboring areas, the new region promised great rewards. It took time and money, however, to follow up such news, and before the slow-moving bureaucracy at Mexico city could do anything, the men of the frontier had taken matters into their own hands and launched a new expedition.

17. Viceroy Don Lorenzo Suárez de Mendoza, Count of Coruña, old and inefficient, died in 1582. For a time the audiencia ruled, but the archbishop, Moya de Contreras, who became viceroy in 1584, kept the king informed of what went on in New Spain in the interim. Gallegos gives the date of his return to Mexico city near the end of his "Relation."
18. "Información de los méritos y servicios del capitán Hernán Gallegos," 1582-1584. A.G.I., *Patronato*, legajo 77. Gallegos was still in Spain in 1589, as this record shows, bombarding king and council with petitions that he be favored with the governorship of New Mexico, or at least with some financial aid, as he had spent everything he had in the king's service and was in debt, both in Madrid and in Seville.

THE ESPEJO EXPEDITION

SUCH WAS THE CHAIN of circumstances that gave rise to the next step in New Mexico's history, the Espejo expedition, which was in itself a marvel of frontier improvisation. The leader, Antonio de Espejo, was one of those adventurous Spaniards who had come to Mexico to seek favor and fortune. He arrived in 1571, in the company of the Chief Inquisitor, Pedro Moya de Contreras, sent by the king to establish the Inquisition as a separate and formal tribunal in New Spain.

At this time, in the 1570's, there was great activity in the northern interior of Mexico, where cattle ranches, mines, missions, and presidios had reached the present limits of southern Chihuahua. As far as the 21st parallel, one hundred and fifty miles or so north of Mexico city, the tribes had been sedentary and docile, living in permanent villages and readily subjected to the yoke of conversion and tribute paying. This was not true of the northern tribes. They were independent, less firmly tied to village life, and either fled to the hills or stood their ground and fought when threatened by an invader.

Along with others, Antonio de Espejo and his brother, Pedro Muñoz de Espejo, had become successful cattle ranchers on this northern frontier. Antonio not only owned a number of estancias in the Querétaro and Celaya districts, but maintained his ties in Mexico city.[1]

Then something happened which changed Espejo's career from that of a rich and prominent official to a fugitive from justice. While preparing for a roundup of his cattle on April 5, 1581, near Celaya, one of his vaqueros, Sebastián López, feigned illness and refused to take part, so runs the story. This infuriated Espejo, who threatened to kill him, as he had another Indian cowboy some time earlier. Thereupon, four men, aroused by Espejo's threats, deserted, reaching Aguas Calientes the next morning, where two of them had gone to get their wives.

---

1. Very little is known of Espejo's early life in Mexico, but see G. R. G. Conway, "Antonio de Espejo, as a Familiar of the Mexican Inquisition, 1572-1578," in *New Mex. Hist. Rev.*, vol. VI (1931), pp. 1-20. Conway found some Inquisition records showing that Espejo in 1572, as a familiar of the Inquisition (that is, a confidential officer), arrested one of the English sailors, then living in Mexico, who had come on the unfortunate "Jesus of Lübeck," John Hawkins' ship. At that time Espejo, age 34, was a cattle trader. Later, in 1578, Espejo (who then gave his age as 36) charged that some of his cattle had been seized and were being slaughtered in the Mexico city slaughterhouse, whereupon he, with two vaqueros, forcibly broke in and drove away about twenty, or perhaps twenty-four, out of the forty-four that had been seized. Though arrested and thrown into jail, he was released on bond, and no further action seems to have been taken against him, "probably because he was protected by the considerable privileges granted to familiars of the Holy Office," says Conway. The inventory of Espejo's effects made at the time of his arrest show him to have lived in refinement and comfort.
 Cf. also Henry R. Wagner, *The Spanish Southwest* (1937), vol. I, pp. 153-163, who discusses chiefly bibliographical knowledge about Espejo. Wagner adds a note that in 1575 Espejo petitioned to have his daughter Juana, age three, born out of wedlock by Elvira Cansina, declared legitimate, that he and his wife were both old, and that he wished Juana to be his sole heir. See "Legitimación de Juana de Espejo, México, 22 de marzo de 1575," in A.G.I., *Audiencia de México*, legajo 100.

Unfortunately for them, Pedro Muñoz de Espejo and a couple of his men, heavily armed, were there also; a fight ensued in which one vaquero was killed and another wounded. One of the survivors of the brawl brought the story to the lieutenant alcalde mayor of Querétaro who made a complete investigation, the record of which has been preserved.[2]

Both of the Espejo brothers were charged with complicity in this murder, and a long drawn-out trial followed in Mexico city. Pedro Muñoz de Espejo, as the actual murderer, received a heavy punishment, but Antonio escaped with a fine—which he made no effort to pay.[3] Instead, he absented himself from the viceregal capital and took refuge on the Chihuahua frontier, where he was fortunate to be on hand about the time of the return of the Chamuscado party in 1582 and so to hear of its great success.

These circumstances, Espejo's voluntary exile, return of the Chamuscado party without the friars, and Franciscan anxiety for the safety of the two brethren who had remained at Puaray, played into his hands, and he was quick to take advantage of the opportunity by offering to lead a rescue expedition, at his own cost. The viceroy, too, was moved by the wonderful accounts of the new discovery, which he verified by obtaining sworn affidavits from several of the participants. He then proceeded to inform himself fully as to the number of soldiers and equipment that might be required to rescue the friars and to bring back more information about the country.

His adviser was Rodrigo del Río de Losa, acknowledged as one of the best frontier experts of the day, who recommended that an expedition of from eighty to one hundred men be sent to New Mexico. However, when it was learned from an Indian servant of Chamuscado named Francisco that the friars had been slain and the land was in revolt, he urged that the number be increased to at least three hundred.[4] Such an armed expedition required the approval of the king; until then nothing could be done. This would clearly involve a long delay, which is exactly what would have happened had it not been for Antonio de Espejo's eagerness to assume the responsibility for sending a small reconnoitering party to New Mexico to ascertain the actual state of affairs.

2. J. Lloyd Mecham, "Antonio de Espejo and his Journey to New Mexico," *Southwestern Hist. Quar.*, vol. xxx (1926), pp. 115-116.

3. *Ibid.*, pp. 117-118.

4. Letter of the viceroy to the king, November 1, 1582, p. 123. Rodrigo del Río's letters are printed in Pacheco and Cárdenas, *Col. Doc. Inéd*, vol. xv, pp. 137-146. Cf. Testimony of Hernando Barrado, p. 139.

The Chihuahua frontier, in the meantime, was alive with excitement, for while the viceroy and his advisers in Mexico city went about the time-consuming and routine business of collecting more information about "the province of San Felipe," the people of the frontier, closer to the scene, were ready and anxious to take the first gamble, believing that great riches were just over the hill, almost within their grasp. By chance, Antonio de Espejo, as related above, was in their midst, though hiding out from the law, a fact not then known to them. He must have appeared to be a smart businessman, eager to participate in new investments and mining explorations. Therefore, when the Franciscans became impatient with government red tape and delays, they readily accepted Espejo's offer to bear the cost of a rescue party. For this purpose a permit would be needed, and when Fray Bernardino Beltrán of Durango offered to obtain "the authorization and permission of his superior," all seemed to be in readiness for the journey.[5] According to Espejo's account, published hereinafter, the permit was actually given by Captain Juan Ontiveros, alcalde mayor of Cuatro Ciénegas, at the request of Fray Bernardino, whereupon Espejo enlisted fourteen soldiers and got together the necessary equipment—one hundred and fifteen horses and mules, some servants, arms, and provisions—preparatory to starting out from San Bartolomé on November 10, 1582. Not all of the equipment or supplies were furnished by Espejo, according to Obregón, who stated that while he gave them everything they needed, the authorities of Santa Bárbara helped as much as possible and invested money in the enterprise.[6]

These may be the essential facts, or Espejo may have glossed them over to soothe official displeasure due to the lawsuits of 1581-1582. Luxán, the best diarist of the expedition, giving a somewhat different account, wrote that "Juan de Ibarra, lieutenant-governor of Nueva Vizcaya, had issued a permit to Fray Pedro de Heredia for the expedition with authority to take along all who might wish to go," and this is corroborated by Obregón. As it happened, there was some confusion about this Fray Pedro, who evidently did not have permission from his superior to leave. One day after the party had started out, a Fray Luis arrived with letters from his custodian ordering Fray Pedro to return and to abandon the expedition. Luxán's account suggests that Fray Luis and two others (Juan Bautista and Francisco de San Miguel) were to go instead, since they had received permission from their prelate.

5. Espejo's "Narrative," p. 215.
6. *Obregón's History*, p. 316.

Two soldiers, Diego Pérez de Luxán and Miguel Sánchez Valenciano (the latter to sell the rest of his property in San Bartolomé and to bring his wife and children), accompanied Fray Pedro. There, evidently at San Bartolomé, the friar received letters from Juan de Ibarra to wait for ten or twelve days, and he would secure a license for him from the custodian as well as authority for Fray Pedro to appoint as captain of the expedition anyone he pleased. When Luxán and Valenciano left to join the party, Fray Pedro sent word with them to travel slowly and that he would catch up. Meantime, he requested Fray Bernardino Beltrán to care for the sacred vestments and to administer the holy sacraments.[7] So far, no leader had been appointed, though it may be assumed that Espejo acted in this capacity, in view of his having recruited the men and paid most of the costs of outfitting them. His election to this position was to come later.

In this manner the little group, including Espejo and the soldiers who had volunteered, began its journey, accompanied by Fray Bernardino Beltrán, the only friar. The other missionaries drop out of the record for the time being, although at least one of them, Francisco de San Miguel, became a part of the pioneer band that accompanied Don Juan de Oñate sixteen years later when he established the first Spanish settlements in New Mexico.

The little party which had left San Bartolomé on November 10, 1582, followed the San Gregorio river to its junction with the Florido. These two streams unite to form the Conchos. Thence the explorers went down the latter in a general way to the Río Grande. Near the towns of San Pedro and Cuchillo Parado, they cut across a mountain ridge, very difficult for the pack animals, and then again followed the Conchos, though they now left behind the Conchos Indians and found themselves among a people called Passaguates by Luxán and Obregón, and Cabris by Gallegos. These Cabris-Passaguates were in the Cuchillo Parado valley. Forbes identifies the Cabris as Julimes.[8]

Continuing on their way, the Spaniards entered the land of the Patarabueyes, a nickname that had been applied to them by soldiers on slave-hunting raids, says Luxán. They were really Otomoacos, or Cholomes. These Patarabueyes were bold enough to attack the Spanish horses, killing three and wounding several, after which the leader posted guards at night and took precautions to avoid the repetition of such incidents. The Indians, fearful of retribution, fled to the hills, and it was with some difficulty that they were induced to return to their

7. See Luxán's "Journal," p. 155.
8. Forbes, *Apache, Navaho, and Spaniard*, p. 47.

villages. This was effected through Pedro, a lad of thirteen years, servant of Diego Pérez de Luxán, who spoke their language and convinced them of the friendly motives of the Spaniards.

The party continued down the Conchos to La Paz, identified as San Juan Bautista, where the people spoke a different tongue from the Otomoacos, "although they are friends and understand one another." Luxán added, "They are all inter-related, and for this reason the whole province is called that of the Patarabueyes."

From La Paz, or San Juan Bautista, the Espejo party left the Río Conchos and struck directly northward to the Río Grande. About five leagues above the junction, they halted at a pueblo they named San Bernardino, on the west bank, "composed of flat-roofed houses half under and half above the ground." Here they were met by Juan Cantor, a friendly Indian of the region who had been to New Mexico with Fray Agustín Rodríguez the year previous and who was an uncle of the lad Pedro, Luxán's interpreter. Most of the local Indians had fled to the hills, but, reassured by Juan Cantor, they soon returned, kissed the hand of Father Bernardino, and offered the Spaniards gifts of food and other things. With the establishment of such friendly relations, the Espejo party remained in this pueblo for eight days, "because some of the mounts were worn out. . . ."

Meantime, Diego Pérez de Luxán, four soldiers, and Father Bernardino, accompanied by many natives, went down the river five leagues to La Junta, junction of the Conchos and Río Grande, where they were well received by a pueblo of the Abriaches (Julimes) nation and given food and other tokens of friendship. While part of the men were occupied in this exploration, the others had remained at San Bernardino, vainly awaiting Fray Pedro de Heredia's return. Reunited again on December 11, the soldiers exchanged stories of their experiences. Especially interesting was a report that Juan Cantor, the interpreter, had picked up from some Conchos Indians to the effect that the friars in New Mexico were still alive—and had not been killed after all. This story animated all of the soldiers, and especially Fray Bernardino, who urged that they wait no longer for Fray Pedro, but set out at once to rescue the missionaries at Puaray.

Until this time no leader had been appointed for the expedition, but now the men met and elected from among themselves one of their comrades, Antonio de Espejo, "as captain and chief magistrate, in the name of his majesty the king," and took the oath of fealty to him. In this manner, Espejo became the official leader as well as the chief financial backer of the party.[9] In his own report to the king, Espejo made no mention of this incident. Perhaps this was because he wanted to leave the impression in the royal mind that he had been the leader of the rescue party from the start, or that he would become the successful conqueror of this vast new region and so be forgiven any past misdeeds.

Setting out from San Bernardino on the Río Grande on December 17, 1582, the expedition followed its course upstream, sometimes leaving it for a distance but always returning to it. At each ranchería, says Luxán, they would get some of its people to accompany them to the next village, and in addition, they kept careful guard over their camp and the stock. For forty-five leagues from La Junta, they were among the friendly Otomoacos (Cholomes), and then, on January 2, reached the Caguates (Sumas), where the grandfather of Pedro, the interpreter, lived. They were akin to the Otomoacos and spoke a related tongue. Here Chamuscado had left a worn-out sorrel horse, which the natives had cared for and now returned to Espejo.

The next four days the party traveled among the Caguates, all of whom were friendly, and then they came to the Tampachoas, or Tampachons (possibly Mansos), near modern El Paso, where the men rested and recuperated for a week. All of these nations were related to the Otomoacos, wrote Luxán, and generally wore the same type of clothing.

During the following three weeks, while the Espejo party traveled from below El Paso to above the Elephant Butte, near the modern Elephant Butte dam on the Río Grande, Luxán makes no mention of seeing any other Indians, but on January 31, 1583, when eleven leagues beyond "the large black rock," i.e., Elephant Butte, he notes that "we found an abandoned pueblo with the houses in ruins." In another three leagues, they came to another abandoned pueblo where they met some Indians with whom they conversed, but only by signs. These people had native chickens, i.e., turkeys, in abundance, and wore clothing of cotton and tanned deerskins. The fields were full of stubble, "which was the salvation of our horses," wrote Luxán. The date was now February 1. Espejo's party had reached the region of the Piro Indians, extending from a few miles south of San Marcial, near the site of the later Fort Craig, to old Sevilleta, about two miles north of La Joya. Obregón wrote that the lands occupied by the Piros were twenty leagues long by six wide and that they contained twelve pueblos, with a total of two hundred and fifty houses.[10]

9. Luxán's "Journal," p. 165.
10. *Obregón's History*, p. 340.

Before leaving the friendly Piros, the Spaniards learned from them by signs that the friars at Puaray had been killed, and that the Tigua were armed and in revolt. Disturbed by the news, the little group debated what to do, some arguing they should build a fortress and leave a part of the men and horses there while the others went to reconnoiter the situation among the hostile Tigua; others argued they "should cross to New Mexico, of which we had heard, and not go to Puala"— just what Luxán meant by this reference to New Mexico is not clear— but the final decision was to keep the party united under their leader, Espejo, put on a bold front, and forge ahead to find out definitely what had happened to the friars.

While waiting to gather such information as they could, Espejo decided to explore a province said to be ten leagues to the east, the Magrias, keeping in mind the idea of building a fortress if a suitable place for one could be found. For this purpose, he took along only Diego Pérez de Luxán, Gregorio Hernández, and some Indian servants. At the end of the first day's march, February 10, 1583, they reached the first pueblo of this people. Many fled, but others were friendly, and soon all returned to greet the Spaniards in peace. Luxán says they erected a large cross in token of possession, but that they did not formally carry out the act for lack of a notary and the necessary paper. Espejo did, however, spend one more day visiting another pueblo before returning to his party on the Río Grande. These Indians, east of the Manzano mountains, were in the Chililí-Quarai area, and belonged either to the eastern Tigua or to the Tompiro group of the Piro. It was here that Father Santa María had been killed when he left the Chamuscado party to return alone to Mexico, but Espejo remained discreetly silent when he learned the news.

Reunited with his men on the Río Grande on February 12, he now set out with them for the Tigua nation, reconnoitering leisurely the pueblos up the river, all of which had been deserted by their occupants. On February 14, the explorers passed what was perhaps Isleta (which they called Los Despoblados), and two days later reached Puala (Puaray), within one league of which were thirteen large settlements whose inhabitants had fled to the hills. The Tigua area extended from Los Lunas to above Bernalillo. Puaray, one of its important towns and the place where Fathers Rodríguez and López had been martyred, was situated between Albuquerque and Bernalillo, though scholars have not been able to agree on the exact site. Some have suggested that it was from three to five miles south of Sandía, while others have maintained that it lay farther north. The discovery and excavation of Kuaua, a large and important ruin on the west bank of the Río Grande across from Bernalillo, convinced some archaeologists that this was the ancient Puaray, and it has been made a state monument by New Mexico under the name of Coronado State Monument. Excavation of its kivas, however, and the discovery of a number of ancient murals on their walls, failed to disclose a picture of the Indians in the act of killing Fathers López and Rodríguez, as described by Captain Gaspar Villagrá, one of Don Juan de Oñate's officers, who says he saw it there in 1598, faintly concealed by a fresh coat of whitewash. But there can be little doubt, according to the researches of modern scholars, that Puaray was located in the Sandía-Bernalillo area.[11]

The Tigua Indians had fled to the mountains, probably the Sandías, from fear of the Spaniards, and did not come back to their pueblos, in spite of friendly overtures by the visitors. Espejo's party waited in vain for the natives for three days, meanwhile supplying themselves generously with food from their stores and listening eagerly to messengers from eight or ten leagues and even farther up the river. These Indians brought gifts of turkeys and invited the explorers to visit them. At the same time, says Luxán, they picked up reports of several other rich provinces, including Mojose (Moqui), and Sumi (Zuñi), the only ones he mentions by name.

Going up the Río Grande four leagues, the party was received in peace by the people of a Queres pueblo, who offered them food, and likewise by other towns of the same nation. They remained among this nation from February 23 to 26, then turned up the Jémez river to Zía. Luxán called the pueblo Ziaquebos and the province Punamees. Espejo, who wrote Pumames, adds that they were told of the seven Jémez pueblos, which he called Emexes, but did not visit them, as the little group was unwilling to divide its forces to do so. At Zía, as elsewhere, Espejo took formal possession "of the city and province" for Spain.

From Zía, the Spaniards set out with a guide on February 28 for Zuñi, skirting the eastern slopes of the mountainous mesa of Cebolleta and Mount Taylor, where peaceful Indian mountaineers (*Indios serranos*), undoubtedly Navajos, brought gifts of food and goods to trade. At the lagoon, later to become the site of Laguna pueblo, Espejo left some of his men, while he and the others visited Acoma. He makes no mention whatever of any native settlement at Laguna. On March 7 all of the party were on their way to Zuñi, following the course of the San José river. On the eleventh, they stopped at Inscription Rock (El Morro),

11. For a discussion of the location of Puaray, see pp. 57, 101, 177.

and on the fourteenth reached the first Zuñi town, called Mazaque (Malaque) by Luxán, actually Mátsaki. He also gives the names of the others and describes the province in some detail, as does Espejo. The province of Zuñi had stone houses three and four stories high. Its people were generous and gave the Spaniards all the food they needed, which impressed them very favorably.

Leaving Fray Bernardino and five men in Zuñi, Espejo and nine others, accompanied by eighty Zuñi warriors, set out for Mojose on April 11, forewarned that these people were hostile and would oppose their entry by force. The small group of Spaniards made preparations to fight, joined by many of their Zuñi friends, who said "they wanted to die wherever the Castilians died." To distinguish them from the enemy Indians, each Zuñi warrior was given a piece of red felt to wear on his head, and the joint Spanish-Zuñi party marched on.

In the province of Mohoce, the Espejo party stopped at a pueblo "that had been attacked and destroyed by Coronado. . . . It was and is situated a league from the pueblo of Aguato," i.e., modern Awátobi. Though it was near sunset, people from Aguato in great numbers came out to welcome the strangers when their presence was discovered, bringing quantities of food and timorously asking for peace. The next day the caciques came to make the same plea, brought more food, and when the Spaniards, at the instigation of their Zuñi friends (who insisted the Hopis could not be trusted), asked them to build a stone enclosure for their horses, they did so immediately. The peaceful, non-warlike nature of the Hopis seems to have been much the same in the sixteenth century as in the nineteenth.

The next day, April 19, the entire Spanish party and their Zuñi allies went to visit the pueblo of Aguato, but only the ten soldiers entered the town, the Zuñis being left outside. Nevertheless, the Hopis were so terrified of the strangers that only an old man was to be seen here and there. The rest remained hidden in their houses. Here in the main plaza of Awátobi, Espejo took possession "with a salvo of harquebus shots," probably frightening the timid natives half to death, and then left to pitch his camp a quarter of a league outside. Almost immediately, a thousand people came to bring food and gifts, including six hundred pieces of cloth, large and small, plain and figured, probably all of cotton.

On the twenty-first, the explorers visited Gaspe (Walpi), two leagues away, and were welcomed by the peaceful inhabitants, who scattered prayer meal on the visitors, their servants, and even on the horses, so that "we looked like clowns in carnival time," wrote Luxán. Thereafter they brought a great quantity of food and another six hundred pieces of cloth as gifts. Espejo marched through the pueblo with flag flying, taking possession in the main plaza with another round of gun-fire. Luxán has left a description of the people and their customs, which are remarkably similar to those noted by American observers in the middle of the nineteenth century.

The following day Espejo visited the two pueblos of Comupaui (Shongópovi) and Majanani (Mishóngnovi) on Middle or Second mesa, and was received with the same courtesies. Here, too, he took possession, after which he went to Olalla (Oraibi), to be welcomed there with even greater courtesy and more gifts. During their stay of two days in Oraibi, the Spaniards learned that there were mines, but situated at a great distance, so the entire party returned to Awátobi pueblo. Here, their temporary headquarters, it was decided to send five of the men, with the friendly Zuñi allies, back to Zuñi, while the other five daringly set out to explore. These latter five were Espejo, Diego Pérez de Luxán, Gregorio Hernández, Bernardino de Luna, and Francisco Barreto. They left Awátobi on April 30, and struck out westward, accompanied by guides provided by the Hopi. In fifteen leagues they crossed the Little Colorado at modern Winslow, passed Sunset tanks in Salt Creek canyon, Mormon lake, Beaver creek, Verde river, and reached a mineral outcrop at Black mountain near the present Jerome, Arizona, five or six miles west of the Verde. The mines proved a disappointment. They were mostly copper, with very little silver, and the explorers started back immediately. Such was the comment of Luxán, in his daily record. Espejo, on the contrary, writing later and with the avowed purpose of becoming the founder of New Mexico, said that the ores were very rich and contained a great deal of silver.

At Zuñi, Espejo and his four companions found the others, all well treated and in good health, but divided in purpose. Father Bernardino and a group of followers, including the alférez mayor, Gregorio Hernández, were determined to return to Mexico, since the expedition had fulfilled its mission. The others, led by Espejo, wanted to seize the opportunity of exploring for mines rumored to exist among the Tiguas and Maguas, and then to return home by way of the Buffalo Plains. Without the discovery of such riches, they argued, the country could not be settled. Hernández raised the royal banner, says Luxán, and demanded that all rally about it and return. Instead, it was taken from him by force, though he was not punished, but was allowed to depart peacefully with his faction. They reached Santa Bárbara, safe and sound, before Espejo's group, but we have no record of their journey.

In his report of the expedition, Espejo says very little of this dissension.

The rest of the explorers, led by Espejo and the alguacil mayor, Diego Pérez de Luxan, numbered only nine, a small group indeed among so many strange people. On May 31, 1583, they left Zuñi with an interpreter "to pacify the Tiguas, whom we had left in revolt." There were many warnings that they would be killed en route. At Acoma, some of the servants belonging to Espejo and Luxán fled, whereupon these two officers, leaving their comrades at Acoma, made a fast and daring trip to the Río Grande to prevent the escapees from joining the Hernández faction. The two men returned after spending three days on the river, reports Luxán, but he does not identify the place where they stayed, nor do we have any other information about this trip.

During Espejo's absence, there occurred a scrape involving some of the camp's servants, one of whom had been killed by the Acomas, causing the latter "and the neighboring mountain people" to take up arms, says Luxán. These mountaineers or Querechos were undoubtedly Navajos, living in the vicinity of Mount Taylor and cultivating patches of corn close to the sierra.[12] The fight concerned especially Francisco Barreto, whose Querecho woman servant, given to him at the Hopi pueblo, had fled, and he, determined to get her back, exposed himself dangerously to the enemy. Luxán came to his rescue in the fight that ensued, but the two of them were no match for the Indians, and Barreto lost his wench! The entire incident is of special historical interest because it shows that the Querechos were found from as far west as the Hopi pueblos, where Barreto had obtained the girl, to Mount Taylor.

Espejo's party, which had set out from Zuñi on May 31, now left Acoma on June 22 for Puaray, most of whose people had fled to the mountains, except about thirty who were to be seen on the housetops. When asked for food "they mocked us like the others," said Espejo, whereupon he attacked, seized the Indians who showed themselves, and set fire to the pueblo. Sixteen were seized and executed. Others burned to death in the kivas where they had taken refuge. "A remarkable deed for so few people in the midst of so many enemies," wrote Luxán. From then on, all of the provinces received the Spaniards very well, except the Tiguas, who were so terrified that they dared not accept an invitation to peaceful association with such fearsome conquerors.

Continuing in search of mines, Espejo left the pueblo of San Felipe on June 27 and went eastwardly for twelve leagues, according to his own

12. Forbes writes, of this incident: "This is the first recorded contact between Navahos and Spaniards, and it is interesting to note that the former were corn users—making *tortillas*—in 1582." Forbes, *Apache, Navaho, and Spaniard*, p. 57.

account, and reached a province he called Ubates, having five pueblos, and thence to the Tanos, with three pueblos. There seems to be some confusion in this story, for neither Luxán nor Obregón mentions the Ubates. Perhaps Espejo in his brief account meant to say that he had heard of the Ubates, possibly the Tewa farther north, and then went on his way to visit the Tanos. This, at least, is the view of Erik K. Reed.[13] Since the faithful Luxán fails to make any reference to Ubates, this solution seems plausible. Luxán's account is much shorter at this point, merely noting that they sought the mines called Santa Catalina, probably near San Marcos and not to be confused with Chamuscado's pueblo of Santa Catalina, and that these mineral deposits were rich. Both reports agree that the pueblos here were of three, four, and five stories, and the population very large.

From here on Espejo's route becomes much clearer—and Luxán's description very good. They visited the Tanos province in the upper Galisteo basin, first stopping at San Marcos, thence three leagues to Jumea, very likely Galisteo, and then went to a large pueblo called Pocos by Luxán, which could be San Cristóbal, and so on to Ciquique, or Siqui, i.e., Pecos. There the native warriors were unwilling to match arms with the Spaniards and brought some food when the latter made a show of giving battle. On July 15, having taken two guides by force, the Spanish party started homeward, along the Río de las Vacas, or Pecos. Espejo says they saw great numbers of buffalo during the first thirty leagues, whereas Luxán, after describing their trek through the pine forest for a few days, states that they "found many buffalo tracks as well as bones and skulls," but no buffalo. Perhaps Espejo was drawing a broad bow at this point, relying on the report of the Chamuscado party of the year previous which had verified the presence of buffalo in eastern New Mexico. Finally, on August 7, they met three Jumano Indians out hunting in the vicinity of Toyah creek, Texas. They told the Spaniards, through Pedro, the interpreter, that they would guide them to the Río Grande, which they did, going possibly via Toyahvale, Fort Davis, and Marfa, reaching the river near the present Ruidoso or Candelaria.[14] From this point the entire group returned to San Bartolomé on September 10, 1583, after an absence of ten months.

Espejo's glowing reports, substantiating those of the Chamuscado-Rodríguez party, lent tremendous support to the optimists who believed that there had actually been discovered an "otro nuevo mundo"

---

13. Erik K. Reed, "The Southern Tewa Pueblos in the Historic Period," *El Palacio*, vol. 50 (1943), pp. 260-262, 282-283.

14. Castañeda, *Our Catholic Heritage in Texas*, vol. I, pp. 178-179.

in the area occupied by the Pueblo Indians. Giving emphasis to this belief was the advanced culture of the Pueblo Indians—the "gente vestida"—as reflected in the architecture of their towns, their clothing made from cotton grown in their own fields, their various food crops, together with their political and religious organization. Even though the Spaniards felt the need for better interpreters to understand this native society more fully, they were experienced in the use of the sign language. Clearly, also, after having lived and traveled among these people for several months, studying them and the resources of the land, they had become convinced, not only of the desirability of establishing a Spanish society among them, but of the opportunity for saving thousands of souls from damnation, and at the same time of finding riches for prospective settlers in encomiendas, mines, and ranches.

In Mexico city the news of the northern discoveries received appropriate consideration. The archbishop reported the event to the king and his Council of the Indies in Spain with the comment that "if what they tell me is true, they have indeed discovered in that region another new world."[15] In the meantime, the king had issued a cedula, April 19, 1583, instructing the viceroy to make a contract with some suitable person for the conquest of the new lands in accordance with the laws and regulations for colonization.[16] This led to a scramble among the leading frontiersmen, including Gallegos, Espejo, and many others, for the appointment. Ultimately, the prize went to Don Juan de Oñate of Zacatecas, member of a family distinguished for its service in subjugating Indians and opening up mines in northern Mexico, and it was he who finally in 1598 laid the foundation of Spanish society in New Mexico.

15. Letter of the archbishop of Mexico, October 26, 1583, in *Cinco Cartas del Illmo. y Exmo. Señor D. Pedro Moya de Contreras*, by Cristóbal Gutiérrez de Luna and Francisco Sosa. Bibliotheca Tenanitla (Madrid, 1962), p. 164.
16. A.G.I., *Audiencia de México*, legajo 1064.

THE CASTAÑO DE SOSA EXPEDITION

IN THE MEANTIME, the fame of the Pueblo country, or as it is called in the Castaño documents, land of the "gente vestida," attracted another pioneering band, that of Gaspar Castaño de Sosa in 1590. Castaño was lieutenant governor of the province of New León when its governor, Luis de Carbajal, was arrested and tried on charges of heresy by the Inquisition in 1589. In a reckless moment, Castaño abandoned his headquarters at the town of Almadén [the present Monclova][1] and started the entire colony on its way to the new country, in spite of the fact that he had not received official permission for such an adventure and indeed had been warned not to go.

Castaño's background was typical of frontier officials in sixteenth-century Mexico. A man of much courage, energy, and aggressiveness, he had become a settler of Saltillo in the jurisdiction of New Vizcaya, and when the villa of San Luis (now the city of Monterrey) was established, sometime in 1582 or 1583, he became its first alcalde mayor, and later lieutenant governor of the province.[2] He participated in the establishment of a number of settlements, among them Almadén, where he made his headquarters, the city of León, the mines of Quabila, the villa of San Luis, and others. During his ten years or so on this frontier, Castaño had nourished the hope of developing New León into a rich province, but its mines yielded very little and settlement was slow. Vito Alessio Robles, distinguished Mexican historian, suggests that he finally had become discouraged and disillusioned by the poverty of the mines and at the same time fascinated by the mirages of Gran Quivira.[3] This was also the theme of Don Alonso de León, historian of New León, writing about 1660. Without citing his sources, de León made the significant statement, with respect to Castaño's colony at Almadén, that since there was so little silver for so many, and provisions were scarce and distant, the proud Castaño hoped to find success in a new discovery, a hope that was nourished by the confused notices then current of clothed people living to the north who might be a source of tribute and treasure.[4]

When, therefore, news of the Pueblo country reached Almadén, perhaps from the accounts of the Chamuscado-Rodríguez and Espejo expeditions, or perhaps from Indians who traded with tribes farther inland—or even from raiding expeditions—he dreamed of becoming its conqueror. The new region seemed to offer the riches he sought, and he proceeded to inspire the colonists of Almadén with his own zest for new conquests (even to the point of dropping a piece of silver into an assay of ores being made from some mines in that direction!), and to send a representative to Mexico city to obtain the viceroy's permission

1. There is some confusion regarding the name of this town. In the contemporary documents, the name is given as the town of Almadén, never with the addition of the word "new." Alessio Robles, on the contrary, called it Nuevo Almadén. See his *Coahuila y Texas en la Época Colonial,* pp. 93, 95. In this study, we have followed the contemporary usage.

2. Vito Alessio Robles, *Coahuila y Texas en la Época Colonial* (1938), pp. 91-92.

3. *Ibid.,* pp. 101-102.

4. Genaro García, *Documentos Inéditos ó Muy Raros para la Historia de México,* vol. xxv (1909), the first publication of Captain Alonso de León's manuscript.

for making such an exploration, in accordance with the Colonization Laws of 1573.

It has now become clear that the above outline of the Castaño story, as hitherto known, is not entirely correct, but that he was apparently trying to force the viceroy's hand by anticipating the royal plan for settling a Spanish colony among the "gente vestida" of the north. Castaño realized, certainly, the need for securing a license from the government before starting out, as is evident from the fact that he sent agents on two occasions to Mexico city for this purpose, and that Captain Juan Morlete came to visit him at Almadén in June 1590 with specific orders from the viceroy requiring him to cease taking and selling Indians as slaves, and forbiding him from leaving for New Mexico without authorization.[5]

The first party that Castaño sent to consult with the viceroy consisted of four men led by Captains Francisco Salgado and Manuel de Mederos. They left Almadén on May 27, 1590. The second was entrusted to Alonso Ruíz, one of the soldiers who had accompanied Morlete to Almadén in June 1590, but this was not until Castaño had first accepted, and then rejected, Morlete's urging that Castaño himself go to Mexico city for consultations with the viceroy.

Of these men, Captain Francisco Salgado was one of Castaño's inner circle, often assigned duties of great responsibility. In earlier years, he had led many excursions on Castaño's orders, into the country beyond Almadén to capture Indians to be sold as slaves—*piezas*, as they were called—for use on the farms and in the mines of northern Mexico. The income from this business seems to have been more stable than from mining, in many places. In fact, it had been a common practice on the frontier since the time of Cortés and, though royal orders had sought to stop it, the business continued to flourish until the time of Governor Carbajal and Lieutenant Governor Castaño de Sosa, when the government took drastic steps to bring it to an end.

As Castaño's "Memoria" reveals, his colony, including a train of wagons in addition to the usual equipment and supplies, left Almadén

5. These new facts come from the following documents in the Archives of the Indies: 1) "Treslado de las ynformaciones, autos y otras diligencias que se hizieron contra el Capitán Gaspar de Sosa y sus soldados. . . ," *Audiencia de México,* legajo 220, expediente 30 (cited hereafter as "Autos y Diligencias"); 2) "Ynformación recivida en la audiencia real de la Nueva España de pedimiento de Domingo Martínez de Cearreta . . . ," February 27, 1592. *Audiencia de México,* legajo 220, expediente 27 (cited hereafter as "Ynformación recivida en la audiencia real . . ."). Castaño's own "Memoria" is printed in Pacheco and Cárdenas, *Col. Doc. Inéd.,* vol. IV, pp. 283-354, and in vol. XV, pp. 191-261. There is a manuscript copy of it in the Juan Bautista Muñoz collection of the Real Academia de la Historia in Madrid, vol. 70, no. 1543, on which these printed versions are evidently based, and another in the Rich Collection of the New York Public Library.

on July 27, 1590, with its full complement of men, women, and children, so that all might participate in the riches expected from the discovery of new lands and peoples in the distant north.

For several weeks the expedition proceeded slowly toward the Río Bravo, that is, the Río Grande, stopping occasionally to rest or pursue Indians, and to await the return of Francisco Salgado and his companions from Mexico city. On September 9 Castaño finally reached this river, where he remained encamped to the end of the month. Meanwhile, he searched for mines, unsuccessfully, and apparently sent out Luis Bogado and other captains on new raiding parties to capture Indians for the slave markets of northern Mexico.[6] This practice was in conformity with the old policy of the frontier, where aggressive captains supplied the mines and ranchos with labor in this manner. Since the messengers that Castaño had sent to Mexico city had failed to return, this activity served not only to keep the men occupied, but to provide them with servants as well as with compensation for their labor and investment in making such an expedition, and thus to prevent discouragement and desertion.

The identification of Castaño's route from Almadén to the Río Grande is difficult, in part because the diarist almost never tells the number of leagues marched each day, nor the direction. Occasionally he mentions names of rivers, but they have little or no meaning today, with the result that such information is not helpful in following the trail. It is our conclusion, however, based on consideration of the available sources and a study of the topography, that Castaño and his party on the first leg of their trek, July 27 to September 9, must have followed approximately the line of the modern railroad from Almadén to Villa Acuña, opposite the later Del Río on the eastern side of the Río Grande. To spend a month in covering this distance of approximately two hundred and twenty-five miles would seem quite possible, in view of the fact that the expedition realized that it had to move slowly to enable the messengers from Mexico city to catch up.

In the neighborhood of Villa Acuña, probably down river from Del Río, Castaño's expedition must have crossed the Río Grande, even though the diarist makes no such specific statement.[7] Two American

6. Castaño's "Memoria"; and also "Autos y Diligencias," in which several soldiers gave testimony that Luis Bogado and others continued to take slaves after the expedition left Almadén.

7. The lower course of the Río Grande is almost a continuous canyon, cutting through the limestone rock to a depth of two thousand feet, nearly as far as Del Río. Robert T. Hill, "Running the Cañons of the Rio Grande," *Century Magazine*, LXI (January 1901), p. 384.

scholars, Dorothy Hull, who wrote a Master's thesis in 1916 on this subject in Herbert E. Bolton's seminar at the University of California, and Carlos E. Castañeda, Texas historian who followed pretty much the conclusions of Miss Hull,[8] assume that Castaño's party did cross to the east bank of the Río Grande in this neighborhood, and then proceeded north-northwestward toward the Laxas river, in two days of travel, and crossed it. This must have been the present Devil's river. The date of departure from the Río Grande was October 1, and of the crossing of the Laxas, October 2. From then on the party floundered almost hopelessly amid ravines, canyons, and mountains, looking for the Río Salado and for water to keep men and animals alive. On October 7 a scouting party actually saw the Salado, but found it impossible to descend to the stream below because of its depth in a steep and impenetrable canyon. Consequently, the expedition proceeded slowly, Castaño sending out various parties to search for a better route, but while they could see the Salado now and then, they did not find a trail down to the water's edge until October 26, after three weeks of desperately difficult travel. The point at which they reached the Salado, or Pecos, may have been in the vicinity of Sheffield, Texas, where the river broadens out and access to its banks becomes somewhat easier.[9] This is the site of one of the river's historic fords, beyond which the stream flows through a canyonlike barrier for about twenty-five or thirty miles northwest of that town when it again flattens out. Since the party must have traveled a roundabout course on account of the roughness of the country, and in view of the difficulty of finding a trail for the wagons, it is impossible to determine with any confidence the spot at which it reached the river.

Explorers who came upon the Pecos in the nineteenth century, before the rise of irrigation and flood control measures, found it a demon to cross. Few dared try it except at established places, and some of these were very treacherous. "Its banks are as perpendicular as the walls of an edifice, rising six feet above the water, to the level of the valley, composed of mud, which on drying, falls into an impalpable powder. An animal may wander along its banks half a day without finding a point where he may drink. Indeed, in my twenty miles' ride along it I saw but

8. Dorothy Hull, "Castaño de Sosa's Expedition to New Mexico in 1590," *Old Santa Fe*, vol. III (October 1916), pp. 307-332; and C. E. Casteñada, *Our Catholic Heritage in Texas*, vol. I (1936), p. 182.

9. Letters of Walter W. Ristow, chief, map division, Library of Congress, September 18, and Chester Kielman, archivist, University of Texas, September 10, 1962, to Hammond.

one point on either side where he could do so; and these were the artificial excavations where we crossed."[10]

Soon after reaching the Salado, the expedition began to find deserted rancherías, and occasionally some Indians. These were undoubtedly Querechos (later named Jumanos), as may be inferred from the excellent description of the travois, or train of pack dogs, references to which are found in the expeditions of other early Spanish explorers who crossed eastern New Mexico and western Texas.

Contrary to the route suggested here, the Mexican historian, Vito Alessio Robles, a native of Coahuila and a distinguished engineer and scholar, held that the expedition, after leaving Almadén, proceeded by easy stages toward Villa Acuña, but at this point, the swampy and marshy nature of the Río Grande forced it to turn westward across the northern portion of the state of Coahuila, as we now know it, and finally to strike the Río Grande at Los Chizos ford, at the extreme southern point of what is now the Big Bend National Park in Texas.[11] The date on reaching the river was September 9, and it was here, therefore, in his judgment, that the expedition awaited the return of Salgado and Mederos from Mexico city, while various captains went out to explore the nearby country. When the entire expedition then resumed its journey on October 1, after Salgado and Mederos had failed to return, Alessio believes it struck northeastward, down the Río Grande, in the direction of the Pecos, and so on up that river into New Mexico. Unfortunately, Alessio makes no attempt to describe the route thereafter, as he treats only of the first part, in territory now under the Mexican flag—a weakness in his study since one must follow the entire trail to get a comprehensive view of it. We have examined Alessio's suggestions in detail, but believe it would have been virtually impossible for Castaño's company to take this route in view of the topography of the area and of its description as given in his "Memoria."

When the expedition resumed its march on October 1, after the long and fruitless wait for Salgado and Mederos, it reached and crossed the Río Laxas in two days. Now, there is no river such as the Laxas near Los Chizos ford, nor is there such a stream in Big Bend National Park or in the area between it and the Pecos that would in any manner fit Castaño's description.[12]

10. Nathaniel A. Taylor, *The Coming Empire; or, Two Thousand Miles in Texas on Horseback* (1877), pp. 326-327.
11. Vito Alessio Robles, *Coahuila y Texas en la Epoca Colonial*, pp. 103-104.
12. Letter of Douglas B. Evans, chief park naturalist, Big Bend National Park, September 4, 1962, to Hammond.

On the contrary, the expedition followed the east bank of the Salado throughout the entire earlier portion of the march, in fact, until November 26. On that date the diarist writes that they had always been on the left or east side of the stream up to that point. If this statement is correct, and we see no reason for doubting it, it would not have been possible for the expedition to make a laborious crossing through northern Coahuila to Los Chizos ford, for example, and then to turn northeast in the direction of the Pecos, through virtually impassable country. Castaño and his captains must have known perfectly well the general location of the Conchos river, the route taken by the Chamuscado and Espejo parties to New Mexico, and if they had wanted to follow that trail, they would not have wasted their resources in the long search for the Salado over the route suggested by Alessio. The fact is, however, that Castaño had conceived the idea of finding a new route to the northern interior via the Salado in the belief that in this area lay new kingdoms, new civilized people, and that they would provide a reward for him and his followers. In his dreams Castaño sought a settled and wealthy society that neither the Chamuscado nor Espejo explorers had found. We must conclude, therefore, that the Castaño expedition must have crossed the Río Grande somewhere in the vicinity of Villa Acuña or Del Río, and then have made the strenuous and fatiguing march into the pueblo area of New Mexico, following the Pecos, at first along its eastern bank, and later, when in the Artesia-Roswell latitude, marching along either bank wherever the going was easiest.

Some evidence of the expedition's progress may be deduced from the pages of Castaño's journal through geographic features or various events that are referred to. On October 29 and 30, for example, the party found some rancherías that had been deserted very recently. Here the soldiers caught four Indians, two men and two women, who used dogs for carrying their baggage, clearly the travois of the Southwestern natives. This was near some marshes with large deposits of very fine salt. The Spaniards could not understand the natives, so gave them some presents and released them. In the following days, they met others, who were hostile and who tried to seize some of the Spanish horses and oxen. These people were doubtless Jumanos, living in the region along the Pecos river, possibly in the vicinity of the old Horsehead Crossing of the Butterfield Overland Stage route between McCamey and Grandfalls, Texas, a distance of a bit more than one hundred miles from the New Mexico border of today. This was Jumano country. The hostility of the natives to the Spaniards may be explained by earlier slave-hunting raids, a common feature of frontier society in the sixteenth century.

Continuing up the Pecos river, the Castaño party on November 20 saw a column of smoke in the mountains four leagues off, probably in the Guadalupe mountains west of Carlsbad, New Mexico, where the Indians, very likely Mescalero Apaches, were signaling the approach of strange or hostile people. By this time the Spanish party had left Jumano territory and did not meet any other Indians for some time. Geographic features may, however, help to identify where the Spaniards were, such as when, on November 26, they found a spring, the first they had seen on the trip. T. F. Stipp of the Geological Survey at Roswell informs us that this might have been Major Johnson spring, twelve miles northwest of Carlsbad, or a large spring at the source of South Spring river near Roswell, most likely the former. Five days later they came to a stream which rose in the mountains to the west, quite possibly the Hondo.

Having now reached a latitude of between 33 and 34 degrees, Castaño knew that he might soon expect to come upon some of the New Mexico pueblos, since both Chamuscado and Espejo had found them in that zone.[13] To investigate this possibility, urgent because of the need for food, Castaño sent his chief officer, Cristóbal de Heredia, on ahead with eleven men and specific instructions to capture some Indian guides, if possible, but not to enter any pueblo, if he found one. Meantime, the main part of the expedition, encumbered with the wagons, came along more slowly, hoping for good news. And news they got, but the good was mixed with a generous portion of the bad.

Heredia, after sending back for supplies a couple of times, eventually returned on December 23. That day Castaño had climbed a hill to examine the landscape and spied in the distance a party of stragglers approaching. When they got close enough to be recognized, he saw that they were Heredia's men, on foot, leading their horses—exhausted, defeated.

The humiliating story of their experiences finally came out. Heredia and his men had found a pueblo, Pecos, and contrary to instructions had entered it, though without any opposition. Finding the Indians friendly and hospitable, the men became careless, left their arms and saddles in some rooms of the pueblo, according to the testimony of

13. The approximate latitude of San Marcial, where both Chamuscado and Espejo had found the first New Mexico pueblos. See Castaño's "Memoria" for further details.

Alonso Jaimez,[14] and wandered peacefully through the pueblo, completely assured of the friendship of the natives. The next day, however, when the Indians saw the Spaniards taking their corn, they suddenly attacked them. In the fray that followed, the men were fortunate to escape with their lives, though at least three were wounded, and they lost half their guns, saddles, and equipment. It was a sad and disastrous story, but there was one gleam of hope in it all, because the party had at last found an Indian pueblo, the prize for which Castaño and his men had been searching for so many weary months.

Castaño now decided to go on ahead in person with twenty chosen men, leaving the main part of the expedition to follow. He left on December 26, after what could not, certainly, have been a happy Christmas, although undoubtedly he looked forward to capturing the pueblo he now knew existed and to obtaining a much-needed supply of food. Since Heredia's course along the river had been tortuous, he followed a ridge farther west to avoid the gullies and ravines.

Castaño reached Pecos on December 31 and entered it with banners flying and bugles blowing, as though he were a conquering hero, but he was cautious. Camping a short distance outside, he ordered the two bronze cannons set up, urged his men to be alert and prepared for the worst, war if necessary. None of the Indians came out, even though the Spaniards circled the pueblo again and again, signaling that they wanted to be friends. It was all of no avail, however, and Castaño was forced to fight. In their attack on the pueblo, the soldiers gradually made headway, killing a number of natives, among them one who seemed to be a prominent chief. This terrified the Indians, many of whom abandoned their positions. In this way Castaño seized the pueblo. Its occupants, recognizing their defeat, cried, "Amigos, amigos, amigos," and made a cross with their hands in sign of peace. But still they remained within their walls and would have nothing to do with the Spaniards. Castaño could not even capture one Indian to serve as guide, which he very much wanted, so he tried a ruse. Making a show of abandoning the pueblo, he actually left four men concealed in the town. Lulled into a false sense of security, the Indians returned to their homes, and two walked into the trap set for them by the wily Castaño, who thus gained the guides he desired.

Without waiting for the main part of the army, which had been left some twenty-five or thirty miles down the Pecos at a place called

14. See especially the testimony of Alonso Jaimez, July 10, 1591, in "Autos y Diligencias." He gives a detailed account of Heredia's escapade at Pecos, quite different from the story in Castaño's "Memoria."

Urraca, probably in the vicinity of Ribera, where the Santa Fé Railway now crosses the Pecos river, Castaño went on ahead with his advance party to explore the country, find other towns, and look for mines. Though his diary is extremely vague at this point and fails to mention the pueblos seen, his itinerary, or his direction, it would appear that he went through Glorieta pass toward present-day Santa Fé, and continued northward, visiting several pueblos, perhaps of the Tewa group, between January 7 and 10, possibly Tesuque, Nambé, Cuyamungué, Pojoaque, and Jacona, though it is necessary to stretch the diarist's leagues into very long ones to reach these towns.[15] Then he went on two leagues to another valley, the Río Grande no doubt, to a large pueblo—possibly San Ildefonso—visited two more towns, and then followed the large river for five leagues in a northerly direction and, on January 13, came to a very great town, "situated in a valley between sierras. . . ." Miss Hull identifies this site with Taos; yet the fact that the distance from the Tewa area to Taos was about fifty miles, that there were about three feet of snow on the ground, that the men carried

15. Cf. Hull, *op. cit.*, pp. 324-325. While it might seem plausible that Castaño visited the Galisteo pueblos from January 7 to 10 rather than the Tewa, since they too were close together and also generally fit the diarist's description, yet this identification of the route would render his subsequent travels up to January 18 very difficult to understand, in the light of the information available. If, for example, he had taken the Galisteo route, and from there gone to the Río Grande, he should have come in contact with the Queres earlier than he did, but the "Memoria" shows that he did not meet them till January 18, after he had returned from the exploration that had taken him up the river and to the great pueblo described as having been seven or eight stories. The latter statement we take to be pardonable "window dressing," used to impress the people at home with the greatness and significance of the discovery.

The above argument places much emphasis on Castaño's mention of the Queres on January 18, when in reality it is the only time that he gives the name of any tribe up to that date on this trip. It is not impossible that he could have been in contact with the Queres earlier, not knowing the names of the different towns; but if he did not go north to the Tewa, he would have had to visit the Tigua country in order to "follow the very large river to the north." Assuming that he went to the Tigua towns from Galisteo, and that he found the great city of seven or eight stories among the Jémez, for example, he would have had to pass through the lands of the Queres to reach that destination, which might indeed have been possible, if he did not know the names of the towns. This might well have been the case. Espejo, for example, did not refer to the Zía group of pueblos as Queres, but as Punames or Pumames. There is no indication that he associated them with the Queres of the Río Grande. The same might apply to Castaño, as there is no evidence that he distinguished between towns of different tribes or nations. If, therefore, we assume that Castaño, after leaving Pecos, visited the Galisteo towns, proceeded southwestward to the Río Grande, possibly among the Tigua, went up the great river some distance, and then westward to the Zía area, and farther up Jémez canyon to the great pueblos situated there—to the town of seven or eight stories—he could, on the return, have met the "Quereses" on his way back to Urraca via the Galisteo pueblos.

For bibliography, consult Marjorie F. Lambert, *Paa-ko, Archaeological Chronicle of an Indian Village in North Central New Mexico* (Santa Fé, 1954), p. 178 *et seq.*; Fred Wendorf and Erik K. Reed, "An Alternative Reconstruction of Northern Río Grande Prehistory," *El Palacio*, vol. 62 (1955), pp. 131-173.

two bronze culverins as well as other equipment and supplies, and that the journey was made in one day, seems to preclude this identification. We think it more likely that Castaño had reached the pueblos at the mouth of the Chama, near San Juan, which would have been physically possible, since that distance would have been about five leagues—not the fifteen or twenty required to reach Taos.

With his men, Castaño now returned "to the pueblos through which we had come," visiting various towns along the great river, which was frozen over, and on the eighteenth reached the Queres, where he "found four pueblos within view of one another," though exactly at what point cannot probably be determined satisfactorily with the evidence at hand.[16] Everywhere, except at the large town visited on the thirteenth, the Indians were friendly and gave freely of their corn, beans, and other supplies, so there was no repetition of the fighting that had taken place at Pecos.

Having seen much of the country, Castaño was now ready to bring the main expedition to the Río Grande, and on January 24 started back for Urraca on the Pecos river where the men had remained in camp. Taking along two Indian guides, he arrived at Urraca on January 27, despite heavy snow. The route is not clear, but one may conjecture that it lay on the border of the Galisteo basin, which would have provided a better trail than through the valley itself, though the diarist merely states that they set out in the direction of the main camp, in spite of the snow, hoping to find a route passable for wagons. Led by their guide—one had deserted—they traveled through thick pine forests, melting snow for water, and pressed forward, either by way of present Lamy and Apache canyon or via Cañada Estacada, White lakes, and Canyon Blanco, an old and natural route said to have been used by the Indians on their way to the Buffalo Plains. Perhaps the bad weather and the desire for haste led the party to ignore the opportunity to visit the pueblos in the Galisteo country, and hence the diarist does not mention them. Reunited with his men at Urraca, Castaño rested a couple of days, and then, on January 30, set out with the entire expedition, including the wagons, for the Rio Grande valley. Since the first pueblo he encountered on entering the Galisteo valley on this trip was San

16. This statement is interesting, and difficult to reconcile with what is known of Queres ruins today, but it may be observed that when Oñate in 1598 assigned various groups of pueblos to the missionaries, Father Fray Juan de Rozas was given the Queres province, and Oñate named a dozen pueblos, though they were not all in this specific area along the Río Grande. Archaeologists state that today's pueblos number only a fraction of those in existence at the end of the sixteenth century. Cf. Frank Hibben, *Digging up America* (1960), pp. 147-150.

Cristóbal, which lies at the eastern extremity of the valley, it seems probable that he came by way of Cañada Estacada.

It was now mid-February and still very cold, so the Spaniards were pleased to stop at San Cristóbal pueblo. This was on February 15. Castaño visited and named several other towns, including San Lucas (Galisteo), and San Marcos, which he entered on February 18. Everywhere he was well received by the Indians, who gave such supplies as were required of them.[17]

Leaving the main expedition in the Galisteo valley, apparently at the pueblo of San Marcos, Castaño selected nineteen men and with them returned to the pueblo of Pecos to re-establish Spanish authority. This time there was no resistance. The Indians treated the visitors well, returned the broken swords and ruined clothing, and gave them some supplies.

With Spanish honor vindicated, Castaño rejoined the main party at San Marcos within a week, and from there continued to Santo Domingo on the Río Grande, apparently on March 9. It was seemingly at this juncture that Alonso Jaimez and a group of conspirators threatened insurrection. Castaño, in a merciful spirit, listened to the pleas of the loyal to spare the plotters, and forgave them, though Jaimez was deprived of his commission as captain of a party that was to have gone to Mexico for reinforcements.[18] As these events happened on the eve of Morlete's arrival, they were quickly overshadowed by more important events, for he had come to take Castaño and his followers back to Mexico as prisoners for having violated the colonization laws.

17. For an excellent study of these pueblos, see Nels C. Nelson, "Pueblo Ruins of the Galisteo Basin, New Mexico," American Museum of Natural History, *Anthropological Papers*, vol. xv (New York, 1914), pp. 24-26; and Erik K. Reed, "The Southern Tewa Pueblos in the Historic Period," *El Palacio*, vol. 50 (1943), pp. 254, 259-260, and 282-283.
18. Castaño's "Memoria," p. 291.

THE MORLETE EXPEDITION

THE ORIGIN and background of the Morlete expedition are somewhat obscure as to details, but there can be little doubt that it was a manifestation of the new policy of the Spanish government toward the Indians on the frontier, outlined in the Colonization Laws of 1573. Up to that time, successful military chieftains could do almost anything they wished, in the name of God and king, exploring the frontier, discovering and reporting on unknown peoples, and hunting for gold and silver mines. Much lawlessness accompanied these expeditions, but as Spanish society in the New World became more firmly rooted, the viceroy was able to establish tighter control over such distant regions than had been possible previously.

The province of New León was one of those settled at the end of the sixteenth century. Its first governor, Luís de Carvajal, began its conquest about 1579. Shortly thereafter he gave the office of lieutenant governor to Gaspar Castaño de Sosa, who, as previously noted, was active in the establishment of a number of settlements in New León and who was stationed in Almadén. Another of the early captains here was Juan Morlete, but he seems to have settled at Mazapil, some two hundred miles farther to the south, whereas Castaño de Sosa remained on the frontier to discover and exploit its mineral resources.[1] Very likely, there was keen rivalry between these two men, Castaño and Morlete, though the former was evidently the governor's favorite. At any rate, he was the one who was made lieutenant governor, and as such was stationed on the frontier where there was hope of new mining discoveries.

When the resources of Almadén and the mines of Quabila proved disappointing and Castaño decided to seek richer fields, as described above, news of his plans seems to have leaked out and the viceroy to have been informed. Indeed, during the month of June 1590, Morlete had been sent to Almadén to notify Castaño of the government's policy forbidding the capture and sale of Indian slaves on the frontier and also to inform him that he would not be allowed to make an expedition to New Mexico without authorization.[2]

Captain Morlete's message was very specific, and Castaño did not fail to recognize its significance. In response to the first warning, that the taking of Indian slaves must stop, he obeyed immediately, issuing an order to the sound of trumpets, as custom required, forbidding his captains to make further raids of this nature and putting a stop to the sale of Indian slaves for use on mines and plantations. Whether the order was observed is rather dubious.

1. Alessio Robles, *Coahuila y Texas*, p. 92 *et seq.*, and testimony of Diego Ramírez Barrionuevo in "Autos y Diligencias," January 6, 1591.

2. There is abundant evidence that Morlete visited Castaño's headquarters at Almadén in June 1590, perhaps toward the end of the month. Two soldiers, Alonso Jaimez and Melchor de Pavía, so testified specifically on July 11, 1591. See "Autos y Diligencias." Two others, Salvador Sánchez and Andrés Pérez, said that thirty days after Morlete left Almadén, Castaño abandoned the settlement and began his march toward New Mexico. Since we know from his journal that he started on July 27, 1590, this would place Morlete's visit in the month of June. See the testimony in "Autos y Diligencias," as well as the testimony of several other soldiers, some of whom had started with Castaño and then had given up the expedition before it reached the Río Grande. Several others testified that they had been with Morlete's detachment on the trip to Almadén.

With regard to the second part of Morlete's message, that Castaño must not abandon Almadén and the neighboring settlements, or go to New Mexico without the viceroy's approval, it is curious that this issue, especially the latter part, should have been raised at all, unless a rumor of his plans was already in circulation. As a matter of fact, Morlete invited Castaño to go to Mexico city to visit the viceroy and to explain these matters in detail. At first Castaño accepted, but after further consideration changed his mind on the excuse that he did not have the proper clothes and equipment for making the trip. Morlete overcame this objection by offering to provide him with money and clothes, but when the news of Castaño's decision to visit Mexico city became known, there was loud murmuring and dissatisfaction among his followers, the soldiers and settlers of Almadén. They objected, assuming that his departure would lead to the disintegration of the entire colony.[3]

The question naturally comes up, did Castaño suspect, on reflection, that a trap was being laid for him? Once removed from his own headquarters, separated from his supporters, his talons would have been blunted, his power broken, and he would be at the mercy of the royal officials, headed by the viceroy and audiencia.

In view of these and similar considerations, Castaño was persuaded to change his mind, and he so informed Morlete, stating that he would send a messenger to Mexico city instead, with full reports for the viceroy. The man selected was Alonso Ruíz, one of Morlete's own soldiers, and to him Castaño entrusted his letters, apparently offering a proper reward for delivery of the messages and a speedy return of the courier.

When Morlete learned that Castaño would not go to Mexico to confer with the viceroy, he became very angry and told Juan Rodríguez Nieto, who had brought the news, that if Castaño left Almadén without the viceroy's authorization, the latter would have to send forty or fifty men to bring him back, handcuffed. "Let them do what they will; I've done my duty by coming here." [A lo qual respondió este testigo el dicho capitán muy enojado: "No se entienden que lo que les combiene es yr Gaspar Castaño á Mexico y tomar horden de su señoría porque si no lo hace y sale de aqui sin ella ha de ynbiar su señoría de el vissorrey tras dellos quarenta o cincuenta hombres y bolber todos maniatados. Por esso hagan lo que quisieren que yo con benir aqui he cumplido y por su bien lo hago. . . ."][4]

---

3. See especially the testimony of Diego Ramírez Barrionuevo, January 6, 1591; Alonso Ruíz, March 29, 1591; and Juan Rodríguez Nieto, July 10, 1591. "Autos y Diligencias," *op. cit.*

4. Testimony of Juan Rodríguez Nieto in *ibid.*

The above information comes from the legal proceedings later brought against Castaño de Sosa for violation of the viceroy's orders. Much of it is in the form of stereotyped questions and answers, which are often vague or inadequate. They do, however, establish the fact that Morlete and his company visited Castaño at Almadén in the month of June 1590 for the purpose of giving him the viceroy's warning not to capture any more slaves or to abandon his post; they reveal also that after Castaño's departure with his colony on July 27, the news reached Saltillo quite promptly, and also Mazapil, where Morlete was stationed. There it was considered by Captains Morlete, Domingo Martínez de Cearreta, and Diego Ramírez Barrionuevo, who decided to inform the viceroy in writing, whereupon the latter immediately commissioned Morlete to take forty soldiers, pursue Castaño, and bring him back under arrest.[5]

The historian, Alonso de León, writing in the seventeenth century, states that there was much enmity between the two men, Castaño and Morlete, but he places the blame on Morlete, who, he says, was a man of ill will, determined to destroy Castaño.[6] This may indeed have been the case, but for the time being, Castaño was a loyal frontier official, no worse than others, so Morlete returned to Mazapil, while Castaño remained at Almadén, plotting just how to proceed.

Meantime, on May 27, 1590, Castaño had sent Captain Francisco Salgado, Manuel de Mederos, and two other men to Mexico city to consult the viceroy about the New Mexico expedition and to obtain his blessing for it. This was obviously before Morlete came to Almadén to warn Castaño, as described above. The next messenger, Alonso Ruíz, was then sent to Mexico, presumably at the end of June while Morlete was conferring with Castaño at Almadén, and of course before the desertion of the colony and its departure for New Mexico on July 27. Thus the die was cast; Morlete returned to Mazapil, while Castaño and all of his colony, in spite of the viceroy's warning, secretly set out for the north.

After Morlete returned to Mazapil, further news soon came from Almadén that Castaño, in direct violation of the viceroy's order, had deserted his post and set out to explore the northern interior. Clearly, the viceroy was informed at once. This is shown by his letter to Morlete, as alcalde mayor of Saltillo, dated September 24, 1590, acknowledging receipt of the news that Castaño had left for New Mexico, and stating that he had decided to send Morlete with forty soldiers, including the

5. Barrionuevo, "Ynformación recivida en la audiencia real," March 18, 1592, *op. cit.*
6. Genaro García, *Documentos Inéditos* . . . vol. xxv, pp. 93-95.

company of Captain Domingo Martínez de Cearreta, to pursue and bring back the errant adventurers.[7] A few days later, on October 1, the viceroy issued official instructions to Morlete to lead an expedition to New Mexico to overtake Castaño de Sosa and his people and to bring them back to Mexico as prisoners.[8]

These instructions authorized Morlete to enlist forty of the finest soldiers he could obtain, all of whom were to be equipped with the best of everything, in view of the possibly dangerous nature of their mission. He was instructed to take along a friar, if one could be found, to take gifts for the Indians, to return the Mexican Indian slaves seized by Castaño and his followers, and to bring back some Indian guides, though paying them a moderate fee for their services!

Morlete's chief purpose, in other words, was to turn back the Castaño expedition, since it was illegal; to curb the injuries and excesses committed against the Indians of the frontier by Castaño and his people; and to return to their homes in northern Mexico any natives who might have been enslaved. To make sure that Castaño would be brought to heel, he was to be arrested and kept in chains, and the entire colony was to be returned to Mexico as prisoners.

If Captain Alonso de León's history of New León is correct in stating that Morlete was a bitter enemy of Castaño, he now had the supreme satisfaction of his life. Castaño, in considerable measure through his efforts, would be reduced to ruin.

Morlete's force was made up of two parts, twenty of his own followers and twenty enlisted by Martínez de Cearreta and his son. There is a document in the Archives of the Indies telling in detail of the New Mexico services of Captain Martínez de Cearreta and his followers, recorded when he asked that the government take an "Ynformación" of them and that witnesses be examined to substantiate the nature of his achievements on this expedition. Although this document does not give the details we should like to have today, it does emphasize the difficulties faced by the expedition and the hardships the men suffered throughout their journey to and from New Mexico in pursuit of Castaño.[9]

While these records do not state specifically the route taken by Morlete's party to New Mexico, it is probable that he followed the traditional route up the Río Grande. He made two major stops on the

---

7. Barrionuevo, "Ynformación," March 18, 1592.
8. "Instrucción al Capitán Juan Morlete para yr al Nuevo México en seguimiento de Gaspar Castaño y sus compañeros," in A.G.I., *Audiencia de México,* legajo 220, expediente 30A.
9. Barrionuevo, "Ynformación."

way that we know of, the first on the Río Bravo at a place called Los Reyes. This was on January 5, 1591. Here he began certain "Autos y Diligencias" against Castaño de Sosa and his soldiers for having entered New Mexico illegally and took the testimony of two witnesses, Diego Ramírez Barrionuevo and Bartolomé de Aviña.[10] They testified in some detail, telling almost exactly the same story of how Castaño conducted himself in the colony at Almadén, his relations with Morlete and other representatives of the viceroy, and his practice of seizing natives throughout the frontier area and selling them in captivity to the miners and farmers of the frontier.

Morlete's second stop was made at a place called Buena Nueva, on March 28, 1591, when he took the testimony of several other men— Salvador Sánchez, Domingo Hernández, Agustín de Villasín, Andrés Martínez Palomo, and Alonso Ruíz. The latter was the man who had been sent as Castaño's representative to Mexico city, but who, instead of returning with the desired permit for Castaño to go to New Mexico, brought orders for his arrest.

There is not sufficient information to judge of Morlete's route, but from the fact that the stop on January 5 was made on the Río Grande, and that there is no reference to the Salado, we assume that he followed the Río Grande to the pueblos of New Mexico, as had the Chamuscado and Espejo expeditions. If he had gone by way of the Pecos river, he would almost surely have found and commented on the traces of the route left by Castaño's party. Instead, Morlete reached New Mexico on Monday of Holy Week, March 29,[11] a few days after Castaño had established his entire colony at Santo Domingo, one of the Queres pueblos on the Río Grande about forty miles north of the present city of Albuquerque.

Morlete happened to reach Santo Domingo while Castaño was away on an exploring expedition. In his absence, the quartermaster, Juan Pérez de los Ríos, was in charge. Surprised by the unexpected arrival of Morlete, Pérez found himself caught between two fires, loyalty to his immediate superior, who was absent, and allegiance to the viceroy,

10. Their testimony was taken on January 6. See "Autos y Diligencias," *op. cit.*

11. Testimony of Juan Calderón, March 18, 1592, in "Ynformación recivida en la audiencia real." With regard to Morlete's route, Viceroy Velasco informed the king on February 23, 1591, that a soldier had written him that Morlete and his men were "proceeding in good conduct and order along Castaño's trail and close behind him," and that they had met some soldiers from his party returning with some Indian captives. This might appear to indicate that Morlete was following Castaño's route up the Pecos, but we doubt that this interpretation would be correct. Rather, it may indicate that Morlete's men were approaching the pueblos in the vicinity of Santo Domingo where Castaño was quartered and where the neighboring Indians would have known of his presence.

represented by Morlete. Pérez did the only thing he could—receive Morlete and his people with the utmost respect and fealty.

Meantime, Castaño had learned from Indians of the arrival of new people in the colony and promptly hurried back to Santo Domingo to meet them. On the way he met three soldiers, Juan de Carvajal, Joseph Rodríguez, and Francisco de Mancha, who had come to notify him of Morlete's arrival "with fifty men." Castaño asked the three soldiers about the newcomers, but in the names they gave he recognized none as the messengers he was looking for. Puzzled by the situation, he hurried to Santo Domingo at a gallop so that he might enter the pueblo by daylight. Dashing into the plaza with his troop, Castaño came face to face with his old rival, Morlete.[12]

After the two men had greeted and embraced each other with typical Spanish courtesy, Morlete showed Castaño the viceroy's order for his arrest, read it to him word for word, and asked him to submit to the royal command. Castaño said he would obey, since it was the king's wish, "for he was entirely subject to his authority," and Morlete immediately had him shackled, unwilling to take any chance on the escape of his able and resourceful prisoner in such a remote place. These galling chains Castaño bore on the long journey to Mexico city, as described so vividly in his pathetic letter to the viceroy of July 27, 1591.[13]

Morlete was evidently in no hurry to return to Mexico. Calderón, a soldier in Morlete's company, testified in the Domingo Martínez "Ynformación" that they spent forty days, "poco más ó menos," in various settlements. From this statement one may infer that they took time to explore the country, either while at Santo Domingo or as they traveled slowly down the river.

There is evidence also that Morlete took along a friar. His instructions provided that he do so, if he could find one, and two of the witnesses in the Martínez, "Ynformación," Calderón and Andrés Martín, suggest that his search was successful. Calderón states that a Franciscan friar said mass and preached to the Indians, and that many of the Indians came from afar to witness the ceremony, with which they were much pleased. Martín, not so lengthy in his remarks, says that a Franciscan friar recited mass on most of the days while there, evidently in Santo Domingo, and that the Indians looked on from the roofs and corridors of their houses.[14] Definite proof of the friar's presence is found in a report of Viceroy Luis de Velasco, who gives the friar's name as

12. Castaño de Sosa's "Memoria," p. 294.
13. See pp. 305-311.
14. Given in "Ynformación recivida en la audiencia real."

Juan Gómez, a Franciscan. Juan Bautista de Lomas y Colmenares, who was soon to become a candidate for the post of governor and adelantado of New Mexico, corroborates this statement.

As Morlete descended the Río Grande on the homeward trek, we find a record of two major stops. The first, on July 10, 1591, was at a place called Siete Mártires (The Seven Martyrs), described as about forty leagues from the last settlements of New Mexico. There he spent a few days formulating official charges against Castaño and taking further testimony to obtain evidence to prove them.[15]

It is interesting to speculate on the location of this stopping place, The Seven Martyrs. Judging by the fact that it was approximately forty leagues from the last New Mexico pueblos, which would be in the San Marcial area, it would have placed the expedition in the Mesilla valley, near modern Las Cruces, a pleasant and fertile spot, well supplied with food and water, bounded on the east by the spectacularly beautiful Organ mountains. These mountain peaks could well have been described by an imaginative observer as The Seven Martyrs. In other words, the distance of the Mesilla valley from the last New Mexico pueblos, its fertility, and the beauty of the spot all suggest this as the location of their camping place.

The testimony of several other witnesses was taken at a place called Las Milpas (the cornfields), on August 24, 1591.[16] Again, we are not sure of the location, though we learn that Morlete had not arrived in Mexico city by November 11, 1591, according to a report of the audiencia to the king.[17] But if one may venture a guess, Las Milpas was doubtless in the settled part of Mexico, the tribulations of the march over, and Morlete in an area where food and supplies were more abundant.

Though Morlete's itinerary on the return trip to Mexico is not outlined in detail, Captain Martínez de Cearreta claimed they came by a new route, two hundred leagues shorter. This raises some questions. Shorter than what? Shorter than the trails of Chamuscado and Espejo, or their own northward route? All of this region was inhabited, he said, except one hundred and twenty leagues, by which he presumably meant the stretch from San Marcial, where the first pueblos were found, to a point below El Paso.[18]

---

15. Six witnesses testified at Siete Mártires from July 10 to 12, 1591. They were Alonso Jaimez, Juan Rodríguez Nieto, Melchor Pabía, Juan de Contreras, Andrés Pérez, and Juan de Virués. "Autos y Diligencias," *op. cit.*

16. That is, Juan Pérez de los Ríos, Cristóbal Martín, and Pedro Yñigo. *Loc. cit.*

17. Audiencia to the king, November 11, 1591.

18. "Ynformación recivida en la audiencia real," *op. cit.* It is difficult to understand what Captain Martínez meant by saying that the return route was two hundred leagues shorter, a good five hundred miles. This may, of course, be a natural exaggeration, for

These statements certainly have some significance. Possibly Morlete left the Río Grande shortly after crossing the stream at El Paso and took a more direct course southward through modern Chihuahua to a point on the Conchos. This was the road subsequently followed by Juan de Oñate and company on their march to New Mexico in 1598, where there was plenty of water and grass to meet the needs of a large expedition.

Most of the new information about the Castaño de Sosa and Morlete expeditions comes from two documents, the "Autos y Diligencias," consisting of charges and testimony against Castaño and his soldiers for having entered New Mexico illegally and for making slaves of the Indians, and the "Ynformación recivida en la audiencia real" regarding the services of Captain Domingo Martínez de Cearreta and his son. Although Captain Martínez headed twenty of the forty men under Morlete's command, his name had dropped out of the New Mexico story almost completely until this document became known. The testimony of the various witnesses against Castaño, all participants in his affairs in New León and New Mexico or in the Morlete expedition, is extremely interesting and, though probably biased, reveals details about events not found anywhere else. One must recognize that Castaño's "Memoria" was designed to give the viceroy and other royal officials the most favorable impression of his achievements; but if this is offset by the testimony against him, which aimed at condemning him as a criminal who had repeatedly and openly violated the law, one gets a better picture of what took place on the northern border, especially of how independent of authority in Mexico city, whether of viceroy or audiencia, these captains felt themselves to be, and how they were looked on as powerful and irresponsible entrepreneurs, dangerous to the viceroyalty itself.

If we conclude, as the historian, Alonso de León, did, that Morlete was out to get Castaño's scalp, it still does not justify the governor's conduct in continuing to take Indian prisoners (which he seems to have

the men who took part in the Morlete expedition felt that they had suffered great hardships on the journey and had been exposed to extreme dangers, both from hostile Indians and from lack of supplies. Juan Calderón testified that they went by one route and returned by another a hundred leagues shorter, but he gives no further details. Francisco de Sant Miguel, a bit more informative, said they discovered a new route, on their return, by way of the Río del Norte, and that it was two hundred leagues shorter. The explanation of this "new route" may be that on the way north the party had followed the Río del Norte rather closely, like the Chamuscado and Espejo expeditions, but that on the way back they took a more direct route to Santa Bárbara, after crossing the Río Grande in the vicinity of El Paso, veering farther to the westward and following a trail at some distance from the river, as did Oñate on his way northward in 1598. See the testimony of the soldiers in "Ynformación recivida en la audiencia real," *op. cit.*

done) after leaving Almadén, or his departure for New Mexico without a permit. Perhaps Castaño saw no other way out of his troubles on the New León frontier—chiefly poverty, due to failure of the mines, and his illegal taking of Indian slaves. He had to be successful; he had to make a tremendous "strike," such as the discovery of a "new" Mexico. Success on a grand scale would condone small errors. And so, when neither Salgado nor Ruíz returned from the capital, Castaño set his steps for the north—without the viceroy's approval. For him, the die was cast. Let the future take care of itself.

Idle speculations, in a sense, but they do point up the changing conditions on the frontier after the publication of the Colonization Laws of 1573, and the difficulty of enforcing them. Castaño's arrest and conviction, though a misfortune to him, suggest the determination of the royal officials to curb ambitious frontier captains, even governors, from continuing the practice of capturing peaceful Indians and selling them as slaves. The authority of the viceroy, as the king's direct representative in New Spain, finally was extended to the remote northern border, although only time could make it truly effective.

Castaño's subsequent fate, after his trial in Mexico city, was as tragic as his earlier career was spectacular. The audiencia of Mexico sustained the charges against him, namely, that he had illegally raised troops, invaded lands inhabited by peaceable Indians, and entered New Mexico in spite of specific orders to the contrary. For these offenses he was sentenced to exile in the Philippine islands for six years, and he sailed with the fleet of Captain Felipe de Sámano during the same year, 1593.[19] Captain Alonso de León relates that he was highly regarded in the Philippines, but that he was killed on a voyage to the Moluccas when the Chinese galley slaves of his boat rose in revolt. In the meantime, the sentence against him had been appealed to the Council of the Indies in Spain, which vindicated him, declared him innocent, and revoked the sentence imposed by the audiencia of Mexico.[20] His name had been cleared, although not until after his death.

19. Castaño de Sosa's Sentence, March 5, 1593; and Genaro García, *Doc. Inéd. ó muy raros para la Historia de México* (1909), vol. XXV, pp. 94-95. The chronicler, Alonso de León, states that he was exiled to China, but our documents do not bear him out.
20. Genaro García, *loc. cit.*

LEYVA AND HUMAÑA, 1593

THE MISFORTUNES of Castaño de Sosa did not lessen the magnetism of the northern frontier in the minds of others. Within three years we find another group of adventurers making an expedition into the same region, also without the sanction of the viceregal authorities.[1] Unfortunately, we have only the most meager record of who took part in it and where they went, but it is enough to show the enormous seductive power of this new frontier. Otherwise, how can one explain the risks these men took in launching out on such distant explorations and under such circumstances?

This new expedition began in 1593, it appears, when Governor Diego Fernández de Velasco of New Vizcaya sent a force under Captain Francisco Leyva de Bonilla to punish certain hostile Indians, especially Tobosos and Gabilanes, including any renegades who might be hiding out on the frontier, robbing the cattle ranches of the province. Taking advantage of the opportunity of having an organized party under his command, Leyva de Bonilla determined on bigger things, namely, to invade New Mexico. Obviously he had learned nothing from the experiences of Castaño de Sosa. When the governor heard of this development, he sent a Captain Pedro de Cazorla to forbid him from going inland, under penalty of being declared a traitor to the king. Though some of his men refused to go along, Leyva persisted and went his dreary way to infamy and disaster.[2]

This account comes from the *Historia* of Villagutierre Sotomayor, but the sequel, even more interesting, was told by an Indian, Jusepe Gutiérrez, one of the invading party who escaped when the rest were destroyed during an exploration of the buffalo country, called by some the kingdom of Quivira. From the meager details that have been preserved, we learn that Jusepe managed to find his way back to New Mexico, where he was questioned by Don Juan de Oñate at the pueblo of San Juan Bautista in 1598.[3]

According to Jusepe's story, he was a native of Culhuacán, a town situated a short distance north of Mexico city, where Antonio Gutiérrez de Humaña induced him to join the proposed expedition, probably as his servant. At Santa Bárbara, others were recruited, so Jusepe testified, and the group entered the pueblo country and wandered about for a year. They made their headquarters at San Ildefonso, one of the Tewa towns on the Río Grande some twenty-five miles north of modern

1. See "Account Given by an Indian of the Flight of Humaña and Leyva from New Mexico."

2. Juan de Villagutierre Sotomayor, "Historia de la conquista, pérdida y restauración del reyno de la Nueba México, en la América Septentrional," MS No. 2822-2823 in the Biblioteca Nacional, Madrid, the essential parts of which relating to New Mexico were published by Alfred Charles Herrera as *Historia de la Nueva México*, Madrid, 1953. See Libro Segundo, pp. 28-30.

3. "Account Given by an Indian," *op. cit.*

Santa Fé. Evidently intrigued by reports of the lands and people in the vast region beyond, they "went inland through the pueblos of Pecos and the Vaquero Indians" to the Buffalo Plains. They crossed two large rivers, and beyond them saw many densely inhabited rancherías. One of these was a very large settlement, through which they traveled for two days. It was situated on one of the two rivers they had crossed. The houses of the inhabitants were built of poles, covered with straw, and stood close together; and there were fields of corn, calabashes, and beans.

Continuing in a northerly direction from the Great Settlement for three days, they "were startled and amazed" at the number of buffalo, which seemed to blacken the plains, but farther on they saw no more rancherías and but few of the humpbacked animals.

In some way, discord developed between Captain Leyva and Humaña. The Indian said it occurred three days after leaving the Great Settlement. He testified that one afternoon, after spending the day in his tent, occupied in writing, Humaña sent a soldier to summon Captain Leyva. As the captain approached, Humaña drew a butcher knife and killed him. Humaña now called the men together, took command, and showed them some papers, said Jusepe. In fact, he had heard of no reason for the killing except Captain Leyva's threat to give Humaña a beating. Later, as Oñate learned on his expedition to Quivira in 1601, the Indians had destroyed Humaña and his followers. In the melee at the settlement, five Indians had managed to escape, but got lost on the Buffalo Plains, only Jusepe and one other reaching an Indian ranchería in safety. Eventually Jusepe, taken prisoner by the Apaches and kept for a year after his companion was killed, heard that there were Spaniards in New Mexico, and made his way to one of the northern pueblos, from which he continued to San Juan Bautista.

The Great Settlement visited by this Spanish party appears to have been the same one that attracted Oñate on his expedition to Quivira in 1601. Bolton (1916) thought it was located on the Arkansas river at Wichita, Kansas. Wedel (1942), an archaeologist with the U.S. National Museum, concluded on the basis of extensive field studies that this Indian civilization, which had proved such a lodestone to these several expeditions, was situated near the junction of the Arkansas and Walnut rivers,[4] i.e., north and east of the Arkansas river and south of the Smoky Hill, covering several counties of southern Kansas.

---

4. Waldo R. Wedel, "Archaeological Remains in Central Kansas and Their Possible Bearing on the Location of Quivira," in *Smithsonian Miscellaneous Collections*, vol. 101 (1942), pp. 18-22.

THE PROBLEM OF IDENTIFYING GALLEGOS'
LIST OF PUEBLOS

THE PROBLEM of identifying the pueblos listed by Gallegos in his "Relation" is difficult and perplexing. In 1917, J. Lloyd Mecham prepared a Master's thesis, in Herbert E. Bolton's seminar at the University of California, entitled, "The Rodríguez Expedition into New Mexico, 1581-1582," in which he sought to locate virtually all of the pueblos recorded by Gallegos. In this effort, he used not only the latter's "Relation," but also the narratives of Espejo, Luxán, Obregón, and the 1598 "Ytinerario" of the Oñate expedition for contemporary sources, while relying particularly on Bandelier's researches of the 1880's for location of ruins then still visible. Bandelier, working alone, did almost no digging or excavating, except at Pecos, but he lived among the Indians, studied their customs and folklore, and sought to learn from them the sites of old and abandoned habitations. No one before him had done anything like this. As a consequence, his research, embodied in the two volumes of his *Final Report* (1890-1892), though very much of a pioneer effort, has been generally accepted as the basic authority in this field. Today it must be supplemented especially by the investigations of the Museum of New Mexico, the School of American Research, the Laboratory of Anthropology at Santa Fé, and the University of New Mexico, notably the archaeological surveys reported by R. G. Fisher and H. P. Mera.

The difficulty of correlating a list of pueblos in 1581, very vaguely described and probably with a certain amount of exaggeration,[1] with ruins that might or might not be visible nearly four centuries later, is certainly great. Modern readers, except expert archaeologists, tend to forget the enormous power of nature in leveling the mud walls of a pueblo in a relatively short time, once it is abandoned. Even today, adobe houses, protected by excellent stucco, will crack, and unless the rifts are promptly repaired, erosion sets in and the walls will decay.

When the Spaniards occupied New Mexico, less than twenty years after the exploration of the Chamuscado-Rodríguez party, many of the pueblos fell into disuse because it was the policy of the new regime to concentrate the Indians into larger communities. Here the friars could

---

1. Gallegos' "Relation" does indeed seem very reliable, and its population estimates are much less inflated than Espejo's own account of the following year, yet it is in many ways both unsatisfactory and exasperating. Gallegos virtually never gives the distance from one pueblo to another, and seldom mentions direction or location, leaving the student to guess or to proceed by trial-and-error method. In other respects it appears that he attempted to give a genuinely accurate description of the wonderful, new Pueblo country.

more effectively bring the rudiments of Christianity and a new mode of life to these neophytes.[2] At the same time, Apache depredations during the sixteenth and seventeenth centuries took an increasingly heavy toll of the pueblos. As a result, a great many of them, large and small, were left to decay, and today less than a fourth of the sixteenth-century New Mexico towns still exist as living organisms. Furthermore, pueblos that were located in areas now under cultivation, as is the case in the Río Grande valley, have been so thoroughly leveled that archaeologists cannot find enough remains to identify them. Any attempt to locate Gallegos' sixty-odd pueblos must be weighed against this background, a fact that makes such an effort difficult and uncertain.

During the decade of the 1930's, the School of American Research, the Laboratory of Anthropology, and the University of New Mexico began an archaeological survey of the Río Grande valley and the pueblos to the east. The first fruit of this project was the Fisher report of 1931,[3] covering the area from Isleta to about two miles above the mouth of the Jémez river. Of the twenty-six sites located that might be considered of pre-Spanish origin, only about half find a parallel in Mecham's location of Gallegos' towns. Nor was this 1931 reconnaissance considered definitive. "One can never know," wrote Fisher, "at what point a section will be finished, or at what time new material may turn up."

The truth of this observation was borne out by a more ambitious archaeological survey under the auspices of the Laboratory of Anthropology at Santa Fé initiated by Mera.[4] The area of investigation was the valley of the Río Grande in central New Mexico, with some extension to the east. The results, published in 1940, revealed a vast number of ruins which were mapped and described briefly. The chief difference between the work of Mera and his predecessors was that he did not seek to relate the old ruins to modern Indian towns or to those inhabited in the early years of Spanish occupancy. But he did give each one a number, and he used modern scientific techniques, especially the study of pottery remains, to establish the age and span of years in which

2. The missionaries sought to congregate the Indians into organized communities, on the assumption that no such order had existed among them previously. They conceived of the natives as living in savagery, dispersed and unregulated, and susceptible to spiritual administration only if congregated in villages or pueblos; or, if they already lived in pueblos, of concentrating them into fewer areas and centering their new life about the church and its functions. Cf. Edward H. Spicer, *Cycles of Conquest*, (1962), p. 288.

3. Reginald G. Fisher, "Second Report of the Archaeological Survey of the Pueblo Plateau," The University of New Mexico Bulletin, Survey Series, vol. I, 1931.

4. H. P. Mera, "Population Changes in the Río Grande Glaze-Paint Area," Laboratory of Anthropology Archaeological Survey, Technical Series, Bulletin No. 9 (Santa Fé, 1940).

each pueblo flourished. The fact is that the names of the individual pueblos of the sixteenth or seventeenth centuries are for the most part irretrievably lost, with the exception of a few like Pecos, Acoma, and the Zuñi and Hopi towns. About their early history we know precious little, even after the arrival of the Spaniards.

In their first publication of Gallegos' "Relation" (1927), the present writers accepted Mecham's conclusions, in the main.[5] Now, after further reflection and the study of such investigations as noted above, we are not so confident of his hypothesis.

Take, as an example, the pueblo of Taos. Did the Chamuscado party actually go that far north, as described by Mecham? We think it did not. In fact, we believe that it is possible to identify specifically only a few of the pueblos mentioned in 1581, and to suggest locations for some others. In general, however, it is feasible to locate them only as nations or linguistic groups.

To come back to Taos. This pueblo was not visited by the Espejo expedition, which with fourteen soldiers was stronger and better organized than that of Chamuscado and Rodríguez the preceding year. The latter had only nine, and one of them, Captain Chamuscado, was ill. Espejo was ambitious to learn everything he could about the country and pursued his explorations vigorously. After the trip to Zuñi, the Hopi towns, and the search for silver mines far to the west, he and his followers returned to Puaray on the Río Grande, but they did not go north to the Chama valley or to Taos. Instead, they explored the pueblos of the Galisteo basin in a vain search for minerals, after which they went on to Pecos, called Cicuye, and then on down the Pecos river as far as Toyah creek in Texas, where they found guides who directed them to the Río Grande, and so got back to Santa Bárbara.

We mention the Espejo expedition first because it is so much better documented than that of Chamuscado. In addition to Espejo's own account, we have Luxán's magnificent day-by-day diary, which eliminates any doubt or uncertainty of the itinerary. We have also Baltasar Obregón's *History*, written in 1584, which gives an excellent summary of both expeditions—Chamuscado's and Espejo's. Obregón not only corroborates the accounts of Espejo and Luxán, as well as that of Gallegos, but his "Summary" of the area explored by Espejo, brief and to the point, outlines the party's itinerary and leaves no doubt of the chief places visited. Nor do any of the chroniclers state that Espejo

5. In *New Mex. Hist. Rev.*, "The Rodríguez Expedition to New Mexico, 1581-1582," vol. II, pp. 239-268, 334-362.

went farther north than the Queres and the neighboring Tanos of the Galisteo basin.

For the Chamuscado party, we have in fact only Gallegos' "Relation," Obregón's *History,* and the sworn statements of Gallegos, Bustamante, and Barrado given before the viceroy in Mexico city soon after their return from the north in 1582, but these are sketchy at best and not of much help in tracing the route of this party through New Mexico. However, if we ignore for the moment Gallegos' "Account of the Pueblos," or "Pedrosa's List of Pueblos," which are virtually identical, and follow the descriptive chapters of Gallegos' "Relation," we find that nowhere does he make any record of having visited the northern New Mexico towns—none farther north than the Queres.

After the Spaniards had taken possession at San Felipe, the first New Mexico pueblo, on August 21, 1581, where they spent the night, says Gallegos, they continued up the river, marching slowly, trying to induce the frightened Piros, who had fled to the hills, to come back to their homes. The Piros are believed to have been Tanoan speaking, dialectally different from the Tigua and other Tanoans.

Gallegos states that they journeyed through the territory of this nation for four days, stopping to rest for two days before entering the lands of another, the Tigua, though he does not mention either of these tribes by name. This would signify that the Spaniards reached the homes of the latter about August 28. The next date mentioned is September 2, when Chamuscado took possession of a pueblo called Cáceres, probably in the Bernalillo area. Here the visitors were in the most densely populated part of the Río Grande valley and we might expect their progress to have been slow. Luxán, whose daily record of Espejo's travels the next year is very detailed, gives the native names of thirteen Tigua pueblos (including Puaray)—none of which, except Puaray, correspond to those of Gallegos—but they do verify the large number of towns in the Tigua nation. One of these, named Malpais, might have been near that spur of the Sandía mountains which extends toward the Río Grande four or five miles south of Bernalillo. There seems to be no other place that would fit the description, even though the land here is not as rugged as the word "malpais" would seem to indicate.

Then Chamuscado and his party continued forward, visiting the Atotonilco valley, evidently the lower Jémez, where they found four pueblos, at the largest of which, called Valladolid—probably Zía—they took possession for the king on September 6, another chronological anchor point of the trip. Moving along at the same pace, they were in the Galisteo basin two days later, on the evening of September 7. There Father Santa María made his famous decision to return alone to Mexico, intending to spread the report of their success in finding such a well-established native society ready for conversion and pacification. In spite of protests from his fellow friars and the soldiers, he left, but was soon killed by the natives, presumably the eastern Tigua. The affidavits relating to his departure appear in this volume.

Nowhere do we find specific identification of the place where Father Santa María left his companions, but after a study of N. C. Nelson's work on the pueblo ruins of the Galisteo basin, and the Laboratory of Anthropology archaeological survey, we believe that the party had reached Tunque pueblo, east of Algodones, and that the good father probably set out from that place. Coming from the Jémez valley, this would be an easy route to travel, and would provide a natural trail to the Galisteo pueblos farther east, or indeed to San Marcos. If the former, they would probably have turned the northern end of the Ortiz mountains and found themselves in the midst of a group of towns in the Galisteo basin, seven or eight of which were occupied at that time. If they went to Malpartida (San Marcos), that would also have been possible. Their itinerary for the next two weeks is purely speculative, as they did not leave for the buffalo country until September 28, and we are told only of their adventures at Malagón before then.

Immediately after the friar's departure, the Indians became alarmed, says Gallegos, believing that he was going to bring more Christians in order to put them out of their homes. The real reason for their dissatisfaction may well have been the Spaniards' demand for food, judging by what happened at Malagón. At that pueblo, situated a league from Malpartida, the natives revolted and killed three horses.[6] This led to open warfare, evidently because the natives refused to give up their food supply—and they were ready to fight to defend their homes. These Tanos appear to have been bold fighters, but they were no match for the visitors, who attacked and partially burned some of the smaller towns.

This episode at Malagón may have taken place soon after September 10, following the abrupt departure of Father Santa María, and before the trip to the buffalo country on September 28, or possibly after the return from that trip. We believe the former is the more likely explanation.

From late in October or early November, when the explorers came

6. See chap. 13 of Gallegos' "Relation."

back from the buffalo hunt, to January 31, 1582, when they left Puaray and started the return journey to Mexico, there is no chronological record of where they went or what they did, with the exception of an exploration that took them to Acoma and Zuñi, but for this trip we have no dates, except Gallegos' statement that it was December and the weather was bad.

Gallegos merely writes, near the end of his "Account of the Pueblos," that from Cáceres (located near Bernalillo), they explored a valley called Santiago, with two pueblos, Puerto Frío and Baños (Jémez towns), and then proceeded to Acoma, for which he gives the proper Indian name, a definite geographic peg on which we can base their itinerary. Hearing of other pueblos to the west, the party went on to the province of Zuñi, for which Gallegos likewise uses the native name and which comprised five pueblos, he wrote, naming four instead of the actual six: Aquima (K'iákima), Maca (Mátsaki), Alonagua (Hálona), Aguico (Háwikuh). This is positive proof of the point the Spaniards had reached on this western journey. Instead of going on to the Hopi country, of which they had heard reports, a land containing five pueblos and a mineral deposit and which Gallegos in his sworn testimony called Osay (Bustamante called it Asay)—clearly the Hopi kingdom—they returned to Puaray, "since it was the month of December and it was snowing heavily" and they were unable to travel further.

One is left to assume at this point that the party may have rested from its recent travels. Their need for a breathing spell must have been very great, for shoeing horses and restoring the strength of both men and animals, but of this necessary side of their adventures, we get only a glimpse. Similarly, we find no timetable for their observation of the native rituals, like the "snake dance," the marriage ceremony, or other customs, which Gallegos describes so vividly in his "Relation," yet these must have consumed some of the weeks not otherwise accounted for.

In spite of the foregoing analysis, there remains the burden of fitting Gallegos' sixty-one pueblos into the New Mexico landscape in some fashion.

Of the pueblos named by Gallegos, none has a familiar or historical sound until we reach Puaray, the nineteenth on the list of towns seen. Its location has created endless confusion among scholars. Bandelier placed it on a bluff on the west bank of the Río Grande, across from Bernalillo, about two miles south of Kuaua. These two sites, Bandelier's Puaray and Kuaua, have been called the two largest and most important ruins on the Río Grande and recognized also as probably the center of Coronado's Tiguex of 1540.[7] Bandelier, who based his conclusion to some extent on the accounts of Indian informants in the 1880's, was supported in his views by Edgar L. Hewett and Chas. F. Lummis. Later, other scholars uncovered several ruins which fitted the historic Puaray pattern better, in their judgment. These sites are east of the Río Grande and from seven to nine miles south of Bernalillo. On Fisher's Archaeological Survey Chart, they are Site 10, near modern Alameda, and Sites 11 and 13, about two miles farther north and closer to Sandía, or approximately three to five miles south of that pueblo.[8]

Charles W. Hackett placed Puaray on the east bank of the Río Grande, about ten miles north of Albuquerque, basing his conclusions on the records of the Pueblo Revolt of 1680.[9] Of course, changes did take place in pueblo life in the century after Chamuscado's day, and it is possible, indeed likely, that during this period more than one of the Tigua towns was referred to as a single "Puaray."[10]

Now, with the first of the pueblos located at San Felipe, that is, near San Marcial, and the nineteenth at Puaray, we still have some forty towns on Gallegos' list to account for, a substantial number of which were Tigua. How far north did Tigua territory extend? Bandelier believed that it began near Bernalillo and went as far south as Los Lunas.[11] The Fisher Archaeological Survey found Tigua ruins from just above the confluence of the Jémez river with the Río Grande, or about five miles from the Queres town of San Felipe, but it did not probe their southern boundary. Mera found the Tigua pueblos of Chamuscado's time to extend from Los Lunas to just above Bernalillo, with sixteen sites along the Río Grande and one on the Puerco, the latter opposite Los Lunas.

After Puaray, we find that the names of towns given by Gallegos, with few exceptions, offer little help in locating them on a modern map. The next town to note especially, however, is Medina de la Torre, number 31 on the Gallegos list, which could be identified with Kuaua,

7. Gordon Vivian, "The Excavation of Bandelier's Puaray," *El Palacio*, vol. 37, pp. 153-159. See also Wesley L. Bliss, "Preservation of the Kuaua Mural Paintings," *American Antiquity*, vol. XIII (1948), pp. 218-223. Bliss believed that Site 11 of the Fisher survey might have been Puaray.

8. Fisher, *op. cit.*

9. C. W. Hackett, "The Location of the Tigua Pueblos of Alameda, Puaray, and Sandia, 1680-1681," in *Old Santa Fe*, vol. II, pp. 381 ff.....

10. Vivian, *op. cit.*, p. 154.

11. Bandelier, *Final Report*, Pt. II, p. 233.

number 187 on the Laboratory of Anthropology survey.[12] Gallegos wrote that it contained two hundred and thirty houses of two and three stories, making it one of the largest in the province, exceeded in size only by Acoma and Nueva Tlaxcala, each with five hundred houses, and Piedrahita and Puerto Frío, each with three hundred.

According to the Gallegos "Relation," it appears that the party next visited a valley called Atotonilco, evidently the lower Jémez, in which they found four pueblos, called Guatitlán, La Guarda, Valladolid (modern Zía, where Chamuscado took possession on September 6), and La Rinconada. Espejo, the following year, reported five pueblos in this same group, and Oñate later gave the number as four. Mera found four ruins at Zía that had flourished late in the sixteenth century.[13]

Chamuscado's party did not spend much time in this visit to the Jémez valley, for on the evening of September 7, while on the way to the Galisteo basin, possibly at Tunque pueblo, Father Santa María left them, as already noted. He took the route east of the Sandía and Manzano mountains, and, as the explorers learned after their return from the buffalo trip, was killed three days after leaving the Spanish party.[14]

On the departure of the friar, the rest of the party set about prospecting for minerals, obtained various samples from the Indians, and then went on to see the sites for themselves. These deposits might have been on the borders of the Galisteo valley, such as at the San Pedro mountains or one of the adjacent mineralized areas, or at Cerrillos, where there were lead outcrops that must have been used by the natives as glaze-paint for pottery.[15]

During this two weeks' period before the start of the buffalo trip on September 28, the soldiers evidently returned to the Río Grande and continued their explorations up that stream as far as Cochití, at the mouth of the Santa Fé river, discovering on the way four pueblos. These were Castilleja (San Felipe), Castildavid or Castil de Avid (LA

12. The original work of the Museum of New Mexico and of the Laboratory of Anthropology, once independent entities but now both functioning within the State Museum organization, has been combined and the site survey continued. Each known archaeologic site is assigned a number, which is recorded in an index book and on the proper map, with pertinent information entered on a file card. All cultural materials derived are cataloged according to the site numbers. Therefore the designation LA 187 shows that this is the 187th site recorded in the Laboratory of Anthropology's survey. To date, over 8,035 locations have been registered in New Mexico.

13. Mera, "Population Changes," pp. 24-26.

14. It is supposed that he skirted the east side of the sierra, up the San Pedro valley. Bandelier and some later writers believed that he was killed by the Indians of Paa-ko, but on the basis of what Espejo learned the following year, it seems more likely that he was killed by the eastern Tigua. Marjorie F. Lambert, *Archaeological Chronicle of an Indian Village in North Central New Mexico* (Santa Fé, 1954), pp. 5-6.

15. Reed, "The Southern Tewa," *El Palacio*, vol. 50 (1943), p. 261.

922), Suchipila (Cochití), and Talaván (LA 35, in Cochití canyon). Thence they continued into the lower Galisteo valley, which they called Valle Vicioso because of its fertility, where they found three pueblos, Castilblanco (Santo Domingo), Buena Vista (LA 182, two miles east of Domingo station), and La Barranca, all of three to four stories, if we can believe Gallegos' "Relation." These towns could not have been situated along the Santa Fé river, for archaeologists have not found ruins of such size on its banks dating from the Chamuscado period, nor indeed for La Barranca.[16]

It is interesting that Gallegos places Castilblanco opposite the pueblo of Castildavid. If the latter was, as we believe, the Queres town at LA 922, on the west bank of the Río Grande, Castilblanco would be almost directly across from it, near the mouth of the Galisteo river, that is, the pueblo of Santo Domingo.

About this time, the Spanish party discovered the great pueblo of Nueva Tlaxcala, which we believe was Pecos, of which they took possession for the king, but no date is given for this act. Whether the trip was made between September 10 and 28 or later is not clear, but we infer that it took place before the buffalo hunt. The soldiers also heard of thirteen other pueblos, but did not visit them due to lack of time and supplies. What towns could these have been? Could the Spaniards have heard of the Tewa and northern Tigua, the Plains Indians, or the eastern Tigua and Tompiro? Since the evidence presented by Gallegos is so frail, it is impossible to be more specific, but the above conclusion does seem to be logical.

Nueva Tlaxcala? Was it really Pecos? This is one of the intriguing questions that arises in a study of the expedition. The chronicler said that it was the largest pueblo on their trip, with five hundred houses, yet he devotes fewer words of description to it than to most of the others. Nevertheless, the soldiers must have considered it of great importance, for Gallegos wrote that they left it "under the authority of his Majesty." The phrase is *Quedó en cabeza de su magestad,* which usually meant that such a town was reserved for the king, that he would get its revenues, and that it would not be given in encomienda to some individual conqueror.[17]

For the reasons already stated at some length, especially the lack of

16. Mera, "Population Changes," p. 29; Stanley A. Stubbs and W. S. Stallings, Jr., "The Excavation of Pindi Pueblo, New Mexico," School of American Research, Monograph No. 18 (1953), pp. 22-23; Lambert, *op. cit.,* p. 6.

17. Bandelier, with much less documentary material than is now available, identified Nueva Tlaxcala with Pecos. "Documentary History of the Río Grande Pueblos, New Mexico," in *New Mex. Hist. Rev.,* vol. v, pp. 337, 384-385.

evidence that the explorers visited the most northerly pueblo groups, and the description of Nueva Tlaxcala as such a large settlement—which would not be true of Taos—we believe Nueva Tlaxcala to have been the great pueblo of Pecos, famous since the time of the Coronado expedition.

We recognize the difficulty of explaining the sworn statements of Bustamante and Gallegos that Nueva Tlaxcala was a one day's journey from "the river," presumably the Río Grande, but that is one of the over-all problems of interpreting the Gallegos "Relation" four hundred years after it was written—and with far too many details of the route of march, and distance, left unspoken. In all probability, the Spaniards followed Indian trails, more direct than present roads, a fact that needs to be considered in judging the regions they visited.

Now came Chamuscado's trip to the Buffalo Plains which occupied the party from September 28 to early November. Owing to the lack of a guide, the soldiers wandered about for some time after leaving the Galisteo valley, but finally, on October 9, they reached some brackish lagoons on the plains of eastern New Mexico, where they found buffalo, though it was not until ten days later that they had shot an adequate number and started back. Gallegos says they returned to Piedrahita, which Erik K. Reed believes was Pecos,[18] a view that does not appear logical to us. Previous scholars, including Bandelier, Nelson, and Mera, identify Piedrahita with San Cristóbal in the eastern part of the Galisteo valley, a conclusion we share.

Assuming the above itinerary to approximate correctly the travels of the Chamuscado party, we still have to account for a valley named Santiago, with two pueblos, Puerto Frío and Baños, which we believe were situated in the vicinity of Jémez pueblo or the sister towns farther north in the San Diego and Guadalupe canyons, where there were several towns at that time. Puerto Frío, says Gallegos, was found "in a gorge close to a river that flows near the pueblo." This must be the gorge of the Jémez river, very narrow, with bluffs rising steeply skyward on both banks, especially to the west. Farther up the valley was the pueblo named Los Baños, perhaps Giusewa, "place of the boiling waters." The Indians for centuries had known its medicinal value and made long journeys, even from Zuñi, it is said, to benefit from its waters.[19]

At these pueblos the Spaniards were told that there were thirteen

18. Reed, "The Southern Tewa," *op. cit.*, vol. 50, pp. 260, 283; and vol. 61 (1954), p. 325.

19. Bertha P. Dutton, "The Jemez Mountain Region," *El Palacio*, vol. 44 (1938), pp. 136-141; Paul Reiter, *The Jemez Pueblo of Unshagi, New Mexico* (Albuquerque, 1938).

other pueblos farther on, but they were unable to visit them due to a heavy snowfall. This description seems to point to the Vallecitos region, where there were several pueblos.

The late Lansing B. Bloom, able New Mexico historian, pointed out emphatically that the early chroniclers distinguished between the "Aguas Calientes" and the "Jémez" groups of pueblos of this tribe. The former was in the San Diego-Guadalupe drainage, and the latter in the Vallecitos region farther east where there were many towns. Bloom reported in 1922 that in the whole Jémez country at least twenty-two sites were known.[20] Castañeda, chronicler of the Coronado expedition, first made the distinction, reporting three "Aguas Calientes" and seven "Jémez" pueblos. Since there would probably have been no material change forty years later when Chamuscado's men visited the area, Gallegos may well have been speaking of the Vallecitos towns, six to seven thousand feet in elevation, in referring to the thirteen that they did not visit because of the weather. In this case, Puerto Frío and Baños were in the Aguas Calientes group on the Jémez river and its nearby canyons.

The best known region visited by the Chamuscado party was the valley of San Mateo. "About five leagues from the Guadalquivir river we discovered another valley, which we called San Mateo." In it the explorers found four pueblos—Piedrahita, Galisteo, Malpartida, and Malagón. These obviously were in the upper Galisteo basin, about twenty-five miles from the Río Grande. All scholars agree on this location, although there is difference of opinion on specific locations for these towns. Most agree that Piedrahita was San Cristóbal; Galisteo, the same; Malpartida, San Marcos; and Malagón, San Lázaro. Reed's assertion that Piedrahita might have been Pecos and that Malagón was San Cristóbal has already been referred to. In part, his reasoning was based on the assumption that San Lázaro was not inhabited in 1581, though it had been both earlier and later and might have been at this time. In this identification no account is taken of Shé or Colorado, situated in Jara arroyo a few miles south and west of San Cristóbal, though both were occupied at the end of the sixteenth century. Shé was a large pueblo, while Colorado was smaller, so it seems entirely possible that the Spaniards might have visited Shé, which lies only six or seven miles south of Galisteo over a good trail.

While at Puaray, on the return from Acoma and Zuñi, the Chamuscado party heard of some salt deposits fourteen leagues away, to the

20. Lansing B. Bloom, "The West Jemez Culture Area," *El Palacio*, vol. 12 (1922), pp. 21-23; Hammond and Rey, *Narratives of the Coronado Expedition*, p. 259.

east of and behind the Sierra Morena, obviously the Manzano mountains. On going to examine them, the explorers discovered the splendid
salines around present Estancia and Willard, New Mexico, and found
five more pueblos, to which they gave Spanish names—Zacatula, Ruiseco, La Mesa, La Joya, and Francavila. They were probably situated
between Tajique, Chililí, and Quarai. The soldiers heard reports also
of others that were larger, possibly Abó and the Tompiro group, but
returned to Puaray instead of going to examine them, since the weather
was snowy and bad. Gallegos, the only one to give it a date, places this
trip in December.[21] From Puaray, the party started the final journey
for home on January 31, 1582.

The geographical names used by Gallegos and his companions for
the New Mexico pueblos can be divided into four main categories:
those of Spanish derivation; some of purely New Mexican tribes; others
of Mexican origin, chiefly Nahuatl; and those named after saints.

From the Tigua pueblo of Cáceres northward (in the vicinity of
Bernalillo), we find seven pueblos to which they gave Spanish names,
all taken from towns in the home provinces of Cáceres, Avila, and
Badajoz. From Cáceres province came five: the pueblos of Cáceres,
Galisteo, Malpartida, Talaván, and Castilleja (Sierra de Castillejo);
from Badajoz, two: Medina de la Torre and Castilblanco; from Avila,
one: Piedrahita. Of New Mexican origin we have only Acoma, the
Zuñi group of pueblos, Puaray, and Asay or Osay (modern Hopi) before the Espejo expedition, when more native towns were named and
identified.

It does not seem fruitful to analyze the application of saints' names
to localities in New Mexico, since each expedition applied its own and
none were permanent. On the other hand, combinations of Nahuatl
terms which the Chamuscado explorers applied to New Mexican
pueblos and geographical features can be found in Mexico. Notable
among these are Atotonilco (Hot Springs), Cempoala, Tlaxomulco,
Mexicalcingo, Tomatlán, and Cuautitlán, all of which are to be found
within a fifty-mile radius of Mexico city. Other names used by Gallegos
occur elsewhere in Mexico, apparently taken from places familiar to
him or other members of the expedition.

Our study of Gallegos' "Relation" has brought out many details of
interest, but it has also revealed the limitations of such a narrative
for the development of a truly complete understanding of the party's
itinerary. Gallegos was writing to impress the viceroy and the crown

21. Testimony of Hernando Gallegos, May 16, 1582, p. 137.

with the discovery of a vast new region, inhabited by people who rivaled in some respects those of the valley of Mexico in culture, and, he hoped, in riches. The party had no topographer to draw a map, and Gallegos obviously had other things to do, as one of only eight soldiers, than to act solely as notary and to keep a record of their experiences. And since none of the three friars survived the expedition, they left no account of what happened, as might normally have been expected. Espejo's expedition the following year, 1582-1583, did much to augment Spanish knowledge of the "New" Mexico, particularly through Luxán's diary, and so did the Castaño de Sosa and Morlete adventures of 1590 and 1591. But none of their chroniclers left posterity a definite description or a map showing locations of the sixteenth-century pueblos or indicating their native names, with a few exceptions.

The first map of New Mexico that has been preserved comes from the Oñate period in 1602.[22] It was made by a cosmographer in Mexico named Enrico Martínez, at the suggestion of Rodrigo del Río, for use by the viceroy following Oñate's unsuccessful expedition to Quivira the previous year. The viceroy was trying to get a clear picture from returning officers and men of what the new country amounted to, so that he might advise the king as to further development of the country, possibly at royal expense. Martínez drew such a map, on the basis of information supplied by a certain Juan Rodríguez, one of the New Mexico soldiers who had accompanied Vicente de Zaldívar, Oñate's chief officer, to Mexico in 1602. Martínez called his map a "sketch," and this defines it exactly. It gives, nevertheless, a faithful picture of New Mexico from the Río Grande to Quivira. As the first map of any part of the American West it is an extraordinary treasure.

The original Martínez map is preserved in the famous Archives of the Indies in Seville, Spain, and is reproduced by courtesy of its distinguished director, Don José de la Peña.

---

22. Reproduced in Bolton, *Spanish Exploration in the Southwest* (1916), at p. 212; and by Carl I. Wheat, *Mapping the Transmississippi West*, vol. 1 (1957), at p. 29. The original is in A.G.I., *Mapas y Planos*, Núm. 49.

PART I

GALLEGOS' RELATION OF THE CHAMUSCADO-RODRÍGUEZ EXPEDITION

RELATION AND REPORT[1] OF THE EXPEDITION MADE BY FRANCISCO SÁNCHEZ CHAMUSCADO AND EIGHT SOLDIER COMPANIONS IN THE EXPLORATION OF NEW MEXICO AND NEW LANDS, AND ITS OUTCOME; ADDRESSED TO HIS EXCELLENCY, DON LORENZO SUÁREZ DE MENDOZA, COUNT OF CORUÑA, VICEROY, GOVERNOR, AND CAPTAIN GENERAL OF NEW SPAIN, BY HERNÁN GALLEGOS, NOTARY AND DISCOVERER.[2]

Most excellent prince:

Since I began serving his Majesty as a youth in this kingdom of New Spain in a military capacity, in the new province of Galicia and that of Vizcaya, by accompanying certain captains against the wild Chichimeco Indians, who have caused so much damage in these regions, there has grown on me constantly, as the years have passed, an earnest desire to serve my king and lord in some important cause worthy of my ambition. Since Francisco Sánchez Chamuscado was offered the leadership of the expedition that he was to carry out in the discovery of New Mexico and the new lands—which had been sought for so many years—and as he had spoken to me about it, I saw that this was an opportunity commensurate with my purpose and aspirations. After weighing and deliberating upon the obstacles and difficulties that would be encountered in an undertaking of such magnitude, we determined, together with seven other companions with whom we discussed the

1. The Gallegos "Relation" of the Chamuscado-Rodríguez expedition to New Mexico is one of the many treasures preserved in the Archives of the Indies in Seville, Spain, (A.G.I.), *Patronato*, legajo 22. The copy is preceded by the following certification:

"I, Juan de Aranda, treasurer of his Majesty in this New Spain, certify that in a book, written by hand, left in my possession with other books and papers at the death and by the will of Don Pedro Moya de Contreras, late archbishop of Mexico, governor and inspector *(visitador)* in this New Spain, and president of the Council of the Indies, of which he was secretary and executor, was found this manuscript."

Moya de Contreras, then archbishop of Mexico, had been appointed viceroy in 1584 at a time of corruption and venality in public affairs. After instituting numerous reforms, he left the office of viceroy in 1585, returned to Spain, and subsequently became president of the Council of the Indies. His papers in Mexico were sent to Spain, presumably while the government was seeking a conqueror of New Mexico.

2. Viceroy Don Lorenzo Suárez de Mendoza y Figueroa ruled New Spain from October 1580, to June 1582. H. I. Priestley, *The Mexican Nation*, pp. 88-89; H. H. Bancroft, *History of Mexico*, vol. II (1883), pp. 678 and 683.

enterprise, to carry out the said expedition, which had for its ultimate object the service of God our Lord, the preaching of His law and gospel to all men, and the extension of the dominions of the royal crown of Castile.

After discussing the matter with some friars of the Franciscan order who gladly offered to go on the expedition, and having obtained in advance the permission and authority of your Excellency, we set out from the valley of San Gregorio,[3] which is included in the jurisdiction and district of the mines and town of Santa Bárbara in the kingdom of Vizcaya. We were three Franciscan friars and nine soldiers, provided with arms and horses at our own cost. Anticipating with good reason the great dangers that we would encounter, not only from war with the innumerable barbarous peoples along the way, but also from hunger and want in the uninhabited areas that we expected to find on such a long journey—especially since our party was so small—and fortified with the hope of attaining temporal and eternal reward, in imitation of the example set by the nine men of fame,[4] and moved by a spirit of determination to die or to discover the desired region, we continued our journey until we reached that land.

On this expedition I noted the important events that occurred in the exploration of the province; but after I had served to the best of my limited ability it seemed to me that I was not even then doing all I should. I chose also to employ the little talent that God had given me in an undertaking that would be of service to God our Lord and to his Majesty, in order not to leave undone anything I could do. Thus, while discharging my duty as a soldier, I wrote, in my scanty spare moments, a brief account of our exploration and the important events that took place, as well as of various customs and rituals that we learned about from the natives. I decided to divide the account into chapters and to dedicate it to your Excellency.

Although this action may seem boldness on my part, because I was born and brought up in humble circumstances, I was nevertheless encouraged by the incident of the poor widow mentioned in the gospel, who was praised by the Lord for the two small coins which she offered in the temple. She was not belittled because she did not give much, but,

3. On June 6, 1581. See chapter 1. San Gregorio was situated a few miles down the Río Parral from the modern town of Parral.

4. The nine men of fame were: three Jews—Joshua, David, and Judas Maccabaeus; three gentiles—Alexander, Hector, and Julius Caesar; three Christians—King Arthur, Charlemagne, and Godfrey of Bouillon. The novel, *Le triomphe des neuf preux* (Dabbeville, 1487; Paris, 1507), was translated into Spanish as *El triumpho de los nueve de la fama,* and printed at Lisbon, 1530, and Valencia, 1532. It went through many later editions.

on the contrary, was held in greater esteem.[5] As a result of this reflection, and finding myself in possession of two mites, I offered them to your Excellency and risked them in this venture. I beg you to take this narrative under your care, mindful of the fact that I gave all I had, and to consider the good will with which I offered it, since your Excellency has such a great part in the enterprise under discussion; for it was by your support and during your term in office that the discovery, so greatly desired by our predecessors, was achieved, although this was not accomplished without the special providence of God. May He protect your very excellent person for many happy years and prosper your state as your Excellency deserves, and as I your humble servant desire.

5. Mark, chapter 12, verse 42.

CHAPTER I

ACCOUNT OF THE PERSONS WHO, AT THEIR OWN EXPENSE, FURNISHING THEIR ARMS AND HORSES, WENT FORTH TO DISCOVER NEW MEXICO AND OTHER LANDS WHERE GOD OUR LORD WAS PLEASED TO DIRECT THEM, IN ORDER THAT HIS HOLY FAITH MIGHT BE TAUGHT AND HIS GOSPEL SPREAD THROUGHOUT THE LANDS WHICH THEY, AS YOUR LOYAL VASSALS, MIGHT THUS DISCOVER IN HIS HOLY SERVICE AND IN THE INTEREST OF THE ROYAL CROWN.

THE PERSONS above-mentioned were Francisco Sánchez Chamuscado, leader of the expedition; Hernán Gallegos, his aide; Pedro de Bustamante; Felipe de Escalante; Pedro Herrera; Pedro Sánchez de Fuensalida; Hernando Barrado; and Juan Sánchez.[1] In order to carry out the enterprise and their good purpose of spreading the holy gospel, they took along the preachers, Fray Francisco López (superior) and Fray Juan de Santa María, together with the lay brother, Fray Agustín,[2] all three being Franciscans from the monastery of New Spain in the city of Mexico. On this expedition all set out together on June 6, 1581, from the valley of San Gregorio, district and jurisdiction of the mines of Santa Bárbara in New Vizcaya.

On the said journey we marched down the San Gregorio river until we came to the junction of this stream with the rivers Conchas and Florido, twelve leagues more or less from Santa Bárbara and from the

1. Also Pedro Sánchez de Chaves, whose name is here omitted. See chapter VII, and later.
2. Fray Agustín Rodríguez.

place where we began the journey. Leaving the junction of these rivers, we determined to follow the largest stream that we might find, and thus we followed the Conchas. Proceeding down this river for a distance of more than fifty leagues we were met by many Indians who lived along it and who received us cordially.

After leaving the Concha nation we came to the Raya, another people who inhabit the same land and use the same language as the Conchas. In this territory of the Raya[3] we took the latitude and found it to be twenty-nine degrees. We had guides who led us at all times through these two nations. Great numbers of Indians, men as well as women, accompanied us; and others came out to meet us with many presents of ground mesquite—as it is commonly called by the Spaniards, because it is a fruit which resembles the carob bean—in addition to quantities of honey mesquite and calabashes. These people are very unattractive in appearance. They go about naked like savages. They are lazy, capable of little work, and dirty, and sustain themselves on quantities of calabashes, ground mesquite, mescal, prickly pears, and fish from the river. They call water "bod," corn "fonet," and they are named "Yoslli."

3. Though Gallegos here states that the Raya were different from the Conchos nation, he then explains that they "inhabit the same land and use the same language." See J. Charles Kelley, "Historic Indian pueblos of La Junta de los Ríos," *New Mex. Hist. Rev.*, vol. xxvii (1952), pp. 257-295, and vol. xxviii (1953), pp. 21-51; and Jack D. Forbes, *Apache, Navaho, and Spaniard*, p. 33.

CHAPTER II

TELLING OF OUR DEPARTURE FROM THE SAID RAYA NATION, OUR PENETRATION OF THE INTERIOR, AND THE MANNER OF OUR RECEPTION BY THE INDIANS.

WHEN WE STARTED OUT we traveled down the aforesaid river.[1] After five leagues, more or less, we were met by numerous Indians of the Cabris nation,[2] who speak a different language from the Conchas whom we had left behind. The Indians of the Cabris nation are very handsome, spirited, and much more active and intelligent than the people met previously. They are very well built. Their faces, arms, and bodies

1. The Conchos.
2. The Cabris were Julimes. The party had reached the ridge separating San Pedro from Cuchillo Parado, which marked a political and linguistic boundary, distinguishing the Cabris from the Conchos. Luxán called these people Passaguates. The Cabris-Passaguates were in the Cuchillo Parado valley. Kelley, *op. cit.*, vol. xxvii, p. 285; Forbes, *op. cit.*, p. 47.

are striped with neatly painted lines. These people are cleaner and more modest than the Conchas. They grow large quantities of calabashes and beans in the proper season. Like those we met before, they go about naked and wear their hair cropped short in the shape of skullcaps. The Cabris Indians gave us large amounts of calabashes, ground mesquite, prickly pears, beans, and mescal, which is what they use for food throughout the year.

They brought us these presents because they had heard how the Spaniards were going to be their friends and would reconcile them with their enemies, who were at war not only with them but with the Spaniards. It seemed that the other Indians had fled into the sierra for fear of the Spaniards, because the latter had taken and carried off many of their people during the raids of the captains who had entered the territory by order of Francisco and Diego de Ibarra and had caused them much harm.[3] In order to pacify the land and to reassure these people, as well as the rest, we gave them to understand through the interpreter we had brought along that we, who were now in their land, had come only to restore friendship between them and their enemies, to help them in their wars and struggles, and to lend them the protection and aid they might need against their foes. We also told them not to fear the Spaniards, who would not cause them any further harm; and that we were there for this express purpose—to insure that in the future no Spaniards would come except as their friends, provided the Indians behaved well, but if they misbehaved, the Spaniards would kill them all. If they wanted to avenge the seizure of their friends, relatives, wives, and children, they should come out into the open quickly; for we eight, who were there among them, would avenge the other Spaniards for what they had suffered.

Our boldness toward the natives was meant primarily to intimidate them so that the news should spread. We fired quite a few harquebus shots, at which the natives were very much frightened and said that they did not wish to quarrel with the Spaniards, but instead wanted to be our friends and to be aided in their wars. They added that, though they had been somewhat afraid of the Spaniards, they would not be so in the future, but on the contrary would take pleasure in not offending us in any way, and that we Spaniards should conduct ourselves likewise. They did not want to fight us because they would soon become demoralized. It was God's will that instilled this fear into these and the other natives, because we knew very well we were not sufficient

3. Slave-hunting raids beyond the older settlements were one of the evils of frontier society in the Spanish colonies. See Introduction, pp. 30, 47.

in number to withstand so many people without the aid of the Lord. With this confidence in divine aid we had set out on the expedition.

After all this conversation we told the Indians, in order that they might know that the Spaniards were their friends and would not harm them further or steal any more of their people, that they should place crosses in their rancherías, so that in case any Spaniards did come with the intention of doing harm they would refrain, on seeing the crosses. The Indians were very much pleased by this and showed their appreciation by embracing us and promising not to remove the crosses from their towns and rancherías. When we placed them in the latter, they were delighted, and raised their hands toward the sun, because they had been told we were children of the sun.

We asked them if there were clothed people beyond their nation, if there was corn, and if there were settled communities, because we wished to see them and wanted to send them notice that we were coming. The natives replied that farther on, very far from there, they had heard that there were many brave people with many houses, an abundance of corn, beans, and calabashes; and that the people wore white clothes like ourselves.[4] In view of the answer of these Indians, messages were sent throughout the land [of our visit].

4. That is, cotton clothing.

CHAPTER III

How we sent notice of our coming throughout the land.

WE LEFT this place[1] after sending word through the land that we were coming to restore peace between these people and the nations with whom they carried on war; for we understood that they waged war against one another. Continuing down the same river [the Conchos], we entered and crossed a region of many very dense ridges, which our pack animals traversed only with great difficulty. In fact, it became necessary to lift up some that rolled down, and others became exhausted and collapsed. This resulted from our not knowing the way. But God was pleased to give us patience and endurance to bear these hardships; and as these are matters directed by His hand we offered our thanks to Him. When we had descended from that mountainous territory, we came to the river; for it was necessary to cross the ridge to

1. The territory of the Cabris Indians.

reach it. This sierra must be about a league across, but the difficult part is short, only about an harquebus shot, which includes climbing to the summit and descending.[2]

Marching down the river [Conchos], we met the messengers we had sent to notify the natives of our coming, and as soon as they reached us we halted on the bank of the river in order to learn at once what they had to say. A short time later many Indians came to meet us, very handsome men and beautiful women. We asked them the name of their language, because it seemed different from the one we had just heard, although the two peoples understand one another. They answered that it was "Amotomanco."[3] These Indians call water "abad," corn "teoy," and beans "ayaguate." They paint themselves with stripes and are cheerful in disposition. They live in houses made of paling plastered with mud, but go about naked like the people we had met earlier. They cultivate very little corn, but calabashes and beans, which form a part of their diet, in quantity. However, their natural food is *xamiscas* [mescal?]. These people received us cordially and gave us of the provisions they had, namely, calabashes, ground mesquite, beans, prickly pears, and also *exicas* [mescal?].

The natives were disturbed, fearful of the Spaniards on account of what they had heard; and so they complained to us. We reassured and quieted them through our Indian interpreters and let them know that the Spaniards would not cause them any further harm, because we had been sent to reassure them by our great lord. They were much pleased at this and became cheerful. They have very fine weapons—Turkish bows and excellent shields of buffalo hide.

After this we summoned two old Indians who seemed to be caciques of that region, in order to inform ourselves concerning the land and people to be found farther on. We asked them through our interpreter what kind of people there were beyond, in the territory bordering on theirs. They replied that in their own land there were many people of their tongue, and from what they indicated their nation extended for

2. The party had left the Conchos river near the modern Cuchillo Parado where it makes a sharp turn to the north around the mountains. There they struck across the Sierra Grande, a very difficult, mountainous trail, and then, reaching the Conchos again, descended it to the vicinity of El Mesquite and San Juan Bautista. Here they went northward to the Río Grande at Porvenir, thence down the Río Grande to La Junta, junction of the two streams, the Conchos and the Río Grande. The La Junta pueblos of the historic period were located either on the Río Conchos or on the Río Grande at and near the junction. Kelley, *op. cit.,* vol. xxvii, pp. 261-262.

3. These were undoubtedly the same as those called Otomoacos by Luxán, or Patarabueyes by Luxán and Obregón. The Patarabueyes, says Forbes, were divided into two groups, the Otomoacos, later known as Cholomes, and the Abriaches, subsequently called Julimes. Forbes, *op. cit.,* p. 56.

more than one hundred leagues; that many more were to be found beyond their land; that along a river three leagues distant from the said Conchas, going upstream toward the north, there were many, so they had been told, who wore white [cotton] clothes like ourselves; and that there were quantities of cotton, corn, beans, and calabashes. In order to ascertain the size of the river they had mentiond and to find out if it fitted their description, we decided to look for it, although the route we chose was not the one toward the north indicated to us by the Indians.

In response to other questions, we learned that in the interior there were many clothed people living in very large houses. Our informants seemed almost to indicate to us that those people spoke the Mexican language, but as they were Indians we did not believe what they said about the language, although we did believe the rest. We were very much pleased by this information, and gave many thanks to God our Lord for the news which the natives of that land had given us to facilitate the dissemination of the holy gospel for the salvation of souls in idolatry.

From this river to the San Gregorio, from which we had started out on the expedition, the distance must be seventy or eighty leagues, rather more than less. The land is all wretched, dry, and unproductive, the worst we encountered on the whole trip in that we were not acquainted with it and therefore did not know where to go.

CHAPTER IV

How we obtained further details of the characteristics of the interior, its inhabitants, settlements, and the buffalo.

WE CONTINUED in the direction the Indians had indicated to us on the previous day, taking along guides who led us to the river of which they had told us at that time. This river formed a valley, the best and most pleasing that we had seen on the trip; we named it Nuestra Señora de la Concepción.[1] Along the river and valley we found many people who lived in similar houses and spoke the same tongue we had heard the day before. It was a permanent settlement and the people were very clean, handsome, and warlike, the best featured we had encountered thus

---

1. The Río Grande, a few miles above its junction with the Conchos.

far. Standing on the housetops, the natives showed great pleasure on seeing us. The houses resemble those of the Mexicans, except that they are made of paling. The natives build them square. They put up forked posts and upon these they place rounded timbers the thickness of a man's thigh. Then they add stakes and plaster them with mud. Close to the houses they have granaries built of willow, after the fashion of the Mexicans, where they keep their provisions and harvest of mesquite and other things. They brought us presents from what they had, for they cultivate and harvest like the people we had met previously.

In order to inform ourselves and get further details in connection with the reports that had been given us before, it was necessary to stop in this valley for almost a whole day. We issued a summons for many people to assemble, and they soon came; and as the Indians we had met before had already been taught to kiss the hands of the friars whom we brought along, we first did so in order that these natives might follow our example. The natives then kissed the hands of the missionaries and raised their own to heaven, blowing toward the sky, because we informed them that the friars we brought with us were children of the sun, that they had come down from heaven, and that we were their children, all of which the Indians believed.

These people are very friendly. To judge from the way they acted, any labor that may be expended in teaching them will bear fruit. They will be well disposed toward any good cause and will remain attached to it. I think, however, that as a naked and barbarous people they will be difficult to settle and congregate in towns, for they do not even wear clothing.

In this valley we found an Indian who seemed to be the cacique and who was obeyed by the others to such an extent that they carried a seat for him, consisting of a very large tanned buffalo skin. These people possess many hides and have fixed domiciles. In their settlement we placed a cross. This pueblo had eight large square houses with many inhabitants, more than three hundred persons altogether.

To reach this river, the largest to be found in the Indies, we left the Conchas on our right, with our backs toward the south.[2] No other river was seen, from the Vera Cruz river to this one, which is lined with so many trees. The valleys are fine for cultivating or raising all kinds of things; for grains or trees, for ranches or cattle raising.

2. That is, at San Juan Bautista they turned northward and reached the Río Grande a few miles above its junction with the Conchos, and then descended the former to the junction. This was the regular route of travel in this area.

CHAPTER V

How we learned more about the land from the trinkets that the
natives had in their possession.

In the said valley of Concepción [i.e., Río Grande] we saw a piece of
copper which an Indian carried about his neck, tied with some cotton
threads. Another carried a tiny copper bell.[1] When we asked them
where they had obtained these things, they told us that it was from the
west and pointed in that direction. They call copper "parba." We
noticed likewise that some of the Indians who came to see and welcome
us wore white and red coral, although not of fine quality, suspended
from their noses, and also some turquoise. We asked them, too, where
they had obtained the ornaments, and they replied by giving us to
understand that it was from the direction of the sea, as they pointed
that way.

We inquired of these and many other Indians whether they knew
from observation or hearsay what there was in the interior, whether
it contained cotton,[2] corn, and many inhabitants. They told us that
thirteen days from the Concepción river, upstream, there were many
clothed people who cultivated and gathered much corn, calabashes, and
beans, as well as much cotton, which they spun, wove, and made into
blankets for covering and clothing themselves, the women as well as
the men; and that they wore shirts. Our informants showed by signs how
the people in question cultivated the land. This pleased us very much.
We asked them whether they had been there, to which they answered
no, but that they had heard about it long ago from the men who hunted
the buffalo and that they considered the report very reliable.

In view of this we offered many thanks to God our Lord for the encouraging information they had given us and for the news concerning
the supplies of corn, which was the thing we most desired. As long as
we did not lack corn and other food we would march on until we came
to the end of the land and saw all that was to be discovered in it, especially the people with fixed domiciles, among whom the holy gospel
might be planted and taught; for this was our main purpose when we
set out on the expedition. The reports given to us earlier by other Indians, and the present reports—which also indicated that the people

1. Copper was in general use among the Indians before the coming of the white man.
Native copper was found in small quantities in Arizona, New Mexico, and elsewhere,
though probably not utilized to any considerable extent. F. W. Hodge, *Handbook of
American Indians North of Mexico*, vol. I, pp. 343-344.
2. *Si avia campeche*, a rather common term for Campeche blankets, *i.e., cotton* goods.

described had very large and high houses, with ladders—made us think that these might be the Mexican Indians; but we decided that this inference was false. We were also influenced by the accounts of those who had gone inland to explore, and who had written chronicles, copies of which we had with us.[3] These accounts informed us that the said settled people were very brave and numerous; but that did not discourage us from going ahead.

While we were in this situation we saw another Indian, who brought us an iron bar about three spans long and shaped like those the Mexican Indians have. When we asked him where he had secured this valuable article, all the Indians pointed in the direction where they had said the clothed and settled people were located. We were very much pleased with the reports already obtained and with this additional information.

We were followed and accompanied by many people, who approached our horses and rubbed their bodies against the animals' haunches, raising their hands to heaven and blowing toward the sky. They did this because we had told them, as we had the others before, that the friars whom we brought with us were children of God and we their children, which the Indians believed. We told the natives that we came only to visit them, to see how they were, and to pass on. They were very pleased at what we said and brought us many presents of prickly pears, ground mesquite, and calabashes. They offered us a share of the things they had—feathers, tanned skins of buffalo and deer, and other gifts— and gave many indications of their satisfaction.

We asked them if any men like us had passed that way, and they replied that a long time ago four Christians had passed through there. By the descriptions they gave, we realized clearly that the leader must have been Alvar Núñez Cabeza de Vaca, because, according to his narrative, he had come by way of these people. However, we now had additional information of finer and very important things which Cabeza de Vaca did not mention. We therefore considered it an event directed by the hand of God that we, who were so few, dared to go among such a multitude of barbarians and treacherous idolaters. There was not a day or night during our journey up the Concepción river [Río Grande] when we were not accompanied by more than three hundred souls. But as these are matters disposed by the Lord, we nourished great hopes of emerging victorious and of preaching the gospel, for this was our aim.

3. The reference may be to Cabeza de Vaca's *Relación*, which was first printed at Zamora, Spain, in 1542, reprinted at Valladolid in 1555, or possibly to hearsay accounts of the Coronado expedition, though these were not actually published until modern times. Cf. the "Testimony of Hernán Gallegos."

CHAPTER VI

CONCERNING THE LAND AND VALLEYS DISCOVERED, AND THE REPORTS WE
GATHERED.

AFTER TRAVELING up the said river for nine days we came to a beautiful
valley which we named Los Carneros.[1] This valley is twelve leagues
from that of Concepción. It was given this name because on passing
through it we discovered an abandoned ranchería where we found many
horns of rams which appeared to weigh upward of sixteen pounds each.
It was an impressive sight, for these horns were larger than those of
steers. Continuing for nine days more, we came to another valley along
the same river, which we called La Magdalena.[2] Here we were told of
some mines and went to examine them, but they seemed to be of no
importance. Nevertheless the people who accompanied us led us to
them.

Many natives went with us as far as this valley, where they told us
definitely what was to be found and then left us. They said that farther
on was a nation speaking another language, who were their enemies,
and that they did not dare to go there for fear the others would think
they were coming to fight and do harm. We wanted to please them,
which was no more than just, in view of what they had done for us;
they and their wives had offered us their Turkish bows, arrows, feathers,
and whatever else they possessed, such as buffalo hides, deerskins, and
provisions. All this they offered and bestowed so willingly that we felt
like giving many thanks to God.

These people accompanied us at night and performed dances for us.
Their nation has a rhythm in its dances, resembling that of Negroes,
produced by beating some skins attached to a vessel in the fashion of
a tambourine. After doing this, the dancers rise and execute their movements, revolving to the rhythm of the music like clowns. They raise
their hands toward the sun and sing in their language, with the cadence
of the dance, "ayia canima." This they do with much unity and harmony, in such a way that though there are three hundred savages in a
dance, it seems as if it were being sung and danced by one man only,
due to the fine harmony and measure of their performance.

The Indians went away very contented; but before parting we asked
them where we might find corn, and clothed people with permanent
homes, which was what we most desired. They answered that five days

1. It was the Río Grande.
2. The Río Grande again.

from there, up the aforesaid river, we would find the things about which we had asked. We were delighted to hear that the settlement we sought, and which they described, was so near; but, on the other hand, we could not help being somewhat apprehensive that, as Indians, they might be lying. Since they were Indians—people who are born liars and in the habit of always telling falsehoods—we questioned them again about what they had related, and they reaffirmed what they had already told us. It was the truth. Realizing this, we commended ourselves to God and went on.

After two days we came to another nation of friendly people, fine men who received us well and offered us of what they had, in the same manner as the others had done.[3] These people call the arrow "ocae," the name given to bamboo by the Mexicans. Among the things they gave us were two bonnets made of numerous macaw feathers. We asked them if they knew anything about the interior: if there were settled inhabitants who wore cotton blankets (like the one we brought along to show them), if they ate corn, and other questions we had asked the Indians encountered before. We also inquired how many days distant those people were, warning the natives to speak the truth, for otherwise we would tell the sun to become angry. To this they replied that they had heard, and indeed knew for sure, that in the interior were many clothed and settled people who lived in large houses three and four stories high. They told us this by means of signs, because we had no interpreter for this nation.

They added that the said people cultivated large areas of land and harvested corn, calabashes, and beans of many kinds; that they had fowls, and many cotton blankets which they wore, for they cultivated and gathered large quantities of that crop, with bolls as big as one's fist, so our informants indicated; that they wore shoes, made pottery from which they ate, and that the settlement was seven days distant. Since the other Indians had told us it was five days off, we asked these people why they said seven, to which they replied that the others did not know or had lied, not knowing as much about it as themselves, who had seen it. We were much relieved by this, as well as by the satisfactory account given. Moreover, the natives told us that the people farther on—who were numerous, very brave and warlike—caused them a great deal of trouble, being members of a different nation; and that for three days we would not see any human beings, although at the end of the three days we would meet many clothed people, who harvested

3. These people were called Caguates by Luxán. They were probably Sumas.

much corn, beans, calabashes, and cotton. After receiving this information, we made our farewells.

The next morning we left this place, went up the river[4] another three days without seeing any one, and came to a marshy valley extending for more than eight leagues, which was suitable for ranches and for the cultivation of anything that might be desired. We named it Los Valientes.[5] We found it uninhabited.

4. The manuscript reads, "down the river," an obvious error.
5. This swampy region began near Guadalupe and extended up the west side of the Río Grande to near modern El Paso.

CHAPTER VII

CONCERNING THE LAND WHICH WE TRAVERSED WITHOUT MEETING ANYONE, SINCE IT WAS UNINHABITED.

ON LEAVING the valley of Los Valientes we went on another four days in search of the settlement of which we had been informed. We did not locate it, so we thought the Indians had deceived us; but we did not lose courage on that account. We pressed forward, going up the same river yet another five days to see if we could find the place; but as we found nothing after fifteen days of travel, we decided to assemble and discuss the question of whether we should return to Christian lands; for, according to what the natives had told us, we were lost. Our latest informants had said the settlements were seven days away; others had previously said five; and we had marched for fifteen days through an uninhabited land without seeing anyone. We had indeed lost our way. We did not know where we were going; and we were without a guide and without provisions to go farther, because we had traveled more than seventy leagues through uninhabited country since last seeing human beings.[1]

So we decided to explore and follow a trail we had found the day before. Those who left on this party were Father Fray Juan de Santa María, Hernán Gallegos, Pedro de Bustamante, Pedro Sánchez de Fuensalida, and Pedro Sánchez de Chaves. We left the camp and continued over a plain for more than two leagues, until we came to the end of it and reached a sierra. On entering the mountainous territory, we saw an Indian brave and two inhabited huts. Taking our horses

1. This uninhabited area extended from a point north of El Paso to the vicinity of San Marcial, where the first New Mexico pueblo was found.

and arms we went in that direction and discovered many people, who fled toward the mountains when they saw us approaching. While we were pursuing them, such a heavy shower fell that we were helpless and unable to make use of our horses. On this account we were not able to seize a single Indian who might give us information and enlighten us as to the actual existence, in the interior, of the things that we had been told about and for which we were searching.

It was God's will that, on our way back to camp, we should meet an Indian about forty years of age. We thought that God had led him to us because we had decided to turn back; and as the Lord is most merciful He remembered us, so that our good purpose, for it was directed to His holy service, should not fail us but should, on the contrary, be furthered. He therefore sent us the Indian, who told us of what there was in the interior—the many houses; the numerous clothed people; the abundant corn, beans, calabashes, cotton, and wild turkeys; and the fact that the inhabitants wore clothes and had houses three or four stories high. He gave us this good news by means of signs, for we could not understand him in any other way. The report brought us great joy, and we gave many thanks to God our Lord for such bountiful favors and for His succor in the moment of greatest need.

CHAPTER VIII

How we left, accompanied by the Indian, and went in search of the houses and corn.

WHEN WE HAD LEARNED what there was beyond, from the account of the Indian, we went on with him as our guide. Farther up the same river we came to an abandoned pueblo that had been inhabited by a large number of people, who must have been very advanced, judging by the buildings, and whose discovery would be of great importance, if they could be found. The said pueblo was walled in; and the houses had mud walls and were built of adobes, three stories high, so it appeared, though they had crumbled from the rains and seemed to have been abandoned for a long time. Here we halted for the night.[1] Asking our guide for the location of the settlement he had told us about, he in-

---

1. The date was August 21, 1581. Here the Spaniards took possession of the entire province, naming the first pueblo, as well as the province, San Felipe. The first town consisted of about forty-five houses of two and three stories. See pp. 54, 102. It was a Piro village on Mulligan gulch south of San Marcial, near the site of the later Fort Craig. Cf. Bandelier, *Final Report,* Pt. II, p. 252; and H. P. Mera, "Population Changes," p. 7 and map.

dicated that it was approximately two leagues away and that he wanted
to go there to notify the people, so that they might bring us corn and
other things from their stores. By unanimous agreement the Indian was
sent, but as he was of a different nation, it seems that he did not go
to the pueblo he had mentioned.

The following morning we left the abandoned settlement and, after
traveling the two leagues which the Indian had indicated, came to a
pueblo of many houses three stories high, but found no inhabitants.[2]
They had left the night before because they had noticed our approach.
In the houses we found many turkeys and much cotton and corn.
Although we did not see any people in the pueblo on entering it, we
did find in the valley many cornfields like those of Mexico, and also
fields of beans, calabashes, and cotton. We did not dare to take any
of the goods, for we wanted the people to know we did not intend to
harm them. We found the houses very well planned and built in blocks,
with mud walls, whitewashed inside and well decorated with monsters,
other animals, and human figures. There were many curious articles
in these houses, more neatly wrought than those of the Mexicans when
they were conquered. The inhabitants have a great deal of crockery,
such as pots *(ollas)*, large earthern jars *(tinajas)*, and flat pans *(comales)*,
all decorated and of better quality than the pottery of New Spain.

We endeavored to locate the people in order to calm them and bring
them to us peaceably, which we managed to do. We appealed to them
by friendly gestures, because otherwise we should not have been able
to see their land. Nevertheless, if they had attempted to prevent our
coming we would have entered by force in order to examine the region
and what it contained, for we had already endured many hardships.
But it pleased God that some Indians should come to us, and we sent
them away in peace, telling them to make the sign of the cross with
their hands as an indication that we did not wish to harm them. The
news that we were coming in peace spread so widely that there was
not a day when we were not surrounded and accompanied by more
than twelve thousand people.

Here we informed ourselves about the land and the Indians. They
indicated to us that there were in their nation twenty-odd pueblos,[3] and
that farther on was another nation, with which they were at war. In

2. This was the pueblo of San Miguel, according to the "List of Pueblos" given below.
Oñate in 1598 found two pueblos at this point, Qualacú on the east bank and Trenaquel on
the west bank. Hammond and Rey, *Oñate, Colonizer of New Mexico*, pp. 318, 346, and 372.

3. These were Piro towns. For a detailed discussion of this nation, see *Benavides' Revised Memorial*, pp. 246-252; and Mera, *op. cit.*, pp. 6-11.

view of this we continued up the river, which we named the Guadal-quivir, as it was large, full of water, and very wide and swift.

After passing the pueblos of the first nation we came to a town with many large houses three and four stories high, whitewashed inside and with well-squared windows. All the houses were decorated in many designs and colors. We journeyed through the territory of this nation for four days, always passing numerous pueblos—indeed, we sometimes passed through two a day—continuing until we reached the frontier of another nation[4] of this populated territory. When we came to the boundary of the other nation we halted two days in order to inform ourselves of what there was farther inland, so that we might continue our journey. There we learned more of what there was in the interior, and that it was thickly populated, news which gave us much satisfaction. We gave many thanks to God because, though only so few of us had come, He had pleased to send us such good tidings. Before this time numerous Spaniards with ample commissions from the viceroys of New Spain had entered the land in an attempt to discover this settlement, and they had not found it.[5] Thus we concluded that our project was directed by the hand of God, who enabled us to find these people and a settlement like this, where the holy gospel might be planted in order that the natives there might come to the true faith. We therefore went ahead very happily and joyfully.

The people sustain themselves on corn, beans, and calabashes. They make tortillas and corn-flour gruel *(atole)*, have buffalo meat and tur-keys—they have large numbers of the latter. There is not an Indian who does not have a corral for his turkeys, each of which holds a flock of one hundred birds. The natives wear Campeche-type cotton blankets, for they have large cotton fields. They raise many small shaggy dogs—which, however, are not like those owned by the Spaniards—and build under-ground huts in which they keep these animals.

4. The Tigua, or Tiwa. Their principal area of occupation extended from Los Lunas to the mouth of the Jémez river. For slightly different views on this subject, see Bandelier, *Final Report*, Pt. II, p. 233; Mera, "Population Changes," pp. 17-20.

5. Gallegos here refers to such expeditions as those of Francisco Vázquez Coronado in 1540 and Francisco de Ibarra in 1565, whose northern explorations had ended in disappoint-ment. See H. H. Bancroft, *Arizona and New Mexico* (1889), p. 70; Bolton, *Coronado, Knight of Pueblos and Plains* (1949); Hammond and Rey, *Narratives of the Coronado expedition* (1940).

CHAPTER IX

HOW WE LEFT THE SAID FRONTIER AND ENTERED THE TERRITORY OF AN-
OTHER NATION; AND OF THE RECEPTION WE WERE ACCORDED.

AFTER WE TOOK our leave of this people, the Indians led us to a large
pueblo of another nation,[1] where the inhabitants received us by making
the sign of the cross with their hands in token of peace, as the others
had done before. As the news spread, the procedure in this pueblo was
followed in the others.

We entered the settlement, where the inhabitants gave us much corn.
They showed us many ollas and other earthenware containers, richly
painted, and brought quantities of calabashes and beans for us to eat.
We took a little, so that they should not think we were greedy nor yet
receive the impression that we did not want it; among themselves they
consider it disparaging if one does not accept what is offered. One must
take what they give, but after taking it may throw it away wherever he
wishes. Should one throw it to the ground, they will not pick it up,
though it may be something they can utilize. On the contrary, they will
sooner let the thing rot where it is discarded. This is their practice.
Thus, since we understood their custom, we took something of what
they gave us. Moreover, we did this to get them into the habit of giving
freely without being asked. Accordingly, they all brought what they
could. The supply of corn tortillas, corn-flour gruel, calabashes, and
beans which they brought was such that enough was left over every day
to feed five hundred men. Part of this the natives carried for us. The
women make tortillas similar to those of New Spain, and tortillas of
ground beans, too. In these pueblos there are also houses of three and
four stories, similar to the ones we had seen before; but the farther
one goes into the interior the larger are the pueblos and the houses,
and the more numerous the people.

The way they build their houses, which are in blocks, is as follows:
they burn the clay, build narrow walls, and make adobes for the doorways. The lumber used is pine or willow; and many rounded beams,
ten and twelve feet long, are built into the houses. The natives have
ladders by means of which they climb to their quarters. These are
movable wooden ladders, for when the Indians retire at night, they

---

1. The party was evidently leaving the country of the Piros and entering the Tigua
pueblos, though Gallegos' description at this point is so very vague that it is difficult to
be sure.

pull them up to protect themselves against enemies since they are at war with one another.

These people, like the others, wear clothing. I have decided to describe their attire here because, for barbarians, it is the best that has been found. It is as follows: [some of] the men cut their hair short and leave on top—I mean, on the crown of their heads—a sort of skull cap formed by their own hair, while others wear their hair long, to the shoulders, as the Indians of New Spain formerly did. Some adorn themselves with pieces of colored cotton cloth three-fourths of a vara in length and two-thirds in width, with which they cover their privy parts. Over this they wear, fastened at the shoulders, a blanket of the same material, decorated with many figures and colors, which reaches to their knees, like the clothes of the Mexicans. Some (in fact, most) wear cotton shirts, hand-painted and embroidered, that are very pleasing. They use shoes. Below the waist the women wear cotton skirts, colored and embroidered; and above, a blanket of the same material, figured and adorned like those used by the men. They adjust it after the fashion of Jewish women, and gird it with embroidered cotton sashes adorned with tassels. They comb their hair, which is worn long.

These people are handsome and fair-skinned. They are very industrious. Only the men attend to the work in the cornfields. The day hardly breaks before they go about with hoes in their hands. The women busy themselves only in the preparation of food, and in making and painting their pottery and *chicubites*,[2] in which they prepare their bread. These vessels are so excellent and delicate that the process of manufacture is worth watching; for they equal, and even surpass, the pottery made in Portugal. The women also make earthen jars for carrying and storing water. These are very large, and are covered with lids of the same material. There are millstones on which the natives grind their corn and other foods. These are similar to the millstones in New Spain, except that they are stationary; and the women, if they have daughters, make them do the grinding.

These Indians are very clean people. The men bear burdens, but not the women. The manner of carrying loads, sleeping, eating, and sitting is the same as that of the Mexicans, for both men and women, except that they carry water in a different way. For this the Indians make and place on their heads a cushion of palm leaves, similar to those used in Old Castile, on top of which they place and carry the water jar. It is all very interesting.

2. A pan for baking bread.

The women part their hair in Spanish style. Some have light hair, which is surprising. The girls do not leave their rooms except when permitted by their parents. They are very obedient. They marry early; judging by what we saw, the women are given husbands when seventeen years of age. A man has one wife and no more. The women are the ones who spin, sew, weave and paint. Some of the women, like the men, bathe frequently. Their baths are as good as those of New Spain.

In all their valleys and other lands I have seen, there are one hundred pueblos. We named the region the province of San Felipe and took possession of it in the name of his Majesty by commission of his Excellency, Don Lorenzo Suárez de Mendoza, Count of Coruña, viceroy, governor and captain-general of New Spain.[3]

These Indians call corn "cunque"; water "pica"; the turkey "dire"; and a woman "ayu." When they want to drink they say "sesa." They call the cotton blanket . . . [there is a blank]. Their language is very easy to learn. They are the most domestic and industrious people, and the best craftsmen found in New Spain. Had we brought along interpreters, some of the natives would have become Christians, because they are a very intelligent people and willing to serve.

3. This was on August 21, 1581. See the "List of Pueblos."

CHAPTER X

HOW WE LEARNED OF THE BUFFALO; AND THE DISTANCE FROM THIS PROVINCE AND SETTLEMENT TO THE REGION WHERE THEY WERE TO BE FOUND.

WHILE WE WERE at the pueblo which we named Malpartida[1]—a league from the one already discovered and which we called San Mateo—we asked if there were many minerals in the vicinity, showing the natives the samples we had taken along for that purpose and requesting them to lead us to the place where such riches might be found. They immediately brought us a large quantity of different kinds, including some of a coppery steellike ore. This mineral appeared to be rich and assayed about twenty marcos per hundredweight. The others assayed less. When we asked them where they obtained the ore, they gave us to understand that there were many minerals near the province and

1. Malpartida may have been identical with the pueblo of San Marcos, located in the Galisteo valley about four miles northeast of Cerrillos or twenty miles southwest of Santa Fé. See Erik K. Reed, "The Southern Tewa Pueblos in the Historic Period," *El Palacio*, vol. 50, pp. 260-261.

pueblo; and they thought that part of what they had shown came from there.[2] We went to investigate and discovered mines of different ores. The natives indicated that the Indians in the region of the buffalo had given them a part of the ore.

Some of these natives paint themselves with stripes. When they told us of the buffalo, we asked them what people lived in that region; whether they had houses and cultivated corn; whether they wore clothes; and how many days it was from their own locality to the buffalo, because we wanted to go and see the animals. We added that we would reconcile them with those other people. They indicated to us that the inhabitants of the buffalo region were not striped; that they lived by hunting and ate nothing but buffalo meat during the winter; that during the rainy season they would go to the areas of the prickly pear and yucca; that they had no houses, but only huts of buffalo hides; that they moved from place to place; that they were enemies of our informants, but nevertheless came to the pueblos of the latter in order to trade such articles as deerskins and buffalo hides for making footwear, and a large amount of meat, in exchange for corn and blankets; and that in this way, by communicating with one another, each nation had come to understand the other's language.

When we heard this and the report on the buffalo, we decided to find the herds and to explore the land in which they lived; for we realized that there must be good grazing in a place where there were as many buffalo as the Indians reported. The region must be fertile and have many grassy plains and plenty of water, to judge by the number of buffalo the natives said there were. Taking up some handfuls of soil, they said that the animals were just as numerous as the grains of sand in their hands, and that there were many rivers, water holes, and marshes where the buffalo ranged. We were much pleased by this news.

In reply to our questions the natives stated that the buffalo were two days' journey away. We asked them why they lived so far from the herds, and they replied that it was on account of their cornfields and cultivated lands, so that the buffalo would not eat the crops; for during certain seasons of the year the buffalo came within eight leagues of the settlement. They also said that the Indians who followed these herds were very brave, fine hunters with bow and arrow who would kill us. But God our Lord inspired us with such courage that we paid no attention to what was said and decided that we would go to see the cattle.

2. Probably from the lead outcrops in the Cerrillos area or in the San Pedro or Ortiz mountains farther south. Reed, *loc. cit.*; Marjorie F. Lambert, *Paa-ko, New Mexico,* p. 6.

We told the natives that some of them should accompany us, inasmuch as the buffalo were so near, and that we would kill game for them. They answered that they did not want to go, because the Indians who followed the buffalo were enemies and very cunning; and that the two peoples would kill each other and start trouble. As we were so few, we did not dare to force these natives to go with us, preferring to travel without a guide by the route they had indicated.

CHAPTER XI

How we left the settlement to go in search of the buffalo; and of the route we took.

We left the settlement and province of San Felipe[1] on September 28 of that year to go in search of the buffalo, in view of the reports that the natives had given us. On the first day we traveled six leagues through plains with good pasture for cattle. Accordingly, we thought the Indians had not told the truth, for we noticed that this pasture was untouched by the buffalo, and that the tracks left by them seemed very old. At the end of the day we slept without a drop of water, both men and horses, which occasioned much anxiety, because we feared that under such conditions our animals would become exhausted.

The following day we went through a forest with many pine trees which appeared to be the largest that had been discovered in New Spain. In addition to pines, there were carine and cypress trees.[2] After five leagues we came to an extensive gorge where we found a large pool of rainwater. Here the horses drank, and we stopped at this spot for the night, being fatigued from the previous day.

On the next day we continued to travel across plains, night overtaking us after we had gone seven leagues. We went without water as on the preceding day; and so we thought we were lost, due to the lack of water and because the Indians had told us the buffalo were only a two days' journey from the settlement. Since we had traveled three full

---

1. This statement might imply that the explorers set out from the pueblo of San Felipe, near San Marcial, which was not the case. Instead, they were in the Galisteo valley and probably set out from Malpartida, so called by Obregón. See his *History*, p. 302. On their return, they halted in the pueblo of Piedrahita (San Cristóbal) to replenish their food supply. Obregón, p. 308. On the whole, this account parallels that of Gallegos very closely for the trip to the buffalo country.

2. This description is characteristic of the mountainous area between Galisteo and the Pecos river. Evidently they wandered circuitously southeastward, emerging finally at the Pecos in the vicinity of Anton Chico.

days and had failed to locate them, it seemed to us that we must have lost our way. But God our Lord inspired us with great courage and emboldened us to penetrate strange and hostile lands.

The next morning, after we had gone forward another league, God was pleased to lead us to a large pool of brackish water in a plain below a canyon, where we stopped to refresh the animals from the fatigue of the foregoing day. On the following morning we continued our march through this canyon, and all along it we found pools of briny water. We called it San Miguel, because we reached it on the day of the blessed Saint Michael. This valley is suitable for sheep, the best for that purpose ever discovered in New Spain. On the same day we went five leagues down the valley and came to a very large pool of water where we halted for the night. We noticed that numerous people had left this place the preceding day, and we found many buffalo tracks. For this reason we thought the people in question must be those who followed the buffalo and that we were close to the herds. This pleased us very much, in view of our desire to see them.

The next morning, after traveling a league, we came to a river with a large volume of water and many trees and we named it Santo Domingo.[3] It contained brackish water suitable for cattle. Accordingly, we thought the buffalo would be found there, because a river as good as this one could not fail to be frequented by cattle and because all along the way we had found their tracks.

Continuing down this same river four leagues we went toward a column of smoke which we had noticed. We wanted to see whether there were people there of whom we could inquire about the buffalo. We came upon a ranchería on this river in which we found fifty huts and tents made of hides with strong white flaps after the fashion of field tents. Here we were met by more than four hundred warlike men armed with bows and arrows who asked us by means of signs what we wanted. We replied that we were coming to visit them and that they were our friends; but they were intent upon fighting us with their arrows. We decided to attack them if necessary but did not actually do so, waiting first to see if they would accept peace. Although on the point of clashing with them, should they provoke us, we restrained ourselves, though there was no fear in us.

So we withdrew our force to see what the outcome would be. Then we made the sign of the cross with our hands in a token of friendship, and the Lord was pleased to fill them with fear while inspiring us with

3. Presumably the Pecos. Cf. Obregón's account, p. 303.

renewed courage. When they saw that we made the sign of the cross as an indication of peace, they, too, made the same sign. Moreover, they welcomed us to their land and ranchería. Then Father Fray Agustín Rodríguez dismounted and took a cross from his neck for them to kiss, in order to let them know that we were children of the sun and that we were coming to visit them. They soon began to rejoice and make merry, and to give us of what they had.

We spent the day in this ranchería, where we called together all the Indians, and then discharged an harquebus among them. They were terrified by the loud report and fell to the ground as if stunned. It was God our Lord who put such fear of an harquebus into these Indians, in spite of the fact that they numbered two thousand men. They asked us not to fire any more, because it frightened them greatly. We were very much pleased by this, although we did not let them know it. We asked them where the buffalo were, and they told us that there were large numbers two days farther on, as thick as grass on the plains. They described the entire region where these herds roamed, but not one native wished to come along with us. Thus we saw that we had strayed and had not followed the route suggested by the Indians of the pueblos.

These semi-naked people wear only buffalo hides and deerskins for covering themselves. At this season they live on buffalo meat, but during the rainy season they go in search of prickly pears and yucca. They have dogs which carry loads of two or three arrobas, and they put leather pack-saddles on these animals, with poitrels and cruppers. They tie the dogs to one another as in a pack train, using maguey ropes for halters. The packs travel three or four leagues per day. These dogs are medium-sized shaggy animals.

The following morning we went down this same river, and since we found no buffalo after two days, we wandered on bewildered. It was not advisable to travel over plains like these without guides, so we returned to the river by command of our leader. We went back to the ranchería, where we had left the many people, in order to get an Indian guide, either willingly or by force, to take us to the buffalo. This purpose was accomplished; we went to the said ranchería, seized an Indian, bound him, brought him to camp, and handed him over to our leader so that we could start at once and continue our journey to the cattle. Noting that the Indians of the ranchería had become angry, we decided to prepare ourselves fully for battle, as we were in the habit of doing under such circumstances; and also to maintain a careful vigil, even though we were tired as a result of keeping guard for six months. This was a tremendous strain, for one can well imagine that keeping watch every single night for a whole year was enough to exhaust forty men, to say nothing of our small group of eight.

Then, in the morning, we started off with the guide and journeyed laboriously for three days, during which we had no water, until we reached a place where we found some small pools where the Indians were accustomed to drink. We opened the pools with hoes, since at first they did not contain enough water for even one of our animals. By God's will, as these pools were opened, so much water flowed from them that it was sufficient for ten thousand horses. We named the pools Ojos Zarcos. Traces of buffalo were found here, and we killed one—the first that we had seen on the trip. This led us to believe that the herds were near by. We remained another day at the pools in order to refresh our horses, which were tired out from the previous day. We had gone without water for more than forty hours, and if we had been without it one more day we should have perished. But God our Lord is merciful. In the time of greatest need, He gives aid, as was especially manifest on this occasion.

We asked the guide whom we took along where the other buffalo were. He said there were many and that we would see them the next day in large numbers at a water hole. So, on the following day, which was October 9, we reached some lagoons of very brackish water. Here we found many such pools in a valley that extends from these lagoons toward the sunrise. We named this valley and its pools Los Llanos de San Francisco and Aguas Zarcas, because they formed such good plains.[4] In these plains there is a spring, the best to be found in New Spain for people afflicted with dropsy.

At the water holes on the plains we found many buffalo, which roamed in great herds or droves of more than five hundred head, both cows and bulls. They are as large as the cattle of New Spain, hump-backed and wooly, with short, black horns and big heads. The bulls have beards like he-goats. They are fairly swift and run like pigs. They are so large that when seen in the midst of a plain they resemble ships at sea or carts on land. According to our estimate and that of the men who discovered them, the bulls must weigh more than forty arrobas each when three years old. Their meat is delicious and to our taste as palatable as that of our beef cattle.

We killed forty head with our harquebuses, to be used as food. It is easy to kill these animals, for as soon as they are wounded they stop moving and, on stopping, they are slain. There are so many buffalo that there

---

4. The assumption is that this was on a branch of the Canadian river.

were days when we saw upward of three thousand bulls. The reason there are so many males together is that at a certain season of the year they separate from the cows. They have very fine wool, suitable for any purpose, and their hides are the best that have been found on any cattle up to the present time.

Here we learned that this valley and its waters extended to the river where the great bulk of the buffalo ranged;[5] according to the natives the herds cover the fields in astonishing numbers. The leader and the discoverers at first resolved to look for the river described, but later they realized that this was not a good plan because they were running short of supplies. Had it not been for that drawback, we would have gone on to explore the river, so that we could report to his Majesty on what had thus been discovered.

Accordingly, on October 19 of that year [1581], we left the valley of San Francisco, turning back toward the settlement from which we had started. From that point to the location of the buffalo, we traversed forty leagues of difficult road, and were on the point of perishing for lack of water and for our original failure to obtain a guide at the settlement. We learned that from this place to the buffalo there were two days of travel, more or less, following the direct route of which the Indians had told us. We went back over the same route we had followed on our first entry, because we knew of no other.

The Indian we had taken as guide from the ranchería we now sent ahead, well laden with meat and very happy because he had seen us kill the buffalo. Indeed, it seemed as if it was the will of God that not one of us should fire his harquebus at an animal without felling it. This greatly astonished the guide who had led us to the herds. After leaving us he told of what he had seen us do, how we killed the buffalo, and other things. In view of this the whole ranchería which he had left behind, and from which we had taken the guide by force, came to meet us peacefully. The inhabitants said that they wanted to take us to the buffalo and would lead us to a place where there were many herds, as they showed us by signs. We gave part of what we had—that is, some of the meat—to those who seemed to be caciques, for they stand out readily. We told them we would return shortly, which pleased them, and they gave us to understand that they would await us. Thus we left them, though we kept our vigil in order that, under the pretext of friendship and peace, they should not try to avenge the seizure of the guide whom we had taken from them to help find the buffalo. He was

5. Could this have been the Cimarron or the Arkansas?

one of their own people. We then turned back toward the said settlement, our starting point.[6]

6. This statement seems ambiguous, since ch. 12 states that they returned to Piedrahita. The fact is, probably, that they went on to establish their camp at this town, as explained by Obregón. See his *History*, p. 308.

CHAPTER XII

TELLING HOW, UPON OUR ARRIVAL AT THE SETTLEMENT, WE GAVE ORDERS THAT THE INHABITANTS SHOULD PROVIDE US WITH FOOD SUPPLIES.

WHEN WE ARRIVED at the settlement, a pueblo which we named Piedra Aita,[1] we decided that we would start there to explain how we had run short of provisions, in order that the natives of this and other towns should give us the food necessary for our sustenance. Moreover, if this pueblo gave us provisions, they would be given to us everywhere in the province. Up to that time, the natives had not been asked to supply anything for our maintenance.

We all assembled to consult with our leader and to determine the method which should be used in obtaining the provisions. It was decided first of all to tell the natives by means of signs that we had used up the supplies brought with us, and that since they had plenty they should give us some because we wanted to go on. When they realized this and saw that the supplies we had brought were exhausted, they thought of starving us to death and acted as if deaf. We told our leader that the natives had paid no attention to us and pretended not to understand.

To this he replied that it was not advisable to use force, for we could see plainly that the people in these pueblos were very numerous and that within an hour after their call to arms three thousand men would gather and kill us. When the leader expressed this opinion, the soldiers argued that, inasmuch as he had authority to seize the provisions we needed for men and horses, he should make use of it, because we preferred to die fighting rather than from starvation, especially since we were in a land with ample food. Since our leader was ill, he replied that we could do what we thought best, provided that we did not incite the natives to revolt and that they gave us the provisions willingly.

When our men found that the Indians rebelled at our request for food, our leader, rising from his sick bed, and seven companions armed

1. The Spanish reads Piedra Aita, an error for Piedrahita.

themselves and went to the pueblo with their horses in readiness for war. When the Indians saw we were armed, they withdrew into their houses and fortified themselves in the pueblo, which was composed of three hundred houses of three and four stories, all of stone.[2] Seeing that the Indians had retired to their houses, we entered the town, and, carrying a cross in our hands, asked them for some corn flour because we had nothing to eat. The natives understood, but held back, not wishing to give it. Confronted with the hostile attitude of the Indians, some of our men fired a few harquebuses, pretending to aim at them in order to intimidate them into giving us the food we needed. We wanted them to understand that they had to give it, either willingly or by force.

In order that no one should complain of having provided much while another gave less, the soldiers decided that each house should contribute a little and that for this purpose a measure should be made which held about half an almud of ground corn flour.[3] Then the natives brought us quantities of ground corn from every house in the pueblo, fearing us and the harquebuses—which roared a great deal and spat fire like lightning—and thinking we were immortal, since we had told them that we were children of the sun and that the sun had given us these weapons for defense. Seeing that we did not ask for anything except food for ourselves, all gave something and told us they were our friends, though the friendship they feigned was due more to fear than to anything else. We remained on our guard lest, being Indians, they should treacherously plan some trick and attack us unawares.

Since this pueblo had contributed nine loads of flour as a present and the news had spread throughout the province, we were given exactly the same amount, no more and no less, at the other pueblos, so that we did not lack food during the entire trip. For all this, and the many favors He had granted us, insuring that we should never be without provisions, we offered thanks to God. All the pueblos thus gave us supplies as tribute; and as they are now accustomed to it, they will not resent giving such tribute when someone goes to start settlements. Together with the supply of corn and flour, they presented us with large numbers of turkeys, of which they have many flocks and do not value highly. Of the provisions that they offered us we took only what was necessary, and what was left over we returned to them. This pleased them very much, and they told us they were our friends and would

---

2. Hence the name, Piedrahita, meaning "bare rocks." Note that this pueblo is described as containing three hundred houses. Reed suggests that Piedrahita might have been Pecos, but in our view it was San Cristóbal, and Nueva Tlaxcala, which was said to have five hundred houses, was Pecos.

3. An almud is an old measure equal to about an English peck.

give us food and whatever else we might need. They did this due to fear rather than from any desire to befriend us. It was presumably because of that attitude and the fact that we had asked for and taken provisions from them that they attempted to unite the province in order to seize us by force and kill us.

CHAPTER XIII

CONCERNING THE ATTEMPT OF THE INDIANS TO KILL US, THE GATHERING THAT THEY HELD, AND HOW THEY OVERCAME THEIR FEAR OF US.

AFTER THE EVENTS related above, and after the natives had given us what we needed for our support, in characteristic Indian fashion, they determined to seize us treacherously by night and kill us if they could. The cause for this was the fact that, after we had seen the settlement (*poblazón*), with which we were very much pleased, Father Fray Juan de Santa María, one of the friars in our party, decided to return to the land of the Christians in order to give an account and report of what had been discovered to his prelate and to his Excellency, the viceroy.[1]

Everyone condemned the decision as inadvisable, for he would not only endanger his own life, but imperil the soldiers, and in addition would jeopardize further exploration of the land. We urged him to wait until we had inspected everything about which the natives had informed us, and had gone to see the buffalo, in order that a complete report of all this might be taken to the friar's prelate and to his Excellency, as any account that he could give now would be incomplete, since we had not seen the most important things. To this advice Fray Juan de Santa María replied that he was determined to return to Christian territory and report on what he had seen. His departure caused much unrest in the land and trouble for us. Without the permission of his superior, he left the party at vespers on the feast of Our Lady of September.[2]

When the natives saw that the friar was leaving, they became alarmed, believing he was going to bring more Christians in order to put them

1. Father Santa María set out for Mexico in spite of the protests of the soldiers and the other friars, but the place at which he left his companions is not stated, though we believe it may have been Tunque. Unfortunately, the affidavit of his leave-taking does not specify where the document was drawn up nor the day of his departure.

2. Gallegos here refers to the birthday of the Virgin Mary, September 8, which seems to conflict with the notarial document mentioned in note 1, above, unless the affidavit was drawn up later.

out of their homes; so they asked us by signs where he was going, all alone. We tried to dissuade them from their wicked thoughts, but, as they were Indians, this did not prevent them from doing evil. They followed the friar and killed him after two or three days of travel. We knew nothing of this until we returned from our trip to the buffalo; and even though the natives told us they had slain the father in the sierra, which we named the Sierra Morena,[3] we pretended not to understand. Seeing that we paid no attention to the death of the friar and that they had killed him so easily, they thought they would kill us just as readily. From then on they knew we were mortal; up to that time they had thought us immortal.

When we learned that the natives had killed the friar and that they intended to slay us also, we decided to withdraw gradually. We stopped at a pueblo which we named Malpartida, and at a distance of one league from that spot we discovered some mineral deposits. While we were at this pueblo, some Indians from another settlement, which we named Malagón,[4] killed three of our horses. We soon missed the animals and learned how the Indians of this district of Malagón had killed them. When the leader and the soldiers realized what had happened, they determined that such a crime should not go unpunished. The leader ordered five of the party—Pedro de Bustamante, Hernán Gallegos, Pedro Sánchez de Chaves, Felipe de Escalante, and Pedro Sánchez de Fuensalida—to go to the pueblo of Malagón, where it was reported the three horses had been killed; to find and bring before him the culprits, either peaceably or by force; and to make some arrests at the pueblo in order to intimidate the natives.

When the five soldiers learned of their leader's orders, they armed themselves, made ready their horses, and proceeded to Malagón, which they found to consist of eighty houses of three and four stories with plazas and streets. Entering the pueblo in fighting order, as men who were angry, they found the Indians keeping watch on the housetops and asked who had killed the three missing horses. In order to protect themselves from the harm that might befall them, the natives replied they had committed no such deed. As soon as we heard this answer, we discharged the harquebuses to make the Indians think we were going to kill them, although we incurred great risk in doing so, for we were only

3. The Manzano range, southeast of Albuquerque.
4. Malagón, generally identified with San Lázaro, while Malpartida was San Marcos. Reed has assayed another interpretation, with Malagón becoming San Lázaro or San Cristóbal, probably the latter. In this case, he thinks Piedrahita would be Pecos. See his article "The Southern Tewa Pueblos in the Historic Period," *El Palacio*, vol. 50, pp. 254-264 and 276-288.

five men facing the task of attacking eighty houses with more than a thousand inhabitants. When we had fired our harquebuses, the natives became frightened, went into their houses, and stayed there. To placate us they threw many dead turkeys down the passageways to us, but we decided not to accept the offering so that they would know we were angry. Then we asked twenty or thirty Indians who appeared on the roofs and who seemed to be the chief men of the pueblo—the cacique among them—to give us either the horses or the culprits who had killed them. To this they replied that their people had not slain the animals; and they asked us not to be angry, declaring that they were our friends.

Since the natives did not surrender those who had killed the horses, Hernán Gallegos, Pedro Sánchez de Fuensalida, and Pedro de Bustamante dismounted and went up to the houses to see if they could find any trace of horseflesh. The other soldiers guarded the pueblo to protect their companions from danger. Hernán Gallegos and Pedro de Bustamante soon found pieces of horseflesh in two houses of the pueblo and came out to notify their comrades of the discovery. We then fired the harquebuses once more, and the Indians, observing our conduct, were more frightened than defiant, since we had expressed our will with such determination. Gallegos and Bustamante then mounted; and all five of us, holding horseflesh in our hands, again asked the Indians who were keeping watch to tell us which men were guilty of killing the horses. We warned them to deliver those men to us, because we wanted to kill them or take them to our leader so that he might have them put to death; and we added that if the natives would not give up the culprits, we would have to kill them all. We challenged them to come out of their pueblo into the open so that we might see how brave they were; but they were very sad and answered that they did not want to fight us, for we were brave men, and that it was the Indians in the next pueblo who had killed our horses, thinking they were animals like the native buffalo.

Then we soldiers attacked the pueblo again in order to capture some Indians. They took refuge in the pueblo, but some hurled themselves from the corridors into the open in an attempt to escape, whereupon Hernán Gallegos and Pedro de Bustamante rushed after them and each seized an Indian by the hair. The natives were very swift, but the horses overtook them. After apprehending them, the soldiers took them to the camp of the leader to be punished, in view of their crime and as an example to the others.

Before this happened and before returning to camp, we decided to set fire to the pueblo so that the inhabitants would not perpetrate such a crime again. Pedro de Bustamante then picked up a bit of hay, started a fire by means of an harquebus, and prepared to burn the pueblo; but his companions would not allow the town to be burned and so many people to perish, lest all should suffer for the guilt of perhaps eight individuals.

Thus we returned to the camp with the prisoners and delivered them to our leader, who ordered that they should be beheaded on the following morning. To this the soldiers replied that he should consider what it meant to imprison these Indians for a day; that it was not good policy; that if they were to be executed it should be done at once, for there were more than a thousand Indians in the camp who might attempt some wickedness on account of the imprisonment of the two Indians. When the leader realized that the soldiers were right, he ordered Pedro de Bustamante, the notary [Gallegos], and the other soldiers to place a block in the middle of the camp's plaza, where the rest of the Indians were watching, and to cut off the heads of the prisoners with an iron machete as punishment for them and as an example to the others. The preparations were carried out as ordered; although, as the friars had decided to remain in that settlement [*en aquella poblazón*], it was agreed that at the time when the Indians were to be beheaded the friars should rush out to free them—tussle with us, and snatch the victims away from us in order that the Indians might love their rescuers, who were resolved to remain in the land.

All was so done. At the moment when the soldiers were about to cut off the heads of the Indians, the friars came out in flowing robes and saved the captives from their perilous plight. As we pretended that we were going to seize them, the Indians who were watching immediately took hold of the friars and the prisoners and carried all of them off to their houses, mindful of the great support they had found in the priests. Because of what we had done and proposed to do, the natives became so terrified of us that it was surprising how they trembled. This was willed by God on high, for we ourselves were but a small force.

The following morning, many Indians from the pueblo of Malagón came, heavily laden with turkeys and other food for our use, entreating us not to be angry with them, since they would not commit such deeds again. In the future they would watch and round up the horses, so that none would be lost. They assured us that they were our friends. We were very much pleased at this, although we did not show it, in order that they and the other natives might hold us in even greater fear.

A few days later the Indians assembled for the purpose of killing us, but that did not deter us from going to explore the land in order to verify the information that we had been given. When we left, and again after we returned to camp, we realized clearly and definitely that they wanted to kill us, and that the people of the entire region were gathering for this purpose; so we decided to take precautions and to continue keeping careful watch, as we had done up to that time. Since we watched with more zeal than in the past, the natives became aware of it. If they had shown great friendship for us before, they showed even more now.

In spite of their fear, we came to the conclusion from their conduct that they wanted to kill us; wherefore we determined to attack and kill them, and to burn some of their small pueblos even though we should perish in the attempt, in order that they might fear the Spaniards. We challenged them many times so that they might know there was no cowardice in us. But as the friars had decided to remain in the said settlement [en la dicha poblazón],[5] we sometimes—in fact, most of the time—relinquished our rights in order that the fathers might remain in the province and be content. Nevertheless, their decision to stay was against the judgment of all, because the natives had killed the other friar and because they were to remain among such great numbers of idolatrous people.[6]

5. By this statement Gallegos clearly does not mean that the friars had decided to remain in Malagón, where this episode was taking place. Rather, he must have reference to the province of New Mexico, and not to any specific pueblo. See also the fourth paragraph above, where he uses a similar expression, namely, that the friars had decided to remain en aquella poblazón, i.e., among the pueblo people.

6. The two friars were Agustín Rodríguez and Francisco López. See the affidavit, translated below, drawn up on Chamuscado's order, opposing the decision of the friars to remain in New Mexico.

CHAPTER XIII A

EVIL PRACTICES OF THESE PEOPLE.

WE LEARNED NOTHING of the rituals performed by the people of this settlement, except that when someone dies they dance and rejoice, for they say that he goes to the one whom they worship. They bury the dead in cavelike cellars, and every year on designated days they place many things as an offering at the foot of the cellars where the bodies lie.

The mitotes, or ceremonial dances, which they perform to bring rain when there is a lack of rainwater for their cornfields, are of the following nature.[1] During the month of December the natives begin their dances, which continue more than four months, at intervals of a certain number of days—every fortnight, I believe. Attendance at the mitotes is general, so the people gather in large numbers, though only the men take part, the women never. The ceremonies, which begin in the morning and last until evening, are held around an altar maintained for this purpose and continue throughout the night. An Indian chosen for the occasion sits elevated in their midst, and the participants dance before him. Close to this Indian are six others holding fifteen or twenty sticks.[2] They walk about and dance. During each movement of the dance, one of them steps out and puts into his mouth seven sticks, three spans in length and two fingers in width. When he finishes putting them in his mouth and taking them out, he pauses, seemingly fatigued. Then he dances with two or three of the said sticks in his mouth. Next, the man who is seated as "lord" receives seven lashes from whips made of light flexible willow for that purpose. These lashes are administered by the Indians standing close to him, for he has six Indians on each side who lash him thirty-six times in the course of each movement, in such a manner as to draw blood, making him look like a flagellant. After inflicting the original seven lashes, they continue to dance and to give him an equal number of lashes until they make the blood flow as if he were being bled. Although they do this until it seems that he will collapse, he shows no sign of pain. On the contrary, he talks to a large snake as thick as an arm, which coils up when it is about to talk. The whipped "lord" calls to it, and the reptile answers in such a manner that it can be understood. We thought this snake might be the devil, who has them enslaved. For this reason God our Lord willed that the settlement and its idolatrous people should be discovered, in order that they might come to the true faith.

At these dances, furthermore, two Indians carrying two rattlesnakes in their hands walk around in the midst of the people. The snakes are real; one can hear their rattles. They coil around the necks and creep all over the bodies of the two Indians who come, dancing and executing their figures, toward the lashed man, whom they acknowledge and obey as "lord" on this occasion. They hold the reptiles in their hands and, falling on their knees before the flayed one, give him the two snakes. He takes them, and they creep up his arms and over his body, making a

---

1. Generally speaking, the long and intricate ceremonies performed by the Indians of the Southwest are invocations for rain, bountiful harvests, and the creation of life. See F. W. Hodge, *Handbook*, vol. 1, p. 382; L. Farrand, *Basis of American History*, p. 187; and *Benavides' Revised Memorial*, p. 294.

2. These were prayer sticks, without which the prayer would be ineffectual.

great deal of noise with their rattles, until they reach his throat. Then the flayed one rises and swings around quickly. The snakes fall to the ground, where they coil and are picked up by those who brought them. Kneeling, the two Indians put the reptiles in their mouths, and disappear through a little doorway.

When this is over two Indian coyotes appear and go around among the dancers, howling in a startling and pitiful manner.[3] As soon as the mitote has concluded, the flayed lord makes an offering of a certain number of sticks, adorned with many plumes, so that the people may place them in the cornfields and waterholes; for they worship and offer sacrifices at these holes. The natives do this, they say, because then they will never lack water. The men flayed are so badly lacerated that their wounds do not heal in two months. The participants are so neat and well adorned in these mitotes and dances that the spectacle is well worth seeing.

The local marriage customs will be described here to show how much wisdom God our Lord has bestowed upon the people of this settlement.[4] Whenever anyone wishes to marry according to their custom, all his relatives and some of the other inhabitants assemble and perform their dances. The wedding and attendant festivities last more than three days. The first thing given the couple is a house in which to live. This is presented to them as a dowry by the father- and mother-in-law, parents of the bride. The house is two, three, or four stories high, with eight or ten rooms. The couple to be married are seated on a bench. At the side of the bride stands an Indian woman as bridesmaid and at the side of the groom an Indian who acts as groomsman. Apart from them stands a very old man, well dressed in colored and nicely woven blankets. He acts as the priest, telling the couple from time to time to kiss and embrace, and they do what the old man commands.

Their colored and ornamented blankets are set before the couple. The groom covers his bride with her blankets and she places his on

---

3. These "coyotes" must have been Indians disguised as coyotes who went around howling and cavorting to amuse the crowd. The cunning coyote played the same role in Mexican folklore as the sly fox did in old European animal tales. Ethnically, coyote denotes a person born to an Indian mother and a mestizo father, with a color resembling that of the coyote. The term evidently was used to refer to men of a darker hue, distinguished in this way from the others. A century later, the term was applied to a Zuñi Indian in a Vargas document. Three natives came to meet Vargas, two of them Moquis, "and the third a coyote named Ventura, an intelligent Indian native of the pueblo of Alona and the province of Zuñi." José Manuel Espinosa, *First Expedition of Vargas into New Mexico* (1940), pp. 210-211. In modern Mexico, the term coyote is applied to someone who engages in shady business, a scoundrel or deceitful cheat, regardless of the color of his skin.

4. Regarding marriage customs of the Pueblo Indians, see Hodge, *Handbook*, vol. I, p. 809; Farrand, *op. cit.*, pp. 185-186; and *Benavides' Revised Memorial*, pp. 44, 239, 241.

him, in such a way that they clothe one another. Then the old man talks. As we did not know the language we did not understand what he was saying, but from his gestures we supposed he was telling them that they should love each other very much, since that was the purpose for which they had been united. When this is over the people place before the bride a grindstone, an olla, a flat earthenware pan *(comal)*, drinking vessels, and *chicubites*. They also put a grinding stone *(metate)* in her hand. The old man tells the bride that the gifts set before her, which are all entirely new, signify that with them she is to grind and cook food for her husband; that she is to prepare two meals every day for him, one in the morning and the other in the afternoon; that they are to dine and retire early, and rise before daybreak. She answers that she will do so.

Then the priest speaks to the groom, before whom are placed a Turkish bow, spear, war club, and shield, which signify that with them he is to defend his home and protect his wife and children. They give him his crate *(cacoxte—cacaxtle)* and leather band *(mecapal)* for carrying burdens. Then they place a hoe in his hand to signify that he is to till and cultivate the soil and gather corn to support his wife and children. He answers that he will do everything indicated. In addition to this, he is given lands in which to plant corn. Then the dances continue. Afterward the couple are taken to their house. All that day there is food in abundance, which consists of turkeys, buffalo meat, tamales, tortillas, and other things. The orderliness with which these Indians perform the ceremony described above is amazing. For a barbarous people the neatness they observe in everything is very remarkable.

CHAPTER XIII B

ACCOUNT OF THE PUEBLOS THAT WERE SEEN; THE NAMES THEY WERE GIVEN BECAUSE OF OUR IGNORANCE OF THEIR LANGUAGE; AND THE INFORMATION GATHERED CONCERNING THE LAND FARTHER ON.

THE FIRST PUEBLO to be seen we named San Felipe.[1] It had about forty-five houses of two and three stories. In this pueblo we took possession of the whole province for his Majesty; and on August 21, 1581, we set out

1. Mera located a Piro ruin on the south bank of Mulligan gulch at its junction with the Río Grande. See chapter VIII, footnote 1.

from it to explore all the other pueblos and provinces located farther up on a river which we named the Guadalquivir and of which the natives had told us.

Close to San Felipe, on the same side of the river, we found another pueblo, about two leagues distant, containing forty-seven two-story houses. We named it San Miguel.

On the opposite bank of the river, across from San Miguel, is another pueblo, which has twenty-five two-story houses. We named it Santiago.

Above the pueblo of San Miguel we discovered yet another. It had forty houses, two stories high. We named it San Juan.

On the other side of the river, opposite San Juan, there is a pueblo containing about thirty-five two-story houses. We named it Piastla.

On this same side, above Piastla, we found a pueblo of about eighty-five two-story houses built around two plazas. We named it Piña. It is located in a large meadow formed by the said river.

Farther up the river, on the side of the Sierra Morena,[2] we discovered another pueblo and named it Elota. It has fourteen houses, two stories high.

On the same side, farther upstream, we found still another pueblo and named it El Hosso. It had fifty houses, two stories high.

Near El Hosso, on the same side, in a bend *(hoja)* formed by the river, we discovered a pueblo containing fourteen two-story houses. We named it La Pedrosa.

Along this same river we found a pueblo of twenty-five two-story houses. We named it Ponsitlán.

Also along this river we found another pueblo containing twenty-five two-story houses. We named it Pueblo Nuevo because its construction had just begun.

Above the pueblo of Ponsitlán we discovered another. It had fifteen houses, two stories high. We named it Caxtole.

On the opposite bank, facing Caxtole, we found a pueblo containing one hundred two-story houses. We named it Piquinaguatengo.[3]

On the other bank of the river, toward the Sierra Morena, there is another pueblo of forty houses, two stories high. We named it Mexical-cingo.

Above this pueblo we discovered another; it had seventy houses of two and three stories. This pueblo is divided into two sections, the one

2. The Sierra Morena was the Manzano mountains, east of the Río Grande.
3. Called Chiquinagua in the Pedrosa list. Venturing a guess, this might have been Isleta.

being an harquebus-shot distant from the other. It was named Tomat-lán.

Fronting Tomatlán, on the opposite bank, we found another pueblo which had one hundred and twenty-three houses of two and three stories. We named it Taxumulco.

Up the river, above Taxumulco, we discovered a pueblo containing one hundred houses of two and three stories. We named it Santa Catalina.[4]

On the opposite side of the river, toward the Sierra Morena, we found another pueblo with fifty two-story houses. We named it San Mateo.

Above San Mateo we discovered a pueblo with one hundred and twenty-three houses of two and three stories. We named it Puaray.[5]

On the other bank we discovered another pueblo containing [there is a blank] of two and three stories.[6] We named it San Pedro. This pueblo is above Santa Catalina.

Above San Pedro we discovered a pueblo of forty houses, two and three stories high. We named it Analco.

Upstream from the pueblo of Analco we found another, with eighty-four two- and three-story houses. We named it Culiacán.

Above Culiacán there is a pueblo consisting of one hundred houses of two and three stories. We named it Villarrasa.

Above the pueblo of Villarrasa there is another, of one hundred and thirty-four two- and three-story houses. We named it La Palma.

On the opposite side of the river, above the pueblo called Puaray, we found another, containing twenty houses two stories high. We named it Cempoala.

Above Cempoala there was a pueblo that consisted of seventy-seven houses of two and three stories. We called it Nompe.

On the same side, farther upstream, we discovered another pueblo of one hundred and twenty-three two- and three-story houses. We named it Malpaís because it is close to some "bad lands."

Above this pueblo of Malpaís, up the river, we found another, which had one hundred and forty-five houses of two and three stories. We named it Cáceres and took possession of it for his Majesty on September 2 of that year, 1581.[7]

4. The Pedrosa list adds that there were many cottonwood trees near this pueblo. It will be noted that Pedrosa occasionally gives a sentence of description not found in the Gallegos account.

5. Located somewhere between modern Albuquerque and Bernalillo, but the exact site is a matter of controversy. See Introduction, pp. 23, 57.

6. The Pedrosa list gives the number of houses as sixty-two.

7. Possibly LA 677, located in the north end of modern Bernalillo. See Introduction, p. 12.

Above this town of Cáceres we found another pueblo, which had seventy houses of two and three stories. We called it Campos.

Opposite Campos, on the other side of the river, we found a pueblo which had eighty houses of two and three stories. We named it Palomares.

Farther up the river we discovered another pueblo with two hundred and thirty houses of two, three, and four stories. We named it Medina de la Torre.[8]

Near Medina de la Torre, in a northerly direction, on a stream that empties into the Guadalquivir river not far from that settlement, we discovered a valley which we called Atotonilco,[9] in which there were four pueblos. The first we named Guatitlán;[10] it contained seventy-six houses of two, three, and four stories. The second we called La Guarda; it had one hundred houses of three and four stories. To the third we gave the name of Valladolid; it had two hundred houses of three and four stories.[11] In this pueblo we took possession for his Majesty on the sixth day of September. The fourth town, which contains sixty houses three and four stories high, we named La Rinconada, because it is in a bend of the said valley.

Farther up this Guadalquivir river, above Medina de la Torre, we found another pueblo on the river bank which had forty houses of two stories. We named it Castilleja.[12]

Still farther up the river, we discovered a pueblo which had two hundred houses three and four stories high. We named it Castildabid.[13]

Continuing upstream, we found a pueblo that had ninety houses of two and three stories. We named it Suchipila.[14]

Above Suchipila we found another pueblo, of eighty houses three and four stories high. We named it Talaván.[15]

Likewise up the river, on a large stream that turned away from the said river in a northerly direction, we discovered another pueblo which had five hundred houses of from one to seven stories. It was called

8. Perhaps this was Kuaua, LA 187.

9. Why was it called Atotonilco, a Nahuatl term signifying "hot springs"? Could it be that the party had actually gone farther up the Jémez valley and discovered its famous hot springs?

10. Guaxitlán, in the Pedrosa list.

11. Possibly Zía. Mera shows a group of ruins around Zía that seems to fit this description.

12. The Pedrosa list states that at this pueblo the natives had a stream of water with which they irrigated their cornfields. It might have been the one now known as San Felipe.

13. Site LA 922.

14. If we are on the right trail, this would be Cochití.

15. Site LA 35 in Cochití canyon.

Nueva Tlaxcala and was left under the authority of his Majesty.[16] In this pueblo the natives indicated by signs that there were others farther on, but which we did not visit for lack of time.

We also discovered a stream carrying a large volume of water which flows into the Guadalquivir from the south. This stream forms a valley which we named Valle Vicioso because it was so fertile and luxuriant. In the valley there were three pueblos. The first was close to the river, opposite the pueblo of Castildabid. It had two hundred houses three and four stories high. We named it Castilblanco.[17] The second pueblo had two hundred houses of three and four stories. We named it Buena Vista. The third had seventy houses three stories high. We named it La Barranca. At the pueblo of La Barranca we learned that in this valley, at a distance of a three days' journey up the river, there were thirteen other pueblos. The natives indicated that these were located toward the south. We did not visit them because we were so few and because our supplies had given out.

About five leagues from the Guadalquivir river we discovered another valley which we called San Mateo.[18] Here we found four pueblos, the first of which had three hundred houses, five stories high. We named it Piedra Hita because it was built entirely of rock. The second had one hundred and forty houses four stories high. We named it Galisteo. The third had one hundred houses three stories high. We called it Malpartida. The fourth had eighty houses three stories high. We named it Malagón. Here we were informed that on the slopes of the Sierra Morena there were two large pueblos, but we did not visit them on account of incidents that prevented us from doing so.[19]

FAMOUS SALINES

Back of the Sierra Morena we found some salines which extended for five leagues, the best ever discovered by Christians.[20] The salt re-

---

16. We believe Nueva Tlaxcala was Pecos. For a discussion of its identification, see Introduction, p. 59. Bolton, in his editing of Bustamante's declaration, thought that Nueva Tlaxcala was in the Jémez valley, but he did not have the advantage of studying Gallegos' "Relation." *Spanish Exploration in the Southwest.* p. 147.

17. Possibly Santo Domingo, since it was opposite Castildabid, which we place in Cochití canyon.

18. The upper Galisteo basin. For identification of the four pueblos noted by Gallegos, see Introduction, p. 61.

19. These two pueblos may have been Paa-ko and San Antonio, located to the southwest of San Marcos and Galisteo between the San Pedro and Sandía Mountains. Both were contemporary with the Chamuscado expedition. See Marjorie F. Lambert, *Paa-ko, Archaeological Chronicle of an Indian Village in North Central New Mexico* (Santa Fé, 1954), pp. 5-7.

20. These salt marshes were in the Estancia-Willard region. With regard to the pueblos east of the Manzano mountains, see Introduction, p. 62.

sembles that of the sea. In the vicinity of these salines we discovered five pueblos. The first had one hundred and twenty-five houses two stories high. We named it Zacatula. The second, containing two hundred houses of two and three stories, we named Ruiseco. To the third, which had ninety houses of three stories, we gave the name of La Mesa. The fourth had ninety-five houses of two and three stories; we called it La Hoya. The fifth contained sixty-five houses two and three stories high. We named it Franca Vila. Here we were told that there were three very large pueblos beyond the salines, and our informants indicated that they were large cities. We did not visit them on account of the heavy snowfall which occurred at that time.

From the pueblo of Cáceres we soldier-explorers went to investigate a valley of which we and our leader and chief had been given fine reports. It was situated five leagues from the Guadalquivir river. In this valley, which we named Santiago, we found a pueblo with three hundred houses of three and four stories. We called it Puerto Frío.[21] This pueblo is situated in a barranca which is near a river, with water, which flows by the said pueblo.

In the valley of Santiago we found another pueblo, with one hundred houses, two and three stories high. We named it Baños. Here our party of explorers was told that there were thirteen pueblos farther up this same valley. We did not visit them on account of the heavy snowfalls.

The chief and soldiers were informed that thirty-five leagues from the Guadalquivir there were many pueblos and a mineral deposit. In view of this report, the leader sent the explorers and conquerors to reconnoiter the land and to learn the truth. Setting forth from the pueblo in the direction the natives had indicated, the reconnoitering party traveled for two days along the river toward the north and found a pueblo built in a strong position.[22] According to the discoverers, it is the best stronghold in existence even among Christians.

A VERY LARGE FORTRESS

This pueblo, called Acoma, has five hundred houses three and four stories high. Here we made inquiry as to whether more settled territory

21. This valley could be the upper Jémez, and its towns the "Aguas Calientes" group, to use Bloom's designation. These were the pueblos extending from Jémez pueblo itself to those in the San Diego-Guadalupe canyons, the best known of which were near the hot springs at Giusewa. Indeed, the latter may have been the "Baños" of Gallegos.

22. Both Gallegos and Bustamante, in their testimony, indicate that they started the trip to Acoma and Zuñi from Puaray. If so, they should have been going west rather than north.

was to be found farther on; and the natives said that at a distance of two days beyond their pueblo of Acoma, toward the south, there were many pueblos and also the mineral deposit we were seeking. The explorers, following the route indicated by this information, took along an Indian as guide for this purpose.

After two days they came upon a valley called Suni [Zuñi] in which they discovered five pueblos. The first had seventy-five three-story houses and was called Aquima. The second had one hundred houses, four and five stories high, and was named Maça. The third, called Alonagua, had forty-four three- and four-story houses. The fourth, Aguico, had one hundred and twenty-five houses of two and three stories. The other pueblo, which was the fifth, had forty-four three- and four-story houses.[23]

In this same valley, the Indians informed us that two days farther on were five pueblos and a mineral deposit. We did not visit that site because we had not brought the necessary provisions.[24] This valley [of Zuñi] is the best that has been discovered, since all of it is cultivated and not a grain of corn is lost. All the houses are of stone, which is indeed amazing; and all of them in this settlement have passageways, windows, doorways, and wooden ladders affording a means of ascent. There is not a house of two or three stories that does not have eight rooms or more, which surprised us more than anything else, together with the fact that the houses are whitewashed and painted inside and out, and the various pueblos have their plazas and streets. It is the custom of the natives to make mats of straw for their rooms, and many make them of fine light palm on which to sleep.

23. All of the Zuñi pueblos are named in the Pedrosa list, with a slight variation in spelling.

24. Bustamante called it the valley of Asay. Actually, it was the Hopi country, and the news of a mineral deposit was doubtless the same that subsequently lured both Espejo and Oñate to send exploring parties in search of it in the region of the present Jerome, Arizona.

CHAPTER XIV

HOW WE TURNED BACK AFTER SEEING THE LAND; WHAT HAPPENED ON OUR DEPARTURE; AND HOW THE FRIARS REMAINED IN THE SETTLEMENT.

AFTER INVESTIGATING everything in the land that could be seen or learned, the leader and the other soldiers decided to return to the land of Christians before any misfortune should befall them and before the natives should attempt to carry out their evil plan. Thus we took leave of the friars, who had decided to remain in the settlement, a pueblo called Puaray, which contains one hundred and twenty-four houses two and three stories high. The decision of the friars to stay was, however, very much against our will, in view of the fact that the Indians had killed Fray Juan de Santa María.

When the leader learned of the decision taken by the friars, he asked them not only once, but three times, in the name of God and of his Majesty, to leave with us and not to remain, for they would be in great danger and the land would revolt if any misfortune befell them. He added that they could not accomplish any good results at present, before there were Spanish forces to compel the natives to obey their wishes; and that they should go to report to their superiors concerning the land so that the latter might send the necessary aid. The leader of our party ordered that testimony of all this should be recorded in writing.[1] In spite of his exhortations and those of the soldiers in this matter, the friars replied that they were determined to remain, that no one could force them to abandon their pious intention of preaching the holy gospel, and that they would excommunicate any person who attempted to thwart them.

When the leader received their reply, he tried to leave the natives in a friendly mood and at peace with us and the friars, letting the Indians know that we intended to return to our land for many more Christians, including women. The natives rejoiced greatly at this and promised to look after the fathers and to feed and treat them well, saying that since we wanted to return to our country we should go and bring back many Spaniards and their wives. They wanted to see what these Spaniards looked like and how they dressed. The Indians also promised that when we came back they would have the fathers fat and well. Since they had shown such good will toward the latter for their decision to stay and toward us in regard to our departure, we left the pueblo of Puaray. Some Indians grieved at our departure and we Spaniards—the friars as well as the soldiers—were all affected, particularly at leaving one another, so much so that some of the soldiers showed a determination to stay; but for certain reasons pointed out by the leader no one dared to remain.

We left this pueblo and the friars on the last day of January 1582, determined to return quickly to Christian territory in order to bring help for the conversion of these natives. We went down the same river

---

1. See the affidavit drawn up on February 13, 1582.

by which we had come. After having gone twenty leagues from the pueblo of Puaray, we discovered six mineral deposits.[2] These are in a very fine locality with abundant water and timber; the veins are rich and well provided with supporting walls. In the opinion of all our men—who were nearly all miners and knew about mines, veins, and minerals—the deposits were, and are, excellent.

After the leader and magistrate of our expedition had seen, taken possession of, and recorded these discoveries of mines, we were informed of six or seven more; but because the supply of iron for horseshoes had been exhausted, we did not go on to explore them. Moreover, we wanted to keep our promise to both the friars and the natives that our absence would be brief. This and other reasons prevented us from going on to investigate those mining sites. Nevertheless, according to the signs made and information given us by the natives, the deposits must be near that place; and, God willing, we shall locate them when the land is settled, for such an abundance of mines is indeed marvelous.

When the leader and the soldiers saw that the land had so many mineral deposits and resources that would facilitate its settlement and the conversion of the natives to Christianity, they were filled with an even more zealous determination to return and report on that land, so that a decision might promptly be reached to send the necessary aid for the protection of the fathers who had remained and for the preaching of the holy gospel. We desired that so many idolatrous souls should not be lost, but should, on the contrary, be brought to the true faith before they, as idolatrous Indians, should attempt some evil deed, killing the fathers and hindering the penetration of the territory.

2. These mineral prospects might have been found in the Magdalena mountains west of Socorro, New Mexico, though the distance from Puaray would have been nearly twice that given by Gallegos. The statement is illuminating also in that it shows the Spaniards made side trips not otherwise recorded. We suspect they followed this practice throughout their New Mexico journey, and that some of their excursions were not reported by Gallegos, whose "Relation" is, of course, our main source of information for the Chamuscado-Rodríguez expedition.

CHAPTER XV

CONCERNING OUR EXPERIENCES ON THE RETURN JOURNEY AFTER THE DIS-COVERY OF THE MINERAL DEPOSITS; AND THE ILLNESS THAT BEFELL OUR LEADER, NECESSITATING A HALT ON THE WAY.

AFTER THE ABOVE EVENTS had transpired, we continued down the river for more than eighty leagues. Then God willed that our leader should be stricken with an old ailment, from which he was already suffering on leaving the settlement. His illness became much worse due to the hardships of travel, so that we were obliged to stop for rest at a place which we named Canutillo. We stayed here four days to give him some relief before proceeding with our trip; and then we left, although his illness grew much more serious from the fatigue of the march. Since his condition was caused by exhaustion, we decided to bleed him. As the equipment which he had brought (the lancelet and the syringe) had been left with the friars, we proceeded as soldiers do in time of need when they draw blood with a horseshoe nail and apply the medicines by means of a horn. These two devices were used for our leader and for the soldiers who were ill.

Indeed, we were beset by many difficulties, for with three or four men sick out of eight soldiers—nine with our leader—we had to stand guard every night wearing armor. We endured great hardship, especially as the illness of our leader became aggravated. Because he was a man of sixty or seventy years, the ailment took firmer hold on him than on the others who were not so old. It became necessary to stop four days more at another place, which we named De los Patos, so that he might have a chance to improve and the illness might decline. Since it did not diminish, but on the contrary took firmer hold on him, we urged him to commend himself to God and to make his last will before Hernán Gallegos, the notary of the expedition, which he did. The affliction was becoming so serious that his hands and feet were paralyzed, and therefore we decided to build a litter which, slung between two horses, could take him quickly to Christian lands where the holy sacraments could be administered, for that was the most important consideration. As we had no tools, because all of them had been left with the fathers for cutting timber, we had to cut branches and poles for the litter with our swords, which we did as well as we could. To make a covering for the litter it was necessary to kill a horse, since the hides we had brought from the buffalo country were not sufficient. We reinforced it to the best of our ability, and when it was finished we placed our leader on it.

Burdened by this device, we traveled with great difficulty. The horses, not used to that sort of work, fell at times, to our great dismay. Thus if we had endured much suffering on our entry, we were meeting with much greater hardship on our return. We gave many thanks to God for such trials, which came to us through His will; and we prayed that since He was sending them to us He would also endow us with patience and fortitude to withstand them. These hardships were due to our very small number, for out of nine men three or four were ill and we still had to keep vigil every night just as we had done up to that time. The Indian servants that we had taken along had, moreover, remained at the settlement with the fathers.

After we had traversed the longest and most difficult part of the way, and when we were at last out of the new land and near Christian territory, within thirty leagues of Santa Bárbara, God willed that our leader should die. We gave him the best burial possible, in a marked place, on a route and in a locality that had to be crossed to reach the said settlement, so that when the occasion should arrive his remains might be taken to the land of the Christians.[1] God alone knows the depression, grief, and pity that we all experienced at seeing him die in such a remote and desolate land, without spiritual or temporal comfort. But as these are things willed by God our Lord and directed by His hand, we gave many thanks to Him because He was pleased to call away from us the leader who had been in our company for a year, who had traveled so many leagues in our party, and who at the moment when it was least expected had left us disconsolate.

1. The next year Luxán observed that the burial place of Chamuscado was at El Xacal, a thatched hut, about two leagues down the Conchos river below the mouth of the San Pedro. Luxán's "Journal," November 24, 1582.

CHAPTER XVI

CONCERNING THE RECEPTION GIVEN US AT SANTA BÁRBARA; WHAT TRANSPIRED BETWEEN ITS INHABITANTS AND OURSELVES; AND HOW THEY TRIED TO ARREST US BECAUSE WE HAD NOT TAKEN POSSESSION ON BEHALF OF THE GOVERNMENT OF FRANCISCO AND DIEGO DE IBARRA.

AFTER BURYING our leader, we decided to push on to Christian territory without delay. Proceeding on our way, we came to Santa Bárbara on April 15, a notable day, as it was Easter. This was the place from which we had originally set out on the expedition. We were well received here and given an especially warm welcome because the inhabitants had thought us dead. We fired a salute to the town with our harquebuses, after which the royal notary (who was present) gave us, at the request of Hernán Gallegos, a written affidavit of the day, month, and year on which we had reached the mines and town of Santa Bárbara. The affidavit stated that, having armed and equipped ourselves and our horses, we were returning from serving God and the king at our own cost and expense.

Notwithstanding we had been given this certification, the settlers and authorities of Santa Bárbara, although they realized that the discovery had been carried out by commission from New Spain, decided to have us arrested; to seize the documents concerning the expedition brought by Hernán Gallegos; and to place the new land under the jurisdiction of Diego de Ibarra that he might take cognizance of this discovery. Hernán Gallegos, notary of the expedition, knew that it was not proper to do such a thing and that, on the contrary, we should report to the viceroy of New Spain, by whose commission the land and people had been discovered and explored, and that we should give him an account of the discovery, as loyal vassals of his Majesty.

When Hernán Gallegos learned that the people and authorities of Santa Bárbara had planned so carefully to take the documents from him, and when the captain of Santa Bárbara saw our determination to resist, that official ordered Gallegos, as the notary of the expedition, to show him the said documents, stating where the explorers and their leader had gone, and what had been discovered and accomplished on the expedition. To this Gallegos replied that in regard to the discovery, the captain of Santa Bárbara did not even have authority to ask him for a report concerning the trip, for their party had entered and explored by commission from New Spain; that if they had done wrong and the officials of Santa Bárbara could not show them in what manner, the members of the party would be punished by his Excellency, the viceroy of New Spain, to whom we should all submit as was our duty; and that he questioned the authority of the captain of Santa Bárbara to issue the aforesaid order.

In spite of all this, the captain ordered Hernán Gallegos, under threat of punishment, to exhibit the documents in question. In order to evade the Santa Bárbara authorities, Gallegos answered that he would bring the papers to the officer. Then, during the early morning of the next day (the day following Easter), we left the jurisdiction of Santa Bárbara, on our way to Mexico, so that we might report on the discovery to his Excellency. We were three companions, Pedro de Bustamante, Hernán Gallegos, and Pedro Sánchez de Chaves, and we took along all the documents concerning the expedition. It was agreed that the rest of our comrades should remain at Santa Bárbara to ward off penetration into the land we had discovered. We therefore went to report to his Excellency, by whose commission we had taken possession of that land, so that he might provide the proper authority and succor and might also command that, until other provisions were made by him, no captain or magistrate of any place whatsoever should enter the land save by his order. This was done at once and the appropriate royal decrees were dispatched in due form to the jurisdictions of Francisco and Diego de Ibarra, Carbajal, and the others involved.

In due time the three companions mentioned reached the post of the general of Zacatecas, Rodrigo del Río de Lossa, in the valley of San Juan, eleven leagues from the mines of Sombrerete. Here it was necessary for one of the party, Pedro Sánchez de Chaves, to go back with certain reports to Santa Bárbara, where the rest of the party had remained. The other two—Pedro de Bustamante and the narrator, Hernán Gallegos—took leave of him and departed for Mexico city, where we proposed to report to his Excellency concerning the discovery.

Pushing on, we arrived in Mexico city on May 8, 1582. We appeared before his Excellency to give an account of the expedition, explaining what had been accomplished; and we brought him samples of what there was in the land, such as clothing, buffalo meat, salt from the salines, and ores from the mines discovered there. Some of these assayed at twenty marcos per hundredweight. We presented him also with specimens of the dishes (chicubites) from which the natives eat, and other crockery made in their settlement, which is like that of New Spain.

We were well received. Indeed, we brought great joy and happiness to the city of Mexico, and especially to his Excellency, the viceroy of New Spain, because we had carried out in such a short time, and during his administration, this enterprise on which his Majesty and his subjects had previously spent much money, but without success. Now nine men had dared to go among the multitude of people in the inhabited area, as well as into the uninhabited region, and had made the discoveries above described.

This was their report—that where five hundred men had failed to discover or explore, eight men had succeeded at their own cost and expense, without receiving any subsidy or other help from his Majesty or from anyone else. Their success brought great relief and inspiration to many people in New Spain.

Hernán Gallegos, one of the explorers and the notary of the expedition, decided to write this report, with the chapters and explanations herein formulated. He wrote it and had it copied on July 8, 1582.

The above report was copied, corrected, and compared with the one found in the aforementioned book, folios 31 to 78, at the instance of Doctor Quesada, fiscal of his Majesty in the royal audiencia and chancellery of the city of Mexico, on May 12, 1602. In certification whereof I attach my signature so that the document may be legal. Its correction was witnessed by Lorenzo de Burgos and Juan Martínez de Aranda, residents of this city. Signed, JUAN DE ARANDA [There is a rubric]

PEDROSA'S LIST OF PUEBLOS

LIST OF THE PUEBLOS IN THE PROVINCE AS DRAWN UP BY MARTÍN DE PEDROSA, NOTARY, BY ORDER OF THE COUNT OF MONTERREY, FROM PAPERS LEFT BY THE COSMOGRAPHER, FRANCISCO DOMÍNGUEZ.

LIST OF THE PUEBLOS[1] in the province explored by the illustrious Francisco Sánchez Chamuscado, magistrate, leader, and discoverer, and by the explorers and conquistadors who came with him to survey and conquer the aforesaid province, which they named San Phelipe. It was discovered and is being conquered by commission of his Excellency, Don Lorenzo Suárez de Mendoza, Count of Coruña, viceroy, governor, and captain general of New Spain. Francisco Sánchez Chamuscado took possession of it for the king by virtue of his commission from the viceroy. The complete list of pueblos is as follows:

1. San Phelipe, capital of the province *(cabeza de la provincia)*. First, a pueblo containing forty-five houses and two plazas was discovered on a hillock, the houses being two stories high. We named the place San Phelipe, and here took possession of the entire province, on behalf of his Majesty, on August 21, 1581. From this pueblo the exploration of the whole province was begun by following upstream a river to which we gave the name of Guadalquivir.

2. San Miguel. There is another pueblo, farther up this river, on the same side of the stream as the first one, San Phelipe, and two leagues distant from it. This second pueblo has forty-seven houses, all two stories high. We named it San Miguel.

3. Santiago. On the opposite bank of the said river, facing the pueblo of San Miguel, there is another, with twenty-five two-story houses, which we named Santiago. It is situated on the top of a little hill, close to a meadow formed by the river.

4. San Juan. Likewise, above the pueblo of San Miguel, we found another, to which we gave the name of San Juan. It has forty houses two stories high. This pueblo nestles against the slope of a small hill.

5. Piastla. Again, on the opposite bank of the river, across from San Juan, another pueblo was discovered, containing thirty-five two-story houses. It was given the name Piastla.

---

1. Pedrosa's list varies sufficiently from that given in chapter XIII B, above, to mark it as an important document. It also comes from A.G.I., *Patronato*, legajo 22.

6. Piña. On the same side and above Piastla, we discovered another pueblo, which had eighty-five two-story houses located on two plazas. We named it Piña. This pueblo is in a large meadow formed by the said river.

7. Elota. Farther up this river, on the side of the Sierra Morena, we discovered another pueblo, of fourteen houses, which we called Elota.

8. El Osso. Also on this side, and farther upstream, another pueblo was found which we named El Oso. It had fifty two-story houses; it is located on a high hill.

9. La Pedrosa. Near El Oso, on the same side and in a bend formed by the bank of the river, we discovered another pueblo, with fourteen two-story houses. We called it La Pedrosa.

10. Pueblo Nuevo. Along the same river we discovered another pueblo, containing twenty houses two stories high, which we named Pueblo Nuevo because construction had just begun.

11. Ponsitlán. Farther up the said river we found another pueblo, which had twenty-five two-story houses. We named it Ponsitlán.

12. Caxtole. Above the pueblo of Ponsitlán we discovered another, with fifteen two-story houses, which we named Caxtole.

13. Chiquinagua. On the opposite bank of the river, across from Caxtole, we found another pueblo, with one hundred houses two stories high, which we named Chiquinagua.

14. Mexicalcingo. Upstream on the other side of the river toward the Sierra Morena, there is another pueblo, containing forty two-story houses. We named it Mexicalcingo.

15. Tomatlán. Above this pueblo, on the said river, another was discovered, with seventy houses of two and three stories. This pueblo is divided into two parts, close to each other. It was given the name of Tomatlán.

16. Taxomulco. Opposite Tomatlán, across the river, we found another pueblo which had one hundred and twenty-three houses two and three stories high. We named it Taxomulco.

17. Santa Catalina. Above Taxomulco, farther up the river, we discovered another pueblo, containing one hundred houses of two and three stories, which we named Santa Catalina. There are many cottonwood trees near this pueblo.

18. San Mateo. Along the opposite bank of the river, on the side of the Sierra Morena, another pueblo was found, with fifty two-story houses. We named it San Mateo.

19. Puari [sic]. Above the pueblo of San Mateo we discovered an-

othcr, containing one hundred and twelve houses two and three stories high. We called it Puarai [sic].

20. San Pedro. On the opposite bank of the river we discovered another pueblo, with sixty-two houses of two and three stories, which we named San Pedro. This is just above Santa Catalina.

21. Analco. Above the pueblo of San Pedro we discovered another which had forty houses two and three stories high. We gave it the name of Analco.

22. Culiacán. Above Analco we found another pueblo; it had eighty-four two- and three-story houses. We named it Culiacán.

23. Villarrasa. Above this pueblo of Culiacán we found another containing one hundred houses two and three stories high, which we named Villarasa. This pueblo is situated on a hill in the meadow bordering the said river.

24. La Palma. Farther upstream, above Villarasa, we found another pueblo, with one hundred and thirty-four houses of two and three stories. We called it La Palma.

25. Cempoalla. On the opposite bank of the same river, above the pueblo called Puarai, we discovered another, with twenty houses two stories high. We named it Cempoalla.

26. Nompe. Above this pueblo of Cempoalla we found another containing seventy-seven two-and three-story houses. We gave it the name of Nompe.

27. Malpaís. Along this same bank, farther up the river, we discovered another pueblo, which had one hundred and twenty-three houses two and three stories high. We named it Malpaís because it was near a stretch of "bad lands."

28. Cáceres. Upstream, above the said pueblo of Malpaís, there is another, which has one hundred and forty-five houses of two and three stories, which was named Cáceres. There we took possession for his Majesty on September 2, 1581.

29. Campos. Above Cáceres we discovered another pueblo, containing seventy houses two and three stories high. We named it Campos.

30. Palomares. On the opposite side of the river, across from Campos, we found another pueblo, with eighty houses, which we named Palomares.

31. Medina de la Torre. Then again, farther up the said river, we discovered another pueblo, which had 23 [230] houses of two, three, and four stories. We named it Medina de la Torre.

[32-] 35. Guaxitlán, Guarda, Valladolid, La Rinconada. Near Medina

de la Torre, in a northerly direction, on a stream that empties into the aforesaid Guadalquivir river close to Medina de la Torre, we discovered a valley and named it Atotonilco. Here we found four pueblos. The first of these, named Guaxitlán, had seventy-six houses two, three, and four stories high. Above this pueblo there is another, which we called La Guarda, containing one hundred houses, of two, three, and four stories. Yet another, which was named Valladolid, has two hundred houses. Here we took possession for his Majesty on the sixth day of the above-mentioned month and year. The fourth pueblo, with sixty houses three and four stories high, was given the name of La Rinconada because it is situated in a bend of the valley.

36. Not named [Castilleja].

Along the said Guadalquivir river, above Medina de la Torre and along another part of the stream, we found another pueblo, with forty houses of two and three stories. A stream of water with which the natives irrigate their cornfields flows near by.

37. Castil de Avid. Farther up the river we discovered another pueblo, containing two hundred houses three and four stories high, which was named Castil de Avid.

38. Suchipila. Still farther up this river we found another pueblo, which had ninety houses. We named it Suchipila. The houses are three and four stories high.

39. Talabán. Above Suchipila another pueblo was discovered, with eighty houses of three and four stories. We called it Talabán.

40. Likewise, farther up the river on a large stream that turned away from the said river in a northerly direction, we found another pueblo which had five hundred houses of two, three, four, five, six, and even of seven stories. It was named Nueva Tlaxcala and was left under the authority of his Majesty. In this pueblo the natives indicated that there were more pueblos farther on which we did not visit for lack of time.

[41-] 43. Castil Blanco, Buena Vista, La Barranca. Likewise, we found a stream with a large volume of water joining the Guadalquivir from the south. This stream forms a valley which we named Valle Vicioso because it was so luxuriant. In the valley we discovered three pueblos. The first, near the river and across from the pueblo of Castildavid, had two hundred houses. We named it Castil Blanco. The second, farther up the said valley, also has two hundred houses, and was given the name of Buena Vista. This pueblo is situated on the summit of a hill. Beyond it and upstream is the third pueblo, with seventy houses, all of which (like those of the other settlements in the Valle Vicioso) are three and four stories high. We named this pueblo La Barranca. In La Barranca

we heard that there were thirteen pueblos upstream, at a distance of a three day's journey from there; and our informants pointed toward the south. We did not go to visit these places because we were so few in number and our supplies were so limited.

[44-] 47. Four pueblos. Moreover, we discovered another valley, five leagues from that of the Guadalquivir, which we named San Mateo. In it we found four pueblos. One, which had three hundred houses four and five stories high, was named Piedra Hita. The second had one hundred and forty houses of three and four stories. We gave it the name of Galisto [sic]. The next pueblo contained five hundred houses of two and three stories; and the fourth had eighty houses three and four stories high.

At this last pueblo it was reported that there were two more settlements close to the sierra, which we named Orena [sic], but we were not able to visit them. Back of the Sierra Morena we found some salines, which extend for five leagues and which produce the best salt in Christendom, just like salt derived from the sea.

[48-] 52. Zacatula, Ruyseco, La Joya, Franca Vila. In this region of the salines, on the slopes of the Sierra Morena, we discovered five pueblos. The first of these, containing one hundred and twenty-five two-story houses, we named Zacatula, The second, with two hundred houses, was named Ruiseco. Its houses are three stories high. The third, with ninety three-story houses, we called La . . . [there is a blank in the manuscript]. The fourth had ninety-five houses three stories high and was named La Joya. The fifth, containing sixty-five three-story houses, we named Franca Vila. Here we were informed that at some distance from the salines there were three very large pueblos, apparently cities, to judge from the signs made by our informants. Lack of supplies and bad weather, with snow, prevented us from visiting them.

[53-] 54. Puerto Frío, Baños. Moreover, from the pueblo of Cáceres, the said magistrate and explorers went on to find another valley, of which we had heard reports, situated five leagues from the Guadalquivir river. In this valley, which was named Santiago, we found a pueblo with three hundred houses of three and four stories. We called it Puerto Frío. This pueblo is in a gorge, close to a river that flows near by. Farther up the valley, we discovered another pueblo, which had one hundred houses two and three stories high. We named it Baños.

[55]. Acoma. We, the said magistrate and explorers, were likewise informed that thirty-five leagues from the Guadalquivir river there were many pueblos and a site where mines had been discovered. In view of this the magistrate sent the aforesaid explorers and conquista-

dors to visit and examine the land and to travel through it. Setting forth in the direction indicated by the information received, they marched upstream for two days, toward the north, and found a pueblo situated on a stronghold, the greatest in Christendom. This pueblo, which has five hundred houses three and four stories high, was named Acoma. In response to questions about what there was in the interior, the inhabitants reported that, two days' march away, there were many pueblos, as well as the mines of which we had heard.

56 [-61]. Aquiman, Maça, Aconagua, Coaquina, Allico, Acana. Continuing our journey, we reached a valley called Suni, where we came upon and discovered six pueblos. One of these, containing seventy-five houses of two and three stories, is called Aquiman. Another, known as Maça, has one hundred houses of four and five stories. Yet another, Aconagua, has forty-four houses of three and four stories. The next, Coaquina, contains sixty houses three and four stories high. The fifth, Allico, has one hundred and eighteen houses of three and four stories. The sixth, Acana, has forty houses three and four stories high.

Moreover, in this same valley, we heard that there were five more pueblos a two day's journey away. It snowed so much that the bad weather made it impossible for us to go on and visit them.

I certify that his Excellency, the Count of Monterrey, viceroy of this New Spain, having ordered me to search through the papers left by the cosmographer, Francisco Domínguez, and to remove those relating to the expedition to the provinces of New Mexico, I found this document among them. By order of his Excellency, I hereby issue the present certification. Mexico city, May 14, in the year of 1600. MARTÍN DE PEDROSA [Rubric]

DEPARTURE OF
FRAY JUAN DE SANTA MARÍA[1]
SEPTEMBER 10, 1581

IN THE PROVINCE of San Felipe, September 10, 1581, his Grace, Francisco Sánchez Chamuscado, entrusted with a commission by his Excellency, Don Lorenzo Suárez de Mendoza, Count of Coruña, his Majesty's viceroy, governor, and captain general in New Spain, determined to carry on his discoveries, as were the others accompanying him, on learning that Father Juan de Santa María of the Franciscan order wished to go to some pacified region of his own choice without his guardian's authorization, requested him not to leave, because of the commotion his departure would create among the natives of the province and among his explorer-companions; because it would be imprudent for him to travel alone through a region he did not know, so far from any pacified land, for the province of San Felipe lies some five hundred leagues from Mexico city; and because he himself, as leader and magistrate appointed for the purpose, would leave shortly to report on their discoveries. On hearing this, the father said that he intended to go to Mexico city and that no one was going to stop him.

When the aforesaid leader and magistrate perceived that Father Fray Juan de Santa María was leaving and that the conquistadors, explorers, and settlers were quite disturbed and excited because they disapproved of the father's departure, he called all the explorers together to ask them whether they acknowledged him as chief and magistrate and whether they knew that he had been commissioned by the viceroy to discover lands and report thereon to his Excellency.

The men replied in unison that they did acknowledge him as their leader and had done so throughout the entire expedition; that if they obeyed him, it was precisely because of the commission his Grace had received from the viceroy;[2] that they had obeyed him thus far and would continue to do so in the future, complying with his every command to them as explorers and loyal vassals of his Majesty; that with this end in view, they were ready to provide arms and horses at their

1. From a copy in A.G.I., *Audiencia de Mexico,* legajo 20. J. Lloyd Mecham published the Spanish text and an English translation in the *Southwestern Hist. Quar.,* vol. 29, pp. 224-231.
2. This fact was emphasized in the "Información de los méritos y servicios del capitán Hernán Gallegos." A.G.I., *Patronato,* legajo 77.

own expense, for, having come so far, they wished to press on in order to discover and investigate the other things reported to be in these lands; and that they were prepared to accompany his Grace henceforth so that he and they together might report to his Excellency in the hope that the king would reward them for the hardships they had endured in the course of these discoveries. Such was the statement they made in reply, which they signed with their names: FELIPE DE ESCALANTE; PEDRO SÁNCHEZ DE CHAVES; PEDRO DE BUSTAMANTE; PEDRO SÁNCHEZ DE FUENSA- LIDA; HERNANDO BARRADO; FRANCISCO SÁNCHEZ CHAMUSCADO. Done in my presence. HERNÁN GALLEGOS.

THE COUNT OF CORUÑA TO THE KING, NOVEMBER 1, 1582

IN NOVEMBER of last year, 1580,[1] there came to me a Franciscan friar who said that his name was Fray Agustín Rodríguez and that he ardently wished to go into the interior to preach the holy gospel in the region beyond the Santa Bárbara mines in New Vizcaya. Since we had information that along the Conchas river there were people where his good purpose could be attained, I granted him permission to do so and to take along some other friars and up to twenty men who might volunteer to go with him as protectors and companions. I also authorized them to take along some articles for trading, but I did not permit a greater number of people to join them, since your Majesty had given instructions that no new expeditions into the interior should be undertaken without your express authorization. And I ordered that whoever was designated by the friar should act as leader and be obeyed by the rest, so that there would be no disorderly conduct.

The party was accompanied by some eight men who volunteered to join it. Apparently the expedition discovered several pueblos provided with good, fertile lands and means of subsistence, and people who were better clothed and of finer appearance than those along the Río de las Conchas, already mentioned. Fray Agustín Rodríguez decided to remain in one of these pueblos with one companion, while the eight men came back to report on what had been seen and discovered thus far. I had the statements of these men taken down, and am enclosing certified copies for your Majesty's attention.[2]

Moreover, since Rodrigo del Río de Losa, lieutenant captain general in the province of New Galicia, was staying here at the time, and since he was a very experienced and conscientious man who had served both in the fleet of Don Tristán de Arellano and in New Vizcaya with Francisco de Ibarra, I consulted him as to what he considered necessary

---

1. Pacheco and Cárdenas, *Col. Doc. Inéd.*, vol. xv, pp. 97-100. There is a defective copy in A.G.I., *Audiencia de México*, legajo 20; and an English translation in Bolton, *Spanish Exploration in the Southwest*, pp. 158-160.

There seems to be a conflict of chronology in this document, since the text reads, "Por Noviembre del año pasado de ochenta," and the document was signed in 1582. Both dates are clearly correct, however. The friar went to Mexico city in 1580 to obtain a license for the proposed trip; and the viceroy wrote this report of what had happened after the return of the expedition in 1582.

2. These are the declarations of Bustamante, Gallegos, and Barrado, pp. 127-140.

for sending out a party to learn what had become of the friars and to seek information about the whole region, so that a report of it might be given here. He gave me the enclosed account, signed with his name.[3]

At this juncture a soldier arrived, accompanied by an Indian who had remained with the friars who told us how he had witnessed the killing of one friar, and that when he fled so that they should not kill him, he heard clamoring and shouting in the pueblo which led him to believe that the natives must have been killing the other friar.[4] I again consulted with the aforesaid Rodrigo del Río concerning this event and sought his opinion as to what would be needed in men and provisions for sending an armed expedition into the region, if your Majesty should be pleased to order such an undertaking. He prepared a comprehensive report, which he signed and which I am enclosing, so that your Majesty may have it examined.

From the reports of these men, we may conclude that the land is well populated and very fertile. Although they state that they saw, among the Indians, indications of the existence of mines, they found no trace of gold or silver, nor evidence that any ore had been extracted.

Your Majesty will give orders for study of the whole question and adoption of such measures as may seem best for the royal service. In the meantime, no further steps will be taken in the matter.

May God protect your royal Majesty's sacred person and multiply your kingdoms and possessions. I remain, your Majesty's most humble and devoted servant. Mexico, November 1, 1582. THE COUNT OF CORUÑA [Rubric]

3. Rodrigo del Río made two statements to the viceroy on this subject, one before the death of the friars was known, recommending an expedition of eighty men, and the other after the Indians had killed Fathers López and Rodríguez, proposing a force of three hundred, on the assumption that the Indians would be hostile and would resist invasion. They are printed in Pacheco and Cárdenas, *op. cit.*, vol. xv, pp. 137-146.

4. This Indian was Francisco, one of the Conchos Indians who had remained with the friars at Puaray. Testimony of Barrado, October 20, 1582, p. 140.

FATHERS LÓPEZ AND RODRÍGUEZ REMAIN AT PUARAY, FEBRUARY 13, 1582[1]

I, HERNÁN GALLEGOS, appointed notary for the province of San Felipe by his Grace, Francisco Sánchez Chamuscado, chief magistrate and leader of explorations for his Majesty in the said province and the buffalo plains, do certify and truly attest to all men who may see these presents that on this day, February 13, 1582, the following events occurred. The aforementioned magistrate and leader had decided to leave the land he had discovered, in order to report to his Majesty and to his Excellency, the viceroy of New Spain (by whose commission he had undertaken the expedition), and to tell what he had found in the land, so that the viceroy might make such provisions as were deemed most suitable for the conversion of the natives in that region. He had learned that Father Fray Francisco López, guardian, and Fray Agustín Rodríguez, friars minor who accompanied him to preach the holy gospel, were desirous of remaining in the said land, though the time was not opportune, whereas Sánchez Chamuscado and his soldier-explorers were resolved to depart in order to render a report. His Grace gave the friars good reasons why they should leave the region with him, since they could not reap any harvest there at the moment without an interpreter. To these entreaties the friars replied that they did not want to go, but wished to stay in order to preach the holy gospel to these heathen people.

Whereupon the aforesaid captain, leader, and magistrate summoned the two friars to appear before him in regard to this matter and told them that they were not to remain in the said land and locality, because they were serving no useful purpose without an interpreter; that they should reflect upon the death of their comrade and subordinate, Father Fray Juan de Santa María; that when his Grace and the other explorers left, they themselves would be killed; that they should consider well what they were doing, for they were tempting God our Lord by remaining and would give great cause for scandal in the land; and that they should depart with Sánchez Chamuscado and the other men, to return at a later time for the purpose of preaching and establishing settlements there.

1. From A.G.I., *Audiencia de México*, legajo 20. Also published by Mecham, *op. cit.*, vol. 29, pp. 224-231.

To all this the two friars replied that they would not leave the land, for they had been sent to preach the holy gospel and intended to stay even against the will of his Grace and the others, and that they were not to be subjected to physical force, under pain of excommunication. In view of this attitude, the chief magistrate again issued his orders—once, twice, and thrice, in the name of God our Lord and on behalf of his Majesty the king—telling the friars that they must not remain, and that they should take into account the grave danger they were running and the disturbances that would ensue in the land. Their answer to this was the same as before; and consequently the magistrate and leader ordered me, the aforesaid notary here present, to give him a statement that would be accepted as a legally certified record.

Accordingly I, the said notary, do hereby certify that everything herein recorded took place in my presence and before the above-mentioned magistrate, who did not sign because he was greatly indisposed; and also that, at his request, I drew up the present document and affidavit in due legal form, as I am authorized to do, appending thereto my signature and customary rubric. Witnesses were Pedro de Bustamante, Pedro Sánchez de Chaves, and Pedro de Herrera, explorers who were present. In witness whereof, done on the date above indicated. HERNÁN GALLEGOS, notary.

This copy was made from the original affidavit, which was returned to the said notary, Hernán Gallegos, at his request and by order of his Excellency, the viceroy of New Spain. It is true and exact. Done in the city of Mexico on November 8, 1582. Witnesses who were present to view the copying, comparison, and correction: Pedro de Valencia and Luis de Ribera, residents of this city. [Signed] JUAN DE CUEBA [Rubric]

TESTIMONY OF PEDRO DE BUSTAMANTE[1]
MAY 16, 1582

TESTIMONY GIVEN IN MEXICO CONCERNING AN EXPLORATION EXTENDING TWO HUNDRED LEAGUES BEYOND THE MINES OF SANTA BÁRBARA IN THE JURISDICTION OF DIEGO DE IBARRA; THIS EXPLORATION WAS MADE BY VIRTUE OF A PERMIT GRANTED IN RESPONSE TO A REQUEST OF FRAY AGUSTÍN RODRÍGUEZ AND OTHER FRIARS.

IN THE CITY OF MEXICO, New Spain, May 16, 1582, his Excellency, Don Lorenzo Suárez de Mendoza, Count of Coruña, viceroy, governor, and captain general of New Spain and president of its royal audiencia, et cetera, issued the following statement:

Whereas, Fray Agustín Rodríguez and other Franciscan friars had informed him that they wanted to go forth to preach the holy gospel beyond the mines of Santa Bárbara and the jurisdiction of Diego de Ibarra, in a certain new land of which they had been told and where they might do much good, he granted them authority, in the name of his Majesty, to go and discover the land and its people; and for their personal safety and to enable them to spread the holy gospel, he gave them permission to take along as many as twenty men. By virtue of this authorization, it seems that the friars went, accompanied by eight men. And yesterday, the fifteenth of the present month, two of those who accompanied the friars appeared in this city and reported that they had traveled two hundred leagues beyond the Santa Bárbara mines, which is in the jurisdiction of Diego de Ibarra, and had found a land dotted with many pueblos, and Indians who wore clothes and lived in an orderly manner like the Indians here in New Spain; and that they had received reports of much more extensive lands farther on with many pueblos and people living in a settled society. Therefore, to find out what all this means, the viceroy decreed that sworn statements be obtained from these two men who, as has been stated, had taken part in the expedition and had returned to this city. This was done in the following manner:

Thereupon oath was taken in due form from Pedro de Bustamante, one of the two men who had returned to this city, who swore by God,

---

1. Pacheco and Cárdenas, *Col. Doc. Inéd.*, vol. xv, pp. 80-88. English translation in Bolton, *Spanish Exploration in the Southwest*, pp. 142-150.

Holy Mary, and the sign of the cross to tell the truth. After he had so sworn, he was questioned as follows:

Asked his name and place of birth, he said that he was Pedro de Bustamante, native of a town called Carancejas in Montaña del Valle de Cabezón, near Santillana.

Asked how long ago he had come to New Spain, he replied about ten years.

Questioned about his activities since coming to New Spain, he said that he had spent the first three years in mining explorations and the other seven as a soldier of his Majesty in the jurisdiction of Diego de Ibarra.

Asked if he was one of the eight soldiers who accompanied the Franciscan friar, Agustín Rodríguez, and the other friars who went with him, who had requested him to join the expedition, and with what aim or purpose he did so, he replied that he was indeed one of the men who had accompanied the friars, and that his principal purpose in going with them as a member of the expedition was to serve God our Lord and his Majesty the king. He added that no one had induced him to go. On the contrary, moved by the desire to be of service, as stated above, he and the said friar had been planning the expedition for more than two years, and it was he who sought to induce the others to join it.

Because of his assertion that he had been discussing and planning the expedition for more than two years, the witness was asked what reports he had heard to make him believe the venture would be successful. He replied that the primary reason for considering it was the fact that an Indian had told him about a native settlement beyond the jurisdiction of Diego de Ibarra where the inhabitants raised cotton and wove cloth for clothing. He was influenced also by the information in Alvar Núñez Cabeza de Vaca's book about his travels from Florida to this land of New Spain.

Then the witness was questioned as to how he and his companions prepared for the expedition, how they managed to supply themselves with arms, horses, and the other necessary equipment, and what servants they had. To this he declared that once the expedition had been agreed upon by himself, the other soldiers, and the friars, they all provided themselves with arms—that is to say, coats and breeches of mail, harquebuses, and armored horses—as well as with an Indian servant for each man. The friars took seven Indians, among them a mestizo, all from the Santa Bárbara mines.

He was asked from what district of the Santa Bárbara mines the expedition started, what route it followed, and through which pueblos and provinces it passed once it had gotten under way. He replied that on June 6 of the preceding year, 1581, he, his comrades, and the friars had set out from the valley of San Gregorio in the jurisdiction of Santa Bárbara in New Vizcaya, marching down that same valley until they reached the Concha river, where they found a small settlement of naked Chichimeca Indians who lived on roots and other products of the fields. Traveling down the said river they reached another stream which they called the Guadalquivir [Río Grande], because it was large and carried a great volume of water. Along its shores they met other Indians, of a different nation and language from those along the Concha, although both groups went about naked.[2] They received the Spaniards peacefully and freely offered to share with them all they had. From these Indians they inquired through an interpreter if there were people like themselves farther on, and they answered in the affirmative, saying that they were naked, unfriendly, and at war with them. Consequently, they pressed forward along the same stream, covering eighty leagues of uninhabited country in twenty days. Then they came to a settlement, and they named it the province of San Felipe.[3]

Here they found a pueblo made up of handsome two-story adobe houses, whitewashed on the inside. The inhabitants wore cotton blankets, and shirts of the same material. The Spaniards were told that at a distance along the river there were many other Indian pueblos of the same nation. The people of these pueblos received the soldiers peaceably and gave them of whatever they had, such as corn, calabashes, beans, turkeys, and various other things used for their own sustenance. Asked through an interpreter if there were other populated settlements, the natives replied that there were.

In view of this information the Spaniards marched on up this same river and found many more pueblos (both on the route they were following and to either side of it), which could be seen from the road. They came to another nation,[4] different in language and dress, where they were likewise received peacefully and joyfully by the Indians, who kissed the hands of the friars. These Indians, too, wore clothes; and they had houses three stories high, whitewashed and painted inside. They had many fields of corn, beans, and calabashes; and they also raised large numbers of turkeys.

2. Generally known as Jumanos, but the chroniclers called them Patarabueyes, Passaguates, or Otomoacos. Cf. Introduction, pp. 10-11.

3. Near San Marcial, New Mexico. For further details, see the "List of Pueblos," pp. 102-105.

4. Evidently the Tigua. See Gallegos, "Relation," chapter VIII, pp. 81-83.

From there the Spaniards went on up the river to another nation,[5] whose people were more highly developed than any of those met before, with better pueblos and houses. These natives accorded the explorers the best treatment, giving most willingly of everything they possessed. They have well-built houses of four or five stories, with passageways and rooms twenty-four feet long by thirteen feet wide, whitewashed and painted. They also have very fine plazas connected by streets, enabling them to pass unhindered from one plaza to another. They are well supplied with provisions like those found among the other Indians. Two or three leagues distant there are additional pueblos belonging to this nation, with three hundred or four hundred houses of the same type as the buildings here. The inhabitants wear cotton clothing like that worn by the people of the nations previously encountered.

Thus far, the Spaniards had traveled steadily toward the north. Now, drawing away from the river for one day's journey, but still following a northerly direction, they saw a large pueblo containing approximately four or five hundred houses. When they reached it and noted the houses of the Indians, four or five stories high, they named the pueblo Tlaxcala,[6] on account of its great size. Here, as in the other pueblos, they were received peacefully. Through an interpreter of these natives, they learned that at a distance of a ten days' journey, there was a very large Indian settlement situated on that very northern route which they were following; but due to a shortage of shoes for the horses and clothing for himself and the other soldiers, they were afraid to go on farther and turned back over the same route by which they had come.

At one of the pueblos they had passed through and had named Castildavid or Castil de Avid, the Spaniards crossed the river to the south and went along a small river which emptied into the other one.[7] Then they went on to visit three pueblos they had heard about. The first two of these pueblos had up to two hundred houses; the other as many as seventy. Here they heard reports of eleven pueblos farther upstream belonging to a different nation from that of the other settlements and having a different language. The Spaniards named the valley in which

5. This would be the Queres, from San Felipe to Cochití, and the pueblos on the lower part of the Jémez river.

6. If Bustamante's narrative is to be taken at its face value, the explorers were now among the Queres, probably in the vicinity of modern Santo Domingo. Here, drawing away from the river, evidently the Río Grande, for one day's journey, they found a large pueblo of four or five hundred houses, says Bustamante, which they called Nueva Tlaxcala. Bandelier, in his "Documentary History of the Río Grande Pueblos," identified it with Pecos, even though he recognized that it would be a hard day's journey. *New Mex. Hist. Rev.*, vol. v, pp. 336-337, 384-385.

7. Gallegos' directions are obscure. The valley seems to have been the lower Galisteo, which they named Valle Vicioso because of its fertility.

the three pueblos were situated Vallevicioso.[8] They did not go to visit the eleven pueblos, but chose instead to make a trip in search of the buffalo, which they had been told would be found in large numbers about thirty leagues from that place.

So they set out in search of the buffalo and covered those thirty leagues in a roundabout course, led by their guides, taking a route which seemed different from the one indicated by the natives. If they had traveled by a direct route, they would have arrived sooner. When they reached some plains with water holes, which they named Llanos de San Francisco and Aguas Zarcas, they saw many trails made by the buffalo that come to drink there, moving in herds of two to three hundred. These animals are humpbacked and hairy, short-horned and thick-set, with low-slung bodies.[9]

In this region, the explorers found an Indian ranchería of a different nation from those previously encountered. The inhabitants were naked people on their way to kill buffalo for food. They carried their provisions of corn and yucca loaded on dogs raised for that purpose.

This witness and his companions killed as many as forty animals with their harquebuses, dried the beef, and returned to the settlement from which they had started out. From there they went back down the river, past the places already visited, until they reached a pueblo called Puaray. Here they heard of a valley and settlement known as the valle de Camí,[10] located to the south, where the people spoke a different language.

Acting on this information, the explorers set out from Puaray and reached the said valley, where they found six pueblos, of thirty, forty, and even one hundred houses, inhabited by many Indians dressed like the ones met before. The houses were two or three stories high and built of stone. At this place the Spaniards heard about the valley of Asay,[11] containing, it was said, five pueblos with many inhabitants. From signs made by the Indians, they deduced that two of these pueblos were very large, and that great quantities of cotton were grown in all five, more than in any of the places yet seen. But as it was snowing, they could not go forward and were forced to return to Puaray, their starting point. There they heard reports of some salines fourteen leagues beyond the said pueblo and went on to examine them, locating them behind a mountain range which was given the name of Sierra

8. This seems to have been the lower Galisteo valley. See Introduction, p. 13.
9. Cf. chapter IX of the Gallegos "Relation."
10. A copyist's error for Zuñi, located to the west.
11. Called Osay in Gallegos' statement. The reference is to the Hopi pueblos.

Morena.[12] The salines are the best thus far discovered and extend over a five-league area, in the opinion of the present witness and his companions, who provided themselves with salt for their own needs and brought back for his Excellency the amount he has been shown.

Near these salines, many more pueblos, similar to the others, were seen and visited. The natives informed them of three other pueblos, which they represented as being near these salt deposits and very large.[13]

From this place the explorers returned to the pueblo of Puaray, where they had left the friars, the horses, and the rest of their equipment; and from Puaray they turned back to retrace the route over which they had come. The friars and their Indian servants, including one mestizo, remained at the aforesaid pueblo. This witness, together with the other soldiers and their leader, returned to Santa Bárbara, whence they had set out, as authorized by his Excellency. They then came to report on what they had seen and discovered, including the fact that in the course of their travels they had found in certain settlements five mining areas which seemed good to them, although the lack of equipment had prevented them from assaying the ores. Neither had they dared to bring back any Indians from those parts. Despite attempts to do so through persuasion and the promise of gifts, the Indians would not come, and the soldiers did not venture to use force lest they anger the natives. In addition to the aforesaid mining sites, the natives told them of many others.

This is the truth, under his oath, and he affirmed, ratified, and signed his testimony. He said that he was thirty-four years old; and that the leader of the expedition, Francisco Sánchez Chamuscado, died at a spot thirty leagues from Santa Bárbara while making his way homeward in the company of the present witness and his companion, Hernán Gallegos, for the purpose of reporting on what they had seen. PEDRO DE BUSTAMANTE. Before me, JUAN DE CUEVA.

12. The Manzano mountains, east of which were the salines, in the neighborhood of the modern Estancia and Willard.

13. Probably Abó and other pueblos of the Tompiro group. Cf. *Benavides' Revised Memorial*, pp. 264-265.

TESTIMONY OF HERNANDO GALLEGOS[1]
MAY 16, 1582

IMMEDIATELY thereafter, on this same day, an oath was administered in due legal form to Hernando Gallegos, who swore by God, the Virgin Mary, and the sign of the cross to tell the truth. Since he was one of the two men who had come to this city to report on their journey, he was questioned as follows:

Asked to give his name and place of birth, he replied that he was Hernando Gallegos and that he was a native of Seville.

Asked how long he had been in New Spain, he replied that it was about nine years.

Asked what he had done since coming to New Spain, he said that he had devoted the entire nine-year period to serving his Majesty, partly in the jurisdiction of Diego de Ibarra, partly in the mines of Mazapil, where he was engaged in punishing the hostile Indians who had rebelled, and partly in exploring for mines, all at his own cost and expense.

Asked if he was one of the eight soldiers who accompanied the Franciscan, Fray Agustín Rodríguez, and the other friars who went with him, what aim and purpose he had in going, and who had asked him to join the expedition, he replied that he was one of the men who accompanied the said friars, and that his chief motive was his desire to serve God our Lord and his Majesty; that no one had persuaded him to go, though he had discussed the matter with the said friar and with Francisco Sánchez Chamuscado, the leader of the party, and that he had told them he wanted to go, and they had encouraged others to join. In this manner the party was organized, after it had been under consideration for more than two years.

Asked what information he had which promised success for the expedition since it had been discussed for two years, he said the basic fact was the many trips inland that he had made beyond Santa Bárbara in pursuit of marauding Indians with the captains and leaders appointed for the occasion. In addition, an Indian captured in one of these forays had related that beyond the district governed by Diego de Ibarra, very far away, there were very large settlements of Indians who had cotton and who made blankets for clothing, and who used

---

1. Pacheco and Cárdenas, *Col. Doc. Inéd.*, vol. xv, pp. 88-95.

corn, turkeys, beans, calabashes, and buffalo meat for food, all of which inspired him and the others with the desire to explore the interior of the land. They were guided also by the information given by Alvar Núñez Cabeza de Vaca in a book which he had written about his journey from Florida to New Spain.

When the witness was asked what authority he and the others had for making the expedition, how they equipped themselves with arms, horses, and other necessaries, and what servants they took along, he replied that after they had decided to make the journey, he and his companions and the friars supplied themselves with coats and breeches of mail, armored horses, harquebuses and helmets, and one Indian servant [each]; the friars took seven Indians from Santa Bárbara, among them a mestizo.

Asked what section of the Santa Bárbara mines he came from, when the expedition set out, what route it took, and through what pueblos and provinces it passed, he replied that on June 6, 1581, he and his companions and the friars set out from the valle de San Gregorio, jurisdiction of Santa Bárbara, in New Vizcaya. They descended the said valley toward the north to the place where it joined the Conchas river, where they found a ranchería of naked Chichimecos Indians who lived on roots and other things of little substance. They continued down this river until they reached another stream, which, because of its great size, they named the Guadalquivir [Río Grande]. There they met other Indians of a different nation and language from those encountered earlier, although they went about naked like the others.[2] These Indians received them peacefully and gave them some of their food. The Spaniards asked them through an interpreter if there were more people farther on, and they replied in the affirmative, indicating that they were naked people like themselves, that they were enemies and carried on war with them.

So the Spaniards traveled up the said river for twenty days, or about eighty leagues, through an uninhabited area, after which they reached an Indian settlement that they named the province of San Felipe.[3] There they found a pueblo with houses of two stories, well built, mud walls, and whitewashed inside. The people wore cotton shirts and blankets. Here the Spaniards were told that there were many other Indian pueblos of their same nation and way of life on both sides of the river and at some distance from it. These Indians received them peacefully and willingly offered a share of their provisions, which con-

2. The Patarabueyes at La Junta. Cf. Gallegos' "Relation," chapter III.
3. Near San Marcial, New Mexico, at the beginning of the Piro pueblos.

sisted of calabashes, beans, turkeys, corn, and other products which they grow for their regular food.

Having been told by the natives by means of signs that there were still more settlements, the visitors continued up the river and found many other pueblos, both along the route they were following and off to the sides. They saw many of these towns or spied them from afar as they traveled steadily northward. They then came to another settled area of Indians, who had a different language and dress.[4] Here, too, they were received in a friendly manner, the natives gladly kissing the hands of the friars when they saw this witness and his companions do so. These people wore cotton blankets and shirts; they lived in houses three stories high, painted and whitewashed on the inside. They are industrious in planting corn, beans, and calabashes; and they raise many turkeys which they keep in large numbers for food.

After the Spaniards had discussed some matters with the inhabitants by signs, since they had no interpreter who understood their language, they marched ahead to another nation, which proved to be more noble and of a finer quality than the ones encountered earlier, with better pueblos and houses.[5] These houses were well built, of four, five, and six stories, with corridors, halls, and rooms, some of which measured twenty-four feet long by thirteen wide. The houses were painted and whitewashed on the inside. In this pueblo there were two or three fine plazas, connected by streets so that the people could pass from one square to the next. They raise quantities of food products of the same kind as the inhabitants they had met earlier. Moreover, at a distance of two or three leagues, there are other pueblos belonging to the same nation containing two, three, and four hundred houses, planned and built in the same style. The people wear cotton shirts and blankets like the ones previously mentioned.

One day's travel from this river, in a northerly direction, they found a large pueblo with some five hundred houses. When they reached it they saw that these were of four and five stories, in which the people must have lived quite comfortably. Because of its size they named it Tlaxcala after the city of the same name in New Spain.[6] Questioning the natives by means of signs, the travelers learned that at a distance

---

4. Evidently the Tigua.

5. The Queres.

6. Gallegos, like Bustamante, leaves the impression that the explorers were among the Queres when they went only a day's travel to the pueblo named Tlaxcala, or Nueva Tlaxcala. We believe that this was Pecos, probably the largest and most imposing town in the pueblo country, with the possible exception of Acoma. See the Bustamante declaration, note 6, p. 130.

of ten days from there, in the same direction as the route they were following, there was a very large Indian settlement with many pueblos and people, though they did not dare to travel farther owing to lack of horseshoes and certain articles needed by the men. So they returned by the same route they had come and reached one of the pueblos which they had passed before and which they named Castildavid.

From there they crossed the river to the south and, following a small river that flowed into it, they went to visit three other pueblos which they had been told were situated in that direction. They found that two of them had up to two hundred houses each and the third about seventy or eighty. There they heard of eleven more pueblos farther up the river in a valley which they named Valle Vicioso.[7] These pueblos belonged to a different nation and spoke a different tongue from the others, but the Spaniards did not go to visit them because they had planned a trip to discover the buffalo, which the Indians indicated by signs were to be found in great numbers on some plains situated in a different direction from there, about thirty leagues away.

Hence they went in search of the buffalo, traveling in circles for about thirty leagues, wherever the natives guided them. If they had gone by a direct route, the distance would have been shorter. Finally they came to some plains with water holes which they named Llanos de San Francisco and Aguas Zarcas.[8] Here they saw many herds of buffalo, numbering from two to three hundred head, that came to drink at the said water holes. These animals are woolly, have small horns, short legs, and are humpbacked. The Spaniards found there also a ranchería of naked Indians who followed the cattle and killed them for meat. These Indians carried their food and other necessary supplies on pack dogs which they breed for this purpose. This witness and his companions killed about forty of these buffaloes with their harquebuses, and dried the meat for use on the trip.

Then they returned to the settlement whence they had set out, and from there they continued their journey down the river, by way of the same places they had passed before until they reached another pueblo, called Puaray.[9]

At this place they were told of a valley with a settlement of Indians

7. See the Bustamante declaration, note 7. The valley was evidently the lower Galisteo. The eleven pueblos could have referred to the Tewa and others on the upper Río Grande.

8. Probably on the Canadian river in eastern New Mexico.

9. From this statement they must have struck the Río Grande, on their return, some distance north of Puaray.

of different language. It is called the valley of Zuñi and extends to the southward.[10] Having received this information they set out for the said valley and there they found six pueblos with thirty, forty, and up to one hundred houses, inhabited by a large number of Indians who wore cotton shirts and blankets and shoes with leather soles. The houses were similar to those of the other pueblos, two or three stories high, and built of stone. At this place the explorers heard of another valley called Osay and were given to understand by means of signs that it contained five large pueblos with numerous people, two of which were especially well populated, and that they raised more cotton there than in any other place we had visited.

Since it was the month of December and it was snowing heavily, the Spaniards were unable to travel farther and had to return to the pueblo of Puaray from which they had set out. While there they heard of some salines located fourteen leagues from the latter pueblo. They went to see them and found them back of a sierra which they named Sierra Morena.[11] The salt is found in some lakes measuring more than five leagues in circumference. They are, in the opinion of this witness, the best salines he has ever seen. Having provided themselves with the salt they needed, the men brought a sample for his Excellency, which he has seen and found satisfactory in quality.

Near these salines the Spaniards saw many other pueblos which they visited and found to be similar to the previous ones; the people there, who are numerous, dress and live in the same manner as the others. In these pueblos the explorers learned that farther on there were three others, with large fine structures, which, as the natives indicated by signs, were situated near the salines. The Spaniards did not go visit them because they did not want to get too far away from their starting point, and so they returned to Puaray where they had left the friars and the horses and other possessions.

At this pueblo of Puaray they decided to leave the friars and Indian servants they had brought, among them a mestizo named Juan Bautista, and to return by the same route over which they had come. This witness, his companions, and Francisco Sánchez Chamuscado, their leader, left this land and returned to Santa Bárbara, from which they had set out by authority of his Excellency.

After the said leader [Francisco Sánchez Chamuscado], Pedro de Bustamante, and this witness had left Santa Bárbara for Mexico to re-

10. That is, westward.
11. The Manzanos, east of Albuquerque.

port to your Excellency on what they had discovered and explored, the former died.[12]

During the course of this expedition they found and visited in some pueblos five mining prospects which seemed good and of high grade, but they were unable to make assays for lack of tools and other equipment. The Spaniards were told also of many other mines which were said to be rich in silver. When they were ready to return, they tried by kindness and gifts to induce some of the Indians from the nations they had visited to come with them, but they were unsuccessful—and they did not dare to use force for fear of angering them. This witness believes that the distance from the city of Mexico to that region must be upward of four hundred leagues, rather more than less. The land is flat and can be traveled on foot or on horseback with pack animals, and it is suitable for wagons.

This is the truth, under his oath, and he ratified and signed his statement. He said he was twenty-five years old, a little more or less. And he said also that he had written a book, in his own hand, in which he recorded all that transpired on the expedition in which he took part. This book he has given to his Excellency.[13] Everything in it is true, because he wrote it from time to time as the events took place and as he observed them. HERNÁN GALLEGOS. Before me, JUAN DE CUEVA.

12. Chamuscado died while the party was returning from New Mexico to Santa Bárbara.

13. This book is presumably the "Relation" that we have translated in this work.

TESTIMONY OF HERNANDO BARRADO
OCTOBER 20, 1582[1]

THEREAFTER, in the city of Mexico, October 20, 1582, the viceroy stated that since he had been informed how the Indians in the said new land killed the friars who had remained to instruct and indoctrinate them in matters of the holy Catholic faith, he was therefore requesting a new report on the affair, so as to be able to inform the king fully of everything. With this end in view, an oath was administered in due legal form to Hernando Barrado, a Spaniard, who is said to have visited the new land with some other soldiers. He took his oath in the name of God our Lord and Holy Mary, His Mother, making the sign of the cross, on which he placed his right hand, and swore to tell the truth.

On being questioned in regard to the matter above-mentioned, this witness said that what he knew about the case was as follows: He himself was one of the eight soldiers who penetrated inland with the leader, Francisco Sánchez Chamuscado, Fray Agustín Rodríguez of the Franciscan order, and two other friars. They visited all the Indian towns mentioned in the depositions of his companions, the two soldiers,[2] which were shown to him. He knows that these statements are true and that the events happened as described, because he was present at all of them.

When the witness went to those lands, in the interior, he took along as servant an Indian called Gerónimo from the Santa Bárbara district of the Conchos nation in the kingdom of New Vizcaya. When the leader and the other soldiers decided to return to New Spain in order to report on what they had seen and discovered, the said Indian, together with two others (named Francisco and Andrés), a mestizo, and some native boys, remained of their own free will with the aforementioned friars at the town known as Puaray.

After having returned to Santa Bárbara in New Galicia [sic], while this witness was at the convent of that town some three months ago, he saw there the said Francisco, one of the Indians who had stayed with the friars. Surprised at this encounter, the witness talked to him and asked why he was there and why he had come back from the land where he had left him. The Indian replied that the natives in the

---

1. Pacheco and Cárdenas, *Col. Doc. Inéd.*, vol. xv, pp. 95-97. Translated in Bolton, *Spanish Exploration in the Southwest*, pp. 151-153.
2. Bustamante and Gallegos.

region of Puaray had killed Fray Francisco López, the guardian; that he himself had seen the friar buried; and that when he conveyed the news to Father López's companion, Fray Agustín, the Indian servants became excited. Without awaiting further developments, Francisco and the two other Indians, Andrés and Gerónimo, escaped through Concho territory by a roundabout route, almost the same one they had followed when entering the land.

As they were leaving the pueblo [of Puaray], they heard a great clamor and tumult, which led them to believe that the Indians had killed the other friar and the Indian boys who had remained there, unable to join in the flight. One of Francisco's companions, Andrés, was slain by some Indians in a settlement through which the fugitives passed, between the Concho nation and the Tatarabueyes. The only person who succeeded in escaping with him was the Indian Gerónimo, a former servant of the present witness. Later, when this witness was traveling through the mines of Zacatecas, he met the Indian Gerónimo, who was being brought to this city by the other soldiers, companions of the said witness. The latter talked to Gerónimo and received the same information that he had been given by the other Indian, Francisco. From these mines they all proceeded together to this city of Mexico. His Excellency saw the Indian [Francisco] and talked with him; but a few days ago the Indian in question disappeared. The witness has not seen him again, and he believes that he has returned to his own land.

This is the truth, under his oath, and he affirmed, ratified, and signed his testimony. He said that he was more than fifty years old. HERNANDO BARRADO. Before me, JUAN DE CUEVA. Copied and compared with the original, which remains in my possession, JUAN DE CUEVA [Rubric]

BRIEF AND TRUE ACCOUNT
OF THE DISCOVERY OF NEW MEXICO
BY NINE MEN WHO SET OUT FROM
SANTA BÁRBARA IN THE COMPANY
OF THREE FRANCISCAN FRIARS[1]

WE, THE NINE MEN above-mentioned, set out on our journey from Santa Bárbara with the sole aim of serving God our Lord and his Majesty and implanting the holy gospel wherever we found an opportunity or wherever the divine Majesty might lead us. We started on June 5, 1581, and after leaving Santa Bárbara, traveled for thirty-one days over land inhabited by naked Chichimeca people who had no food other than roots and prickly pears, being very poor indeed.

Proceeding on our way, we left these people behind and traveled for nineteen days without seeing any human being or other living thing. We suffered many hardships and afflictions, but finally, on the eve of the feast of Our Lady of August, our Lord was pleased to send us a naked Indian whom we asked by means of signs where we could get some corn. He replied, when we showed him two or three kernels, that one day's journey farther on we should find corn in abundance. He told us there was a great deal of it, and indicated that the natives wore clothes the color of our shirts and lived in houses. All this information was conveyed through signs and marks made on the ground.

We rejoiced greatly, because we were already short of provisions; and we kept the Indian with us for three days so that he might lead us to the place he had indicated. He did so, and we found that all he had said was true, for on August 21, we discovered a pueblo with forty-five houses two and three stories high, and we saw also extensive fields of corn, beans, and calabashes.[2] Here we earnestly thanked the Lord for providing us with the food we needed.

We entered this pueblo all together, well equipped and arrayed for war in case that should prove necessary, although we had no warlike intentions but on the contrary meant to attract the people to the fold

---

1. Pacheco and Cárdenas, *Col. Doc. Inéd.*, vol. xv, pp. 146-150. English translation in Bolton, *op. cit.*, pp. 154-157.
2. This was San Felipe, near San Marcial, New Mexico, as told by Gallegos, Bustamante, and others.

of our holy Catholic faith with peace and affection. In our midst were three friars, each carrying a cross in his hand and wearing one around his neck. We entered the pueblo in that fashion, but found no one there at all, because the inhabitants had been afraid to wait for us, not knowing what manner of beings we were, since we came on horseback and were armed. Consequently, we left the settlement at once and marched through cornfields for about half a league, soon finding five more pueblos. We pitched camp on level ground and agreed not to leave that place until we had won over the natives peacefully and made friends of them.

After two days, a cacique came with three other Indians to find out what kind of people we were. We greeted each other in sign language, and the Indians approached us. We gave them some iron, sleigh bells, playing cards, and various trinkets, thus winning their friendship, and they called the other natives, many of whom came to look at us, telling each other that we were children of the sun. They gave us corn, beans, calabashes, cotton blankets, and tanned buffalo skins. We stayed among them for four days, and during that time we learned from them by means of signs that both farther ahead and on either side of the river, there were numerous pueblos.

From this place we traveled fifty leagues upstream, discovering and visiting, in the course of approximately one day's march, either on the riverbank or away from it, sixty-one pueblos, all inhabited by clothed people. These pueblos were located on excellent sites with good, level land; and the houses, clustered together, contained plazas and streets, all very well planned. The inhabitants had native fowls, which they raised. We agreed that in the sixty-one pueblos that we saw and visited there must be more than one hundred thirty thousand persons, all clothed.

We did not see an equal number of additional pueblos in that province, which were among the largest, because we were unable to visit them, nor should we have dared to do so. A great deal of cotton is grown in these settlements.

Fray Bernardino Beltrán, a Franciscan friar who entered that region ten months later with Antonio de Espejo and fifteen soldiers, reports that he found five pueblos in the said province, containing more than fifty thousand souls, whose inhabitants gave his party two thousand cotton blankets. Subsequently, according to their report, they discovered eleven more pueblos, heavily populated. They were told also of a large lake, with many towns and inhabitants, where the people rode in canoes bearing large, bronze-colored balls in the prows. They report that Antonio de Espejo and eight companions are going in search of this lake. Father Fray Bernardino Beltrán will give an extensive and complete account of this whole matter.[3]

We, the said nine men and three friars, discovered also, about thirty leagues to one side of the above-mentioned pueblos, a vast quantity of humpbacked cattle, who have humps on their shoulders a cubit high. These animals range over a continuous area more than two hundred leagues in length. We do not know its width. The cattle are not very fierce nor very swift. Their meat is more tasty than that of the cattle here, and the animals are larger.

We discovered also in the said land eleven mining areas with extremely rich veins, all containing silver deposits. Samples from three of the ores were brought to this city and delivered to his Excellency. He gave orders to have them assayed by the assayer at the mint. He did so and found that one sample contained one-half silver, another, twenty marks per quintal, and still another, five marks. In regard to all this I refer to the aforementioned assayer, for whatever he says, we will accept. Moreover, in that same settled region we discovered a very rich saline containing great quantities of very good salt, samples of which were brought for his Excellency. This saline is five leagues in circumference.[4]

With respect to all of the foregoing statements, if his Majesty will authorize us to return as settlers to undertake the salvation of the many souls enslaved by the devil in those regions, we are quite ready and thoroughly equipped to go and settle and save so many souls by teaching and instructing them, *berbo ad berbo*,[5] as we say here.

Furthermore, there are reports of many other things in the said regions, which would redound to the service of God our Lord and to the great enrichment of the royal crown, both in subjects and royal fifths. For when the Spaniards have once entered the land, they will seek and find many mines, in addition to those we have already discovered, since the region is rich in them, as well as in woods, pastures, and water. The climate tends to be cold, although not excessively so; and the temperature is similar to that of Castile. If this land is not settled quickly, the souls now there will be in great danger, and it is

3. The only accounts of the Espejo expedition known today are those of Obregón, Luxán, and Espejo, the last two translated in the present volume, and the account printed in González de Mendoza's *Historia de las Cosas mas notables, Ritos y Costumbres del Gran Reyno de la China* . . . (Madrid, 1586, and later editions).

4. It was near the modern Estancia and Willard, New Mexico.

5. Word for word.

evident that the royal crown of his Majesty will suffer great loss. FELIPE DE ESCALANTE. HERNANDO BARRANDO [BARRADO]. By order of the most illustrious archbishop of Mexico, I had this copy made from the original report, with which it agrees. Mexico, October 26, 1583. JUAN DE ARANDA [Rubric].

COUNCIL OF THE INDIES TO THE KING
MARCH 14, 1583[1]

To his Catholic Majesty:

Captain Hernán Gallegos, a native of Seville, states that he went to the provinces of New Spain some ten years ago, moved by the desire to employ all of his energies and abilities in the service of your Majesty. It was God's will that his desire should be fulfilled, for Captain Gallegos, not content with such progress as he could achieve through following the aims and methods adopted by others, chose to risk his person and possessions by proceeding to the discovery of New Mexico (a region entered also by Cabeza de Vaca, Francisco Vázquez Coronado, and some others who did not succeed in this discovery), of which he brings a report authorized by the royal audiencia of Mexico.

Eighteen cities and fifty-three towns were found, in addition to six mining areas, for which the viceroy ordered an assay that showed a content of thirty-six marks per quintal, as is indicated in the report and memorandum presented by Gallegos on this point; and there were other important things which merit consideration and appraisal.

He beseeches your Majesty to favor him by examining everything recorded in the documents he brings, for they will reveal the services rendered by him, his expenditure of more than eight thousand pesos— aside from the dangers encountered, and the benefits that may be derived from the whole undertaking for the service of God our Lord and your Majesty. And he also asks that, in recognition of the laborious efforts and costly expenditures involved in his journey of exploration, your Majesty will graciously grant to the explorers, in conformity with the ordinances, authority to make the said expedition, as well as the offices of factor and of alguacil mayor for the province of San Felipe of New Mexico, and aid for the proposed expedition in the form and manner customary for such administrative responsibilities.

Placing his trust in our Lord and mindful of the things he has seen and heard as well as the perils and captivity endured, he hopes that the territory already discovered and the region still to be explored (incomparably greater in extent and finer in quality than he has declared them to be) will prove as valuable as the richest discoveries made anywhere

1. A.G.I., *Audiencia de Guadalajara,* legajo 7.

in New Spain. There are cities with houses of from one to seven stories, a great number of cattle, fertile soil adapted to many products, and extensive river valleys, in addition to the mines already mentioned, and towns for their exploitation. Since he has come to report to your Majesty on all the matters recorded here, in the capacity of leader of the party engaged in the aforesaid exploration, and since it is advisable that the undertaking be resumed without delay, he begs your Majesty that he be speedily aided and sent on his way. Having come on the recently arrived mail boat, through the help of the viceroy, he solicits from your Majesty the same kind of assistance in his sojourn here and on the return trip, for it is very important for him to leave with the fleet that is now being made ready.

[*Endorsed:*] Captain Hernando Gallegos. March 14, 1583. Suitable measures have already been taken in this matter.

PETITION OF HERNÁN GALLEGOS
TO THE KING, MARCH 30, 1583[1]

Mighty Sovereign:

I, Captain Hernán Gallegos, discoverer of New Mexico, state that I have submitted a petition, report, and various papers which record how I came from the province of New Spain, on your viceroy's order, to report to your Majesty how I, accompanied by eight soldiers and three friars, went on the discovery of New Mexico, with the viceroy's authorization, and to inform you of what befell my comrades and me on that journey, as explained in the papers now in the possession of your council, in which I implore your Majesty to favor me by ordering that the conquest and pacification of that land be granted to me in accordance with the laws and ordinances and with the procedure used in the cases of others who have undertaken similar discoveries.

It seems that your Majesty did not grant my petition because it did not specify that the conquest was to be conducted at my expense; yet my aim is and always has been to serve God our Lord and to bring those barbarous people into the fold of our holy mother, the Church of Rome, and to make them subjects of your Majesty's government, acknowledging you as their lord and king. In this letter I hereby offer, if it please your Majesty, to take five hundred men for the pacification of that land at my responsibility and cost, subject to the same terms and conditions which your Majesty granted to Francisco de Ibarra (your former governor of the province of Chiametla, which is the nearest of the Christian lands to the province of New Mexico), and such other terms as may be desirable to attain the pacification of that province.

I further state that while it is not necessary to send people from these parts for the conquest, though many men in New Spain would gladly join me in the proposed expedition, I have nevertheless learned that there are many persons in this capital [Madrid] and in the city of Seville

1. A.G.I., *Audiencia de Guadalajara*, legajo 7. It is clear from this document and the following one that Hernán Gallegos, soon after reporting to the viceroy in May 1582, went to Spain to confer with the king's advisers. This petition, evidently written in Madrid, shows that Gallegos had hoped to become the conqueror of New Mexico. Proof of this statement appears in the "Información de los méritos y servicios del capitán Hernán Gallegos." As late as 1589, he was still petitioning the king for favorable action on his request to become the founder of New Mexico. A.G.I., *Patronato*, legajo 77.

who have served your Majesty in numerous expeditions of discovery, both in the lands of the Chichimecos and elsewhere, and who would prove very useful and valuable because of their ability to act as army officers in this venture. I earnestly implore your Majesty to order that I be granted permission to take as many as thirty soldiers for that purpose, as such a measure would befit your Majesty's service. HERNÁN GALLEGOS [Rubric]

[*Endorsed:*] Captain Hernán Gallegos to his Majesty. Let him appeal to the viceroy. [Rubric]. Madrid, March 30, 1583.

THE KING RECOMMENDS HERNÁN GALLEGOS
APRIL 20, 1583[1]

To the Count of Coruña, our kinsman and viceroy, governor, and captain general in New Spain; or to the person or persons charged with the government of that land in his absence:

Hernán Gallegos has informed us that, after serving us in the land of New Spain on various occasions, he pressed on in the company of other persons, with your authorization, to the discovery of New Mexico and the province of San Felipe, where he and his companions found many towns, settlements, and fully established pueblos and where he rendered us service at his own expense—with his person, arms, and horses—at great risk to his life, all of this being set forth (as he has stated) in certain papers submitted to our Council of the Indies wherein he beseeches us to entrust him, in consideration of these facts, with the task of exploring the said region of New Mexico, or with whatever other commission we may be pleased to confer.

Now that the matter has been studied by the members of our Council, it is our wish that Hernán Gallegos be favored, in view of the facts above-stated, and we hereby command that you regard him as recommended and appoint and employ him in offices and commissions in our service of a nature befitting his personal worth and ability, as well as his past labors, so that he may serve us with honor and advantage, and that you extend to him, in every other way possible, your aid, esteem, and favor, whereby I shall consider myself well served. Given in Madrid on the twentieth day of April in the year 1583. I, the King. Countersigned by Antonio de Eraso, and bearing the rubrics of the members of the Council.

1. A.G.I., *Audiencia de México,* legajo 1091.

THE KING TO THE AUDIENCIA
OF NEW GALICIA

THE KING TO THE PRESIDENT AND JUDGES OF OUR ROYAL AUDIENCIA IN THE CITY OF GUADALAJARA, PROVINCE OF NEW GALICIA, OCTOBER 18, 1583.[1]

GONZALO RODRÍGUEZ, acting in the name of Hernán Gallegos, a resident of Mexico city in New Spain, has presented us with a report stating that from the time Gallegos was old enough he began to serve us in various wars which arose; and that he, together with Francisco Sánchez Chamuscado and eight other persons, took part recently in the discovery of New Mexico, during which he endured great hardships and spent everything that he possessed, having received no aid whatever for this purpose from the royal treasury, so that he is now in want. All of this was set forth in the papers he submitted to our Council of the Indies, wherein he besought us to grant him favorable attention, in view of the facts above-stated, which would provide him with such honorable employment as we might choose to bestow.

Now that the matter has been examined by our Council, and in consideration of these facts, it is our wish that favor be shown to the said Hernán Gallegos. We hereby command that you regard him as commended to your attention, that you appoint and employ him in offices and commissions in our behalf befitting his personal worth and ability, as well as his past labors, so that he may serve us with honor and advantage; and that you extend to him in every other way your aid, esteem, and services.

Given in San Lorenzo on the eighteenth day of October in the year 1583. I, THE KING. Countersigned by Antonio de Eraso, and bearing the rubrics of the Council members. [Rubric]

1. A.G.I., *Audiencia de Guadalajara,* legajo 230.

PART II

DIEGO PÉREZ DE LUXÁN'S ACCOUNT OF THE ANTONIO DE ESPEJO EXPEDITION INTO NEW MEXICO, 1582*

I, MARTÍN DE PEDROSA, ROYAL NOTARY, BEING ORDERED BY HIS LORDSHIP, THE COUNT OF MONTERREY, VICEROY OF THIS NEW SPAIN, TO SEARCH AMONG THE PAPERS OF FRANCISCO DOMÍNGUEZ, COSMOGRAPHER OF THE KING OUR LORD, FOR THOSE RELATING TO NEW MEXICO, WHICH I DID, STATE THAT AMONG THE PAPERS EXAMINED I DISCOVERED THE FOLLOWING REPORT.

TWO FRIARS AND THIRTEEN COMPANIONS SET OUT FROM THE VALLE DE SAN GREGORIO, NOVEMBER 10, 1582.

In the name of God our Lord and that of the Virgin Mary, His holy Mother: We set out from San Gregorio[1] on Saturday, at nine o'clock in the morning, on November 10, 1582, the very reverend Father, Fray Pedro de Heredia, Fray Bernardino Beltrán,[2] both of the order of Saint Francis, Antonio de Espejo, Diego Pérez de Luxán, his brother Gaspar de Luxán, Bernardino de Luna,[3] Gregorio Hernández, Miguel Sánchez Valenciano,[4] his son Miguel Sánchez Nevado, his nephew Cristóbal Sánchez, Pedro Hernández de Almansa, Juan de Frías, Francisco Barreto, Alonso de Miranda, and Juan Fernández, in order to go with the said friars to gather together the native Indians and to preach the sacred teachings. And although the authorities of the mines of Santa Bárbara interfered with and attempted to prevent us from going on the expedi-

---

* From the copy in A.G.I., *Patronato*, legajo 22. Hammond and Rey issued an English edition of this diary as Volume I of The Quivira Society Publications in 1929. The present translation has been thoroughly revised.

1. Espejo and Obregón state that they started from the valley of San Bartolomé, which was identical with the present Allende and was situated on the Río Valle Allende. San Gregorio was eight miles northwest of San Bartolomé on the Río Parral. Espejo, a man of some means, had provided the party of fifteen men with a hundred and fifteen horses and mules, some servants, and a supply of arms and other necessaries. See Espejo's own narrative, translated hereinafter; compare also Hammond and Rey, *Obregón's History*, p. 316.

2. Father Beltrán was from New Vizcaya. See p. 18. Father Heredia's name is omitted by Espejo, but included by Obregón, pp. 315-317.

3. This soldier, Bernardino de Luna, gave Obregón his information of the Espejo expedition. "He gave me the account of the entire expedition and the discoveries made by Antonio de Espejo and his companions." *Obregón's History*, pp. 333 and 340.

4. Valenciano brought along his wife and three children, the youngest only twenty months old, as Luxán explains a little further on in the narrative.

tion, we had a permit from Juan de Ibarra, lieutenant-governor of New Vizcaya, which the said Father Fray Pedro showed, and which stated that all who wished might go with the said father, Fray Pedro de Heredia.[5]

That day we went three leagues down the San Gregorio river, where that night a Franciscan friar named Fray Luis arrived with letters from the custodian for Father Fray Pedro de Heredia, in which he ordered the latter under pain of disobedience to abandon the expedition and to turn back, because Father Fray Luis and the two other friars who accompanied him had been chosen for Nueva Tlaxcala.[5a]

When the companions saw that if Father Fray Pedro de Heredia turned back we could not proceed with the journey and would be ruined, because some of us had spent our fortunes, we entreated Father Fray Pedro not to desert or abandon us, for he could appreciate how much the expedition had cost us. To this he answered in writing, as we requested, that he would come with us. Then Father Fray Luis stated that he and the other two friars who had come would accompany us because they had permission from their prelate; and he asked that one of the men return with him so that he could come back with the rest of the party. Thus Diego Pérez de Luxán went with him.

When Miguel Sánchez Valenciano saw the opportunity which was presented, he returned for his wife to San Bartolomé where he had left her. Here he sold the rest of his possessions in order to complete his equipment.

On the following Monday, November 12, while the three newly arrived friars, Fray Luis, Fray Juan Bautista, and Fray Francisco de San Miguel, were in the aforesaid valley preparing to go on the expedition, there came on this very day Father Fray Pedro from the place where the major portion of the party had remained, for he did not notify anyone of his departure. The new friars were not in accord about the other friars accompanying us, so they decided to write to their custodian.

Father Fray Pedro de Heredia told Diego Pérez de Luxán and Miguel Sánchez to proceed slowly with the expedition, saying that he would

5. In the above list of soldiers, Luxán omits one, Juan López de Ibarra, but mentions him later. Espejo says he took along a friar and fourteen soldiers, and gives their names, but he remains silent regarding the friars other than Father Beltrán. See Introduction for a discussion of Espejo's authority to make the expedition.

5a. Although the plan to colonize Tlaxcalans in the north of Mexico did not come to pass till 1591, when four hundred families were settled at Nueva Tlaxcala, it is likely that efforts in this direction were made much earlier. Perhaps the friars might have taken a few Tlaxcalans with them into that area before that date, but it is curious that no one but Luxán seems to have used the name Nueva Tlaxcala before then. Cf. Charles Gibson, *Tlaxcala in the Sixteenth Century* (1952), pp. 181 ff.; France V. Scholes and Eleanor B. Adams, *Advertimientos* (1956), p. 28.

overtake them. The delays were many, especially since Domingo de Ygarza came from Guadiana on this day with letters from Juan de Ibarra, lieutenant-governor, in which he told Father Fray Pedro to wait ten or twelve days, adding that he would bring the father a license from the custodian, and that the said father might give the commission of captain for entering and discovering new lands to whomsoever he pleased.

The next day Diego Pérez de Luxán and Miguel Sánchez left, the latter bringing along his wife, Casilda de Amaya, his oldest son Lázaro Sánchez, and two smaller ones—Pedro, three and one-half years old, and Juan, of twenty months. They overtook us and brought Father Fray Bernardino a key for the sacred vestments and a request that he administer the holy sacraments to us.

The party left the above-mentioned place on the twelfth day of the said month. We went down the river four leagues to a place which we named Los Alamos.[6]

We left Los Alamos on the thirteenth and proceeded four leagues down the river. This place we called Los Charcos Hondos, because the pools there resembled lakes.

We set out from this place on the fourteenth of the month and went four leagues down the said river to a place which we named La Barranca.

AFTER TRAVELING EIGHTEEN LEAGUES THE SPANIARDS CAME TO THE CONCHOS RIVER, VERY LARGE, AND SETTLED BY MANY NAKED PEOPLE WHO COVER THEMSELVES WITH RABBIT SKINS. THESE INDIANS ARE PEACEFUL AND TIMID; THEY FIGHT WITH BOWS AND ARROWS. SOME OF THEM CAME TO SEE THE SPANIARDS AND BROUGHT A CERTAIN KIND OF BREAD AND SOME RABBITS IN TOKEN OF FRIENDSHIP.

Leaving La Barranca on the fifteenth of the month, we went three leagues to a place one league beyond where the rivers San Gregorio, San Bartolomé, Florido, and Conchos unite. This Conchos river flows from the east toward the west, I mean from the west to the east, carries much water, and is settled by a large number of Conchos Indians,[7] naked people, who cover themselves with skins of rabbit and deer. They go about with their privy parts exposed, except the women, who cover them with the said skins, but not their breasts. They live in peace and

6. They were following the San Gregorio, as had Chamuscado the year before.
7. Bandelier insisted that the word was originally written "Conchas," but that the spelling was perverted to "os" by Espejo. *Final Report*, Pt. I, p. 79.

support themselves on fish, mesquite,[8] and mescal. They make mescal from the leafy portion of a small tree resembling maguey.[9] They fight with bows and arrows; the people are timid. Here some natives came to see us, bringing mescal and a few rabbits in token of friendship.

We left this place on the eighteenth of the month and traveled three leagues down the Conchos river. We named the spot El Mesquital. We set out from here on the nineteenth and went four leagues down the river to a place we called El Bado. Here many Conchos Indians, dressed like the others previously encountered, came to meet us peacefully. We left El Bado on the twentieth of the month and went on this day three leagues down the river to a small gorge. From here we departed on the twenty-first and proceeded three leagues down the river. This place we named El Mohino. Indians similar to the others came to meet us here.

On the twenty-second of the month we left this spot and continued three leagues down the river. We named this place Los Sauces, because of the willow trees and because the river was densely fringed with groves.

FARTHER ON THE SPANIARDS MET MORE NAKED CONCHOS PEOPLE, WHO CAME PEACEFULLY AND BROUGHT FISH AND OTHER THINGS.

We left Los Sauces on November 23 and after a march of four leagues came to the San Pedro river, which flows from west to east.[10] This stream carries only a small volume of water and does not flow during some periods of the year, in the dry season. It contains abundant fish, because it has large pools. It is thickly settled by Conchos Indians, naked like the rest. This river flows into the Conchos. We were met there by

8. From the Aztec *mexquitl*. The mesquite plant is native to the southern United States and extends south through Mexico and the Andean region to Chile and Argentina.

9. Mescal (from Aztec *mexcalli*) was obtained from the fleshy leaves and trunk of the maguey or *Agave americana*. John Russell Bartlett, who served with the commission surveying the Mexican-American boundary in the years 1850-1853, describes how it was prepared. "A hole is first dug some ten or twelve feet in diameter, and about three feet deep, and is lined with stones. Upon this a fire is built and kept up until the stones are thoroughly heated. A layer of moist grass is then thrown upon the stones, and on this are piled the bulbs of the maguey, which vary in size, from one's head to a half bushel measure, resembling huge onions. These are again covered with a thicker layer of grass; and the whole is allowed to remain until they are thoroughly baked. . . ." After this the outer skin was stripped off and the mescal was then sweet and rather pleasant to the taste. It was widely used by the Indians over a large part of the Southwest. *Personal Narrative of Explorations* (New York, 1854), vol. I, pp. 290-292; Hodge, *Handbook*, vol. I, pp. 845-846.

10. The San Pedro, a western branch of the Conchos.

natives who brought us fish, *tecomatcs*,[11] and *xícaras*,[12] and we gave them of what we had brought along.

Leaving the San Pedro river on the twenty-fourth of the month, we went two leagues and camped at the aforementioned Conchos river, at a place called El Xacal.[13] It is so named because Lope de Aristi, a captain from Santa Bárbara, took captives there and, in order that the people should not get wet, built a hut *(xacal)* where they remained until they returned with the Spaniards to Santa Bárbara. Here we found a cross. Captain Chamuscado had been buried in this place. Conchos Indians, naked as the former, came to meet us there peacefully.

We set out from El Xacal on the twenty-fifth of the month and traveled five leagues over difficult mountain roads, halting for the night near a small water hole. There was no water for the horses, nor firewood, and on this account we named the place El Paraje Seco.

We left here on the twenty-sixth and on this day went six leagues to a place named La Chorrera. It was given this name because in the highlands were many miry pools and water holes. There is a stream in this place; the water falls from above as if through a channel, but scatters in many directions. We rested here a few days because the animals were worn out.

THE SPANIARDS LOCATED MINES WHICH SEEMED GOOD BUT WHICH THEY DID NOT CLAIM, AS THERE WERE NO WOODLANDS NEARBY.

We left this place on December 1 and continued three leagues to a gorge where there were several small water holes. In this locality, and close to these pools, within two leagues, are large numbers of promising mines. We did not claim them because there were no woodlands in the neighborhood.

TEN OR TWELVE CONCHOS INDIANS CAME OUT TO MEET THE VISITORS PEACEFULLY AND WENT AWAY WITH THEM.

We departed from this locality and went to the Conchos river on the second of the month, a distance of three leagues. This place we named

11. Tecomates (Aztec *tecomatl*) were dishes or vessels made from gourds.

12. Jícaras (Aztec *xicalli*) were small cups or vessels made from gourds. The word is also used to denote a pitch-covered, bottlelike receptacle of basketry for use as a canteen. It was from this skill in making baskets that the Jicarilla Apaches got their name. Hodge, *Handbook*, vol. I, pp. 631-632.

13. El Xacal was located approximately at the site of the modern town of Julimes, Chihuahua.

El Calabazal, because there were many fields of abundant calabashes which the natives had gathered. Conchos Indians, like the others, came to meet us there and ten or twelve of them accompanied us.

Leaving this place on the third day of the month, we went two leagues to the Conchos river, but did not travel farther on account of the swollen stream. We called the spot La Barreta, because the Indians stole a small bar from us.

We left La Barreta on the fourth of the month and traveled four leagues by a trail over which the natives took us to the marsh where there were some water holes. We named this place La Ciénega Llana.

THE SPANIARDS ENTERED THE LAND OF THE NAKED AND WARLIKE PASSA-GUATES INDIANS. THANKS TO THE INTERPRETERS WHO WERE BROUGHT ALONG, THE PASSAGUATES APPROACHED PEACEFULLY AND TOLD US THAT THE PATARABUEYES NATION WAS AWAITING US IN ORDER TO FIGHT.

We set out from La Ciénega Llana on the fifth of the month and went to the Conchos river, four leagues away. On crossing the boundary of the Conchos nation we entered the land of the warlike Passaguates,[14] who were naked like the Conchos. These Passaguates were friends of both the Conchos and the Patarabueyes; they speak all three languages. We named this place El Puerto de la Raya de los Conchos. On this day native Passaguates came to see us here. Thanks to the Conchos interpreters we brought along, as well as a boy named Juan—a Passaguate native belonging to Gregorio Hernández—and another boy, a Patarabuey native belonging to Diego Pérez de Luxán, they came peacefully and warned us that the Patarabueyes Indians were awaiting us in order to fight. We took this as a joke.

THE SPANIARDS CAME TO A PATARABUEYES RANCHERÍA IN REVOLT. AT MIDNIGHT THE INDIANS ATTACKED THE HORSES, KILLING THREE AND WOUND-ING SIX OR SEVEN.

We departed from this locality on the sixth of December, traveled four leagues, and came to a ranchería of the Patarabueyes. The name "Patarabueyes" was made up by the soldiers when people from this

14. Of the Passaguates we know only what is told by the explorers of this period—Gallegos, Espejo, Luxán, and the Oñate chroniclers. Jumano territory began apparently near the Río Grande and extended far eastward into Texas. See Introduction, p. 11. Forbes, "Unknown Athapaskans," *Ethnohistory*, vol. 6, pp. 108-111. The La Junta area appears to have been a place where various tribes came to trade or to hold social intercourse.

same ranchería were taken by Mateo González, chieftain of Juan de Zubia, captain from the mines of Santa Bárbara; for this very nation, which they named Patarabueyes, is called also Otomoacos.[15] We found the settlement up in arms. That night at midnight they attacked our horses by breaking through some dense mesquite groves and killed three of them, two belonging to Diego Pérez de Luxán and one to Miguel Sánchez Valenciano. They also wounded six or seven others. Owing to the alertness of the guards who watched over the horses and stock, no more or greater damage was done that night. Much care was exercised with the camp and animals from then on.

On the following morning there were many opinions in regard to punishing the marauders. It was finally decided to observe them closely but not to harm them, if they submitted peacefully, otherwise they were to be punished. Immediately four Conchos Indian servants who had come with us went to watch them, and one hour later one of the servants came back saying that the Indians had spent the night in a gorge and that they were fleeing to the sierra. In view of this, five of our soldier companions, Diego Pérez de Luxán, Gregorio Hernández, Francisco Barreto, Cristóbal Sánchez, and Juan de Frías, went there, as the other spies were carrying on a bow and arrow fight with the said Otomoacos. When they reached the foot of a very high ridge which the Indians had climbed, they looked for a place of ascent, but found none. They called to the Indians through an interpreter brought by Diego Pérez de Luxán, a boy of about thirteen years, a native of this said ranchería. He was one of those taken by Mateo González in the capture already mentioned and had been brought up by Pérez de Luxán. He was called Pedro and was of great utility in this province and others where he was understood, as the story will reveal.

Thus the said Pedro shouted in his tongue, telling the natives not to fear but to come down and be friends with the Christians, who did not wish to harm them. The chieftain of the Otomoacos then asked the interpreter to identify himself; and the boy told who he was and whose son, exchanging many other questions and answers. The Otomoacos asked that a Christian come to the foot of the ridge and said that they would descend to see what was wanted. Then Diego Pérez de Luxán went to the base of the sierra with the interpreter, having taken off his helmet. The other companions remained within harquebus range.

15. Their name was "Amotomanco," according to Gallegos. Obregón states: "They next reached the Patazagueyes, among themselves called Jumana, who live along the same rivers, the Conchas and Del Norte, which the discoverers named Guadalquivir." *Obregón's History*, p. 317.

Four of the most important Indians came down, full of suspicion, and Diego Pérez de Luxán gave them some tortillas and talked of peace. They agreed to go to the ranchería that afternoon, and some actually came.

THE OTOMOACOS WERE PACIFIED BY MEANS OF THE INTERPRETER.

The next day, Saturday, the day of Our Lady of December, many of these natives came and were settled peacefully. We erected crosses for them and left signs stating that they had been pacified, but that any passersby should nevertheless be cautious. We told these natives that we were going to kill them because they had killed our horses, but that the friar who accompanied us had begged us not to do it. They said the slaughter had been committed not by them but by the people at the junction of the rivers called Del Norte and Conchos, along which we were traveling. Even though we knew very well that they were lying and that they had committed the deed, we were glad they tried to exculpate themselves.

THE PEOPLE ARE PRACTICALLY NAKED, ALTHOUGH THEY DO USE COVER-INGS OF WELL-PREPARED BUFFALO HIDES. THE WOMEN USE THEM FOR SCAPULARIES, SKIRTS, AND CLOAKS, AND WEAR THEIR HAIR TIED UP.

These people go practically naked, with their privy parts exposed. They cover themselves with well-tanned skins of the cíbola (bison). These hides they tan and beat with stones until they are soft. They fight with bows and arrows. The bows are Turkish, all reinforced and very strong, and the strings are made from the sinews of the buffalo.[16] For these people ordinarily go after meat and skins where the buffalo range, which is about thirty leagues from this province. The women

16. Both Luxán and Obregón repeatedly speak of "Turkish bows" in referring to the weapons of the Indians of the Río Grande area, though we find no specific explanation of how they were made, except that they were "all reinforced and very strong," and they had "Turkish bows reinforced with sinews," probably indicating they were backed with bison sinew. Purchas, in *His Pilgrimes*, published in 1625 (vol. II, p. 1295), refers to Turkish bows made of buffalo horn intermixed with sinews.

E. Douglas Branch, *The Hunting of the Buffalo* (New York, 1929), p. 29, wrote: "Bows were usually made of wood, but the best and strongest were made of pieces of bone and horn—buffalo, elk, or mountain sheep—spliced and glued together, and wrapped with sinews of buffalo. Strands of buffalo sinew made the bowstrings."

Saxton T. Pope, in his monograph, "A Study of Bows and Arrows," describes the Turkish bow as a powerful weapon, capable of throwing an arrow a great distance. This may have been its most distinctive feature. See University of California, *Publications in American Archaeology and Ethnology* (1923), vol. 13, pp. 350 and 373.

wear tanned deerskin bodices of some sort, resembling scapularies, for covering their breasts, and other tanned deerskins as skirts, using as cloaks tanned hides of the cattle. These Indians wear [part of] their hair long and tied up on their heads. The men have their hair cut very short, up to the middle of their heads, and from there up they leave it two fingers long and curl it with minium paint in such a way that it resembles a small cap. They leave on the crown a long lock of hair to which they fasten feathers of white and dark birds such as geese, cranes,[17] and sparrow-hawks. They cultivate corn, beans, and calabashes, although very little in this ranchería. There are large numbers of this people all along the Conchos river; they farm together.

Two caciques came forth peacefully.

We left this place on the eighth of December and went two and one-half leagues down the river, taking along some native Indians. We halted by the river and named the place La Paz, because on that afternoon two caciques came from the people at the junction of the rivers[18] to find out whether we were coming in peace or in war. For this is a settlement of people different from the Otomoacos, where a different language is spoken, although they are friends and understand one another. They are all interrelated, and for this reason the whole province is called that of the Patarabueyes. The Indians of La Paz are called Abriaches. They told us that the Otomoacos had sent word to them that we were going to seize them, and on that account they had all taken to the hills.[19] We reassured them through Pedro, the interpreter. The caciques knew him, because a year before the boy had come to that province with one of our men, Gaspar de Luxán, brother of Diego Pérez de Luxán, mentioned above. Being reassured, they sent word to their people that they were safe.

17. The word is *grullas*. When Lieutenant J. W. Abert was reconnoitering in New Mexico during the Mexican war he saw the large grullas, or blue cranes, evidently the same bird as here mentioned by Luxán. Report of the Secretary of War, 30th Congress, 1st Session, *Senate Executive Document No. 23* (Washington, 1848), p. 45.

18. That is, from the junction of the Conchos and Río Grande. Kelley identifies La Paz, on the northern bank of the Conchos, with the modern San Juan Bautista. Kelley, "Historic Pueblos," *op. cit.*, vol. xxvii, p. 290.

19. Kelley notes that these La Junta tribes, "all interrelated," in the words of Espejo, represented a linguistic rather than an ethnic group. He maintains that the Patarabueyes—the several loosely federated groups at La Junta—were a fairly homogeneous cultural unit, distinct from the Jumano, with whom they have been generally confused. J. Charles Kelley, *Jumano and Patarabueye: Relations at La Junta de los Ríos*, Ph.D. thesis, Cambridge, 1947. See Introduction, p. 11.

THE SPANIARDS ARRIVED AT ANOTHER REBELLIOUS RANCHERÍA. PER-
SUADED BY AN INTERPRETER, ALL THE PEOPLE CAME IN PEACE AND OFFERED
GIFTS TO THE FRIAR.

We left this place on the ninth of December and went three leagues
to the Río del Norte. On the way we were met by a friendly Indian
whom the Spaniards called Juan Cantor. He had been taken as an
interpreter by Father Fray Agustín and on the way back had remained
there because it was his land. He was versed in the Mexican language,
was an uncle of the interpreter we had brought along, and had other
relatives. This Indian, Juan Cantor, was known by all the others in the
party and so we were pleased to see him.[20]

This day we halted by the Río del Norte, close to the ranchería of
the Indian, Juan Cantor. The ranchería resembled a pueblo, as it was
composed of flat-roofed houses, half under and half above the ground.
This pueblo we named San Bernardino.[21] When we arrived, there were
only a few old Indians in the ranchería, as the others were in the sierra,
having fled in fear. After we had reassured them through the interpreter
and the said Indian, Juan Cantor, all the people came down within
half an hour, making musical sounds with their mouths similar to
those of the flute. They kissed the hand of Father Fray Bernardino, who
was with us; and all, both old and young, offered everyone corn, beans,
mescal, dry calabashes, gourd vessels, buffalo hides, and Turkish bows
and arrows.

We found here a cross which had been erected by Fray Agustín when
he passed through, and we repaired it. We rested for eight days at this
place because some of the mounts were worn out, owing to the very
cold weather, bad roads, and lack of pasture. We decided to go from
there to the junction of the rivers to pacify those pueblos, especially
some that were known by the interpreter and by Gaspar de Luxán, who
the year before had been there by commission of Juan de la Parra,
captain of Indehe, to take captives, and had left them in peace.[22]

---

20. Obregón makes similar observations about Juan Cantor. *Obregón's History*, p. 318.
21. Located on the west bank of the Río Grande, about twelve miles above the
Conchos junction. Kelley, "Historic Pueblos," *op. cit.*, vol. XXVIII, pp. 21-23.
22. The practice of enslaving the Indians prevailed throughout most of the Spanish
colonial period, in spite of stringent laws against it by the crown. The entering wedge of
legality for the slave-hunters was the permission originally given by King Ferdinand to
capture Caribs, cannibals, and other groups in rebellion against the government. See
Lesley B. Simpson, *The Encomienda in New Spain* (Berkeley, 1929, ch. 3; or rev. and
enlarged edition, 1950, ch. 2).

THE EXPEDITION CAME TO A PUEBLO OF THE ABRIACHES NATION WHERE
THERE WAS A CROSS † ERECTED THE YEAR BEFORE BY SPANIARDS. THE IN-
HABITANTS RECEIVED THEM WELL, KISSED THE HAND OF THE FATHER, AND
OFFERED GIFTS OF CORN, VEGETABLES, BLANKETS, AND OTHER ARTICLES.

Thus Diego Pérez de Luxán with four other soldiers and Father Fray
Bernardino went down the river, accompanied by many natives who
were singing and dancing. On that day, after going five leagues, they
arrived at the junction of the rivers and a pueblo of the Abriaches nation where there was a cross † which Gaspar de Luxán and other
soldiers of Juan de la Parra had erected the previous year. The natives
received us well and kissed the father's hand, offering gifts of corn,
beans, and other vegetables, together with a few native blankets and
arrows. The cacique of this pueblo was called Baij Sibiye.

THERE WERE ABOUT SIX HUNDRED PERSONS IN ALL, CLOTHED, AND LIVING
IN HOUSES.

There were in this pueblo about six hundred persons, young and old.
These people have houses, clothes, and arrows of the same type as the
other Otomoacos Indians. From there we traveled about half a league
farther on that day. We named the said pueblo Santo Tomás and left
a sign there so that if any Spaniards should pass by they would know
that it was friendly.[23]

THE SPANIARDS REACHED A PUEBLO WITH A SUBURB AND MANY FLAT-
ROOFED HOUSES. THE INHABITANTS KISSED THE HAND OF THE FATHER AND
BROUGHT PRESENTS AS IN THE OTHER PUEBLOS. THE SPANIARDS FOUND
ANOTHER CROSS †, SIMILAR TO THE PREVIOUS ONE; THIS WAS IN A VERY
WELL-KEPT PLAZA.

On this day, as previously stated, we went half a league farther to a
pueblo situated on the opposite bank of the river, called Del Norte by
Chamuscado's men.[24] The pueblo was on a high ridge and contained
many flat-roofed houses; below were many other houses forming a sort
of suburb. Its cacique was called Casica Moyo. In this pueblo the in-

23. Santo Tomás was San Francisco de la Junta, located at the junction of the rivers.
Kelley, "Historic Pueblos," *op. cit.*, vol. XXVII, p. 292.
24. Gallegos called it Nuestra Señora de la Concepción, located in the vicinity of
the Conchos river, and Guadalquivir after reaching the pueblos in New Mexico.

habitants kissed the hand of the father and brought presents as in the others. The Spaniards called the pueblo San Juan Evangelista.[25] Here they found another cross † which the said Gaspar de Luxán and his companions had erected; it was in a neatly kept plaza.

THE SPANIARDS FOUND ANOTHER PUEBLO, LARGER THAN ANY HERETOFORE; AND THE NATIVES KISSED THE FATHER'S HAND AND BROUGHT PRESENTS LIKE THE REST. IN ALL THESE PUEBLOS THE VISITORS WERE RECEIVED WITH MUCH REJOICING AND MUSIC SIMILAR TO THAT OF THE FLUTE BUT MADE WITH THE MOUTH. THE INDIANS OF THIS COMMUNITY ARE ALL FARMERS; EVEN THOUGH THEY LIVE IN PUEBLOS, THEY HAVE FLAT-ROOFED HOUSES IN THEIR FIELDS. BESIDES THESE THREE CITIES THERE ARE MANY OTHERS AND MANY RANCHERÍAS.

The Spaniards slept there that night and the next morning they went to another pueblo, the largest of all, whose cacique was called Q. Bisise and was respected by the rest of the caciques. Here the inhabitants kissed the hand of the said Father and brought gifts just as the others had. In all these pueblos the Spaniards were received with much rejoicing and music made with the mouth, as described above. In this pueblo, as in all of them, they told us of how Cabeza de Vaca and his two companions and a Negro had been there. All the Indians of this community are farmers, the river being very appropriate for agriculture, because it forms many damp islands and bays; and even though they live in the pueblos they have flat-roofed houses in their fields where they reside during harvest time.

In addition to these three cities there are many others and many rancherías along the river, all being settled, both up the Del Norte river as well as below the junction of the Del Norte and the Conchos. On this day the Spaniards gave the name "Santiago" to the pueblo of the cacique, Q. Bisise,[26] and returned to the said camp at the pools of San Bernardino where the other companions had remained.

The eight days that we relaxed at this camp, and the other days of rest on the journey, were spent in that way not only because the animals were exhausted, as I have stated, but also in order that we might wait for Father Fray Pedro de Heredia. In this camp the native Indians, and

25. Situated on the east bank of the Río Grande, just above its junction with the Conchos.
26. The pueblo of Santiago was evidently down the Río Grande from La Junta. Kelley, *op. cit.*, vol. XXVIII, pp. 29-34.

especially Juan Cantor, told us that the report that the friars were dead was false; that on the contrary they were alive,[27] that the Conchos Indians who had brought the news had fled, having made the statement in fear of punishment. In view of this, Father Fray Bernardino requested us to go to the relief of the friars, and we offered to do so. Thus we did not wait any longer for the said Father Fray Pedro, lest our supplies give out.

Antonio de Espejo elected as leader.

As we still had no chief to lead and govern us, we met and elected from among ourselves one of our comrades, Antonio de Espejo, as captain and chief magistrate, in the name of his majesty the king, Don Philip our Lord—may God keep him. We took the oath of fealty to him, as is stated in the commission which we gave him. Thus we began to prosecute the said expedition.

The Río del Norte, named Turbio by the Spaniards, is inhabited by naked people who always met us in a friendly manner.

We left San Bernardino on the seventeenth of December [1582], going up the river named Del Norte, to serve God our Lord and his Majesty and to bring succor to the friars. This part of the Río del Norte we named El Río Turbio because it is exceedingly muddy; it always flows northwest.[28] We followed it all the time, leaving it sometimes at a distance of a league but always stopping along it for the night or else near some pools formed by a freshet. It flows through a plain so gently that it does not make any noise in spite of being very large in some places. This stream is three leagues in the widest part, when it becomes swollen, and is thickly grown with cottonwood and willow groves, although there are along its course few willows or trees of any kind aside from those named. It is inhabited by naked people like the Otomoacos. These people always received us peacefully. In spite of this, however, and the fact that we always took along some of their number from one ranchería to another, we were on our guard and very cautious in watching our camp and stock.

27. According to Obregón's version, Cantor said that "one of them had been killed by the natives of that land and that the other two were still alive." *Obregón's History*, p. 318.

28. The author means from the northwest.

FARTHER ON PEOPLE CAME PEACEFULLY AND OFFERED GIFTS FROM WHAT
THEY HAD.

This day we traveled three leagues to the eddy of the Río Turbio,
calling the place Pozo del Río Turbio. Here we were met peacefully
by people from the Otomoacos who offered us presents from what they
had.

We departed from this place on the nineteenth of the month and
went four leagues up the river, stopping at a place which we named
La Daga. All the rest of this river is lined with trees resembling the
screw bean, which produces a fruit like harquebus screws, yellowish in
color and showing between the twists some small seeds similar to those of
the prickly pear.[29] All along the river, on the opposite bank, among the
hills, there are quantities of mesquite plants, so abundant that we no
longer carried anything in our pack saddles but fodder.

We left La Daga on the twentieth of the month and continued three
leagues up the river to a place we named El Estrecho de Santo Tomás.
It was given this name because the river narrows here and forms a
channel. We rested in this location the following day, which was the
feast day of Saint Thomas, whom we considered and still consider as the
patron saint allotted to us. We left this place on the twenty-second and
marched three leagues up the river to a place which we named
Potreadero.

FRIENDLY PEOPLE CAME OUT TO MEET THE SPANIARDS.

We set out from this locality on the twenty-third of the month and
proceeded five leagues to a place we named La Hoya. Here we were
met by peaceful people of the language and dress of the Otomoacos.

Leaving La Hoya on the twenty-fourth of the month, we traveled
three leagues up the river to a place we named La Alamedilla. The
route all along this river is so rough, sandy, and thorny that there is
not a league in its whole course which one could call smooth.

We rested during Christmas and did not leave La Alamedilla until
the twenty-seventh. On that day we continued four leagues up the
river to a place we named Las Bocas, because the river here came out
between two craggy ridges and again flowed between two others.

---

29. The tornillo (Prosopis pubescens) is often called the screw-bean, or screw-pod
mesquite, from the fact that the pods are twisted into a dense screwlike spiral.

THE SPANIARDS WERE MET BY FRIENDLY PEOPLE WHO BROUGHT PRESENTS, THE SAME AS THE OTHERS.

We left Las Bocas on the twenty-eighth and went three leagues up the river through a sierra to a place we named La Sabana Llana. Here we were met by Indians from the same Otomoacos nation, who brought us presents the same as the other people. We departed from this locality on the thirtieth of the month and proceeded three leagues up the river to a place we named El Real de Santa María Magdalena.

THE SPANIARDS FOUND MANY ANIMALS EXHAUSTED; MORE THAN TWO HUN-DRED INDIANS, MEN AND WOMEN, CAME AND PRESENTED THEM WITH BLANKETS, TANNED DEERSKINS, AND ADORNMENTS IN THE SHAPE OF FEATHER CAPS, AND HELD A GREAT CELEBRATION.

Setting out from this place on the last day of the month, we traveled five leagues up the river and crossed a large ridge four leagues long. The trail was bad, and we stopped at the river. We named the place La Deseada. Many animals were exhausted when we got there. Upon our arrival, there came to us, in procession and singing, more than two hundred Indians, men and women, from the same Otomoacos nation. They presented us with shawls, tanned deerskins, mescal, and ornaments like colored feather bonnets which they said they obtained from the direction of the sea.

On this night the natives staged great dances and festivities.[30] They make music by beating their hands while sitting around a big fire. They sing, and in time with the singing they dance, a few rising from one side and others from the opposite, with two, four, or eight persons performing the movements to the rhythm of the song. Some of these people accompanied us.

INDIAN MEN AND WOMEN CAME FORTH PEACEFULLY AND BROUGHT MANY GIFTS.

We set out from La Deseada on the first of January of the year of our Lord 1583. We named this place El Año Nuevo. Proceeding four

---

30. Gallegos described similar dances, performed when the Chamuscado party passed through this region. Since leaving the pueblo of San Bernardino on December 17, 1582, and up to this point and through the next day's travel, January 1, 1583, the party had been in the territory of the Otomoacos, or Cholomes. They next entered the lands of the Caguates, i.e., the Sumas, traversing their domain for four days.

leagues to another point, we were met by many Indian men and women from the same Otomoacos nation who brought a lot of mescal.

THE SPANIARDS WERE MET BY A CACIQUE.

We left this locality on the second of January and went four leagues to a place we called La Guardia del Caballo. An old cacique from the Caguates nation named Guaxi came to us here.[31] He was a grandfather of Pedro, the interpreter, servant of Diego Pérez de Luxán. The natives are friendly. They are intermarried with the Otomoacos and have almost the same language. This cacique had a sorrel horse, for it seems that Francisco Sánchez Chamuscado had left it there, exhausted, when he returned. They had built a manger for it and gave it a large quantity of mesquite and talked to it as if it were a person. When we were leading the animal, as we were about to depart, they took leave of it and gave it more mesquite to eat. We were met here by more than three hundred people, men and women. They performed impressive dances after their fashion and offered us gifts from what they had. From here the natives led us to some mines which were of little value. We erected crosses for these people.

We departed from this place on the third of the said month and went four leagues to a spot we named Las Vueltas del Río del Punzón.

FRIENDLY PEOPLE CAME OUT TO MEET THEM.

We left this location on the fourth and proceeded four leagues to an inlet which we named Los Reyes. Here we were met peacefully by people from the Caguates nation.

THE SPANIARDS FOUND MUCH SALTY EARTH; THEY BOILED SOME AND OBTAINED GOOD SALT.

We set out from this place on the seventh of January and continued three leagues to a spot we named Las Salinillas. In this locality there is an abundance of saline soil, and as we were short of salt we boiled some and obtained very fine salt.

---

31. The party was south of El Paso, in the area of the Suma Indians. This is approximately correct for their habitat. See Kelley, "Jumano and Patarabueye," p. 88; Forbes, "Unknown Athapaskans," pp. 108-111; Carl Sauer, *Distribution of Aboriginal Tribes and Languages in Northwestern Mexico*, pp. 65-76, who notes that the Manso area of occupancy began north of El Paso, along the Río Grande, and went southward toward the Sumas.

We left Las Salinillas on the eighth and traveled four leagues to a site which we named La Ciénega Grande. This swamp is formed by the Turbio river when it overflows its banks. It contains an abundance of game such as ducks, geese, and cranes. There are large salines around it.

NUMEROUS PEOPLE, MEN AND WOMEN, CAME TO THE SPANIARDS, AND IN THE SEVEN DAYS THEY STAYED THERE THE NATIVES PRESENTED THEM WITH A LARGE QUANTITY OF FISH AND OTHER PROVISIONS.

We left this place on the ninth of the month and went three leagues, stopping at some pools near the river formed by it. We named this site Los Charcos del Canutillo, because there were numerous reeds and large marshes and pools with quantities of fish close by the river. A large number of Indian men and women from another nation, called Tanpachoas, came to this place.[32] During the six or seven days that we rested there in order to refresh our horses, they brought us a large quantity of mesquite, corn, and fish, for they fish much in the pools with small dragnets. They are people of the same blood and type as the Otomoacos, and of the same dress, except that the men tie their privy parts with a small ribbon.[33]

THE NATIVES FIGHT WITH TURKISH BOWS AND ARROWS AND WOODEN BLUDGEONS HALF A YARD LONG. THE SPANIARDS PROVIDED THEM WITH CROSSES LIKE ALL THE PEOPLE VISITED.

Their mode of fighting is with Turkish bows and arrows, and bludgeons as much as half a yard in length, made of tornillo-wood, which is very strong and flexible. We all made stocks for our harquebuses from this tornillo-wood because it was very suitable for the purpose. These stocks were fashioned by an Indian whom we brought with us, a good man, and a fine soldier and harquebusier named Gregorio de Tlaxcala. We went to this ranchería with Father Fray Bernardino and erected crosses; this we did wherever we found people.

32. The marshland seen on January 9 was below El Paso. The Tanpachoas may have been the Mansos, who occupied an area extending both above and below El Paso. Benavides, in his "Memorial," described the Mansos in glowing terms and urged that they be placed in a mission, but this did not come to pass until 1659.

33. Some Indians of South America, it is interesting to observe in this connection, wore penis-envelopes as a charm to protect the member against evil spirits. Cf. Rafael Karsten, *The Civilization of the South American Indians* (New York, 1926), pp. 150-152. The Piro Indians, when engaged in certain ceremonies, tied the prepuce with a feathered string. See below, under date of February 1.

ON THE WAY, THE SPANIARDS FOUND SOME SALINES OF VERY GOOD WHITE ROCK SALT, AND ON THE OPPOSITE BANK MANY MOUNTAINS WITH ORES.

We left this place on the fifteenth and went five leagues. Midway we found some salines of white rock salt, wonderful beyond comparison, and very plentiful. On the opposite bank of the river there are many mountains with quantities of ores. We did not go to them because it was late and we were unable to cross the river. We stopped at some pools which we named Las Salinas.

We set out from Las Salinas on the sixteenth and traveled five leagues till we reached a pool formed by the river when it overflows its banks. We named it El Charco de San Antonio. We left this place on the nineteenth and in five leagues came to the said river to camp at a spot which we named Las Vueltas del Río, because here it starts to wind as far as the settlements.[34] Leaving this locality on the twenty-first of the month, we continued five leagues to a prominent place overlooking the river. This we named La Barranca de las Vueltas.

THE SPANIARDS LOCATED A STRAND WITH SALINES.

We set out from this place on the twenty-second of January and went five leagues to a spot we named La Playa de las Salinas. These were the first salines that we saw along this river.

We left La Playa de las Salinas on the twenty-third and traveled four leagues to a place we named La Ciénega Helada, a marsh formed by the river. It was frozen so hard that it was necessary to break the ice with bars and picks in order to get drinking water. We took our horses to the river to water.

A MOUNTAINOUS DISTRICT WITH LARGE VEINS FOR MINING.

Leaving La Ciénega Helada on the twenty-fourth of the said month and going five leagues, we came to a place on the river which we named El Frontón de las Minas, because on the way half a league before reaching this spot, there is a mountainous district containing large veins. These mines we did not assay. During this entire trip we never met any people, although we found numerous traces of them and many abandoned rancherías.

34. This would indicate that the party was in the vicinity of El Paso, which fits pretty closely with the distance traveled from there to the site of the first pueblos of New Mexico.

From this place, on the twenty-sixth, we traveled three leagues up the river. Starting with that day's march, we went straight toward the north, that is, the direction from which the Del Norte flows. We halted at an arm of this river which we named Los Humos, because there were many smoke columns on a high sierra on the opposite side of the river.

THE SPANIARDS CAME TO ANOTHER RIDGE WITH NUMEROUS VEINS OF SILVER EXTENDING FOR MORE THAN TEN OR TWELVE LEAGUES. ALL THE SIERRAS AND RAVINES ARE THICK WITH JUNIPER TREES, WHICH ARE GOOD FOR THE EXPLOITATION OF SILVER.

We left Los Humos on the twenty-eighth of the month and on that day traveled five leagues through a mountainous district close to the said river. This ridge contains numerous veins of silver, which extend for more than ten or twelve leagues. We stopped by the river and called this place El Peñol de los Cedros. It was given this name because here there is a large black rock,[35] and all the ranges and gorges are covered with juniper trees and, in some parts, oak groves, a fine asset for the exploitation of silver.

We left this place on the thirtieth and went seven leagues, stopping at the river. We named the spot La Punta de Buena Esperanza.

THE SPANIARDS LOCATED AN ABANDONED PUEBLO.

We set out from this place on the thirty-first of January and went four leagues to a marsh which we named El Mal País, because it is close to some bad lands. On our way, about a league from this site, we found an abandoned pueblo with the houses in ruins.[36]

Departing from this place on February 1 of the said year, 1583, we traveled five leagues. On the way, after going three leagues, we came to another abandoned pueblo. We stopped by the river at a place close to the first pueblo of the province, which is called San Felipe.[37] In

35. This large, black rock was almost certainly the Elephant Butte, now partially submerged in the waters of Elephant Butte Dam on the Río Grande. Luxán states that it was about ten leagues from this point to the first pueblos, or thirty miles, which is about the distance to the first pueblo, i.e., San Felipe.

36. This was a Piro village, perhaps identical with the one called San Felipe by Gallegos. See Gallegos' "Account of the Pueblos," chapter VIII, note 1.

37. When the Chamuscado party took possession of the land on August 21, 1581, they named it San Felipe. The Piro, whose towns Espejo had now entered, formed one of the principal groups of Pueblo tribes at this time and for a century afterwards. They comprised two divisions, one occupying the Río Grande valley from the vicinity of the present San Marcial northward to within about fifty miles of Albuquerque. The other was the eastern Piro, or Tompiro. See *Benavides' Revised Memorial*, pp. 246 ff.

this first pueblo we did not find anyone who understood us, nor were we able to learn the name of this nation, except through signs, by pointing to each of the articles on which we questioned them. They are good people and seem to be native Otomites. Thus they wear their hair in the shape of a queue. Most of the men cover their privy parts with small pieces of cotton cloth; others leave them uncovered, tied near the prepuce with a cord of maguey fiber. Some wear tanned deerskin jackets and others tanned deerskins tied to their bodies. Most of them have, especially for sleeping, quilts made of turkey feathers, because they raise cocks and hens in quantities. The women wear their hair tied up on their heads, and cover their privy parts and bodies with cotton blankets and tanned deerskins, and on top of these, feather quilts in place of cloaks. They wear shoes of tanned buffalo leather and tanned deerskins fashioned like boots. They are an industrious people who plant and gather very fine corn, beans, and calabashes in abundance. Thus the entire river is bordered with sown fields; we found them full of stubble, which was the salvation of our horses.

THE SPANIARDS FOUND ANOTHER PUEBLO OF ABOUT FIFTY HOUSES AND FOUR HUNDRED PERSONS, CLOTHED, SHOD, CLEAN, NEAT, AND AFFABLE. THE INHABITANTS HAVE HOUSES OF SEVERAL STORIES, AND SO FORTH.

The pueblo must contain about fifty houses and four hundred people, young and old.[38] They are clean and tidy, and do not smell, as is the case with other Indian nations. Their houses are of mud, built by hand, the walls like small adobes half a yard wide. They contain upper and lower floors and have bedrooms. The people climb to the upper floors by means of movable hand ladders; and the lower part of the pueblo can be dominated from above. They have large cellars,[39] and in the lower part they have their granaries, pantries, and kitchens.

At the end of these they have mills where they grind the corn, as for the making of tortillas. They grind it raw or toasted and knead it with hot water; they make very fine tortillas. Their mills are of the following type: four or five and even eight mills are placed together, depending on the capacity of the house. They are a yard long and two-thirds wide. They are made of whitewashed stones, built low, right on the ground, and resemble metates, with a border one span high and in the center an indented stone like the metate, about half a yard in length and a third wide. The Indians grind with another stone.

38. Luxán is evidently describing the pueblo called San Miguel by Gallegos.
39. These cellars were the kivas or ceremonial chambers.

They have earthen jar stands on which they keep their water jars. The rooms are small and whitewashed. The doors are shaped like a "U" so as to allow only one person to go through at a time. These people do not seem to be bellicose, because they fight [chiefly] with flint-edged clubs [*macanas*] and hide-wrapped stone bludgeons about half a yard long. They have few and poor Turkish bows and poorer arrows. They brought us turkey cocks and hens, beans, corn, calabashes, and raw and toasted pinole. We erected crosses for them.

THE SPANIARDS CAME UPON FIVE PUEBLOS, EACH WITH FIFTY HOUSES AND FOUR HUNDRED INHABITANTS, EXCEPT FOR ONE WITH ONE HUNDRED HOUSES AND EIGHT HUNDRED INHABITANTS, ALL WITH PLAZAS.

We left this place on the fourth of February and went three leagues, camping at the said river in the midst of five pueblos of the same nation and type as the first.[40] Four of these pueblos had about fifty houses and four hundred souls each, including children and adults. The other one had about one hundred houses and eight hundred souls. In each pueblo, in the center of the plazas, are some very large cellars two and one-half *estados* deep, with an entrance in the shape of a trap door and with a stepladder. They are all whitewashed and provided with stone benches all around. Here the people perform their games and dances. On one side are their *temascales* where they bathe.[41]

THE NATIVES PRESENTED THE SPANIARDS WITH TURKEYS, CORN, AND OTHER THINGS, AND MANY ACCOMPANIED THEM. THEY COVET IRON GREATLY AND STEAL IT.

In all these pueblos the inhabitants presented us with turkeys, corn, beans, and pinole. Many Indians accompanied us from pueblo to pueblo. They covet iron very much and whenever they can steal some they do not postpone it till the next day! We named this place El Gallo.

We left this site on the seventh of the month and traveled five leagues, stopping by the river at a point which we called Jueves de las Comadres, because we reached this place on that very day.[42] On our way we found four large pueblos in ruins and abandoned, and a small hamlet of twenty houses.

40. The party was among the Piros, below Socorro. Cf. Gallegos' list of pueblos.
41. Temascales (Aztec *temazcalli*) were sweathouses. The large cellars were the celebrated kivas, or ceremonial chambers, of the Pueblo Indians
42. Jueves de las Comadres was the last Thursday before the beginning of Lent.

Two pueblos two harquebus shots apart, one containing sixty houses and the other twenty, made of stone taken from the river. The natives gave the Spaniards turkeys and provisions.

Setting out from this place on the eighth of February, we went three leagues and camped at the said river between two pueblos two harquebus shots apart. They belonged to the same nation and had the same characteristics as the others, except that the walls are of stone from the river. The one had about sixty houses and the other twenty. Here the natives gave us turkeys, pinole, beans, and corn. We named this place El Término de Puala, for the Puala are a different nation from this and speak a different tongue.[43] The friars had remained among the people of Puala. Here the Indians told us by means of signs that the friars had been killed.

There was a great deal of discussion at this place among some of the companions because the natives said that the Indians of Puala were in revolt and secretly armed. Some, the majority, were of the opinion that we should cross to New Mexico, of which we had heard, and not go to Puala; others suggested that we should seek a convenient place in which to build a fortress where the camp might remain with seven men while the other eight went on to explore the land. But Diego Pérez de Luxán and Bernardino de Luna said that it was not feasible for the expedition to do anything but go forward, because the men were few and some poorly armed and lacking in animals; and that they would be lost if they separated. Furthermore, we were reminded that in the province of the Patarabueyes we had chosen among ourselves Antonio de Espejo as our captain and chief magistrate, in order to go and succor the friars; and that it would make a bad impression to alter our route on account of the tales of barbarians who spoke through signs, without going to see whether the friars were dead or alive.[44]

The Spaniards saw a province not seen by Chamuscado.

Finally the captain decided to travel lightly and examine a province ten leagues away which had not been seen by Chamuscado's people.[45]

43. That is, the party was now at the end of Piro territory and about to enter that of the Tigua (the chronicler called the latter Puala), so he named the most northerly Piro pueblo El Término de Paula, i.e., The Boundary of the Puala.

44. Obregón adds some details on this controversy as to the future course of the explorers. *Obregón's History*, pp. 321-322.

45. This was the province of the Magrias, or Maguas (the Manguos of Obregón, p. 322), i.e., Tompiros, but Luxán is in error in saying that Chamuscado did not visit it.

He went with the intention of building a fortress if a suitable place should be found, taking along only Diego Pérez de Luxán, Gregorio Hernández, and some Indian servants.

THE SPANIARDS REACHED THE FIRST PUEBLO, AND WHEN THEY WERE OB-SERVED MOST OF THE PEOPLE FLED, WHILE OTHERS CAME TO MEET THEM PEACEFULLY. THOSE WHO FLED CAME THAT NIGHT AND OFFERED GIFTS OF TURKEYS AND CORN.

We left on February 10 and at sunset reached the first pueblo of the province of the Magrias. Most of the people of that pueblo began to flee when they observed us, while others came to meet us peacefully. We at once reassured them, and that night all the people came and gave us turkeys and corn. That night we kept watch with much care. We erected a large cross † in token of possession, but as no notary accompanied us and as we had no paper we did not take possession in writing.

THESE PEOPLE ARE MORE BELLICOSE THAN THOSE MET BEFORE; AND THEY ARE WELL ARMED. THE HOUSES ARE OF SLABS AND ROCKS, WELL BUILT AND WHITEWASHED INSIDE.

The people of this province are of the same sort as those of the previous one, except that they seem to be more warlike, being well armed with bows and arrows. There were two large plazas in this pueblo. The houses were of slabs and rocks, well built and white washed inside. The people are idolatrous, for that pueblo had four caverns [kivas] in the plazas where they have their dances and their baths; and these places served as a community center and lodging place for strangers. In front of each one, outside the entrance, is a black stone four fingers in thickness, three spans wide, and one estado above the ground; and on each kiva [?] is a badly painted figure of an Indian with a flaming crown. Everyone has these idols in his house.

Actually, Gallegos, his chronicler, described it in some detail and gave the names of five of its pueblos.

Espejo's narrative says that the expedition to the Magrias was made after the party had reached Puala, while Luxán here states that they made the trip while among the Piro and before going to Puala. The same view is given by Obregón. Both Espejo and Obregón say that there were eleven pueblos, while Luxán merely says that there were many pueblos. Their descriptions suggest that the Magrias were eastern Piro, including possibly some of the eastern Tigua. See Espejo's "Narrative," p. 222; Bandelier, *Final Report*, Pt. II, p. 254 ff; and Scholes and Mera, *op. cit.*

THIS PROVINCE HAS MANY PUEBLOS, FORESTS OF PINE AND JUNIPER TREES, AND MINES.

The next day we went to another pueblo of the same characteristics as the first. Each of these pueblos must have about eight hundred people, young and old. From there we returned next day to the camp [on the Río Grande], where it was decided to proceed on our way. This province contains a great number of pueblos. It has many forests of pine and juniper trees and many mines, but as we were only three we did not examine the land.

We left this place[46] on the thirteenth of the month and traveled four leagues, camping at a pueblo of the same type as the others close to the said river. We named the place El Corvillo, because the day was Ash Wednesday. There were some small pueblos and many deserted ones on this trip.

THE SPANIARDS REACHED TWO PUEBLOS WHOSE PEOPLE FLED THROUGH FEAR; ONE HAD ABOUT TWO HUNDRED AND FIFTY HOUSES WITH ABUNDANT SUPPLIES.

We left El Corvillo on the fourteenth, went four leagues, and stopped between two pueblos whose people had fled to the sierra through fear, thinking they would be killed for having murdered the friars.[47] We called this place Los Despoblados, because we found both pueblos deserted, as was also the case with another situated along the way, where we came upon a quantity of corn, beans, and calabashes, and also four Indians who were waiting to see what the outcome would be. We sent them to bring the people peacefully, resting a day in the hope that they would come, but as they did not we continued forward. One of the pueblos had about two hundred and fifty houses, and we found abundant provisions of corn, beans, potatoes, calabashes, and other dried vegetables which the natives keep for their sowing.

ANOTHER PUEBLO IN FLIGHT LIKE THE ABOVE.

Setting out from this place on the sixteenth we marched five leagues. On the way we found one of the pueblos that had taken part in the

46. Espejo and party were now back at the Río Grande after the trip to the Magrias or Tompiro pueblos, and continued up the river, where they soon found themselves among the first of the Tigua towns.

47. One of these pueblos may have been Isleta. Bandelier (*Final Report,* Pt. II, p. 233) noted that the earliest mention of this pueblo was 1629, when it already had a mission with a resident priest—in other words, a substantial population—from which he inferred that it existed in the sixteenth century.

murder of the friars. The people had fled. We stopped at the said river near a pueblo of the same league as the Indians who had fled. Here we found many turkeys and abundant provisions. Throughout this nation the people have many masks which they use in their dances and ceremonies. We named this place Los Guajolotes.

THE SPANIARDS FOUND THIRTEEN PUEBLOS AND STOPPED NEAR THE ONE NAMED PUALA. ALL THE INHABITANTS HAD FLED, OWING TO THE MURDER OF THE FRIARS. IT HAS FOUR HUNDRED HOUSES OF TWO AND THREE STORIES. ALTHOUGH THE SPANIARDS SPOKE TO THE NATIVES, THEY COULD NOT SUBDUE THEM. THE NAMES OF THE THIRTEEN PUEBLOS ARE GIVEN ON PAGE 203.

Leaving this place on the seventeenth of February, we went two leagues, and within one league found thirteen large settlements.[48] We stopped by the said river close to the pueblo of Puala, where the Indians had murdered Fray Agustín and his companion and the servants who had remained with him. For this reason we named it Puala de los Mártires.[49] The pueblo of Puala has four hundred houses, most of them two stories high, not counting the ground floor, which makes three stories. The inhabitants of all these settlements had fled to the sierra because all had taken part in killing the friars.[50] Some Indians soon came to find out what we wanted to do and we sent them to bring the others in peace. There was one among them playing an instrument resembling a flageolet.

Seeing that the others did not want to come, we decided to seek them in the sierra, and we found them there, about a league from Puala. Those who went were Captain Antonio de Espejo, Diego Pérez de Luxán, Gregorio Hernández, Juan López de Ibarra, Gaspar de Luxán, Alonso de Miranda, Pedro Hernández de Almansa, and Juan de Frías. When the natives saw us, they fled into the sierra, where we saw seven or eight thousand Indians. We appealed to them in a friendly way and dismounted from our horses. Then some came down and asked for peace by means of signs, agreeing to return to their pueblos because they said their women and children were suffering greatly from cold.

48. This was the province of Tiguex, situated in the Albuquerque-Bernalillo region.
49. The location of Puala, or Puaray, long a subject of speculation, is believed to have been on a bluff, on the west bank of the Río Grande, opposite Bernalillo, identified with Kuaua. In recent years, excavations by archaeologists from the University of New Mexico, Museum of New Mexico, and the School of American Research, have revealed the ruins of pueblos of the historic and prehistoric periods at this site. One of these, Kuaua, has been developed as the Coronado State Monument. Thousands of tourists visit it annually. For other ideas as to the location of Puaray, see Introduction, p. 57.
50. Presumably to the Sandía Mountains, east of the Río Grande.

After this we returned to our camp where we awaited them for three days.

THE SPANIARDS EXAMINED SOME OF THESE ABANDONED PUEBLOS AND FOUND ABUNDANT PROVISIONS.

During this time we inspected some pueblos. All were deserted, but contained large quantities of corn, beans, green and sun-dried calabashes, and other vegetables; also dew-lapped cocks and hens, and a lot of pottery. We provisioned ourselves well with these things. In the meantime we met some Indians who said that the people from Puala were very frightened and for this reason would not come down.

PEACEFUL INDIANS CAME FROM EIGHT TO TEN LEAGUES WITH TURKEYS AS GIFTS. THEY ASKED THE SPANIARDS TO VISIT THEIR PUEBLOS SO THAT THEY MIGHT SERVE THEM AND SAID THAT TEN OR TWELVE DAYS AWAY THERE WAS A VERY RICH PROVINCE WITH MEXICAN PEOPLE, AND THAT ANOTHER THIRTY DAYS FARTHER ON WERE THE PROVINCES OF MAXOSA AND SUNI, WHICH THE SPANIARDS DECIDED TO GO AND SEE. THE PEOPLE WHO HAD FLED ARE NEAT AND CLEAN. THEY SLEEP IN ESTUFAS, POSSESS WHITE-WASHED HOUSES, AND USE VERY GOOD POTTERY.

During this time Indians came from eight or ten leagues up the river with presents of turkeys, telling us they were friendly and begging us to go to their pueblos, where they would serve us. We were informed in this locality that ten or twelve days farther on was a very rich province with Mexican people; and that thirty days still farther on were the provinces called Maxosa and Suny.[51] In view of this we decided to set out the next morning. Our Lord permitting, I shall give an account of what may befall us. Here I merely say that this province of the Tiguas, from this pueblo of Puala onward, contains neat and cleanly people, for so they are in eating and sleeping. They sleep in estufas [kivas], have whitewashed houses, and use very good pottery.

51. Maxosa, the present Hopi pueblos, and Suny, Zuñi. The origin of the term Maxosa is unknown, but it may have come from the Laguna (Queres) name for the Hopi (Mósǐchǎ in Laguna, Mo-ts in Acoma, Mótsǐ in Zía, Cochití, and San Felipe, etc., whence Espejo's "Mohace" and "Mohoce" and Oñate's "Mohoqui"), or from that of the Zuñi (Ahmukwe). The word Zuñi is also of Queres origin. Benavides' Revised Memorial, pp. 289 and 295.

THE SPANIARDS CAME TO A PUEBLO NAMED CACHITI, INHABITED BY VERY PEACEFUL PEOPLE. THEY GAVE US CORN AND TURKEYS AND TRADED BUFFALO SKINS FOR SLEIGH BELLS AND SMALL IRON ARTICLES.

Leaving this place on the twenty-third of February, we went four leagues up the river, persuaded by some Indians of the Quites [Queres] nation belonging to another group who had been present at the death of the friars. We stopped at a place an harquebus shot from the pueblo of these natives who called their town Cachiti.[52] The people are very peaceful. They gave us corn, tortillas, turkeys, and pinole. We bartered sleigh bells and small iron articles for very fine buffalo hides.

PEOPLE FROM ANOTHER PUEBLO CAME AND ASKED THAT THE SPANIARDS GO THERE. THE NATIVES, WHOSE HOUSES ARE THREE STORIES HIGH, ARE RULED BY A CACIQUE.

People from other pueblos came to meet us and asked us to visit them. We named this place Los Confiados, because the natives did not become disturbed.[53] Most of the houses are three stories high. These people are governed by caciques, as they do not have any ruler who has authority beyond his own pueblo. In their dress and in other respects they are similar to the people of Puala.[54]

THE SPANIARDS REACHED A FRIENDLY PUEBLO WHERE THEY WERE GIVEN PROVISIONS.

We left this place on the twenty-fourth, I mean the twenty-fifth, and traveled a league and a half, camping close to a pueblo of the peaceful Quires nation. Here they gave us turkeys, corn, pinole, and other things we needed. We named this place La Milpa Llana.

GOING WESTWARD, THE SPANIARDS LOOKED FOR SOME VERY RICH PROVINCES.

Setting out from this locality on the twenty-sixth, we traveled five leagues westward in search of certain very rich provinces and halted

52. Espejo says that the "Quires" province was six leagues farther up the river (Río Grande), that it contained five pueblos, and had about fifteen thousand souls. See pp. 223. Later in the Luxán narrative, the names of all these pueblos are given. Cachiti was doubtless identical with the modern San Felipe (Katisthya in Queres).

53. Los Confiados was one of the Queres pueblos.

54. On pueblo government and religion, consult Elsie Clews Parsons, *Pueblo Indian Religion* (University of Chicago Press, 1939), two vols., and for a recent study, showing the trend of development in modern pueblo life, Charles H. Lange, *Cochiti: A New Mexico Pueblo, Past and Present* (University of Texas Press, 1959).

at a fine river with a good volume of water, though it was not so large as the Del Norte.[55]

THE SPANIARDS FOUND A VERY IMPORTANT CITY OF OVER ONE THOUSAND HOUSES WITH MORE THAN FOUR THOUSAND MEN OVER FIFTEEN YEARS OF AGE, BESIDES WOMEN AND CHILDREN. IT WAS CALLED ZIAQUEBOS, AND WAS RULED BY THREE CACIQUES. IT HAD LARGE PLAZAS AND MANY SMALL ONES; THE PEOPLE WERE CLOTHED AND SHOD. POSSESSION WAS TAKEN FOR HIS MAJESTY.

There was here an important city of more than a thousand houses, inhabited by more than four thousand men over fifteen years of age, and women and children in addition. This city, called Ziaquebos, belonged to the province of the Punamees[56] and was governed by three caciques. One was named Quasquito, another Quchir, and the third Quatho.[57] There are in the city five large plazas and many smaller ones. The dress of the men consists of blankets, some draped like a towel for covering their privy parts, and others like knotted cloaks worn shawl-fashion, and also leather shoes in the shape of boots. The women wear a blanket over their shoulders tied with a sash at the waist, their hair cut in front and the rest plaited into two braids, and above a blanket of turkey feathers. It is an ugly dress indeed.

A CROSS WAS ERECTED AND ITS SIGNIFICANCE EXPLAINED TO THE NATIVES. THEY GAVE CORN AND TURKEYS. THE HOUSES ARE OF THREE AND FOUR STORIES, WELL BUILT AND VERY HIGH. THEY ARE A CLEANLY PEOPLE.

In this city and province we raised the flag in the name of his Majesty and took possession. A cross † was erected and its meaning explained to the natives. They gave us many turkeys, such a large quantity of tortillas that they had to be returned to the pueblo, and also a quantity of corn

55. The Jémez river.
56. Ziaquebos was clearly identical with the present Zía pueblo. Compare the account of Espejo, printed below, in which he said that the province comprised five pueblos. Obregón called the town Queraque, but his description identifies it with Ziaquebos. Punames was the Zía group of villages. Cf. Obregón's *History*, p. 323; *Benavides' Revised Memorial*, pp. 262 and 275-276.
57. It is difficult to say whether these are personal or priestly names. Quchir suggests *Koshare*, the common spelling of the name of the sacred clowns—the "delight makers" of the Queres. For comment on the latter, see A. F. Bandelier, *The Delight Makers*, pp. 7-11, 31-35, 134-142, and *passim*; Parsons, *op. cit.*, vol. I, pp. 117-122; and Lange, *op. cit.*, p. 298 *et seq.*

and other vegetables. The houses are of three and four stories, extremely high and well built. The people are cleanly.

We left this city and locality on the twenty-eighth and went four leagues westward in search of the provinces of Zuñi.[58] We took a guide from Ziaquebos for that province, halting at a ravine in which there were some springs issuing from a rock where there was a frozen pool. Because of this we named the place La Fuente Helada.[59]

Setting out from the ravine on the first of March, 1583, we traveled six leagues and stopped at the foot of a mountain without any water. For this reason we named the place El Sequedal.

THE SPANIARDS MET FRIENDLY INDIAN MOUNTAINEERS WHO BROUGHT THEM SOME CORN.

We left El Sequedal on March 2, going two leagues to a marsh which extends from a mountain. We found here peaceful Indian mountaineers who came down to bring us tortillas, even though we did not need them as we had abundant provisions. We named this place La Ciénega Deseada del Pinal.

We set out from this locality on the fourth of the month and continued four leagues, camping at a large lagoon where a small river disembogues. It originates along the route from Suny.[60]

58. There has been some question as to whether the Espejo party visited the Jémez pueblos before the trip to Zuñi, but the evidence is fairly convincing that it did not. Espejo's account is ambiguous, for he first says that, after leaving Zía, and traveling six leagues, he found a province of seven pueblos, called Emexes, and then went fifteen leagues to Acoma. Obregón states that "From the pueblo and city of Cia the captain and soldiers went to visit and examine the strong town of Acuco." With regard to some ore given them, he notes that "The natives said the metal had been brought from the province of the Emixis. They affirmed that the largest town in the provinces of the Emixis was three times larger than theirs. They said it contained four thousand houses like their own and that it was twice as large as Cia." Luxán, finally, makes no mention of any visit to Jémez, but on the contrary explains in some detail the route from Zía to Acoma. We conclude, therefore, that Espejo got his information about Jémez by hearsay and did not actually visit that group of pueblos. See *Obregón's History*, p. 324, and Espejo's Narrative, pp. 223.

59. This spring must have been located between Zía and the Río Puerco, possibly at the base of Mesa Prieta, since the distance was only four leagues, or about twelve miles from Zía, their point of departure, whereas it is some twenty miles to the Puerco. Curiously, Luxán makes no mention of crossing this stream. The next day he says they went six leagues to the foot of a mountain, probably Cebolleta mesa, and then another six leagues to a large lagoon, the site of modern Laguna, and four more to Acoma. This fits both the distances traveled and the country Luxán describes.

Old maps of New Mexico locate a cold spring near Paguate, forty five miles from Zía as the crow flies, a location incompatible with the record of the trip kept by the diarist, Luxán.

60. The "small river" was the San José, and the "large lagoon" was formed by this stream. Laguna, established over a century later, took its name from a lagoon west of the present pueblo, perhaps on the site of an ancient settlement of some sort.

THE SPANIARDS LEARNED OF THE PUEBLO OF ACOMA AND WENT THERE. IT IS SITUATED ON A HIGH AND ROCKY HILL, WITH FOUR CARVED-OUT FLIGHTS OF STEPS.

We learned that close to this place was a pueblo called Acoma. So we left the camp by this lagoon while Captain Antonio de Espejo, Diego Pérez de Luxán, and six other companions went to this pueblo, which was four leagues distant. Because of its conflict with the Querechos Indians, who are like the Chichimecos, it is built on a high and rocky cliff.[61] The pueblo has four ascents made of steps carved in the very rock, up which only one person can climb at a time. Even the doors of the houses are like trapdoors. They keep watch day and night.

THE NATIVES CAME OUT TO MEET THEM WITH GREAT REJOICING AND MERRIMENT, AND GAVE MANY BLANKETS, TANNED DEERSKINS, TURKEYS, AND A QUANTITY OF CORN.

The natives came out to meet us and in order to honor us they performed a very impressive dance after the Mexican fashion, in which the women took part, wearing Mexican blankets, very elegant with colors, feathers, and other trappings. There they gave us many blankets, tanned deerskins, turkeys, and a quantity of corn.

THE VISITORS FOUND MANY IRRIGATED FIELDS WITH CANALS AND DAMS BUILT AS IF BY SPANIARDS.

We left the aforesaid place on March 7 and went four leagues up a river which flows through some bad lands. We found many irrigated cornfields with canals and dams, built as if by Spaniards. We stopped by the said river, calling the place El Río de San Martín.[62]

Setting out from this locality on the eighth, we traveled four leagues,

61. These Querechos were undoubtedly a Navajo band, who, as shown here, inhabited the mountainous area about Mount Taylor. In Spanish times, the term Navajo was used to refer both to the tribe and to a band subdivision inhabiting the classic Dinetah region, in the Largo-Gobernador basin. According to Navajo tradition, there were local band groupings of this people before the introduction of clans. Early Spanish travelers, in their slight contact with these tribes, had an imperfect understanding of their social and political organization. Espejo's contact with them, and the accounts of his expedition, though they contain the best information recorded to that date, did not give the Spaniards very much enlightenment of this nature. Perhaps it would be more accurate to say that they did not take the trouble to write it down. After all, they were not concerned about studying or understanding the Indian's way of life, but rather of uprooting his heathen beliefs and substituting Christian principles instead.

62. This was the present San José, the waters of which were used by the Acoma Indians to irrigate their cornfields.

halting at a place one and a half leagues beyond the spot where the river flows into a marsh. We named that stopping place El Salitrar. We left El Salitrar on the ninth and continued four leagues, camping at some bad lands without water.[63] It snowed so hard that we were forced to halt there.

We departed from this place on the tenth and went seven leagues until we came to a large pine forest. We slept in the woods because it snowed so much that we were unable to proceed. We retired without water, and this day drank snow water melted in pots and pans. We called the place El Helado.[64] We set out from there on the eleventh of the month and marched three leagues, stopping at a water hole at the foot of a rock. This place we named El Estanque del Peñol.[65]

We left this spot on the thirteenth, I mean the twelfth, and traveled seven leagues. We camped at a small arroyo with water,[66] and because there was a very high rock in the shape of a sugar loaf we named the site El Real del Pilón. Here, at the request of the party, two aides to the captain were chosen, Gregorio Hernández and Bernardino de Luna. They granted, in the name of his Majesty, the office of alférez mayor to Gregorio Hernández, and to Diego Pérez de Luxán that of alguacil mayor of the camp and of the new jurisdiction *(gobernación)* of New Andalusia, as well as of the first town or city of that province to be founded, with a vote in its cabildo.

THE VISITORS DISCOVERED THE PROVINCE OF ZUÑI AND SIX PUEBLOS CALLED MAZAQUE, QUAQUEMA, AGUICO, ALONA, QUAQUINA, AND CANA. POOR PEOPLE.

We set out from this place on the fourteenth, went a league, and halted at the first pueblo of the province of Zuñi, called Malaque by the natives, where we had a row of houses for our use. They gave us to eat of what they had until we went to other neighboring pueblos. The people of this province, which comprised six pueblos, are poor. One was called Mazaque, another Quaquema, another Aguico, another

63. The lava beds in this region, west of McCarty's along U.S. Highway 66, cover many square miles.

64. On this day's march, the party passed from the vicinity of Grant to Guadalupe, or Zuñi, canyon and on across the Zuñi mountains toward El Morro.

65. El Estanque del Peñol was El Morro, better known as Inscription Rock, where there is a pool of permanent water. It is intriguing to speculate that some members of the party might have inscribed their names on the towering sandstone cliff, but there is no evidence that anyone did so before Oñate, on his return from the Gulf of California, April 16, 1605, left his name on this remarkable monument.

66. The Zuñi river. The men evidently camped where it flows through the "gateway," east of Zuñi.

Alona, another Quaquina, and another Cana.[67] For even though they wear the same sort of dress as the others, the cloth is of agave fiber,[68] since they gather little cotton because the land is cold. The women wear their hair done up in large puffs.

THE SPANIARDS FOUND CROSSES, ALL WELL BUILT, BECAUSE CORONADO AND CHAMUSCADO HAD BEEN THERE, AS THE INDIANS STATED. THEY ENCOUNTERED MEXICAN INDIANS HERE AND SOME FROM GUADALAJARA, BROUGHT BY CORONADO.

We found very well built crosses ✝✝ in all these pueblos, and also in all the areas discovered by Fray Agustín and Francisco Sánchez Chamuscado, because Coronado had been in this region, as the natives told us everywhere. Here we found Mexican Indians, and also a number from Guadalajara, some of those that Coronado had brought.[69] We could understand each other, although the Indians spoke Spanish with difficulty. Here also we found a book and a small old trunk left by Coronado.

REPORT OF MINES; THE PEOPLE OF THESE PROVINCES ARE INDUSTRIOUS AND PEACEFUL; THEY ARE GOOD FARMERS AND THE SOIL IS PRODUCTIVE; THERE ARE HOUSES OF STONE, MOSTLY OF SANDSTONE, THREE AND FOUR STORIES HIGH.

Having received news of mines, God willing, we are going to discover them. I shall give an account of whatever takes place. At present I merely wish to say that if there are good mines this will be the best land ever discovered, because the people of these provinces are industrious and peaceful. There are many mountains, lands for cultivation, and the natives are great farmers. The houses are all of stone, mostly sandstone, three and four stories high.

THE SPANIARDS WENT TO ANOTHER PUEBLO, AGUICO, WHERE THEY STAYED FROM MARCH 15 TO APRIL 7, LODGED IN GOOD HOUSES AND SUPPLIED WITH GAME IN THE FORM OF HARES AND RABBITS.

---

67. Obregón has Masaque, Zaquema, Alona, Quequina, Acinco, and Cana. They are identical with Mátsaki, K'iákima, Hálona, Kwákina, Háwikuh, and K'iánawa. F. W. Hodge, *History of Hawikuh, New Mexico, One of the So-called Cities of Cíbola* (Los Angeles, 1937), p. 58 ff.

68. This agave fiber was really yucca.

69. Espejo says there were three, Andrés, Gaspar, and Antón. Obregón gives the names of four. Espejo's "Narrative," p. 225; *Obregón's History*, p. 326.

From this pueblo we came to another, called Aguico,[70] which is four leagues from the first one in this province. We stayed here until the seventh of April, lodged in good houses and provided with plenty of hares and rabbits. This was the time for planting the fields, as it was Easter. There were frequent mists as if it were in the heart of winter, for most of the showers in this land come in the form of snow.

It seems that the natives have an estufa for every fifteen or twenty residents, built underground, with heavy timbers, roofed, and all lined with slabs in such a way as to keep so warm that in the coldest weather they sweat while naked, in these estufas. The Indians spin cotton and weave cloth. They say, however, that they obtain part of the cotton in trade from the province of Mohose [Hopi], which is a temperate land. The clothing which the men and women wear is made of agave fiber, so well carded that it resembles coarse linen.

THE PEOPLE ARE PURE MEXICANS IN EVERYTHING, AND VERY INDUSTRIOUS.

Men and women are pure Mexicans in the way they walk, cry, and even in their dwellings, but neater than the Mexicans. They are very industrious.

We learned from the interpreters that two of Coronado's captains were in this pueblo for two years, that from here they went to discover some provinces,[71] and that when Coronado was at Puala de los Mártires (where the friars had been killed) he came to the above-mentioned pueblo of Acoma, made war on the inhabitants, and they surrendered. In Acoma, he was informed that the inhabitants of Puala, who are Tiguas, and those of the surrounding district, had killed ten of the horses left there by Coronado for the people in the garrison. When Coronado heard of the incident, he set out for Puala, whose people are Tiguas, and besieged them near a pueblo encircled by mountains. He pressed them so hard that those who did not die at the hands of the Spaniards—Coronado's people, whom the natives called Castillos—died of hunger and thirst. (Chamuscado and his men were not ignorant of this. They knew it all, but refrained from telling about it in order that others might come to settle the land.) Finally the people of Puala surrendered and threw themselves on Coronado's mercy, and he took as

---

70. Aguico is identical with Háwikuh. Luxán means that they went four leagues to Aguico from Mátsaki, the pueblo in which they had "a row of houses" during their stay there. It was the first pueblo that would be seen in coming from the east.

71. Here Luxán inserts a paragraph about Tiguex on the Río Grande which had served as Coronado's headquarters during his stay in New Mexico. The region he went to discover was the kingdom of Quivira.

many, both men and women, in his service as were necessary, and returned to this pueblo. From here he set out for the valley of Samora, which must be one hundred leagues distant from this province.[72]

THE PEOPLE OF THESE PROVINCES ARE HEALTHY, AS THE SPANIARDS DID NOT SEE ANY CRIPPLES OR INVALIDS, BUT ONLY MANY OLD PEOPLE.

In this pueblo,[73] about one-fourth of a league away, there is a large marsh with many water holes which enables the natives to irrigate some fields of corn. There are two canals with water and ample facilities for building a city or town, as there are abundant woods and good lands. The people are extremely healthy, for neither in this province nor in the others we crossed have we seen any sick or crippled persons, but only many old ones.

Here in this pueblo of Aguico and in the others are some small prayer houses where the Indians speak to the devil and give him offerings of ollas and earthen bowls containing pinole and other vegetables. Father Fray Bernardino erected a cross † next to one of them, and when some of the servants went inside to get earthen bowls, the old men said the devil was no longer in the house, that he was angry because of the cross † which the Christians had erected, and because they had entered his house.

We now determined to go to the province of Mojose and to the mines, because if there was silver this would be the best land in the Indies. Here, as I have stated, on the seventh of April, we decided to go to the aforesaid province: Captain Antonio de Espejo, Diego Pérez de Luxán, Bernardino de Luna, Gregorio Hernández, Gaspar de Luxán, Francisco Barreto, Juan López de Ibarra, Alonso de Miranda, and Juan Fernández.[74] Father Fray Bernardino Beltrán, Miguel Sánchez and his sons and nephew, and Juan de Frías did not wish to proceed farther but wanted to go back to Santa Bárbara, so there was much controversy.

On this day we reached the pueblo of Alona, the dwelling place of the Mexican Christian Indian brothers, Andrés and Gaspar, who had been left there by Coronado. They told us that in the province of Mojose the Indians were awaiting us in order to give battle, that we

72. This is a very sketchy account of the Coronado expedition. For greater detail, see Herbert E. Bolton, *Coronado, Knight of Pueblos and Plains* (Albuquerque, 1949).

73. Evidently Háwikuh. The water supply Luxán speaks of must have been that of Ojo Caliente, where there is now a Zuñi farming village.

74. Espejo adds the name of Pedro Hernández de Almansa, making the number in the group ten. Espejo's "Narrative," pp. 226.

should go prepared, and that some friends from this province wanted to go with us. So at their request we waited for two days.

WHILE IN SEARCH OF THE PROVINCE OF MOJOSE THE SPANIARDS WERE AC-
COMPANIED BY EIGHTY SUMI INDIANS WITH BOWS AND ARROWS TO HELP
THEM AGAINST MOJOSE. THE SUMI PEOPLE ARE VERY GENEROUS, SO WHEN
OTHER INDIANS COME TO THEIR HOMES THEY FEED THEM; THUS FAMINE
OR PLENTY IS SHARED. THEY HAVE ONLY ONE WIFE EACH, AND SO FORTH.

Leaving this locality for the province of Mojose, we traveled six leagues and stopped at a small lagoon which had some water holes. We named this place the Laguna de los Ojuelos. The day on which we departed was the eleventh of April. Eighty men carrying bows and arrows came with us from the pueblos of Sumi, saying they wanted to help us against Mojose. These good people of Sumi are very generous, for whenever any Indians come to their homes they give them food at once, and thus they share in common, either famine or abundance. They have only one wife each, the same as Christians.

We left this place on the twelfth of April and went five leagues to camp at a water hole. We named this spot El Cazadero, because the friendly Indians caught many rabbits which they presented to us. Our direction was continuously toward the west.

We set out from El Cazadero on the thirteenth, and having traveled five leagues, stopped at a small marsh where we made some dams with our hands so the horses might drink. Seven of us arrived here. The other three had gone with the captain on this day after two Conchos Indian servants who had fled the night before. On the way we met an Indian, accompanied by three women and three boys, from the province of Sumi, who were coming from Mojose. They told us that two pueblos, the largest in that province, were waiting to make war upon us; that for this purpose there was a great gathering of wild and warlike people to oppose us; that the other pueblos were awaiting developments since they had not decided either for war or peace; and that the children, women, and girls were in a sierra with their flocks.[75]

We stayed here in this place two days with the friendly Indians, waiting for our companions. When they arrived and brought the Indians, we made preparations to fight. Since about thirty of these friendly natives had come with us from the province of Sumi, influenced by

75. These flocks were presumably turkeys. Coronado had brought the first sheep to New Mexico, but there is no evidence that any of them survived his stay. The sheep industry of the Southwest dates from Oñate's time.

the Mexican Indian brothers, Andrés and Gaspar—two of those left by Coronado—and these warriors showed a fine spirit, saying they wanted to die wherever the Castillos died, we cut up pieces of red felt and put a colored sign on each man's head so that all could be recognized, and determined to attack unless the enemy submitted peacefully at once. There were games and a playful spirit among the friendly Indians.

We left this place in good order on the sixteenth of the month, proceeded six leagues, and camped at a small marsh where there was a foul-smelling pool. So we called it El Ojo Hediondo.

THE SPANIARDS ARRIVED IN THE PROVINCE OF MOJOSE AND MANY INDIANS CAME TO MEET THEM PEACEFULLY WITH PRESENTS OF FOOD, AND SO FORTH.

Setting out from this place on the seventeenth of April, we traveled six leagues and halted in the province of Mojose, at a pueblo that had been attacked and destroyed by Coronado because the natives had killed five of the nine men he had sent to discover Mojose while he remained in the province of Sumi.[76] When Coronado heard the news he fell upon

76. In the 1929 edition of the Luxán "'Journal," published as Volume I of the Quivira Society series, we gave it as our opinion that "The name of this destroyed pueblo is not recorded. It has been assumed that the pueblo first visited by Tovar and Padilla of Coronado's expedition was Awatobi, but Luxán shows plainly that this was not the case. Probably the settlement here referred to as a league from Awatobi was Kawaika or Mishiptonga, the ruins of which have been more or less excavated."

Since then, the pueblo of Awátovi—to use the spelling now preferred—has been studied extensively, the ruins excavated by the Peabody Museum of Harvard University, and the subject of Awátovi and Spanish contacts with it analyzed in some detail. This has resulted in another interpretation of Luxán's account, namely, that it should not be taken to mean that Coronado's men "destroyed" any such pueblo in 1540, but that the people of Awátovi, some three miles down the rim, had spotted the Espejo party and had come out to meet them. They hold that Luxán's story does not fit in with the known Coronado documents, and that, during the forty-three years since the time of Coronado's adventure, many "stories full of truths, half-truths, and complete fabrications" had doubtless sprung up, both among natives and Christians, and that Luxán's account of a Hopi pueblo "destroyed" by Coronado is one of these.

In weighing these views, which should be duly considered, it is well to recall that Luxán, writing of events as they took place, is the best and most reliable chronicler of the Espejo expedition, that he gives the most detailed account of where the party went and what happened, and that he states specifically the "destroyed" pueblo "was and is situated a league from the pueblo of Aguato." We must remember also that Castañeda, the Coronado historian, wrote many years after the event, and that there is no evidence that he told everything that happened, such as recording the incidents that were unfavorable to Coronado and his lieutenants. This is fully demonstrated in the records of the Coronado and López de Cárdenas trials, as well as by the many details of outrages against the Indians of Tiguex province revealed in these same documents. Bolton, *op. cit.*, pp. 201-230.

For further discussion, see Erik K. Reed, "Kawaika-a in the Historic Period," *American Antiquity*, vol. VIII (1942), pp. 119-120; J. O. Brew in "Franciscan Awatovi . . . ," *Papers of the Peabody Museum of American Archaeology and Ethnology*, vol. 36 (Cambridge, 1949), pp. 5-7.

the pueblo with his men and attacked and destroyed it. It was and is situated a league from the pueblo of Aguato.[77] Our arrival being noticed by the natives, a few of the bravest came out to meet us. Even though it was almost sunset, so many people came from Aguato in a short time with tortillas, tamales, roasted green-corn ears, corn and other things, that although our friends were many, they had half of it left over. The natives asked for peace, and with trembling said it was a rumor falsely raised against them that they wanted to make war on us.

THERE ARE IN THE PROVINCE OVER TWELVE THOUSAND INDIANS WITH BOWS AND ARROWS, AND MANY CHICHIMECOS; AND ALL TREMBLED BEFORE TEN MEN. BY COMMAND OF THE SPANIARDS, THEY BUILT A STOCKADE OF DRY MASONRY IN ONE DAY.

The lord willed that the whole land should tremble for ten lone Spaniards, when there were over twelve thousand Indians in the province, armed with bows and arrows, and many Chichimecos, who are called Corechos. Thus the next morning the caciques of all the pueblos came and tremblingly asked for peace,[78] and the Indians brought large quantities of provisions. We asked them to build a stockade of dry masonry in which to keep the horses, because the friendly Indians told us that we could not trust these people. It was built this same day, which was Thursday the eighteenth [of April].

On Friday morning disagreement arose among the soldiers in regard to a proposal for sending their goods to the stockade and leaving two harquebusiers with the servants to guard the camp and the horses, while the other eight men went with the friendly Indians to inspect the pueblo of Aguato. Finally we decided to visit the said pueblo all together, with our entire camp, because even though we were only ten companions we appeared to be many more with our servants and the swarm of friendly Indians.[79]

---

77. Aguato was the pueblo of Awátovi, destroyed in 1700. It was situated on a mesa about nine miles southeast of Walpi, near modern Tallahogan.

78. This evidence as to how the pueblos of New Mexico were governed corroborates that given by Castañeda, who noted that the Zuñi Indians did not have chiefs as in New Spain, but that they were ruled by a council of elders. "They have no rulers as in New Spain, but are governed by the counsel of their oldest men. They have their priests, whom they call papas, who preach to them. These priests are the old men. . . . " Hammond and Rey, *Narratives of the Coronado Expedition*, p. 253; Hodge, *History of Hawikuh*, p. 44.

79. The reference is to the friendly Zuñi Indians who accompanied Espejo's party to the Hopis, glad to have such powerful support.

TEN LONE MEN ENTERED THE GREAT PUEBLO OF AGUATO; THE NATIVES
WERE SO AFRAID THAT, EXCEPT FOR SOME OLD MEN, THE INHABITANTS DID
NOT APPEAR, BUT REMAINED HIDDEN IN THEIR HOUSES.

Thus we left on the morning of this day, which was Friday, the
nineteenth, and went over to the great pueblo of Aguato, which must
have been a league from where we set out. Carrying our flag unfurled,
we halted with our camp and only the ten companions entered the
pueblo. The fear of the natives was so great that, except for an old
man here and there, the people did not appear; they remained hidden
in their houses.

POSSESSION WAS TAKEN IN THE PLAZA FOR HIS MAJESTY. THE SPANIARDS
PITCHED CAMP ONE-FOURTH OF A LEAGUE AWAY. IT WAS HARDLY ESTAB-
LISHED WHEN ONE THOUSAND INDIANS CAME, LADEN WITH PROVISIONS,
BLANKETS, AND SO FORTH.

Possession was taken for his Majesty in the main plaza with a salvo
of harquebus shots. We established our camp one-fourth of a league
from the said pueblo. Hardly had we pitched camp when about one thousand Indians came, laden with corn, ears of green corn, pinole, tamales,
and firewood. They offered all these as a gift, together with six hundred
pieces of cotton cloth, small and large, white and figured, so that it
was a marvelous sight to behold.[80]
They brought so much food that we told them to stop bringing more
as it was going to waste. Likewise they brought some venison and dried
rabbit meat, for there was no time to go hunting as we decided to pass
on immediately to the other pueblos.

THE SPANIARDS WENT TO THE PUEBLO OF GASPE; HALF A LEAGUE BEFORE
THEY REACHED IT, MANY PEOPLE CAME OUT TO MEET THEM WITH FOOD,
AND SO FORTH.

We left this pueblo and locality on the twenty-first of April, and,
after traveling two leagues, reached the pueblo of Gaspe, which is very
high and rocky.[81] About half a league from the pueblo many people,
men and women, came to meet us all along the way until we reached
it. Each one carried his bag and bowl (*jicara*) of pinole, scattering some

---

80. Obregón states that the Indians gave the Spaniards "a thousand cotton blankets,
many pieces of cloth, and well-tanned deerskins." *Obregón's History*, p. 329.
81. The Hopi pueblo of Walpi. Obregón called it Xoalpe and Oalpes. *Loc. cit.*

of it on the road and some over us and on the horses and servants.[82] All this is done as a sign of peace. When we arrived we looked like clowns in carnival time. Along the way were many large earthen jars with water and much food, which was very surprising.

WHEN THE SPANIARDS ARRIVED AT THE PUEBLO MORE THAN ONE THOUSAND INDIANS CAME, LADEN WITH WATER AND SUPPLIES IN ABUNDANCE, AND SO FORTH.

Upon our arrival, more than one thousand souls came, laden with very fine earthen jars containing water, and with rabbits, cooked venison, tortillas, atole (corn-flour gruel), beans, cooked calabashes, and quantities of corn and pinole, so that, although our friends were many and we insisted our hosts should not bring so much, heaps of food were left over. Then they presented us with six hundred pieces of figured and white cloth and small pieces of their garments.

IN THE PLAZA WAS A WHITEWASHED CROSS WITH AN INSCRIPTION AFTER OUR FASHION. THE INSCRIPTION AND THE GROUND WERE COVERED [WITH MEAL AND FEATHERS]. POSSESSION WAS TAKEN FOR HIS MAJESTY.

This day we marched through the town with our flag unfurled, armed for battle. In the main plaza, there was a cross †, newly erected and whitewashed, with an inscription after the Spanish custom, with many feathers and much pinole scattered over the sign and on the ground. Here possession was taken in the name of his Majesty with a salvo of harquebus shots. Horses cannot be kept in this pueblo owing to the lack of water, which the inhabitants obtain from very deep wells.

THE LAND IS VERY FERTILE FOR EVERYTHING PLANTED; THE CLIMATE IS TEMPERATE, AND SO FORTH.

The soil is very fertile for corn, cotton, and everything sown in it, as this is a temperate land. The natives cultivate sandy places without difficulty because they carefully guard the moisture from the snow.

---

82. This was sacred prayer meal—corn meal—commonly used in many Pueblo rites and ceremonies, as an offering to their deities. There is virtually no Pueblo Indian ceremony of which it does not form a part. *Benavides' Revised Memorial;* Elsie Clews Parsons, *Pueblo Indian Religion.*

THE PEOPLE ARE HEALTHY.

The people are very healthy. The men cover their privy parts with a piece of cloth similar to a hand towel, figured and with tassels. When they feel cold they wear cotton blankets.[83] The women are always well dressed and have their hair done up in puffs.[84] Their houses are of stone and mud, small, which is due to the lack of lumber,[85] and in appearance and in their estufas they are quite similar to those of the province of Sumi.

THE SPANIARDS REACHED TWO PUEBLOS, THE LARGEST OF WHICH IS CALLED COMUPAUI AND THE OTHER MAJANANI. THE NATIVES CAME FORTH TO RECEIVE THEM WITH WATER AND PROVISIONS.

We left this pueblo[86] the next day, in the morning, which was Monday, April 22. After going two leagues, one of them through cotton fields, we came to a plain between two pueblos separated scarcely half a league from each other. The larger of these is called Comupaui and the other Majanani.[87] Here in these two pueblos the natives came to meet us with the same sort of things as in the others. They brought us plenty of water in large earthen jars and vessels, as well as calabashes, cooked vegetables, and corn, and whatever was necessary, as in the other pueblos.

83. The growth and use of cotton by the Pueblo Indians was extensive and continued down to the middle of the nineteenth century. Only the introduction of sheep and the availability of yarn and cloth at trading posts caused its decline. See Volney H. Jones, "A Summary of Data on Aboriginal Cotton in the Southwest," The University of New Mexico Bulletin, *Anthropological Series*, vol. I, no. 5 (1936); and F. L. Lewton, "The Cotton of the Hopi Indians: A New Species of Gossypium," *Smithsonian Miscellaneous Collections*, vol. 60 (1912).

84. This Hopi custom was in vogue until modern times and they are still worn on ceremonial occasions. The puffs, or cart wheels, symbolized the flower of the squash, the emblem of fertility, and were worn by marriageable girls. Hodge, *Handbook*, vol. I, p. 19; Edward P. Dozier, *The Hopi-Tewa of Arizona* (1954), pp. 301, 317, 328-329.

85. That is, on account of the scarcity of timbers suitable for roofing larger rooms, as there were no forests or trees near the Hopi pueblos.

86. Gaspe, or Walpi. It will be noted that the villages of Hano and Sichúmovi on First Mesa, and Shipaúlovi on Second Mesa are not mentioned by Luxán, as they were built much later, *Benavides Revised Memorial*, p. 299.

87. Comupaui is the present Shongópovi, and Majanani is identical with Mishóngnovi. They are situated on the Middle or Second Mesa. Obregón confused these difficult Hopi names in his text, which should read: Alpe (Walpi), Moxonami (Majanani, Mishóngnovi), Xomupa (Comupaui or Shongópovi), and Olayyola (Olalla or Oraibi). *Obregón's History*, pp. xii, 329; Hodge, *Handbook*, vol. I, p. 871, vol. II, pp. 553-554; *Benavides' Revised Memorial*, p. 299.

Possession was taken; the Spaniards found two crosses newly erected like the previous ones.

We took possession here as elsewhere. The Indians brought us about six hundred large and small pieces of cotton cloth. We found here two crosses, newly erected like the previous ones. These two pueblos are situated in two very stony sierras which the horses climb with difficulty.

The Spaniards went to the pueblo of Olalla, the largest in the province.

We left this place on the twenty-fourth, traveled three leagues, and reached the pueblo of Olalla, which is the largest in the province.[88] We established our camp at its foot, close to a well with water, to which one descends by stone steps. The water gave out this day, and then the natives brought us some for the animals, in gourds and kettles, from other wells. The greatest handicap in this land is the lack of water.

The Spaniards were well received and given food and blankets.

The natives received us very well here, giving us raw and prepared food in great abundance. They presented us with over eight hundred pieces of cotton cloth, large and small, as well as a quantity of spun and raw cotton which, with some other mantas, we gave to our allies.[89]

Possession was taken.

We stayed two days in this place and, as there were no more pueblos in this province, we procured guides to go to the mines. Possession was taken in the name of his Majesty as in the other pueblos and we returned to Aguato.

Each pueblo of this province is ruled by three or four caciques. The land is more temperate than Sumi.

Every pueblo in this province is ruled by three or four caciques and the cacique has as little power as the ordinary Indian; hence they are

88. Olalla is the present Oraibi, the largest and most populous of the Hopi villages until the split, in 1906, between the conservatives and progressives (the Hostiles and the Friendlies), when the conservatives left the old pueblo and founded the villages of Hotevila and Bakabi. Hodge, *Handbook*, vol. II, pp. 142-143; *Benavides' Revised Memorial*, p. 299.

89. Espejo says they were given four thousand cotton blankets (mantas), "colored or white, hand towels with tassels at the ends. . . ." These evidently were the robes and sashes woven of native cotton used in their ceremonies by many of the Pueblos, who procured them through trade. Espejo's "Narrative," pp. 226-227.

all equal.[90] The land is more temperate than that of Sumi. The inhabitants are idolaters as in the province of Sumi. They have shrines along the roads and houses of worship in the pueblos where they talk to the devil.

THE CAMP WAS DIVIDED AND ONE-HALF WENT TO DISCOVER THE MINES.

We stopped two days in this pueblo and the next day, Saturday, the twenty-seventh of the month, went back to the pueblo of Aguato. Even though it was already late, the natives brought us a large quantity of food. We remained here two days, learning through the interpreters that the mines were far away, that there was a scarcity of water, and that the route was over difficult ridges. Therefore, seeing that the [entire] camp could not go, as this would put it in danger, we commended ourselves to God and decided that five of our party of ten men, with the friendly Indians, should return with the camp to the province of Sumi (which, as I have said, was called Síbula by the natives), while the other five were to go to discover the mines. This plan was carried out, although we saw that it was a matter of great temerity to penetrate into the midst of so many barbarous people who could kill us by merely throwing handfuls of dirt. So of the fifteen in our party, we found ourselves divided into two groups. Thus there were left with the camp Gaspar de Luxán, Pedro Hernández de Almansa, Alonso de Miranda, Juan López de Ibarra, and Pedro Hernández; to the mines went Captain Antonio de Espejo, the alguacil mayor Diego Pérez de Luxán, the alférez Gregorio Hernández, Bernardino de Luna, and Francisco Barreto. They all left at the same time, each one on his trip, on the last day of April of the said year, 1583.[91]

NAMES OF THE CACIQUES OF THIS PROVINCE OF SUMI, OR CÍBOLA, WHICH IS ALL THE SAME.

The caciques of the pueblos of this province are the following. In Aguato: Aco, Onala, Na-mo-sse, Calajo;[92] and in the pueblo of Oalpe

90. The word for the ordinary Indian is macegual (Aztec *macehual or macehualli*), meaning a vassal, a commoner, hence signifying the democratic nature of Pueblo government. See Parsons, *Pueblo Indian Religion*.

91. The first group returned to Zuñi, while the others turned westward to explore the mines that had been reported by the natives.

92. J. O. Brew, who conducted the excavations at Awátovi, has some interesting comments on these names, especially on that of Na-mo-sse. "Franciscan Awatovi," *op. cit.*, p. 7.

[Walpi]: Cocopi, Mahanami, Gongua, Quitigua, Jimopaue, Turri, Amaulase, Enjola, and Aougamina.

We five companions left the pueblo of Aguato for the mines on the last day of April, taking along with us the necessary guides.[93] On this day we went five leagues to a water hole which was insufficient for the horses, so they were two days without water. We named this place El Ojo Triste.[94]

THE SPANIARDS REACHED A LARGE AND BEAUTIFUL RIVER WHICH FLOWS FROM THE SOUTH TOWARD THE NORTH. ITS SHORES ARE SETTLED BY WAR- LIKE MOUNTAIN PEOPLE.

We left this place on the first of May, two hours before daybreak. Overcome by drowsiness and out of consideration for the guides, as well as because of the bad road, we halted midway for the siesta. We traveled ten leagues today and reached a beautiful and exceptionally fine river, almost as large as the Del Norte, containing many groves of cotton- woods and willows.[95] This river flows from the south toward the north. Its shores are settled by warlike, mountain people.

We left this spot on the second and continued six leagues, camping at a deep stream where there were many large pools of rainwater which would provide an ample supply throughout the year.[96] This route is rich in abundant pastures and juniper forests. These trees bear a fruit the size of hazelnuts and are quite tasty.[97]

We set out from this locality on the fourth of the month and went six leagues over a mountain dense with juniper forests and ash trees.[98] We found many water holes and small marshes,[99] stopping by a large

93. In the original publication of Luxán's "Journal" in 1929, we assayed an identifica- tion of Espejo's route to the mines, based on information then available. Subsequently, Miss Katharine Bartlett of the Museum of Northern Arizona in Flagstaff has worked out a new and probably definite trail of how they reached the mines, based on a study of the local terrain and its flora. Though she presents three alternative routes, she believes that Espejo followed her first choice. "Notes Upon the Routes of Espejo and Farfán to the Mines in the Sixteenth Century," *New Mex. Hist. Rev.*, vol XVII (1942), pp. 21-36.

94. From Awátovi, Espejo's party, with Hopi guides, headed for Sunset Crossing of the Little Colorado, modern Winslow. El Ojo Triste may have been Comar spring or Pyramid Butte spring.

95. The Little Colorado.

96. Possibly Sunset Tanks in Salt Creek canyon, where there is permanent water.

97. Miss Bartlett, on the authority of Mr. A. F. Whiting, curator of botany at the Museum of Northern Arizona, states that there are at least two species of junipers with large single-seeded edible berries in this area, *Juniperus utahensis* and *Juniperus mono- sperma*. She adds that some of the berries remain on the trees until springtime.

98. The party may have been entering Chavez Pass canyon.

99. Miss Bartlett writes that Luxán's description here well depicts such places as "Jay Cox Tank, Hay Lake, Cow Lake, etc. The lakes are very shallow even when full." Bartlett, *op. cit.*, p. 29.

and attractive marsh two leagues in circumference, surrounded by numerous pines, junipers, and water pools which can be utilized for irrigation.[100]

The Spaniards discovered a temperate land with warlike mountain people.

This region is inhabited by mountain people, for it is a temperate land. During the night some of them approached our horses but fled when they heard unfamiliar sounds.

We left this place on the fifth of the month and traveled seven leagues through dense, rough woodlands with bad trails, a very dangerous route in an enemy country.[101] We descended a slope so steep and perilous that a mule belonging to Captain Antonio de Espejo fell and was dashed to pieces. We went down by a ravine so bad and craggy that we descended with difficulty to a fine large river which runs from northwest to southeast.[102] At this place the river is surrounded by an abundance of grapevines and by many walnut and other trees. This is a warm land in which there are parrots.[103] The whole region is warm rather than cold. This river we named El Río de las Parras.

The Spaniards met warlike mountain people who fled at first and then offered peace near a large painted cross with four small ones on the sides. They had crosses on their heads.

We found a ranchería belonging to a mountain people who abandoned it and fled from us, as we could see by their tracks. We saw plants of wild flax similar to that of Spain and numerous prickly pears.[104]

We left this place on the seventh of the month and, after going six leagues, reached a little marsh which flows into a small water ditch

---

100. Only Mormon lake in this region, Miss Bartlett points out, is large enough to fit Luxán's description, even though this was in May when every lake and pool would be full.

101. The region between Mormon lake and Rattlesnake tank, observes Miss Bartlett, "is full of cinder cones and weathered lava flows, and it is rough. The forest is thick and would have been dangerous, because they could not see an enemy approaching."

102. Probably Beaver creek, which the party reached by one of its steep tributary canyons.

103. There are no parrots in this region today, but it could have been the Thick-Billed *Rhynchopsitta pachyryncha*, which is found in southern Arizona and northern Mexico. Bartlett, *loc. cit.*

104. Prickly pears are a prominent feature of the vegetation in the Beaver creek area, even today.

where we discovered an abandoned pueblo.[105] We traveled at times close to the Parras river. The mountain people, who were in flight, as I said above, awaited us midway, near this river. They had built a hut of branches. Six paces from it was a large painted cross, with four small ones on the sides. All the men, women, and children were seated in a row, with their heads low, singing of the peace they wished with us. They had crosses of colored sticks on their heads and gave us bowls of mescal with piñon nuts and bread made from them.

THE NATIVES GAVE ORES IN ADDITION TO FOOD AS A SIGN OF PEACE; MANY WENT TO POINT OUT THE MINES. LATER THE SPANIARDS FOUND FRIENDLY MOUNTAIN PEOPLE.

They gave us ores as a sign of peace and many of them came to show us the mines. In this locality we found many peaceful mountain people who received us well. They had planted corn. We named this marshy site La Ciénega de San Gregorio.[106]

We left this place on the eighth and traveled four leagues to the mines on the mission of discovery we had undertaken. Midway we found a large river, carrying a great volume of water, which flowed from north to south. We called it El Río de los Reyes.[107] Close to it was a marsh into which flowed a stream of water.

MANY MOUNTAIN PEOPLE AWAITED THE SPANIARDS ALONG THE ROUTE, WITH CROSSES ON THEIR HEADS, EVEN THE CHILDREN. THEY GAVE OF WHAT THEY HAD. THEY WENT WITH THE VISITORS TO THE MINES, WHICH WERE IN A VERY ROUGH SIERRA; AND SO POOR THAT NOT A TRACE OF SILVER WAS FOUND—ONLY COPPER, AND LITTLE OF THAT.

Many mountain people waited for us with crosses painted on their heads, even the children. They gave us of what they had. Many of them accompanied us to the mines, which were in a very rough sierra,[108] and so worthless that we did not find in any of them a trace of silver, as they

105. Erik K. Reed, archaeologist of the U.S. National Park Service, has suggested that this could be Montezuma's well, with its famous ditch. There is a large pueblo ruin beside the well, and there are many others down the valley. Bartlett, *op. cit.,* p. 30.

106. A swampy place along the river, Beaver creek, down which the party was descending, in the direction of Montezuma's castle.

107. This was the Verde river.

108. Miss Bartlett locates the mines on the east side of Black mountain, five or six miles west of the Verde river.

were copper mines, and poor.[109] We therefore determined to return to the camp at once. On our way we stopped for the night in the rancherías of these mountaineers, who showed us much friendship. Nevertheless, we slept with great caution and kept better guard than in the past.[110]

We left this locality on May ninth, proceeding in the direction of the province of Sívola, which the natives call Sumi, where we had sent the other companions. The mountaineers came out along the way to receive us. We stopped one league and a half from the pueblo of Aguato by a small marsh. The natives of this pueblo, which, as I have stated, is in the province of Mojose, at once sent us corn and many loaves of corn flour. We traveled very fast and reached Síbola, the pueblo of Alona, on the seventeenth of the month. Here we found our companions in good health and well treated by these people, who were loyal and faithful. They had not yet met the father or the other five companions.

A FRIAR REBELLED AND WAS FOLLOWED BY SOME PEOPLE. FOR THIS REASON THE TRIP IN SEARCH OF THE REPUTED MINES WAS NOT CONTINUED, AND THE PEOPLE TURNED BACK.

In order to decide on our course we agreed to attend mass together in this pueblo of Masa[111] on Trinity Sunday. Then, after hearing mass, we decided—inasmuch as we had come from lands so far away and had spent our fortunes, and since we had not found mines aside from one lone discovery—that we should go together to the provinces of the Tiguas and Maguas to look for them, since these provinces were situated on our route and there were reports of mines there. For it was evident that if there were none, the land could not be settled nor all of these many souls saved. If our Lord willed that mines should not be located, we would go back to the land of peace by way of the province of the buffalo [i.e., the Pecos]. To this proposal the father (may God forgive him) and those who followed his views—who will be named here—replied that they were not willing to look for mines, but would return to the land of peace.

It seemed that the one who was leading this dissension was Gregorio

109. The discovery was in the vicinity of modern Jerome, where fortunes have been made in recent times. Major value of the ore is copper, with an admixture of silver.

110. These Indians may have been the Yavapai. See Bandelier, *Final Report*, Pt. I, p. 109.

111. Masa is the pueblo called Masaque by Obregón. It is Mátsaki, one of the Zuñi group abandoned at the time of the Pueblo revolt in 1680. *Obregón's History*, p. 326; Hodge, *History of Hawikuh, New Mexico*, p. 60 ff.

Hernández, whom we had appointed alférez mayor in the name of his Majesty in order to avoid factions and discord. He claimed to be a Galician. He told everybody it was possible to escape from the land alive, and in this manner he was trying to promote his own interests and sow dissension among all. Hence he rebelled and raised the flag, demanding that the captain and the other comrades follow the king's standard. He declared that he meant to take the father and Miguel Sánchez' wife, who was pregnant, to the land of peace. Hernández was requested and ordered under penalty of death, loss of property, and conviction of treason to continue the discovery of the land, for which purpose he had been given the said flag and had taken the oath of loyalty. Since he would not desist but insisted on leaving, the flag was taken away from him by force. He was not arrested or punished, because we were so few, and also because we did not wish to cause disturbances among the natives. With him went Miguel Sánchez Valenciano, Lázaro Sánchez, his son Miguel Sánchez Nebado, and his nephew Cristóbal Sánchez, both native mestizos; also a certain Juan de Frías, a native of Aranda de Duero; and the father. The same request was made of these followers and a report of the incident was drawn up. We nine men were left alone in the land, with more courage than strength, trusting in God that we might discover whatever there was in that region.[112]

Those left were Captain Antonio de Espejo, resident of Mexico and native of Torre Milan; our alguacil mayor, Diego Pérez de Luxán, and his brother, Gaspar de Luxán, natives of Seville; Bernardino de Luna, from Aragon, native of Villa de Castro; Pedro Hernández de Almansa, from the town of Almansa; Juan López de Ibarra, Biscayan, from the town of Ybar; Alonso de Miranda, Galician, a native of the town of Pontevedra; Francisco Barreto, Algaravian, resident of the city of Tavira; and Juan Fernández, a Portuguese, native of the city of Porto.

On the following day, after Corpus Christi, which was the last of May, we set out from the province of Cíbola, called Sumi, for the provinces of the Tiguas and Maguas. We took an interpreter to pacify the Tiguas, whom we had left in revolt. Their province is the place where the friars had been killed.[113] On our way so much news was brought to us to the effect that all the provinces were waiting to kill us, that it

112. Espejo says nothing of these dissensions, merely noting that Gregorio Hernández returned with Father Beltrán, in spite of the fact that he had been urged to stay. Espejo's "Narrative," p. 229.

113. That is, at the pueblo of Puaray, where Fathers Rodríguez and López had remained in 1582, on the return of Captain Chamuscado and his party to Mexico.

would have frightened any group of persons, even if they had been many, and the more so nine soldier companions, some poorly equipped. But trusting in God we marched steadily toward the place where we were told the largest number of people awaited us.

From the Sumi river previously mentioned, we came to the cultivated fields of Acoma on the fourth of June of the said year where we found the people of the pueblo in rebellion. The next night, before dawn, several Indians fled, laden with blankets and clothes, namely, a free Conchos Indian servant of Captain Antonio de Espejo, and two servants of Diego Pérez de Luxán, a Tonaltecan Indian named Juan García, with his wife Lucía, a native Concha. When the said captain and Diego Pérez de Luxán, their masters, noticed this, they went after the fugitives hurriedly in order that they might not be killed, urging upon their companions special watchfulness. They left on Friday at seven o'clock in the morning, and on Saturday at nine they reached the Del Norte river, believing that the servants were going with the friar and the other rebels. Much diligence was exercised with the native Indians in order that if the fugitives passed by, the natives should not kill them, but just apprehend them. After three days at the Del Norte river, Espejo and Luxán turned back.

At sunset on the day after they had started in pursuit of the Indians, which was Saturday, the Indian Lucía came to the camp saying that the Indians of Acoma had killed her husband because they wanted to steal from the fugitives what they carried. So Gaspar de Luxán and Francisco Barreto went to look for him, but as it was night they were unable to find him. Sunday morning they found him alive, with three arrow wounds, from which he died that day. He stated that he had been shot by the Indians of Acoma because they wanted to take his goods from him; that he had fled, incited by Fray Bernardino Beltrán, who personally had asked him to do so with the promise that they would wait for him on the road and would give him horses with which to travel; and that the Conchos Indian named Juan had returned to Síbola.[114]

The people of Acoma and the neighboring mountain people rebelled on account of this death, and kept shouting at us from the hills night and day. When we reached the Cieneguilla de los Curechos[115] with the

114. Obregón summarizes briefly the story of the attempted escape, told here in such detail by Luxán. *Obregón's History*, p. 332.

115. This was the Cieneguilla del Rosal of Obregón, identical with the modern Acomita, a few miles west of Laguna. *Loc. cit.* The Curechos (Corechos) of Luxán were the Navajo Apaches. Bandelier, *Final Report*, Pt. I, p. 180; Forbes, *Apache, Navaho, and Spaniard*, p. 57.

camp and saw the impudence of the Indians, we decided to give them a surprise that morning. While our mounted men got ready to attack them, for the sierra was close to the camp and was very rough, they surprised us with a shower of arrows and much shouting. When this was heard by the guards, we rushed at once to the horses, firing our harquebuses. For this reason the Indians wounded only one horse, belonging to the captain. They continued to shout at us until daybreak. Half of our men with all the servants went to the ranchería and set fire to the shacks. We destroyed also a very fine field of corn belonging to the natives, something they felt a great deal.

The next day the others went to destroy, and did destroy, another Indian cornfield, although the natives defended it with a fusillade of arrows from a very rough sierra, at the foot of which was the cultivated land. All this was caused by the father and the rebellious ones with him because they had left us. May God preserve us for His holy service and keep us under His protection, for we are truly in distress.

On the afternoon of the following Sunday there were peace parleys between us and the Curechos. It was agreed that they should return to us one of the Curechos women given us at Mojose (belonging to one of the companions, Francisco Barreto, although she had fled from us the morning of the skirmish); and that we should give them a girl we had taken from them. This exchange was left for the following day.

Accordingly, on Monday morning, the Corechos determined to put over a wicked plan. It was as follows: as they had sent the Indian woman belonging to Francisco Barreto to her land, they took one of their relatives and sent her over, wearing her feather crest so that we should not recognize her, with the intention of recovering their own girl and giving us nothing but a discharge of arrows. This was planned with the help of the interpreter, who was another Indian woman (belonging to Alonso de Miranda) and who was trying to escape. The Corechos clamored to make the exchange, and Francisco Barreto took the woman interpreter as well as the one who was to be exchanged, tied with two maguey ropes. He was accompanied by another companion, on horseback.

The Indians did not wish to come down, pretending they were afraid of the horse and that Barreto should ascend the sierra a short distance, after which they would make the exchange. Barreto told his companion to go back, that he wanted to carry out the business alone; and although there was much talk back and forth, the companion obeyed. When Diego Pérez de Luxán saw this, he realized the intention of the Indians, mounted his horse, and went to join Francisco Barreto. The latter had left his sword and harquebus and had the Indian woman tied to his body, as a man inexperienced in war, although a good and brave soldier. He asked Diego Pérez de Luxán to go back. After much discussion he [Luxán] took the woman interpreter, dismounted from his horse, and left his harquebus in the saddle-tree, much against his will and at the entreaty of Francisco Barreto, who, being a Portuguese, thought that all the Indians in the world would not be sufficient to harm him.

The Indians were leading them little by little into the sierra, holding the disguised woman. When they were about to deliver her, she pretended they had let her go. When Diego Pérez de Luxán perceived the scheme and saw that Francisco Barreto had come without arms, he urged that they go down, because the Indians had evil designs and they themselves would not fare well, as they were on foot in the sierra. Francisco Barreto, eager to recover his Indian woman, persisted, requesting Diego Pérez de Luxán to proceed with the business; the treacherous woman interpreter was also urging it insistently. When Diego Pérez de Luxán saw this situation, he determined angrily to continue farther into the sierra, and left Francisco Barreto to bring the woman interpreter with a rope tied to her foot. Then Luxán made a leap, seized the disguised Indian woman by the hair, and at the same time let loose the woman held by Francisco Barreto. The people shouted at Diego Pérez de Luxán, who ran down the sierra with both Indian women. The woman interpreter wrestled with him, took from him a knife that he carried in his boot, and threw it to the Indians. Then, like a lioness, she grasped his sword, seizing it by the guard, which Diego Pérez de Luxán could not prevent without letting the two Indian women escape, because his hands were occupied in holding them. He threw them to the ground and dragged them down the hill, even though the Indians shot many arrows and threw many stones to force him to let the women go. Then Francisco Barreto came and seized the disguised woman, but there was such a discharge of arrows that two pierced his right cheek and right arm. When they had reached the plain, the captain and other companions came to help. With all this, Francisco Barreto had to let go of the Indian woman; if he had not done so, the soldiers might have fared much worse; nevertheless, they regretted very much having lost the woman in the skirmish.

THE SPANIARDS DECIDED TO RETURN BY WAY OF THE THIRTEEN PUEBLOS WHICH THEY HAD PASSED AND LEFT AT WAR. THEIR NAMES ARE: POGUANA, COMISSE, ACHINE, GUAGUA, GAGOSSE, SIMASSA, SUYTE, NOCOCHE, HACALA, TIARA, TAYCIOS, CASSA, AND PUALA, WHERE THE MARTYRDOM OF THE FRIARS TOOK PLACE. THEY COULD NOT SUBDUE THE NATIVES, AND SO FORTH.

Since only eight of us able to fight were left, not counting the sick or wounded, we determined to go back by way of the Tiguas, our enemies. These are the thirteen pueblos where the friars were killed, namely: Poguana, Comise, Achine, Guagua,[116] Gagose, Simassa, Suyte, Nocoche, Hacala, Tiara, Taycios, Casa, and Puala, which is the place where the friars were killed. Diego Pérez de Luxán acted as guide and in two and one-half days brought the camp to the Río del Norte close to the insurgent pueblo of Puaguana.[117] Here we caught three Indians and a few warriors at some huts on the day we arrived, and through them we talked of peace with the Tiguas. In order to reassure them we freed the prisoners. The next day, the twentieth of June, we passed near Puala, where we rested the following day.

EFFORTS WERE MADE TO SUBDUE THESE INDIANS PEACEFULLY, AND ALTHOUGH THEY SAID THEY WERE FRIENDLY, THEY SCOFFED WHEN ASKED FOR FOOD, AND SO FORTH. FOR THIS REASON AND TO AVOID BEING KILLED, THE SPANIARDS DECIDED TO PUNISH THEM.

Efforts were made to have the Indians come peacefully to us, but though they said they were our friends, they would not bring their women to the pueblos. Instead, they remained in the sierra and mocked us. Seeing that unless we administered some punishment they would soon become impudent and try to kill us, we determined to do what I shall record below.

Our camp left this place on the twenty-second of June, going in the direction of the pueblo of Puala. In two pueblos near Puala there were many Indians who said they were our friends, but when we asked them for food they scoffed.

116. Guagua certainly looks and sounds like the modern Kuaua.

117. From the paragraphs that follow, it would seem that Espejo reached the Río Grande below the pueblo of Puala, or Puaray. Cf. Note 49, above; Gallegos' "Relation," p. 104. Bandelier, *Final Report*, Pt. II, p. 225.

When the Spaniards arrived in Puala, [most of] the people were in the sierra and about thirty men were on the roofs; when asked for food, as friends, they scoffed. The Spaniards punished some by garroting them and then setting fire to the pueblo.

Thus we reached Puala. The people were all in the sierra except for some thirty Indians on the flat roofs of their houses. When we asked them for food, as they were our friends, they mocked us like the others. In view of this, the corners of the pueblo were taken by four men, and four others with two servants began to seize those natives who showed themselves. We put them in an estufa. And as the pueblo was large and the majority had hidden themselves there, we set fire to the big pueblo of Puala, where we thought some were burned to death because of the cries they uttered. We at once took out the prisoners, two at a time, and lined them up against some cottonwoods close to the pueblo of Puala, where they were garroted and shot many times until they were dead. Sixteen were executed, not counting those who burned to death. Some who did not seem to belong to Puala were set free. This was a remarkable deed for so few people in the midst of so many enemies.[118]

The news of the punishment spread and all the provinces trembled and received the Spaniards very well. There are five pueblos in this province, Catiste, Gigue, Tipolti, Cochita, Sieharan. The natives brought many turkeys, and so forth.

This day we reached the province of the Quires, the pueblo of La Tiete, where we were well received. The news of what had happened at Puala spread throughout the provinces and the people were very much afraid and all served and regaled us. They brought us many turkeys from this province, in which there are five pueblos: Catiete,[119] Gigue,[120] Tipolti,[121] Cochita,[122] Sieharan.[123]

118. Neither Espejo nor Obregón, whose accounts are indeed much shorter than Luxán's, makes any mention of this second visit to the Tiguas and the resultant difficulty with them.

119. Catiete and La Tiete were doubtless the same pueblo, the names having been confused by the copyist. It is identical with San Felipe, whose tribal name is Katishtya. Oñate spelled it Castixes. The pronunciation of these names is so striking that there can hardly be any doubt that they are one and the same. Cf. Hodge, *Handbook*, vol. II, p. 432.

120. Gigue may be the same as Oñate's Gipuy, one of the predecessors of Santo Domingo. *Ibid.*, vol. I, pp. 492-493.

121. Tipolti, by the process of elimination, may be Santa Ana. It was called Tamy and Tamaya by Oñate. See Hammond and Rey, *Oñate, Colonizer of New Mexico*, pp. 337, 346, 371.

122. Cochita is almost certainly identical with Cochití.

123. Sieharan is probably Zía, or one of the nearby pueblos.

THE SPANIARDS SUMMONED THE TIGUAS TO ACCEPT PEACE, BUT THE LATTER SAID THEY WERE AFRAID AND WOULD NOT COME.

Here we summoned the Tiguas to accept peace. They said they were very afraid of the Castilians and did not dare to come. We stayed in this place until the twenty-sixth of the said month [of June].

NEW ROUTE. THE SPANIARDS WENT IN SEARCH OF THE MINES OF SANTA CATALINA, SO NAMED BY CHAMUSCADO; AND ALTHOUGH THEY FOUND SOME, THE COUNTRY WAS NOT EXPLORED BECAUSE THE MEN WERE SO FEW; BUT NOT MANY PLACES OFFER BETTER CONDITIONS FOR MINES.

We left the above-mentioned pueblos and went to the mines of Santa Catalina, so named by the friars and by Francisco Sánchez Chamuscado. We traveled seven leagues and reached the said pueblo of Santa Catalina on the twenty-seventh.[124] From this pueblo, called [like the mines] Santa Catalina, we went out to examine the land and discovered some ores. We did not dare to explore the region thoroughly because we were so few and it was not feasible for us to separate. But I understand that there are not many places with more favorable conditions for mines.

124. The identification of Espejo's route after leaving the Queres is not very clear. The party did not, in all probability, visit all five of the Queres pueblos mentioned above. Luxán says they remained at the pueblo of La Tiete, that is, San Felipe, until the twenty-sixth. From San Felipe they went to the mines of Santa Catalina on June 27, a distance of seven leagues. Luxán speaks of this place both as "mines" and as a "pueblo." The reference to a "pueblo of Santa Catalina" is made twice, but he gives no further hint as to the nature of the town. It was not identical with Chamuscado's town of the same name.

The next day Espejo's party, says Luxán, went three leagues to the pueblo of Jumea, in the province of Atamues, and then two leagues to the very large pueblo of Pocos, or Pocoje. From there they went seven leagues through a pine forest to Siqui, or Pecos, and thence down the river on the way home. This is Luxán's version. Obregón's is a bit different, while that of Espejo is too abbreviated and confused to be useful.

Erik K. Reed has attempted a reconciliation of Espejo's trip from San Felipe to Pecos as recorded in these various chronicles—Espejo's, Luxán's and Obregón's. After leaving San Felipe, the first stop was at Santa Catalina, seven leagues, probably San Marcos. Thence they went three leagues to the pueblo called Jumea by Luxán and Xameca by Obregón, identifiable with Galisteo. The next stop was two leagues farther on at the large pueblo of Pocos, or Pocoje, so called by Luxán, and Tepocoty by Obregón. This pueblo, therefore, becomes San Cristóbal, from which the soldiers went three leagues the next day to Siqui, or Pecos. Of its identification there is, of course, no doubt. Reed, "The Southern Tewa," El Palacio, vol. 50, pp. 260-262.

The province of the Tanos suffered a similar fate in being called by a variety of terms, due in part to copyists who misread the proper names or to the different sounds picked up by interpreters. Thus Espejo called it the province of the Tamos; Luxán wrote Atamues, and Obregón Tamones, yet there is no doubt of what was meant. It was the Tano province in the Galisteo basin.

No mines were found in a large area covered. There were different sorts of people, some warlike and others peaceful.

We left this place on the first of July and, going three leagues, came to the pueblo of Jumea [Galisteo ?], in the province of the Atamues [Tanos], a people more bellicose than those of the other provinces. They possess well-built houses, as is characteristic of people astute in war, and the flat roofs have drainage troughs. The houses are three and four stories high, with movable ladders, so that when these are raised the inhabitants cannot go up. They wear their hair like the Pataragueyes, with a sort of skull cap made of it. The women are better looking than those of the other provinces; they dress like the others. The natives gave us turkeys, pinole, and some of the other things they had. The women are not at all opposed to hiring themselves out to the men, nor are the men particularly opposed to hiring the women. In all these provinces we found that the people are alike in this practice; that the men take whatever women they like and the latter the men they fancy.

From this pueblo we went two leagues farther for provisions, to the very large pueblo of Pocos [San Cristóbal ?] of this province. It must have over fifteen hundred warriors armed with bows and arrows. The houses are of four and five terraces, with wooden palisades in front of them as a defense in case of war. The inhabitants did not wish to give any provisions to four men who went to ask for them. They said they did not have any, that there was a lack of rain, and they were not certain they would gather any corn. They climbed up their ladders and not one would come down. Thus the Spaniards turned back, not wishing to cause trouble in the land.

We set out from this locality and pueblo on the third of the month and, after going seven leagues, stopped at the pueblo of Siqui,[125] belonging to this province. We went the entire way through a forest of pines, mostly juniper and white pines. The pine trees were all laden with cones the size of unshelled walnuts. Each cone contains at the most about thirteen or fourteen good-sized kernels. This pueblo is very large, similar to the one before. It must have contained about two thousand men armed with bows and arrows. When asked to give us some pinole, the Indians replied that they had none, and acted in the same manner as the people of Pocoje. Thereupon six armed men entered the pueblo, determined to burn it, and the people were so frightened that they gave us the food against their will.

125. Siqui was the pueblo of Pecos.

We left this place on the fifth of the month of July and took two Indians by force to direct us to the buffalo. We traveled six leagues on this day through a very dense forest of white pines and juniper. The trail was bad and the march quite difficult, with the result that when we reached our destination the clothes of those in the train were more in condition to be renewed than repaired. We halted by the Río de las Bacas.[126] It is a medium-sized river with very good water, surrounded by numerous trees, vines, roses, roseberries, and pennyroyal.

We left this locality on the seventh of the month and continued five leagues through the forest and sometimes along the river, stopping by this river at a place which we named Las Roselas.[127]

Proceeding on our way on the eighth, we went five leagues through the forest, by a good trail, stopping by a stream of water which we called El Arroyo de los Alamillos.[128] Leaving this place on the tenth, we traveled six leagues and halted at a stream of water close to a small saline, where we gathered salt to season the meat. We named this place, where there are large holes of brackish water, La Salinilla.[129]

We set out from La Salinilla on the twelfth and went four leagues to a stream lined with cottonwoods. This place we called El Arroyo de las Garrochas, because we found many goad sticks with which the Indians kill the buffalo. The land is all very level, containing fine pastures and many water holes. Through the entire four days of travel we found many buffalo tracks as well as bones and skulls.

Leaving this place on the thirteenth of the month, we went six leagues and camped. This was at the junction of the Río de las Bacas with another fair-sized stream which runs from the east toward the west.[130] We left this locality on the sixteenth and, after going four leagues, stopped by the said river. This place we named El Rastro.

On the seventeenth we started out again and, after traveling six leagues, halted by the same river. This place we called El Mosquitero, because there were a lot of mosquitoes there.

We left it on the eighteenth of the month and went six leagues, halting by the river. We named this place El Mesquital because of the heavy growth of mesquite near by. Leaving El Mesquital on the nineteenth of July, we traveled six leagues, stopping by the same river. We

126. This was the Pecos river.
127. The Spaniards were going southward down the Pecos.
128. Evidently the present Gallinas river, which joins the Pecos about fifteen miles east of Anton Chico. Castañeda, *Our Catholic Heritage in Texas*, vol. I, p. 176.
129. Possibly in the vicinity of Santa Rosa.
130. This might have been in the Fort Sumner area.

gave this place the name of El Carrizal. We left this locality on the twentieth and halted by the river after marching six leagues. We called the place La Ranchería.[131]

Resuming our journey on the twenty-third, we continued six leagues through marshy land along the river. We stopped by the river and named this place El Salado, because the river is more salty here than before, on account of the brackish water from the many springs that empty into it.[132]

We left El Salado on the twenty-fourth and traveled three leagues through the many marshes that we found on our way. We named this place El Ancón de la Laguna, because a lagoon formed a bay near the river.[133]

On the twenty-fifth we continued and went six leagues, halting by the said river close to a marsh. We called the place El Mosquitero, because of the many mosquitoes. In all this trip we did not find any buffalo, nothing but many tracks. Hence we came to a stop, greatly troubled by lack of food.

We left this locality on the twenty-sixth of the month, and after traveling six leagues, stopped by this same river. This place we named El Mesquital, because there were many mesquite trees, although they were small.

We proceeded from there on the twenty-seventh and, after going six leagues, halted by the river at a fresh water inlet with many walnut trees. There was fishing for *mojarra*,[134] which was quite a treat. Leaving here on the twenty-ninth and continuing six leagues, we stopped by the said river. We called the spot El Tunal, because there were many prickly pears.

We set out from El Tunal on the last day of the month of July and, after traveling two leagues, halted by the same river, where a large stream, bordered by many walnut trees, empties into it. We named this place El Dudoso, because we noticed the sierra of the Pataragueyes and wondered whether it was the stream which the native Pataragueyes had told us emptied into this Río de las Bacas. Although the whole

131. Forbes places this ranchería a day's journey below the junction of the Río Hondo and the Pecos, or a few miles south of modern Roswell. Forbes, *Apache, Navaho, and Spaniard*, p. 64. Perhaps it was near the Bottomless lakes.

132. Castañeda identified this stream with Salt creek, which enters the Pecos from the west a dozen miles north of Roswell. Castañeda, *op. cit.*, vol. I, p. 176. If this is correct, the ranchería would have been farther north than located by Forbes, which seems doubtful. We are informed that there are ponds or lakes of brackish water on the west and, in places, on the east side of the Pecos.

133. Assuming that the above identifications are somewhere near the mark, these marshes would have been in the vicinity of modern Artesia.

134. Probably the "cow pilot" fish.

region is full of dung and bones, God willed that we should not see any buffalo.

Continuing on our way on the second of the month [August], we marched five leagues and stopped by the said river. We named the spot Las Vueltas, because the river formed a big bend there. We set forth again on the third, went three leagues, and halted by the river at a place which we called El Mal Bebedero. This was because the horses went there to drink, fell into the river, and made their way out by swimming to another point.

We left this place on the sixth of the month and traveled six leagues, stopping by the river at a spot which we named El Quesital [Mesquital?], because there was a very dense *quesital* there, stretching for more than a league.

We left El Quesital on the seventh and marched six leagues. We met three Jumana Indians, who were out hunting, and we were able to understand them through Pedro, a Pataraguey Indian belonging to Diego Pérez de Luxán. They said that the Río de las Bacas came out very far below the Conchos river; that they would take us by good trails to the junction of the Río del Norte with the Conchos, which is among the Pataragueyes. This brought us no little joy, as men who had eaten nothing but pinole. We halted for the night at a large marsh where there were many water holes, some of brackish water and others not. On account of this we called the site La Ciénega Salada.[135]

We left La Ciénega Salada on the eighth and went five leagues, three of them up a stream. We found many Jumana Indians from the ranchería of the people who were guiding us. They were on their way to the river, to the mesquite trees. We stopped by this stream, where the ranchería was situated.[136] The Indians, men and women, received us with music and rejoicing. As an additional sign of peace and happiness, a dance was held amid the tents of the Indian men and women. We rested for a day because we had an opportunity to catch some catfish, *mojarra*, and sardines;[137] some were half a yard in length, a difficult thing to believe. The food was delicious.

Setting out from this locality on the tenth we proceeded up the river for six leagues before stopping at the source of the stream, near some springs where the water flowed out.[138] On our way we found settled

135. Probably south of the town of Pecos, near Toyah lake, Texas.
136. Evidently Toyah creek.
137. Not true sardines, but perhaps one of the small silvery chubs (*Notropis dilectus*), which formerly abounded in various New Mexican streams.
138. Present Toyahvale, near Balmorhea, Reeves county, Texas.

people of this nation, who in their clothing, appearance, and habitat are similar to the Pataragueyes.

We set out again on the eleventh and went four leagues to a marsh formed by the sierra, where there was a ranchería of the same nation. The people received us with merriment after their custom and presented us with roasted and raw calabashes and prickly pears.

Continuing on the twelfth, we marched four leagues over a bad trail, mountainous and rocky. We stopped at a valley with many holm oaks, where a stream of water flowed. We named this spot El Encinal.[139] That was the first holm-oak grove we had seen in this land.

We left El Encinal on the thirteenth and went eight leagues, most of the way through a canyon with holm-oak groves, wild grapevines, and many Mexican cherry trees with ripe fruit. A stream of water flowed the length of this valley.[140] We stopped at a canyon with holm-oak groves where there was a pool of rain water.

Leaving this place on the fourteenth, we marched eight leagues over plains, stopping at a very large valley where there were some pools of rainwater.

We resumed our journey on the sixteenth and traveled six leagues over bad trails through a very rough sierra. We reached the said Río del Norte nine leagues from the pueblo, which seems to be San Bernardino of the Pataragueyes.[141] All the rancherías there gave us a great reception, according to their custom, and presented us with quantities of ears of green corn, cooked and raw calabashes, and catfish. They put on great dances and other festivities as a sign of peace. The same was done at the pueblo of San Bernardino, where all the caciques of the pueblos came to welcome us. Our feeling of security was so great that we went about almost in shirt sleeves.

We departed from this locality of the pueblo of San Bernardino on the twentieth of the month and traveled nine leagues in two days. On the way and in the said pueblo the natives received us very well, and while we were traveling they brought us fruit of the screw bean, roasted and raw calabashes, ears of green corn, and beans. The cacique of San Bernardino ordered small fish, catfish, and *matalotes*[142] brought to us. We rested here for a day.

---

139. This must have been in the neighborhood of Fort Davis, the only practicable road from present Balmorhea to this point. Castañeda, *op. cit.*, vol. i, p. 179.

140. The present Alamito creek, passing through modern Marfa.

141. In other words, they struck the Río Grande nine leagues north of San Bernardino, possibly near the present Ruidoso or Candelaria, Texas.

142. Another kind of fish.

We set forth on the twenty-second of the month and marched five leagues, well accompanied by natives. We stopped at the Conchos river, at the pueblo of Santo Tomás, where it joins the Río del Norte.[143] Not being able to ford the river because it was too high, we rested here for three days. The companions all traded in blankets, of which the natives had many, buffalo skins, and Turkish bows reinforced with sinews. These are the best and strongest there are in the land that has been discovered. The inhabitants gave us calabashes, beans, and ears of green corn. They are fine, bright people who would readily accept the holy faith.

We left Santo Tomás on the twenty-sixth and traveled eight leagues, coming to a stream of running water where we found an old Toboso Indian. The people had fled, having taken warning from the captives that had been seized there. So we called this stream El Toboso. We left it on the twenty-seventh and went three leagues, stopping by some pools which we named Los Charcos de la Cañada.

Leaving these pools on the twenty-eighth, we traveled six leagues to a spring which issues from a stony hill. Soon two Toboso Indians approached, saying that they were friends and wished to come in peace.[144] We gave them food and sent them away, bidding their people to come, for we were all their friends. Those who were to watch that night chose not to do so and in the morning we found two he-mules and a good war horse belonging to Diego Pérez de Luxán wounded by arrows. The Indians did not kill all the horses, either because they did not want to or because the damage was the work of a spy. The soldiers insisted on taking prisoners, but Diego Pérez de Luxán said that even if the Indians should kill all of his horses, there would be no captives taken on his account. We named the place La Fuente de la Mala Paz.

Setting out on the twenty-ninth, we marched six leagues, stopping at some pools in a plain. There seemed to be plenty of water in them all the year around. This place we named Los Charcos de los Llanos.

We left these pools on the thirtieth of the month and traveled eight leagues, halting at the pools of La Elona, where there was a ranchería of Conchos, friends of the residents of Santa Bárbara. Two leagues from this place there is a very large saline of good salt.

We left this spot on the second of September of the said year and marched five leagues, halting at the pool of El Espíritu Santo.

---

143. Also called San Francisco de la Junta. See p. 163, note 23.
144. The Toboso Indians lived to the north of Santa Bárbara and east of the Conchos river. Forbes, *Apache, Navaho, and Spaniard*, pp. 33 and 36.

We resumed our journey on the fifth of the month and, after going eight leagues, stopped at some very large water pools situated along the way.

We left the pools on the sixth and went another eight leagues, halting at the Florido river. We departed from this place on the seventh and went seven leagues up the river and came to a stop at the said river.

We set out again on the tenth of September and marched nine leagues, stopping at the valley of San Bartolomé, where Diego Pérez de Luxán ended this expedition.

I, Martín de Pedrosa, royal notary, certify that having been ordered by his lordship, Count of Monterrey, viceroy of this New Spain, to search among the papers left by Francisco Domínguez, cosmographer of his Majesty, for those which in any way might relate to the expedition to the provinces of New Mexico, I did so and found this report in precisely the form in which it is transcribed. So that there may be a record of the fact, and by his order, I so certify. Mexico, May 14, 1602. MARTÍN DE PEDROSA, royal notary.

Taken from the original, which remains in possession of the fiscal of his Majesty. I attach my signature in testimony of the truth. MARTÍN DE PEDROSA, royal notary. [Rubric]

REPORT OF ANTONIO DE ESPEJO

REPORT OF THE EXPEDITION WHICH I, ANTONIO DE ESPEJO, RESIDENT OF
THE CITY OF MEXICO, NATIVE OF THE CITY OF CÓRDOBA, MADE AT THE
CLOSE OF 1582 IN COMPANY WITH FOURTEEN SOLDIERS AND A FRANCISCAN
FRIAR TO THE PROVINCES AND SETTLEMENTS OF NEW MEXICO, WHICH I
NAMED NEW ANDALUSIA IN REMEMBRANCE OF MY HOMELAND.[1]

FOR THE BETTER and easier understanding of this report, it should be
noted that in 1581 a Franciscan friar named Agustín Ruíz [Rodríguez],
living in the valley of San Bartolomé, had heard from some Conchos
Indians who were in communication with the Pazaguates, that in a
region to the north there were some unexplored settlements, and he
requested permission to enter them with the purpose of preaching the
gospel to these natives. In June, 1581, having obtained the authorization of his prelate and the viceroy, Count of Coruña, this friar entered
the said settlements in the company of two others, Fray Francisco López
and Fray Juan de Santa María, and with seven or eight soldiers under
the command of Francisco Sánchez Chamuscado, penetrated as far as
the province we named Tiguas, two hundred and fifty leagues north
of the Santa Bárbara mines in the jurisdiction of New Vizcaya, the
starting point of the expedition. There, in Tiguas, the natives killed
Fray Juan de Santa María.[2]

Seeing that the Indians were many and the Spaniards few, the soldiers
and their leader, ready for either peace or war, turned back to those
same Santa Bárbara mines, proceeding from there to Mexico, one hundred and sixty leagues distant, in May 1582, to report to the viceroy.

1. Two copies of Espejo's "Report," with minor textual variants, were printed in
Pacheco and Cárdenas, *Col. Doc. Inéd.*, vol. xv, 101-126 and 163-189. Bolton published
an English translation in his *Spanish Exploration in the Southwest*, pp. 168-192.

The first report of Espejo's journey to be printed appeared in the earliest Madrid
edition of the immensely popular history of Juan González de Mendoza, *Historia de las
Cosas mas notables, Ritos y Costumbres del gran Reyno de la China* . . . (Madrid, 1586).
There were other editions of this work, without Espejo's *Itinerario*, beginning with the
first one issued in Rome in 1585, and many later editions, in Spanish, French, and English,
with it. An English printing of the *Itinerario* was made in London, probably in 1587, for
Thomas Cadman (reprinted in a limited issue by F. W. Hodge in 1928), and Parke's translation of González de Mendoza's "History" appeared in London the next year. The latter
was published by the Hakluyt Society in two volumes in 1853-1854. Henry R. Wagner
gives a lengthy discussion of the subject in *The Spanish Southwest* (1937), vol. I, pp. 116-153.

2. See the Gallegos "Relation," chapters X and XIII. Santa María was killed by the
eastern Tiguas, not by the Tanos, as has been asserted in the past.

The two friars, eager for the salvation of souls, refused to leave and remained in the province of the Tiguas, which had been visited a long time before by Francisco Vázquez Coronado on his way to the conquest and exploration of the pueblos and plains of Cíbola. They thought they would be safe among the natives of that province, and so they stayed, keeping with them three Indian boys and a mestizo. This decision caused grave distress in the Franciscan order, whose members felt sure the Indians would kill the friars and their companions. Because of this fear they sought to find someone who would enter the land of the Tiguas in order to help those who had remained behind and get them out of there.

Another friar of the same order, Fray Bernardino Beltrán, a resident of the convent in the villa of Durango, capital of New Vizcaya, offered to undertake an expedition for this purpose with the authorization and permission of his superior. As I was in that area at the time and had heard about the just and compassionate wishes of the said friar and the entire order, I made an offer—in the belief that by so doing I was serving our Lord and his Majesty—to accompany the friar and to spend a portion of my wealth in defraying his costs and in supplying a few soldiers both for his protection and for that of the friars he meant to succor and bring back, provided that I was given authorization or an order to do so, from the royal authorities, in the name of his Majesty. Captain Juan Ontiveros, his Majesty's alcalde mayor in the towns called Cuatro Ciénegas (situated in the eastern section of the aforementioned jurisdiction of New Vizcaya, seventy leagues from the said mines of Santa Bárbara), when he heard of the pious zeal of the said friar and of my own aim, issued orders and instructions at the request of the said Fray Bernardino, authorizing me to enter that new land with some soldiers, for the purpose of succoring and bringing out the friars and other people who had remained there.[3]

Accordingly, by virtue of this order and commission I enlisted fourteen soldiers, namely, Juan López de Ibarra, Bernardo de Luna, Diego Pérez de Luján, Gaspar de Luján, Francisco Barreto, Gregorio Hernández, Miguel Sánchez Valenciano, his sons Lázaro Sánchez and Miguel Sánchez Nevado, Alonso de Miranda, Pedro Hernández de Almansa, Juan Hernández, Cristóbal Sánchez, and Juan de Frías. I supplied these men or most of them with arms, horses, munitions, provisions, and other necessities for such a long trip over new territory.

3. See Introduction for a discussion of Espejo's permit to enter New Mexico. In the study, *Los Judíos en la Nueva España* (Mexico, 1932), p. 341, Carvajal makes the statement that Espejo went by his authority—"y lo hizo con comisión mia, Antonio de Espejo."

We started our expedition on November 10, 1582, at the valley of San Bartolomé, nine leagues from the mines of Santa Bárbara, with a hundred and fifteen horses and mules, some servants, and quantities of arms, munitions, and provisions. For two days we marched directly north, going five leagues each day, and met numerous Indians of the Conchos nation dwelling in rancherías. Many of them, numbering more than a thousand came out to meet us along the roads we traveled. We learned that these natives lived on rabbits, hares, and deer (which they hunted and found in abundance), and on the corn, calabashes, Castile melons and watermelons (resembling winter melons) which they sowed and cultivated. They also ate fish and mescal, the pulpy part of the agave *(lechuguilla)*, a plant half a yard tall with fleshy green leaves on the stumps. By boiling these plants they made a very sweet preserve, similar to quince preserve, which they called mescal.

These natives go about naked. For houses they have straw huts, and for weapons they have bows and arrows. They are governed by caciques, whom they obey. According to our observation, they had no idols, nor did they practice any form of sacrifice. We gathered together as many natives as we could, erected crosses in their rancherías, and explained to them through interpreters of their own language whom we had brought along, the meaning of the crosses, as well as some other matters pertaining to our holy Catholic faith. They accompanied us from their rancherías for six additional days, in which we went some twenty-four leagues toward the north over territory inhabited by people of this nation. The inhabitants came out to greet us peaceably, the caciques having notified one another of our coming. They all welcomed us and our horses, patting men and beasts with their hands, giving us some of their provisions, and doing so in a very friendly manner.

After these six days of travel we came to another nation of Indians, called Pazaguantes,[4] whose rancherías, huts, and food are like those of the Conchos. We treated them in the same way as we did the Conchos nation. These Indians accompanied us for four days, during which we must have covered fourteen leagues. The caciques notified one another so that each leader would come out to welcome us as the others had done. In the course of this four days' march, we found in certain places many silver lodes of fine quality, according to those who knew about such matters.

On the first day after leaving this nation, we came upon another

4. These were the Cabris of Gallegos, and the Passaguates of Luxán's "Narrative," p. 158, note 14.

people, called Jobosos,[5] who were shy and consequently ran away from their huts in the settled localities through which we passed. It was said they did so because other soldiers had already been there and had carried away some of their people as slaves. We summoned a number of these Indians, offering them presents, and several came to our camp. We gave a few articles to the caciques and explained to them through interpreters that we had not come to take them captive or to do them any harm, which reassured them. We set up crosses in their rancherías and instructed them in some matters relating to God our Lord. They seemed to be pleased and several of them accompanied us thereafter to the limits of their territory. These Indians eat the same type of food as the Pazaguantes, use bows and arrows, and wear no clothes. We traveled for three days in their land, which seemed to have but few people; in these marches we must have covered eleven leagues.

Upon leaving this nation we entered the territory of another, known as the Jumanos, whom the Spaniards call also by a different name, "Patarabueyes."[6] This nation seemed to have many people in large permanent pueblos. We saw five settlements containing more than ten thousand Indians, with low, flat-roofed houses well arranged into pueblos. The people of this nation are of large build; they paint their faces in stripes. They have corn and calabashes, game beasts and birds, beans, and many varieties of fish taken from two large rivers, one of which flows straight from the north into the Conchos, being about half the size of the Guadalquivir, while the other, the Conchos, which empties into the North sea, is of approximately the same size as the Guadalquivir. There are in this territory salines from salt-water lakes which, during certain parts of the year, harden and produce salt like that obtained from the sea.

On the first night, when we pitched camp close to a small pueblo belonging to this nation, the natives killed five of our horses with arrows and wounded another five, even though we had posted a watch.[7] Then they withdrew to a sierra where six of us went the next morning, accompanied by Pedro, the interpreter (*naguatato*), a native of their nation. We found the natives, whom we calmed and pacified, and restored them to their own pueblo. We also explained things to them,

5. Luxán does not mention the Jobosos by name, but from his day-by-day description of the journey down the Conchos river, it seems that this group was the same as the one he called Otomoacos.

6. These Jumanos or Patarabueyes were the Otomoacos and Abriaches of Luxán, whose account is more accurate than Espejo's. They correspond to the Cholomes and Julimes, respectively.

7. This was on the night of December 6, as recorded by Luxán. His account of this incident parallels that of Espejo very closely.

as we had to the other Indians, and told them to advise their people not to run away or hide, but to come out and see us. I gave beads, hats, and other articles to some of the caciques so that they would bring back their people peaceably, which they did, and inhabitants from these pueblos accompanied us wherever word had been sent ahead that we were coming as friends and not with intent to harm them; and thus a great number of natives came along to show us the above-mentioned Río del Norte.

The banks of the river, for a distance of twelve days' travel, are settled with people of this nation.[8] Some live in flat-roofed houses, others in straw huts. The caciques came out to welcome us, each one accompanied by his people, without bows or arrows. They gave us some of their food, and a few presented us with very well dressed chamois skins and buffalo hides. The chamois is made from deerskins as well tanned as the ones from Flanders. The hides are from humpbacked cattle called "Cíbola" (buffalo)—the hair resembling that of Irish cattle. The Indians tan these hides in the same manner that elk leather is tanned in Flanders, and use them to make footwear. They dress other skins, worn by some of the natives, in various ways.

Apparently these Indians have already received some enlightenment regarding our holy Catholic faith; for they point to God our Lord while looking up to the heavens, calling Him "Apalito" in their language and saying that He is the One they acknowledge as their Lord and Who provides them with everything they have. Many men, women, and children came to have the sign of the cross made over them by the friar and the other Spaniards, showing great pleasure at this gesture. They told us, or explained through interpreters, that three Christians and a Negro had passed through their land; and from their descriptions it seemed that they referred to Alvar Núñez Cabeza de Vaca, Dorantes, Castillo Maldonado, and a Negro, all survivors from the fleet with which Pánfilo de Narváez came to Florida. We left these natives at peace, calm and contented. Some of them accompanied us and helped us as far as the aforesaid Río del Norte.

Traveling on up the river, always toward the north, we were met by numerous Indian men, women, and children who wore clothes, some of chamois skins. We did not learn to what nation they belonged, because we lacked interpreters.[9] They brought us many articles made of feathers of different colors, and also cotton shawls, striped blue and white, resembling some that are imported from China. They explained

8. That is, Otomoacos, or Cholomes.
9. Possibly the Caguates of Luxán's account, later called Sumas.

to us by means of signs that the people of another nation, bordering on theirs to the west, brought these articles in trade for other goods possessed by this nation; namely—to judge by the signs made—dressed buffalo and deerskins. When we pointed out some shiny ores of the kind which elsewhere usually contain silver and showed them other similar specimens which we carried, they pointed toward the west, indicating a five days' march and saying they would take us to places where there was an enormous amount of those minerals, as well as many people of their own nation. They accompanied us during a four days' journey covering twenty-two leagues.

From the place where we left these Indians, we traveled upstream another four days and came upon large numbers of people who lived near several lakes through which the Río del Norte flows.[10] These people, numbering upward of one thousand Indians of both sexes, dwelling in rancherías and straw houses, came out to welcome us— men, women, and children—each one carrying a present of mesquital (made from a fruit resembling carob beans), and many varieties of fish, which abound in those lakes. They brought also other samples of their food, in such great quantity that most of it was wasted because of the amounts they gave us. During the three days we spent among them, they performed their *mitotes* day and night, both dances of their own and others like those of the Mexicans. They gave us to understand by signs that there were many people of their nation at some distance from there, but we failed to learn what this was, for lack of interpreters.

Among these people we found a Conchos Indian who told us by means of signs, pointing toward the west, that a fifteen days' journey away there was a very large lake, on whose shores were numerous settlements with houses of many stories. He added that Indians of the Conchos nation dwelt there, people who wore clothes and had abundant supplies of corn, turkeys, and other provisions. The natives offered to take us to that lake, but we did not go, as our itinerary called for a continued march northward in order to succor the above-mentioned friars and the persons who had remained with them. In this ranchería and its vicinity the land and climate are very good, and near by there are buffalo herds, abundant game beasts and birds, mines, many forests and pasturelands, water, salines of very rich salt, and other profitable resources.

Continuing up this same river, we traveled for fifteen days away from

10. The marshy area below El Paso inhabited by the Tanpachoas of Luxán's narrative.

the site of the lakes, without meeting any people.[11] We passed through mesquite groves and cactus fields, and over mountains wooded with pine forests producing piñon nuts like those of Castile, as well as with savins and junipers. At the end of this march, we came upon a thinly populated ranchería containing a number of straw huts. Here we found many deerskins as well dressed as those brought from Flanders, quantities of excellent white salt, some jerked venison, and other provisions. The Indians of the ranchería welcomed us and accompanied us for a two days' journey from that spot to some pueblos, always keeping to the course of the aforesaid Río del Norte, which we had consistently followed upstream ever since reaching it. There were sierras on both sides of the river, bare of woods for the whole distance, until we came near the pueblos known as those of New Mexico, although along the river banks there were many cottonwood groves and some patches of white poplars four leagues wide. We never left the Río del Norte from the moment of reaching it until we came to the settlements called the pueblos of New Mexico. On its banks, in many places along the way, we found quantities of grapevines and Castilian walnut trees.

On reaching the said pueblos, we proceeded upstream for two days and found ten inhabited pueblos on both sides of the river and close to its banks, in addition to others which seemed to be off the beaten track.[12] Passing through these settlements, we estimated that they contained more than twelve thousand people, including men, women, and children.

As we crossed this province the inhabitants of each town came out to meet us, took us to their pueblos, and gave us quantities of turkeys, corn, beans, and tortillas, with other kinds of bread, which they make more skillfully than the Mexican people. They grind raw corn on very large stones, five or six women working together in a single mill, and from the flour they make many kinds of bread. Their houses are two, three, or four stories high, each house being partitioned into a number of rooms; and in many of the houses there are estufas for the winter weather. In the pueblos each plaza has two estufas, which are houses built underground, well sheltered and tightly closed, with benches inside to sit on. At the entrance to each estufa there is a ladder for going down into it, so that strangers may find shelter there, and a large stack of wood.

11. The uninhabited area extending from the vicinity of El Paso to the first New Mexico pueblos just south of modern San Marcial.
12. Espejo's party was now among the Piros.

In this province some of the natives are clad in cotton blankets, buffalo hides, or dressed chamois skins. They wear their blankets like the Mexicans, except that over their privy parts they have small pieces of colored cotton cloth; and some of them wear shirts. The women have cotton skirts, often embroidered with colored thread, and over the shoulders a blanket like that worn by the Mexican Indians, fastened at the waist by a strip of embroidered material, with tassels, resembling a towel. The skirts are worn like slips, next to the skin, the lower portion loose and swishing. Each woman displays such an outfit to the best of her ability; and everyone, man or woman, wears shoes or boots with soles of buffalo hide and uppers of dressed deerskin. The women arrange their hair neatly and prettily, winding it with care around moulds at each side of the head. They do not wear any head covering.

All the pueblos have caciques, allotted according to the number of inhabitants. Thus there are the principal caciques, who in turn have other caciques under them, that is to say, their *tequitatos*, the latter functioning like sheriffs to execute the orders of their superiors in the various pueblos, exactly as in the case of the Mexican people. When the Spaniards ask for something from the principal caciques of the pueblos, these officials summon the *tequitatos*, who then proclaim the order aloud throughout the pueblo concerned and in a very short time all bring what they may have been asked to provide.

In the painting of their houses and in other matters—relating to their dances and music and so forth—these Indians are very much like the Mexicans. They drink toasted pinole, made from ground corn mixed with water, and are not known to use other beverages or anything intoxicating.

In every one of these pueblos there is a house to which food is brought for the devil. The natives have small stone idols which they worship; and also, just as the Spaniards have crosses along the roads, these people set up, midway between pueblos, their artificial hillocks (*cuecillos*) built of stones like wayside shrines, where they place painted sticks and feathers, saying that the devil will stop there to rest and talk to them. They have fields planted with corn, beans, calabashes, and tobacco (*piciete*) in abundance. These crops are seasonal, dependent on rainfall, or they are irrigated by means of good ditches. They are cultivated in Mexican fashion, and in each planted field the worker has a shelter, supported by four pillars, where food is carried to him at noon and he spends the siesta; for usually the workers stay in their fields from morning until night just as do the people of Castile.

This province boasts of many pine forests which produce piñon nuts like those of Castile; and it also has many salines. On both sides of the river there are sandy stretches extending for more than a league, naturally adapted for the production of abundant corn crops.

The weapons used by the natives are bows and arrows, flint-edged wooden clubs *(macanas)*, and shields *(chimales)*. Their arrows are made of fire-hardened shafts with sharp-edged flint tips which can easily pierce leather armor. The shields are made of buffalo hide, oval in shape; the battle clubs—half a yard long and very heavy at one end—are used as defensive weapons by persons inside their own houses. We did not hear that these Indians were at war with any other province. They respect each other's boundaries. Here we were told of another province with similar characteristics farther up the same river.

We left this province after spending four days there and came to another, half a league away, called the province of the Tiguas, containing sixteen pueblos, one of which is named Pualas [or Puaray]. Here we learned that the Indians of this province had killed Fray Francisco López, Fray Agustín Ruíz [Rodríguez], three boys, and a mestizo, the persons whom we had come to succor and take back. Here we heard, too, a reliable report of how Francisco Vázquez Coronado had been in this province, how the natives had killed nine of his soldiers and forty horses, and how he therefore destroyed the people in one pueblo of the province.

The natives of these pueblos told us about those events in sign language which we understood. Believing that we had come to punish them because they had killed the friars, the people ran away to a sierra two leagues from the river, before we arrived in the province. We tried by all possible means to persuade them to come back peacefully, but they refused. In their houses we found quantities of corn, beans, calabashes, and turkeys, as well as many ores of different colors. Some of the pueblos of this province, and the houses there, were bigger than those in the province we had crossed just before, but the planted fields and the character of the land seemed to be the same. We were unable to find out how many inhabitants there were, because they had fled.

When we arrived in the province of the Tiguas and discovered that the people whom we had come to find—the friars, the mestizo, and the Indians who stayed with them—had all been killed, our first impulse was to return to New Vizcaya whence we had set out. But as the Indians there told us of another province to the east, saying it was close by, and as it seemed to me that the whole region was heavily settled and that we found increasingly larger pueblos as we went farther inland, with inhabitants who received us peaceably, I thought this was a good opportunity for me to serve his Majesty by visiting and exploring the lands so new and so remote, with a view to informing his Majesty about them while incurring no expense to him for their exploration. Consequently, I decided to press forward as long as my strength permitted. After consultation with the friar and the soldiers, who expressed agreement with my plans, we continued our expedition and explorations in the same way as heretofore.

In this place of the Tiguas we heard of another province, called Maguas, located two days' travel to the east.[13] Leaving the camp behind in Tiguas, I set out in search of Maguas with two companions and reached it in two days. I there found eleven pueblos with a great many inhabitants, more than forty thousand souls, in my estimation, counting men, women, and children. In this area there are no running streams or springs of which the natives can avail themselves. They do have abundant corn, turkeys, and other supplies, as in the province previously visited. The Maguas province borders on the land of the so-called Cíbola cattle. The natives clothe themselves with the hides of these animals, cotton blankets, and chamois skins. They are governed like the people of the provinces already mentioned. They have idols which they worship in the same manner as those other Indians. There are indications of mining possibilities in the mountains of this province, for I saw the signs while traveling through it. We noticed much antimony along the way, and ordinarily one finds rich silver ore wherever there is antimony. Moreover, in this province we found metals in the houses of the Indians.

We learned that in this place the Indians had killed a friar named Juan de Santa María,[14] who had entered the land together with the other friars accompanying Francisco Sánchez Chamuscado and his soldiers. They killed him before the said Chamuscado departed for the land of peace. We made friends with these natives without touching on the subject of the killings. They provided us with food, and after observing the characteristics of the land we left. It is a region wooded with many pine forests producing Castilian piñon nuts, and also with

13. These were the eastern Tiguas and Tompiros, around the Salines, and not the Tanos, as supposed by Hodge and Bandelier. See *Benavides' Revised Memorial*, p. 266; Bandelier, *Final Report*, Pt. II, p. 87; Lambert, *Paa-ko, New Mexico*, p. 6; Reed, "The Southern Tewa," *El Palacio*, vol. 50, pp. 259-260.

14. In other words, he was killed among the eastern Tiguas.

savins. We then turned back to the Río del Norte from which we had set out.

Upon returning to camp we learned of another province, called Quires,[15] situated one day's travel farther up the Río del Norte, some six leagues from the place where we had set up camp. The entire group marched to the Quires province, and while we were still a league away, a large number of Indians came peaceably to meet us and invited us to visit their pueblos. We went with them and were very well received, for they gave us cotton blankets, many turkeys, some corn, and portions of everything else they possessed. This province had five pueblos with numerous inhabitants, amounting, so we guessed, to fifteen thousand persons. Their food and clothes resemble those of the people in the province just visited. They are idolaters. They have many fields of corn and other things. In this place we saw a magpie kept in a roughly fashioned cage, like those in Castile. We saw umbrellas like Chinese parasols, painted with the sun, the moon, and the stars. At this place we took the latitude and found we were at 37.5 degrees directly north. We also heard of another province a two days' journey to the west.

We left the province of Quires and, after two days of travel covering fourteen leagues, came to another, called Pumames,[16] containing five pueblos. The principal town, named Zía, was a very large pueblo, through which I walked with my companions. It had eight plazas, and better houses than the ones previously described. Most of these houses were whitewashed and painted in colors with pictures in the Mexican style. Zía is situated on the banks of a medium-sized river which flows from the north and joins the Río del Norte. Near a sierra in this province there were large numbers of people, apparently more than twenty thousand. Here the Indians gave us cotton blankets and ample supplies of corn, turkeys, and bread made of corn flour. They were very neat, both in the preparation of their food and in everything else, more so than the inhabitants of any other province we had seen thus far. Their clothes and form of government were similar to those of the people we had seen previously. Here we were told of another province to the northwest, which we made plans to visit. In this pueblo we heard that there were mines near by, in the sierra, and they showed us rich ores obtained from them.

After traveling one day toward the northwest, about six leagues, we

---

15. The Queres.
16. This was the province of the Jémez Indians. Zía was then and is now a Queres pueblo.

found a province with seven pueblos, called the province of the Emexes,[17] which had numerous inhabitants, perhaps as many as thirty thousand. The natives said that one of these pueblos, situated in the mountains, was very large. Fray Bernardino Beltrán and some of the soldiers thought that our forces were too small to go to such a large pueblo, and consequently we did not see it, as we were unwilling to divide our forces. These natives were similar to the people we had met before, with equally abundant provisions as well as the same type of clothes and government. They had idols, bows and arrows, and the other weapons mentioned in connection with the provinces already described.

We left the province of the Emexes, and after going west for three days, some fifteen leagues, came to a pueblo named Acoma, which we thought had more than six thousand souls. Acoma is built on top of a lofty rock, more than fifty estados high, and out of the rock itself the natives have hewn stairs by which they ascend and descend to and from the pueblo. It is a veritable stronghold, with water cisterns at the top and quantities of provisions stored in the pueblo. Here the Indians gave us many blankets and chamois skins, belts made from strips of buffalo hide that had been dressed like Flanders leather, and abundant supplies of corn and turkeys.

These people have their fields two leagues distant from the pueblo, near a medium-sized river, and irrigate their farms by little streams of water diverted from a marsh near the river.[18] Close to the sown plots we found many Castile rosebushes in bloom; and we also found Castile onions, which grow wild in this land without being planted or cultivated. In the adjacent mountains there are indications of mines and other riches, but we did not go to inspect them because the natives there were numerous and warlike.

The mountain dwellers, who are called Querechos,[19] came down to serve the people in the towns, mingling and trading with them, bringing them salt, game (such as deer, rabbits, and hares), dressed chamois skins, and other goods in exchange for cotton blankets and various articles accepted in payment. Their form of government and other

17. The Jémez pueblos. Luxán makes no mention of going to visit these towns, probably situated near the Hot Springs, so either Espejo meant that they had heard of these towns, or Luxán failed to record the trip. They arrived at Zía on the evening of February 26, apparently, and left on the twenty-eighth, the dates given by Luxán. This would hardly have given sufficient time for a visit to the pueblos in San Diego and Guadalupe canyons.

18. The San José river, near modern Acomita.

19. These Querechos were Navajos. Bandelier, *op. cit.*, Pt. II, p. 294; Forbes, *Apache, Navaho, and Spaniard*, pp. 57-59.

characteristics were the same as in the rest of the provinces. They held a solemn ceremonial dance for us, in which the people dressed very gaily and performed juggling tricks, including some with live snakes that were quite elaborate, all of which was most interesting to watch. These Indians presented us with ample provisions of everything they had, and then, after three days, we left their province.

After traveling twenty-four leagues to the west in four days, we finally came to a province with six pueblos, known as Zuñi, or Cíbola, where there were many Indians, apparently more than twenty thousand, which we learned had been visited by Francisco Vázquez Coronado and some of the captains who accompanied him. In this province we saw crosses erected near the pueblos; and here we found three Christian Indians who gave their namees as Andrés of Cuyuacán, Gaspar of Mexico, and Antón of Guadalajara, and who said that they had come to the land with Governor Francisco Vázquez Coronado. By refreshing their memory of the Mexican language, which they had almost forgotten, we learned from them that Coronado and his captains had reached this province and that Don Pedro de Tovar had explored inland after hearing of a large lake where the natives claimed there were many towns. These people told us that there was gold in the lake region, that the inhabitants wore clothes, with gold bracelets and earrings, that they dwelt at a distance of a sixty days' journey from the place where we were, and that Coronado's men had traveled twelve days beyond this province before turning back because they found no water and had used up all they were carrying.

Our informants gave us very good descriptions of the lake and the riches of the Indians dwelling there. Although some of my companions and I wanted to visit the lake, others were opposed. In this province we saw a quantity of Castile flax, which seeems to grow in the fields without being planted. The natives gave us much information about what there was in the provinces bordering on the large lake, and about how the Indians in this place had given Francisco Vázquez Coronado and his people many ores, which the Spaniards had not smelted because they lacked the necessary equipment.

In this province of Cíbola, at a pueblo named Aquico,[20] Father Fray Bernardino, Miguel Sánchez Valenciano, his wife Casilda de Amaya, his sons Lázaro Sánchez and Miguel Sánchez Nevado, Gregorio Hernández, Cristóbal Sánchez, and Juan de Frías, who accompanied us, declared that they wanted to return to New Vizcaya, our starting point,

---

20. Háwikuh. See Hodge, *History of Hawikuh, New Mexico.*

after learning that Francisco Vázquez Coronado had not found either gold or silver and had turned back. They, too, wanted to turn back, and they suited the action to the word. The customs and rituals of Cíbola were the same as those of the provinces we had already visited. The natives have quantities of game; they wear cotton blankets or others which look like coarse linen. Here we heard of more provinces toward the west.

After a four day's journey of seven leagues each, we came at last to a province called Mohoce,[21] with five pueblos, which in our judgment contained more than fifty thousand souls. Before we arrived in that province, the natives sent us a warning not to go there lest we be killed. Accompanied by nine men who had remained with me, namely, Juan López de Ibarra, Bernardo de Luna, Diego Pérez de Luxán, Gaspar de Luxán, Francisco Barreto, Pedro Hernández de Almansa, Alonso de Miranda, Gregorio Hernández and Juan Hernández, I went on to Mohoce, taking along one hundred and fifty Indians from the province we were leaving,[22] as well as the three Mexican Indians already mentioned.

A league before we reached Mohoce, more than two thousand Indians laden with provisions came out to welcome us. We gave them some trinkets of little value that we had with us, thus indicating that we had not come to harm them; and we asked them to build a strong stockade for our horsees, which were vicious and might kill them. The natives complied with this request. Then a great many Indians came to meet us, and with them came the caciques of a pueblo in this province called Aguato. They accorded us a grand reception, throwing corn flour over the places we were to pass so that we should tread upon it.[23] They were all joyful and asked us to visit the pueblo of Aguato. There I bestowed presents on the leaders, giving them some things I had brought along for this purpose.

The principal Indians of this pueblo sent word at once to the other towns in the province, whose leaders came with many followers to invite us to visit their own pueblos, saying this would give them great pleasure; and we accepted the invitations. Seeing the good treatment and gifts I gave to their chief men and *tequitatos,* the natives gathered together from various parts of the province more than four thousand cotton blankets, colored or white, hand towels with tassels at the ends, and many other things, including some of the blue and green ores sought by

21. The land of the Hopis.
22. That is, Zuñi Indians.
23. The pueblo was Awátobi, and the corn flour was sacred corn meal.

them for coloring their blankets. They gave us all these goods and even thought that they were not doing enough, for they asked us if we were satisfied. The food of these natives is the same as that of the people in the provinces previously described, except that we saw no turkeys there. A cacique and some other people told us that they knew about the above-mentioned lake where there were riches of gold, and their statements on this point were exactly the same as those of the people in the province we had just left.

During the six days we stayed there we visited the pueblos of the province. Since we believed that these Indians were friendly, I left five of my companions with them in their towns, so that these men could return with the baggage to the province of Zuñi. Taking four others with me, I traveled directly west for forty-five leagues in search of some rich mines I had heard about in this locality, accompanied by guides given me in Mohoce for this purpose. I found the mines, and took from them with my own hands ores which, according to experts on the matter, are very rich and contain a great deal of silver. Most of the area around the mines is mountainous, as is the route leading to them.

There are some mountain Indians in that region, and in some places the inhabitants came out to meet us with crosses painted on their heads. They gave us a portion of their food, and I presented them with a few articles. The general aspect of the land where the mines are located is good; there are rivers, marshes, woods, and also—on the riverbanks— great quantities of Castile grapes, walnut trees, flax, mulberries (*morales*), maguey plants, and prickly pears.

The Indians in that land plant cornfields and have good houses. They told us by means of signs that beyond the mountains (we were not able to understand clearly just how far away) there was a very large river, more than eight leagues wide, to judge by the signs, flowing toward the North sea. They also said that there were large towns on both banks, that they crossed the river in canoes, that in comparison with the provinces and towns along its shores, the provinces we were then visiting were insignificant, and that in the land thus described were many grapes, walnuts, and mulberries.

From here we turned back toward the place to which I had sent my comrades, the distance from the aforesaid mines to Zuñi being about seventy leagues. We wanted to return by a different way so as to have a better opportunity for observing and appraising the characteristics of the land, and I found a route more level than the one followed in going to the mines.

On my arrival at the province of Zuñi,[24] I found there the five men I had left behind, and also Father Fray Bernardino, for they had not yet gone back. The Indians of this province had provided all of them with the food they needed. We all rejoiced greatly on being together again. The caciques came out to welcome me and my companions, furnishing us with abundant provisions and also with Indians to serve as guides and porters. When we took leave of them they made many promises, asking us to come back again and to bring with us a large number of "Castillos," their name for the Spaniards; for in this expectation they were planting a large corn crop that year in order to have enough for everybody. Father Fray Bernardino and the people who had remained with him took their departure from this province, as did also Gregorio Hernández, who had accompanied me as alférez, although I urged them not to leave but to stay and look for mines and other benefits in the service of his Majesty.

After Fray Bernardino and his companions had left, I turned back with eight soldiers, determined to explore upstream along the Río del Norte by which we had entered the land. Having traveled ten days, over sixty leagues, we reached the province of the Quires. From there we marched east two days, covering six leagues each day, and came to an Indian province named Ubates, containing five pueblos.[25] The Indians there received us peacefully and gave us many provisions, including turkeys, corn, and other things. From the Ubates we went on to look for some mines we had heard about, and we found them after two days' travel. Moving in various directions, we obtained some shiny ores and returned to the pueblo where we had started out. There are many people in these pueblos, numbering approximately twenty thousand, in our estimation. They wear white or colored cotton blankets and dressed chamois or buffalo skins. They are governed in the same manner as the inhabitants of the adjoining provinces. These people have no rivers; they depend on springs and marshes. There are many forests of pines, junipers, and savins. The houses in these pueblos are three, four, and five stories high.

Having heard that there was another province at a distance of a day's travel from this one, we went to see it and found that it contained three

24. The Spanish reads "Ami," a copyist's error.

25. Scholars have been unable to explain these Ubates satisfactorily. Luxán does not mention them, but does tell of the visit to the Tano pueblos in the Galisteo basin, as does Espejo after referring to the Ubates. Reed suggests that possibly they were the Tewa villages farther north and that Espejo simply meant he had heard of them. Reed, "The Southern Tewa," *El Palacio*, vol. 50, p. 262. For a different interpretation, see *Benavides' Revised Memorial*, p. 266, identifying them as Tano.

very large pueblos with more than forty thousand souls, so we judged. It was called the province of the Tamos. Here the natives refused to furnish us with food or even allow us to enter. For this reason, and because some of my companions were sick, the natives numerous, and we had no food, we decided to start on our way back.

At the beginning of July, 1583, we obtained an Indian from this community to guide us along a different route from the one we had taken when we came; and half a league from a pueblo of this province named Ciquique, we found a river which we called Río de las Vacas,[26] because in the course of a six days' march along it, covering some thirty leagues, we saw great numbers of the native cattle [buffalo]. Following this river for one hundred and twenty leagues toward the east, we came upon three Indians out hunting. They were from the Jumana nation, and through our interpreters we learned that we were a twelve days' journey away from the Conchos river, which we estimated as a distance of slightly more than forty leagues.[27]

We crossed to the said Conchos river, finding along the way many watering places in arroyos and marshes. Here we met a large number of Indians from the Jumano nation who brought us quantities of fish of different kinds, prickly pears, and other fruits; they also gave us buffalo hides and chamois skins. From this point we went on to the valley of San Bartolomé where Father Fray Bernardino Beltrán and I, with the other persons mentioned above, had started our expedition. We found that Father Fray Bernardino and his companions had arrived many days earlier in this province of San Bartolomé and had gone to the town of Guadiana [Durango].

Everything above described I saw with my own eyes, and it is accurate, for I was present throughout. I made excursions in the company of several men, or sometimes with only one man, to inspect and appraise the qualities of the land with a view to informing his Majesty of all the facts, so that he might issue the decrees deemed suitable for the exploration and pacification of those provinces, in the service of God our Lord and for the dissemination of the holy Catholic faith, thus enabling those barbarous nations to come into the knowledge of that faith. My comrades and I made all possible efforts to achieve this purpose and to meet the requirements of the present report as well as those of the proceedings and inquiries conducted during the expedi-

26. Ciquique was the pueblo of Pecos, and the Río de las Vacas was the Pecos river.

27. The soldiers continued along the Pecos to the vicinity of Toyah creek, Texas, thence southward via the later Fort Davis and Marfa to the Río Grande near Ruidoso or Candelaria, where they were on familiar ground and made their way back to San Bartolomé.

tion, on which there is testimony supported by such authoritative confirmation as we were able to secure in those regions. We are not able to write down everything that happened; nor could I report it all in writing, as the record would be too long, since the lands and provinces visited in the course of our expedition were many and extensive.

We traveled by direct route to the limits of the provinces which we had entered. The journey from the valley of San Bartolomé covered more than two hundred and fifty leagues; and the return, by the route we took, more than two hundred. In addition, we traveled more than three hundred leagues while exploring those provinces and moving from one part of them to another over rough territory, plains, lakes, marshes, and rivers, amid great perils and hardships. We found many differences in language among the natives there, different modes of dress, and different customs. Moreover, what we saw and what I am reporting represents only the smallest part of what exists in those provinces; for as we traveled through them we received reports and information about large towns, very fertile lands, silver mines, rumors of gold, and peoples better governed, all in the direction of our march.

We saw, had dealings with, or heard about large settlements, but because my companions and I were few in number and some of them were afraid to go farther, we explored only what I am describing. Although we were considered too bold in doing even this much, we acted in the belief that we were thereby serving God our Lord and his Majesty. With the purpose of shedding some light on the matter, and in order not to waste the opportunity presented to us, we employed all the means at our disposal in an attempt to see and understand everything, inquiring into the truth through interpreters wherever they were available and, where there were none, using the sign language. When the Indians of the said provinces showed us, by drawing lines on the ground and by gestures, the number of leagues from one province to another and the number of pueblos in each province, we did our best to understand them.

The natives of all those provinces are large, more vigorous than the Mexicans, and healthy, for no illness was noted among them. Their women are fairer than the Mexican women, and they are an intelligent and orderly people. There are attractive pueblos with plazas, and well-arranged houses. This indicates that the inhabitants would learn quickly any matter dealing with good government. In the greater part of those provinces, there is an abundance of game beasts and birds: rabbits, hares, deer, buffaloes, ducks, geese, cranes, and pheasants and other birds. There are also fine wooded mountains with trees of all kinds, salines, and rivers containing a great variety of fish. Carts and wagons can be driven through most of this region; and there are good pastures for cattle as well as lands suitable for vegetables or grain crops, whether irrigated or depending on seasonal rains. There are many rich mines, too, from which I brought ores to have assayed and to determine their quality. I brought also an Indian man from the province of Tamos and an Indian woman from Mohoce, so that they might enlighten us regarding those provinces and the route to that region, if its discovery and colonization are undertaken anew in the service of his Majesty, my intention being that these two Indians should learn the Mexican language and other tongues with this aim in view. In all respects I refer to the proceedings and record of inquiries made on the subject. They will help to establish the purpose and intent with which my friends and I served his Majesty in the said expedition, and the just grounds we thus had for reporting to his Majesty, in whose service I wish to spend my life and property.

I prepared this report at the mines of Santa Bárbara in the jurisdiction of New Vizcaya at the end of the month of October, 1583, having arrived at the valley of San Bartolomé, which is in the same jurisdiction, on September 20 of the said year, the day of our return from the expedition. ANTONIO DESPEJO [Between two rubrics]

ESPEJO TO THE ARCHBISHOP OF MEXICO
OCTOBER, 1583[1]

Most Reverend Sir:

Some twenty-five days ago I arrived at the mines of Santa Bárbara, in this jurisdiction, very worn and tired after traveling for more than a year, in which I covered eight hundred leagues, examining and exploring the provinces of New Mexico, to which I gave the name of New Andalusia because I was born in the district of Córdoba. I entered those provinces on a pious mission, as your Reverence may be pleased to observe from the accompanying report on my whole expedition, which I hope will produce excellent results, by the grace of God, for His service, that of his Majesty, and the promotion of the Catholic faith. In addition to the lands and towns that I visited and the great number of nations and people I saw, I heard reports of many others, larger and richer, situated beyond but on the borders of the localities we visited. Because we were few in number and our supplies were exhausted, we did not press on farther.

I should have liked to go in person to pay my respects to your Reverence immediately after learning, in Santa Bárbara, that his Majesty had commissioned your lordship with the inspection of the royal audiencia, but I would not dare to appear before you without first establishing my innocence of the charges brought against me, which I pray God I may be able to do soon. However, I am resolved to dispatch some suitable person in my name who will inform his Majesty of my travels and will beg him to favor me by entrusting to me the colonization and exploration of those lands and any others I may discover.[2] I shall not rest content until I reach the coasts of the South and North seas. Although part of my estate has been attached,[3] I shall not lack what is needed to undertake the expedition with a sufficient number of people and adequate provisions, military equipment, and other sup-

1. Pacheco and Cárdenas, *Col. Doc. Inéd.*, vol. xv, p. 162. Translated in Bolton, *Spanish Exploration in the Southwest*, pp. 193-194.

2. On April 23, 1584, Espejo appointed Pedro González de Mendoza, his son-in-law, to represent him before the Court in Spain, and gave him full powers of attorney to act in his name. See p. 234.

3. On Espejo's return to Santa Bárbara, the papers and treasures he had received in New Mexico, including several thousand mantas given him by the Indians, were confiscated by the local alcalde. Later, however, they were restored, by order of the audiencia, an indication of Espejo's political prestige. *Obregón's History*, p. 338.

plies, if his Majesty does grant me this favor, as his most Christian liberality entitles us to expect. I ventured to write to your Reverence only because this business was so important for the service of God and his Majesty, and because you were acting as the king's representative.

May the Lord keep and prosper your Reverence's person and estate for many years, as all of us, your servants, desire. From the valley of San Bartolomé in New Vizcaya at the end of October, 1583.

Most Reverend Sir: Your servant kisses your Reverence's hands. ANTONIO DE ESPEJO.

[*Endorsed:*] To the most reverend the archbishop of Mexico, visitor general of New Spain, and my lord.

ESPEJO TO THE KING, APRIL 23, 1584[1]

To his Royal Catholic Majesty:

The accompanying report[2] will inform your Majesty of the lands and provinces which, as a loyal and faithful subject, I have been discovering and exploring with God's favor and a desire to serve your Majesty and increase the royal patrimony, ever since the month of November, 1582, when I left the jurisdiction of New Vizcaya, accompanied by a friar and fourteen soldiers, urgently impelled by a most pious and benevolent motive; and consequently I shall refrain from listing those lands and provinces in this letter.

I beg that your Majesty will indulge my zeal, since it is so truly directed to your service; and that it may be your pleasure for me to spend the rest of my life in the continuation of these discoveries and colonizing activities, wherein, because of the wealth, information, and friends at my disposal, I am able to place at your Majesty's service more resources than are available to any other person from among those who are seeking a contract with your Majesty for this undertaking. I beseech your Majesty to be so gracious as to order that I be given the contract,

1. Pacheco and Cárdenas, *Col. Doc. Inéd.*, vol. xv, pp. 100-101; translation in Bolton, *Spanish Exploration in the Southwest*, p. 195.

2. By the "accompanying report," Espejo presumably refers to his long statement, completed at the end of October 1583, at San Bartolomé, immediately after his return from New Mexico. See p. 231.

thus conferring upon me a boon, an honor, and a favor in consonance with my fervent desire to extend your Majesty's domains, to propagate the holy Catholic faith through the conversion of millions of souls now lacking a knowledge of the truth, and to enhance my prestige so that I may better serve your Majesty and more fully merit your patronage. May our Lord prosper and preserve your Majesty for many years, in conformity with the need that we, your subjects, feel. San Salvador, April 23, 1584.

To his royal Catholic Majesty, from the humblest of his servants. ANTONIO ESPEJO [Between two rubrics]

POWER OF ATTORNEY TO
PEDRO GONZÁLEZ DE MENDOZA, ET AL.[1]

Be it known to all who may see these letters that I, Antonio de Espejo, resident of the city of Mexico in New Spain, being at present in this town of San Salvador, hereby bestow and acknowledge the grant of my full powers, in compliance with the requirements of the law, to Pedro González de Mendoza, my son-in-law, who is about to leave for the kingdoms of Castile; to Juan García Bonilla, notary of the crown residing at his Majesty's court; and to Diego de Salas Barbadillo, solicitor at the said court, vesting these powers in all three of them and in each one individually *(insolidum)*, with the express purpose of enabling them to appear in my name and on my behalf, as my personal representatives, before his royal Majesty the King, Don Philip our sovereign, and his royal Council of the Indies, and members of other councils, in order to beg and beseech of his Majesty that he be pleased to favor me with the task of conquering, pacifying, governing, and administering the provinces of New Mexico, known also as the new kingdom of Andalusia. These provinces I discovered, and I took possession of them in the name of his Majesty and for his royal crown.

The aforementioned persons are empowered to enter into contracts in my name, drawing up and reaching agreements concerning all matters and situations considered by them suitable or necessary for the

---

1. Pacheco and Cárdenas, *Col. Doc. Inéd.*, vol. xv, p. 189.

said conquest and pacification, even with respect to matters particularly calling for my presence and for more specific powers. Such agreements and contracts, drawn up and concluded by them in the form and manner acceptable to all or any one of them, I herewith accept and confirm, pledging my person and my goods for their observance and execution, just as if they had been expressly embodied in this instrument. In regard to those agreements and contracts, my representatives may do whatever is appropriate or necessary, as I myself should do if I were present.

In the matter of seeking and obtaining the above-mentioned favor, or such other favors as his Majesty may choose to grant me in compensation for the services I have rendered him in those provinces at my own expense and on my own initiative, they may submit any of the petitions, testimony, and reports which they are taking with them for his purpose; and they may draw up new ones, as well as any other legal records or documents that may be desirable or necessary whether in or out of court, as I should do if I were present. For each and all of these purposes and every aspect thereof, I grant and give this power of attorney, to be freely and generally exercised, with the ratification and bond required by law. For the fulfillment of the foregoing provisions I pledge my person and the goods I now possess or that I may acquire in the future.

This instrument was given and executed at the aforesaid town of San Salvador in New Spain on April 23, 1584. It was signed by the grantor, who is known to me, as I the notary certify. Witnesses: Alonso Hernández Pulido, Lázaro de Calzada, and Juan de Garay, present in this said town. ANTONIO DE ESPEJO

Before me, Fernán Sánchez Castillejo, his Majesty's notary [Rubric] [Five other notaries certify to the official position of Sánchez Castillejo.]

FRAY PEDRO OROZ TO THE KING
AND THE COUNCIL OF THE INDIES
APRIL 22, 1584[1]

To his Catholic Majesty:

THE COMMISSARY GENERAL of the seraphic order of Saint Francis humbly salutes your Majesty and states that your Majesty has here in your kingdoms of New Spain a most faithful vassal, Antonio de Espejo, who is very active in the service of God our Lord and the king. This man—moved by a keen desire to serve the Lord, disseminate our holy Catholic faith, convert the souls created in the image and likeness of God, and expand your royal domain—has penetrated many leagues, by dint of laborious personal efforts and lavish expenditures of his estate, beyond the territory of Zacatecas into the northern regions, where he has discovered numerous well-populated provinces and towns, supplied with goodly means of subsistence and other things important for human life, as he himself is reporting more fully to your Majesty. Consequently, he deserves to be pardoned for a certain unfortunate episode of past years in which he became involved in these your kingdoms;[2] and he merits your indulgence, since he has served and wishes to continue serving your Majesty with such zeal.

The land he discovered is very extensive, exceeding fourteen hundred leagues in length from the so-called Strait of Anián to the tip of Labrador, and being more than a thousand leagues wide in some places. Furthermore, it is firmly believed that this entire region is thickly populated and that its discovery will contribute greatly to the service of God our Lord and your Majesty.

May God preserve your Catholic Majesty in His holy service. April 22, 1584. Your Majesty's most humble vassal, FRAY PEDRO OROZ [Rubric] [*Endorsed:*] Noted. No reply is necessary.

---

1. A.G.I., *Audiencia de México*, legajo 20. Oroz was commissary general of the Franciscan order in New Spain, 1582-84.

2. Presumably the charge of murdering two of his vaqueros, Marcos Ramos and Andrés Gutiérrez. See "Espejo Pleads for Pardon," p. 241.

FRAY DIEGO RENGEL TO HIS MAJESTY KING PHILIP, OUR SOVEREIGN, IN PERSON[1]

Your Royal Majesty:

As one who has traveled over a great portion of the lands inhabited by the savage Chichimecas and other nations, and has long been informed of everything that happens there, I have already reported my opinions to some of your Majesty's officials, with a view to easing the burdens of your royal conscience, encouraging the conversion of those barbarous nations, and promoting the steady growth and development of your domains.

Now, however, I have acquired additional information about New Mexico and, in particular, about Antonio de Espejo, who, being duly authorized, penetrated the interior, accompanied by fourteen Spaniards, for the purpose of succoring and assisting the friars of our order who had gone along on an exploration and had been left there by the captain, who had taken them among those savages. Espejo found that the friars had been slain by the Indians, but he went on to explore many other provinces.

In view of all this, I thought it appropriate to call to your Majesty's attention the fact that there is a grave obligation to succor these people who so readily entered the fold of the Church, unarmed and with no means of defense. The person best qualified to make this expedition in a satisfactory and Christian manner is Antonio de Espejo, since he is a man of great experience and has many friends who have offered to accompany him at their own expense without any cost to your Majesty, either for his needs or for their own. Antonio de Espejo has spent a large part of his fortune on this undertaking, and therefore deserves that your Majesty should grant him the favor of forgiveness for a certain unfortunate episode in which he was involved.[2] His services merit this pardon, and it befits your Majesty's royal dignity to extend kindness and mercy to your humble vassals.

I, the writer of this letter, have worn the Franciscan habit in these regions for thirty-five years, ceaselessly ministering to the natives. At present I am the unworthy guardian of the convent of Saint Francis in

1. A.G.I., *Audiencia de México*, legajo 20.
2. See p. 242, note 2.

Mexico city, and principal definitor of the province. As one who is dedicated to the well-being of the aforesaid natives, to the service of God our Lord, and to that of your Majesty, I have decided to write all that is set forth above.

May our Lord protect and prosper your Majesty for many years in His holy service, adding new kingdoms and territories to your domain. From the convent of San Francisco in Mexico, Mexico city, May 23, 1584.

To his Catholic Majesty. Your royal Majesty's humble subject and chaplain, FRAY DIEGO RENGEL [Rubric]

ESPEJO'S OFFER TO SETTLE NEW MEXICO
NOVEMBER 16, 1584[1]

To his Catholic Majesty:

Antonio de Espejo, a resident of Mexico city, states that your Majesty has already been informed of how he traveled to the north and discovered a great kingdom called New Mexico, where he found eleven provinces and heard about many others. Owing to the good customs and way of life in that region, he stayed among the Indians eleven months, giving the caciques and principal men such articles as he had brought along for this purpose. In view of the fact that he knows the quality of the land and the customs of the Indians, he believes that if your Majesty will entrust him with the pacification and settlement of that kingdom, he will perform the task in a manner beneficial to the service of God and Your Majesty, and that the goal sought can be attained in the following manner.

First: Your Majesty will command that the aforesaid Antonio de Espejo be accompanied on this expedition by twenty-four Franciscan friars who can remain in the various provinces opened to colonization,

---

1. A.G.I., *Patronato,* legajo 22. This extract from Espejo's offer to undertake the conquest and settlement of New Mexico is indicative of the high hopes he held for its future. His death in 1586 at Havana while on the way to Spain left the field open to others. Wagner believes he might well have become the conqueror of New Mexico except for his untimely death. *The Spanish Southwest,* vol. I, pp. 161-163.

in order to administer the sacraments; and the friars are to be sent entirely at your Majesty's expense.

Item [2]: The said Antonio de Espejo will take with him four hundred men, one hundred of them married, with their wives and children, and all experienced in warfare and of suitable age, to be recruited by him from the Zacatecas mining region, situated eighty leagues from Mexico city on the very route to be followed in approaching the aforementioned land of New Mexico. From Zacatecas the men will travel in a body by way of the mines of Santa Bárbara, or valley of San Bartolomé, the most remote pacified area in New Vizcaya, as far as the southern boundary [of New Mexico], and the force will include four captains to command it as well as the other officers needed.

Item [3]: This force will be divided into four companies, organized as follows: Antonio de Espejo, accompanied by one of the aforesaid captains and a hundred soldiers, will start out first, entering New Mexico through the province of the Conchos . . .

Item [4]: The party will take with it a thousand mares . . . and the necessary number of stallions.

Item [5]: The party will take four thousand cows and bulls.

Item [6]: It will take eight hundred horses.

Item [7]: It will take fifty boxes of assorted iron objects, including nails and tools.

Item [8]: Also, fifty pack animals laden with provisions.

Item [9]: The necessary quantity of hardtack and flour.

Item [10]: One thousand sheep, male and female.

Item [11]: Dried beef from five hundred cows.

Item [12]: A supply of iron bars.

Item [13]: Bellows and pipes for work on metals and tools.

[Endorsed]: To the President of the Council of the Indies: Let this be filed with the other papers relating to New Mexico. November 16, 1584.

RECOMMENDATION OF ESPEJO
NOVEMBER 16, 1584

FILE AND REPORT ON THE EXPEDITION CONDUCTED BY ANTONIO DE ESPEJO IN THE COMPANY OF FOURTEEN SOLDIERS AND A FRANCISCAN FRIAR, AGUSTÍN RODRÍGUEZ, WHO WAS CHARGED WITH THE TASK OF PREACHING TO THE NATIVES.[1]

ANTONIO DE ESPEJO, a resident of Mexico, begs that your Majesty will give orders for the processing of certain documents submitted by him in regard to the exploration of New Mexico, inasmuch as speedy action is required to insure that your Majesty be best served; delay will prove injurious, quite aside from the losses he is suffering from the expenses which his son-in-law is incurring in this capital.

The aforesaid Antonio de Espejo, resident of Mexico city, states that more than twenty-four years[2] have passed since he went to New Spain to serve your Majesty, as he has indeed done on every possible occasion, and most recently in 1582, when, in his zeal to serve God and the king, he pressed northward toward New Mexico, a venture described in the report which he presents with this document and also in a letter addressed to your Majesty. He took with him entirely at his own expense fifteen [sic] soldiers, equipped with arms and horses, and one friar, penetrating into a zone of the interior that exceeds four hundred leagues in longitude and seven hundred leagues in latitude. He discovered and explored the region on which he reports, and it contains everything mentioned in the account and description which he is presenting to your Majesty. He requests that you graciously order an examination of this whole matter and deign to entrust him with the exploration, pacification, and settlement of the said region, granting him such favors as are customarily bestowed upon the conquistadors and colonizers of new lands; and he binds himself to carry out this task of exploration, pacification, and settlement at his personal cost, with no contribution

1. A.G.I., *Patronato*, legajo 22. The lone friar with the Espejo expedition was Bernardino Beltrán, not Agustín Rodríguez, who was one of the three friars with the Chamuscado party.
2. Note that this would place his arrival in New Spain in 1560. Espejo actually arrived there in 1571 with Moya de Contreras, who came to Mexico to set up the Inquisition in that year. Later, Moya de Contreras became archbishop and also viceroy for a time. Bancroft, *Mexico*, vol. II, pp. 678 and 683.

whatsoever from your Majesty; he will furnish adequate guarantees in Mexico to that effect.

He requests your Majesty to command that a swift decision be taken regarding the project, as is expedient for the service of God our Lord and your Majesty, both in order to rescue so many thousands of souls from idolatry and because, on the expedition he made, he left the majority of the leaders in most of the settlements in a pleased and grateful mood, owing to his promise to return soon with richer gifts. Should these leaders be lost to us, which is possible if action is delayed, since some of them are old, fresh efforts would then be required in order to gain the good will of other persons. Furthermore, Espejo is keeping on hand at his own expense the men who went with him before, in the hope that your Majesty will make a speedy decision; for it is very important not to lose them, since they will be much better fitted for the proposed venture than newly recruited persons who have never seen the land in question.

To his Catholic Majesty [on behalf of] Antonio de Espejo. November 16, 1584.

[*Endorsed:*] To the President of the Council of the Indies. Let this be filed with the other papers. [Rubric]

ESPEJO PLEADS FOR PARDON[1]

Mighty Sovereign:

I, Juan de Aldaz, wish to state that I submitted to your Majesty, on behalf of Antonio de Espejo, a resident of Mexico city in New Spain, a certain document and a petition in his name, in the hope that your Majesty, having noted the documents and mindful of the considerations therein set forth, would mercifully pardon him for [his alleged share in] certain deaths. Up to the present time no favor has been shown him, and I therefore beg and beseech that, in tribute to this holy season and taking into account the services he has rendered, together with

1. These two short documents are found in A.G.I., *Audiencia de México*, legajo 109. The first document bears no place, but the year "1585" appears in the upper right-hand corner. Presumably it was drawn up in Spain. The second has neither date nor place of issuance.

the other factors already indicated, you will grant the said pardon, which he will regard as a great favor. JUAN DE ALDAZ [Rubric]

Mighty Sovereign:

I, Antonio de Espejo, a resident of Mexico city in New Spain, hereby state that your Majesty favored me by issuing your royal decree[2] to the effect that whatsoever notary had been or still was in possession of the record of proceedings, orders, and sentence or sentences against me formulated by the criminal judges of the audiencia [in Mexico] in regard to the deaths of Marcos Ramos and Andrés Gutiérrez, should furnish me with a signed copy thereof, drawn up in due form, for presentation to your royal Council of the Indies. In compliance with that decree, Diego Mardones Barahona, notary of the said audiencia, gave me a copy of the proceedings in question, and it is this document that I am presenting. Accordingly, I beg and beseech your Majesty to accept it, and that I be pardoned and cleared of any blame or accusation that may be directed against me in consequence of those proceedings, in consideration of the many services I have rendered to your Majesty— especially my recent service in the exploration of New Mexico, for which I spent a large portion of my estate, as your Majesty will have learned through the reports and certifications I have submitted to your royal Council—and also by the fact that there is no party demanding redress of me; and thereby I shall consider myself mercifully favored. [Rubric]

    2. Dated April 16, 1585.

PART III

CASTAÑO DE SOSA'S "MEMORIA"

REPORT ON THE EXPLORATORY EXPEDITION TO NEW MEXICO UNDERTAKEN ON JULY 27, 1590, BY GASPAR CASTAÑO DE SOSA WHILE HE WAS LIEUTENANT GOVERNOR AND CAPTAIN GENERAL OF NEW LEÓN.[1]

A REPORT on the exploration of New Mexico undertaken by Gaspar Castaño de Sosa, lieutenant governor and captain general of New León, in the name of King Philip our sovereign, pursuant to orders issued by the governor of that province as the king's deputy, as is stated more at length in the said orders, the pertinent royal cédulas, and the book of new laws for colonizers decreed for all residents of that kingdom. In compliance therewith, Lieutenant Governor Gaspar Castaño de Sosa set out from the villa of Almadén [now Monclova] on July 27, 1590, in a convoy of wagons with provisions and all other necessary supplies for a colonizing venture, as is more fully set forth in the legal proceedings drawn up by his direction, for the purpose of making a record of events occurring on the expedition before a suitable site for colonization should be reached. An account of all these matters is preserved, with complete accuracy, in this book,[2] in conformity with his Majesty's commands.

On July 27, 1590, Gaspar Castaño de Sosa started out with his entire force, including wagons, and spent the night at a marsh two leagues from the town, leaving behind many friendly natives who were deeply grieved by his departure because of their association with the Spaniards and their friendship for them. Two days earlier an Indian named Miguel came to the town. He was a native of Caqualco who had lived among the Cacuares for fourteen years,[3] having been left with that tribe

---

1. Printed in Pacheco and Cárdenas, *op. cit.*, vol. IV, pp. 283-354, and in vol. xv, pp. 191-261, which we will call versions A and B. Version B, entitled, "Memorial del descubrimiento que Gaspar Castaño de Sosa hizo en el Nuevo México, siendo teniente de gobernador y capitán general del Nuevo Reino de León," has been used as the basis for this translation. The differences between the two are slight, chiefly in spelling of proper names and in punctuation. There is a manuscript copy in the Juan Bautista Muñoz collection at the Real Academia de la Historia, Madrid, vol. 70 (new numbering), expediente 1543, and another in the Rich collection of the New York Public Library.

2. Nowhere do we find a clear statement of authorship of this "Memoria." If it was not written by Castaño, perhaps the secretary, Andrés Perez de Verlanga, did so, or at least supervised its composition.

3. These native names are characteristic of early Coahuila history. From one of these, "Quabila," the modern name of the state is clearly derived. For a discussion of its origin, see Vito Alessio Robles, *Coahuila y Texas en la Epoca Colonial*, pp. 94-98.

by a group of soldiers. Miguel had learned the native language of the
region, which pleased Gaspar Castaño and the army very much, since
he could serve as an interpreter. After Castaño had clothed him like the
other members of the expedition, he gladly gave up his association of
fourteen years with the Cacuares.

On the twenty-eighth of the month we reached the Río de los Nadadores, where we remained for several days.[4] During this time many
Indian chiefs, including some who had previously been friendly, came to
us with protestations of amity; and Gaspar Castaño ordered that they
be given written guarantees of protection, which they had not had before. While the camp was relying on the sense of security thus established, reports reached us that the natives were stealing horses, whereupon the lieutenant governor set out in pursuit with twelve soldiers
and overtook the culprits at the foot of a mountain to which they were
taking the animals. He seized three of the Indians; and these captives,
besides being caught with the loot, confessed when they were brought
back to camp. As a warning to the rest of the Indians in the camp, as
well as to admonish the natives of the region through which the army
would later pass, Castaño ordered two of the thieves to be hanged; the
other, who was very young, he entrusted to a soldier in the company.

On August 8 we left this river and camped for the night at Charcos
de Vaca, where many Indians came peaceably to see us. They were given
security warrants.[5]

The ninth we reached the small water hole of Tetipala, where we
met many Indians who had already sworn obedience to the king our
lord, and they were given similar guarantees. On August 10 we
journeyed on to Potrero, accompanied by a large number of natives.
The eleventh we went to Boca del Potrero, where we saw many Indians on a mountain. The lieutenant governor sent for them, but they
refused to come down. He sent a second summons on the following
day, but despite all our exhortations and kind words, we could not induce them to descend from the mountain.

On the thirteenth of the month we left Boca del Potrero and spent
the night at Charco del Río Seco; and on the night of the fourteenth

----

4. The route of the expedition from Almadén was northward, following generally
the line of the modern railroad, though the diary gives too few details to make identification
wholly satisfactory.

5. These "security warrants" were apparently written documents, giving assurance
that the holders were peaceful, had sworn allegiance to the Spanish king, and should not
be disturbed.

we reached Estero del Venado, where we were visited by a friendly cacique named Ciborpara.

We set forth again on the sixteenth and camped for the night at Encinillas, where we received visits from four caciques—named, respectively, Troman, Cipopara, Chicoa, and Bitiara—accompanied by many of their people. The lieutenant governor showed them every possible courtesy and asked them to render obedience to his Majesty, trying to convince them that they owed this to the king our Lord. They were pleased and agreed to pledge allegiance, which they did; and each captain was given a security warrant.

On the eighteenth we went on and spent the night at a place where we were drenched by a heavy downpour, making it impossible to travel, for the wagons mired down.

We left this place on the twenty-first and went as far as the marshes of the river thought to be the Salinas,[6] where we were visited by a friendly cacique named Jácome, whom the lieutenant governor treated kindly. Jácome was asked to pledge obedience to the king our lord, which he did, and thereupon received a security warrant. We remained here for several days to await the return of Francisco Salgado, Manuel de Mederos, and two other men whom our leader had sent to Mexico

---

6. Identification of Castaño's route, especially in its initial stages, is beset by many uncertain factors. The diarist almost never gives the number of leagues marched each day, nor the direction, leaving the geographer to postulate his own theory of the route taken, based on such knowledge of the terrain as he might possess, and on the meager data in the diary.

C. E. Castañeda, Texas historian, following the study of Dorothy Hull, published in *Old Santa Fé* for October 1916, pp. 307-332, states that Castaño's force, from Almadén, went northeast toward the Río Grande at Del Río, Texas. Marching by easy stages, the expedition spent twenty-four days in traversing a distance of approximately two hundred and twenty-five miles. In addition, they stopped several times, waiting for Francisco Salgado, Manuel de Mederos, and others to return from Mexico with news from the viceroy.

Vito Alessio Robles, distinguished Mexican engineer and historian, and a native of Coahuila, identified only the Mexican portion of Castaño's route, but he did not agree with Hull and Castañeda. He believed that when Castaño approached the Río Grande, near Villa Acuña, opposite Del Río, he was not able to get near the river because of swamps and marshes. Instead, Alessio had the party turn westward across northern Coahuila, following Los Cedritos arroyo, over the Sierra del Carmen via Las Cruces pass, reaching the Río Grande at Los Chizos ford, near the southern tip of Big Bend National Park. Here the party forded the river, which at that point turns northeastward a distance of some seventy-five miles, and followed it generally until he came to the Salado, or Pecos. Beyond that point, Alessio made no effort to follow the wanderers, but his identification of the route would place the explorers west of the Pecos, whereas the diarist says, under date of November 26, that they had always been on the left or east bank of the stream. The evidence thus points to the Hull-Castañeda route as the one probably followed by Castaño's party. Cf. Hull, *op. cit.*; C. E. Castañeda, *Our Catholic Heritage in Texas*, vol. I, pp. 181-183; and Vito Alessio Robles, *op. cit.*, pp. 103-104.

city with letters for the viceroy.[7] During this period of waiting, the lieutenant governor set out in person with a number of soldiers and natives to explore the sierras in that region, hoping to discover some mines, and saying that if he located any, he would colonize the valley, as it was the best and most suitable to be found anywhere in the world. He made every possible effort to trace the mines, since there were old reports of their existence; but he was unable to locate any, nor could the natives who accompanied him give any information about them. So, finding none in that area, he decided to go on; and, while still searching for the mines, he and his companions came to two rancherías, where the people—men, women, and children—received them gladly. The lieutenant governor and his men treated the Indians well, and they in return gave many of the small articles they had in their rancherías.

On the twenty-fourth we resumed our journey and spent the night near the Río de las Salinas, where we were met by friendly natives to whom we gave a security warrant.

We left this place on the twenty-fifth and camped by the Río de los Ratones. The twenty-sixth we journeyed on and halted for the night by the Río del Gato. On the twenty-seventh we camped at Barranca, where Viruega's horse got mired down in some deep pools. The twenty-ninth we left Barranca and spent the night in some hills where we found a large water hole. On the thirtieth we left this place and camped in a gully or ravine where some showers fell, supplying us with water. Otherwise we should have had none; and thus the Lord cared for us.

On September 1 we started out again and passed through a ravine where our big cart broke down and the oxen were sent back. The second we went on to spend the night in another ravine, without water. On September 3 we continued our journey and camped in a walnut grove where we found many nuts. The fourth we went on and spent the night by the Río de Roldán. On the sixth we halted for the night at the Río de Viruega, where there were many nuts and grapes. The eighth we left this place and camped near a large lake where nuts and grapes were plentiful, and where we also caught many fish.

7. In his letter of explanation and apology to the viceroy, July 27, 1591, written while in the custody of Morlete on the return from New Mexico, Castaño said that he had sent Salgado and three other men with messages for the viceroy, and that the time limit for their return was two months. According to Castaño, Salgado had assured him that if he did not rejoin the expedition on the Río Bravo in that time, it could proceed on its way with confidence. See pp. 305-311.

On the ninth we traveled on to spend the night at the Río Bravo,[8] where we tarried many days waiting for Francisco Salgado, Manuel de Mederos, and a number of other men who were expected with the viceroy's answer. The lieutenant governor had told them that he would wait for them at the Bravo to receive the viceroy's orders, for which purpose he had sent them to Mexico city. Seeing that they were so long in coming back, the lieutenant governor commanded that all corn and wheat be measured in order to find out what provisions were left, and we found that there were only one hundred fanegas. This grieved him, for he thought we had more provisions than that. The cause for the scarcity was the fact that the supplies had not been distributed carefully, since the grain was carried in large baskets and no record had been kept, as the food was in the care of Juan Pérez de los Ríos. The lieutenant governor had not failed to tell him days earlier that he should distribute measured rations to everyone; but Pérez countered on several occasions by saying that his people were not going to be put on short rations, and in order to please him our leader did not compel him to ration the grain. Now, when the corn and wheat finally were measured, the lieutenant governor ordered that the grain should be distributed among the wagons in definite amounts and that the various groups should account for the quantities entrusted to them. He also ordered that from then on each person be given one almud per week; and this command was obeyed.

Meanwhile, in view of the delay in the return of Salgado, Mederos, and their men, and mindful of the scanty provisions, the lieutenant governor decided to go ahead with the expedition. In the process of establishing the route that the army would have to follow, many points of view were expressed by the men, who all differed from the leader with the exception of Captain Cristóbal de Heredia, Francisco López de Ricalde, Martín de Salazar, and Juan de Carvajal. The opinion of this group was that they should look for the Río Salado. In the end the lieutenant governor instructed Captain Cristóbal de Heredia to start the search. In compliance with this command, Juan Pérez de los Ríos and several companions set out in search of the said river, but could not find it because of the difficult nature of the terrain.[9] Pérez came back

---

8. Note that the diarist here speaks of the Río Bravo, i.e., the Río Grande, as the stream at which the expedition was encamped. We believe this must have been in the vicinity of Del Rio, Texas.

9. This search culminated in the discovery of the Salado, the present Pecos, on October 7, after innumerable hardships due to the rugged nature of the terrain and the lack of water for men and animals. The river reported here by Juan Pérez was probably the Laxas, or present Devil's river.

with news of a different river, saying that it could be followed, though with difficulty because of the ruggedness of the land bordering it. He added that the trail lay at some distance from the river, and that it would be laborious and costly to send the oxen and horses to the stream itself on account of the many rocks.

The lieutenant governor was satisfied with the report of the river and route; but he again sent out a number of soldiers from his company, giving them instructions to explore another river farther on, in case this was the one he should follow. The soldiers reached the river that had been discovered by Juan Pérez de los Ríos and his men and turned back, saying that it was absolutely impossible to go that way. This grieved the lieutenant governor, since he himself thought it was the route he ought to take. Being weak and in poor health, he could not go in person to find out what he was so eager to learn, and therefore he sent Cristóbal de Heredia on a third mission in another search for the Río Salado. The captain accordingly set out to look for it, taking along Juan Rodríguez Nieto, Juan de Contreras and Pedro Flores. He reached the river previously found, discovering a ford not noted before which the wagons could cross. Continuing over the hills that extended to the Río Bravo, he reached this last-named river and then returned to camp, reporting we could follow that same route to the Río Salado. When Heredia realized that he had found a route he was very pleased, although others held different views, as related above.

On October 1 the lieutenant governor ordered the captain to get the entire expedition ready to start out on the journey, which he did. As we were about to set forth, many differences of opinion again arose in regard to the route we should follow. The captain therefore asked the lieutenant governor to decide which route we were to take and was told that he should head for the Río Salado and should act as guide. Captain Cristóbal de Heredia did as he was ordered, and we went on to spend the night in a ravine where we found some pools of water.

We resumed our journey on the second and camped for the night by the Río de las Laxas, which we crossed with great difficulty.[10] The fourth we started out again and reached a ravine where we found abundant water.

On the fifth we pursued our quest for the Río Salado until we came to another and very deep ravine. The sixth we reached some small oaks where there was plenty of water.

---

10. This was the Devil's river, which parallels in a general way the Pecos and flows into the Río Grande about twenty-five miles below the Pecos, just above the town of Del Rio.

The seventh we continued in search of the Río Salado, the object of our journey; and Captain Cristóbal de Heredia sent out Juan de Carvajal, Martín de Salazar, Domingo de Santiesteban, and Blas Martínez de Mederos for this purpose. They succeeded in finding the river, which pleased them very much. Domingo de Santiesteban came back to convey the good news that he and his companions had at last discovered the Salado, although it was impossible to reach it because of the many high rocks and gullies.[11] We spent the night in a ravine where there was a pool that supplied water for our people; but the oxen and horses were sent back. We tried every means of reaching the stream, but to no avail; and so we turned back to look for the other river, which we had noted before. Captain Cristóbal de Heredia went ahead to see if it was far away and soon found it, about three leagues from the spot where we had halted.

We set out again on the ninth and spent the night a league from the Río de las Laxas. The eleventh we continued on our way and stopped at some huts where there was no water.

The twelfth we left this place and reached some hills where we found a small pool of water; since we looked in vain for the Río de las Laxas, which was no longer visible, we sent the oxen and horses back to that river and continued vigorously to search for the Río Salado. Salazar, Diego Díaz de Berlanga, and Cristóbal Martín went on this mission. In three or four leagues they again caught sight of it and returned to camp saying that we could not get down to it. Nevertheless, we decided to proceed on our way; and, as we started out, God sent a heavy shower for our relief. We trusted that He would provide, for we knew He was merciful to us.

The fourteenth we left this place and moved on, camping for the night at the place where Cristóbal de Heredia was given his commission as maese de campo. Then the lieutenant governor, realizing that the journey was being drawn out too long, ordered that only one half an almud of wheat or corn should be given to each person per week; as the ration was small, he tried to buy some oxen from Juan Pérez de los Ríos, to be slaughtered and the meat to be distributed among the people in the camp. In the course of the negotiations with Juan Pérez de los Ríos,

---

11. While the diary here states they found the river on October 7, they could not get down to it, and it was not until the twenty-sixth that they succeeded in doing so. In the meantime, they had sent out numerous exploring parties in various directions to find a road. Not only did they encounter extremely rugged country, but they learned that the Pecos throughout its lower course lay at the bottom of a deep and narrow canyon, impossible of access. This situation extended almost as far north as Sheffield, Texas, in the extreme easterly part of Pecos county.

who could see that the need was great, he replied that he would not sell a single animal, but that if the lieutenant governor needed oxen in this emergency, they were all available and he would make a gift of them in the name of the king our lord. The lieutenant governor accepted the offer and immediately held a roll call of all his people. Finding that there were upward of one hundred and seventy persons, he ordered the distribution of one and a half pounds of meat per day for each person. With this ration and the grain portion above-mentioned, we were able to get along; but we began at that point to roast maguey in order to supplement the shortage.

On the sixteenth we continued as far as the Laxas, where we camped for the night and where a good shower fell, much to our relief, since we could not reach the river.[12] At this place we roasted a quantity of mescal. The seventeenth we went to La Cañada, where Alonso Jaimez and Ponce got lost.

When we set out again on the eighteenth, Cristóbal de Heredia and some soldiers went ahead to see if there was an approach to the Río Salado. In the course of his search we found that it could not be reached because of the bad terrain and complete lack of water; so he sent Francisco López de Ricalde and Jusepe Rodríguez back to camp while he himself rode on with the rest of his men. The two who came back told the lieutenant governor that there was no possible way of going forward, since they could not find the river, which must have turned abruptly to the west, and since the wagons could not travel by that route. This information displeased everyone, particularly Juan López [Pérez] de los Ríos, who feared that his capital would be lost, though he was even more concerned about his wife and children than his possessions. He complained bitterly, blaming the lieutenant governor for leading him astray. This was what grieved him most. As far as he was concerned, if things turned out badly, he could withdraw to a ranchería and end his days there, since the lieutenant governor had chosen a different route from the one he wanted to follow.

The lieutenant governor listened to all the hysterical complaints of Pérez and others. Then, during a lull, he called the people together and asked them what they thought should be done. There were some who expressed the opinion that they ought to go back and pick up the route that a number of the men had wanted to follow in opposition to the choice of the lieutenant governor. The latter, since the other route was the one he favored, encouraged us as kindly as he could, urging us

12. Evidently they were traveling between Devil's river (Laxas) and the Pecos (Salado).

all—men, women, and children, including the Indians—to commend ourselves to God and to have faith that He and His holy Mother would guide and enlighten us, giving wisdom to our leader so that he would not be wanting in anything, for it was his desire to serve God our Lord and his Majesty. Accordingly, he gave orders to leave this place and to go on, which we did.

Immediately afterward, the lieutenant governor sent some men to look for water along the route we were to follow. When we had gone about a quarter of a league, Francisco López de Ricalde came to the governor (who was bringing up the rear, as was his custom) to tell how Juan Pérez de los Ríos, downhearted and weeping, had asked him to intercede with Castaño to turn back, for the love of God. As soon as Ricalde broached the subject, our leader told him angrily that he did not want to have anyone talk to him about the matter; that, if the Spaniards showed fright, it would be taken as a sign of weakness on their part and they would lose their rights; and that Ricalde should tell Juan Pérez to hold his peace and go on with the trip, instead of discouraging the people. For he, the lieutenant governor (as he had already said) trusted in God, who would not let them lack water, but would provide it for them.

The lieutenant governor now withdrew from the army and marched to one side, accompanied only by a servant named Juan López. After going about half a league he came to a very large pool of water, which delighted him, for in that area such a big pond had never before been found. It seemed that the Lord had indeed provided it, as He always makes provision. Our leader hastened to the wagons and halted them so that the oxen and horses could be driven to water, as was done. Here we decided to wait for Cristóbal de Heredia. He arrived the following day, reporting that he had been unable to reach the river. Some thought that it had disappeared from our route, as had the Laxas.

In the midst of this uncertainty, the lieutenant governor sent Alonso Jaimez and some other men, including Diego Díaz de Berlanga, Cristóbal Martín, Juan López and Francisco de Mancha, with orders to follow certain human tracks found there and to procure, with the help of their interpreter, another Indian who might serve as interpreter for that land and furnish information about it.[13] He, the governor, would follow their trail with the wagons. They set out the next day.

We left this place on the nineteenth, intending to follow the route taken by Alonso Jaimez to some water found two leagues from our

13. These natives were probably Jumano Apaches, as the expedition was approaching their territory. Forbes, "Unknown Athapaskans," *Ethnohistory*, vol. 6, pp. 128-129.

starting point, according to a report sent by him through an Indian named Juan de Vega, whom he had taken along as a courier. Not being satisfied with this information, the lieutenant governor dispatched Cristóbal de Heredia to go and see the water, which he did. Finding that it was very scanty and that the route was quite different from the one we were supposed to follow, Heredia returned in great haste and said that Jaimez's road was not the one we meant to take. On being informed of this, the lieutenant governor ordered him to abandon that route and to go straight ahead, which he did. We went on to spend the night near some flat rocks and some water found by Cristóbal de Heredia.

On the twentieth we resumed our journey, much troubled by the scarcity of water, since we had not half the amount needed for that day and night. As was customary, the lieutenant governor dispatched many of his men to search for water in rocky pools or arroyos, since there were no springs anywhere in the land. God favored us, and Domingo de Santiesteban came back to report that in a canyon ahead there were large pools of water. We went on joyously, arrived there at eleven in the morning, unyoked the oxen, and remained at the pools for a couple of hours. Then we yoked the animals again and continued on our way, stopping two or three hours at some hills during the night.

We set forth once more on the twenty-first; and while we were traveling along at midday, we found a pool of water in some rocky shallows where all the people and some of the horses drank a little, but without getting enough, since we had run out of water the preceding night. We marched on and spent the next night in a dry ravine, although a half league away we found enough water for the people, and some of the horses also drank there. That night, owing to the scarcity of water, the lieutenant governor instructed Maese de Campo Crsitóbal de Heredia to send some men to look for the Río Salado, with orders not to return until they had seen it and to send someone back to report if they found water.

The maese de campo immediately dispatched Juan de Carvajal, Juan Estrada, Martín de Salazar, Juan Rodríguez Nieto, Pedro Flores, and Gonzalo de Lares, who left that very evening to discharge their commission. After marching about two leagues, they rested for a while during the night, but before dawn they were under way again in accordance with their instructions. The men were intent upon their search for the said river and resolved not to return before finding it, a purpose in which they held firm, when God willed that they should come upon some very large pools. This pleased them immensely on account of the severe shortage of water. In compliance with orders, Pedro Flores went back posthaste to report this discovery. It must have taken him less than an hour to reach the army, while the other men went on to look for the river.

At this stage of our journey the goats got lost and Pedro Pinto rushed back to say that the Indians were stealing them. The lieutenant governor and two or three soldiers went in the direction the Negro had indicated as the route of the supposed thieves, and within about a league he overtook the animals. Actually, the goats had not been stolen by Indians, for they were running away of their own accord, driven by thirst. A large number of the oxen also stampeded, goaded by the same need; but Diego de Viruega rounded them up about two leagues from the camp.

On the twenty-third, as we were yoking our oxen and getting ready to leave, Pedro Flores arrived with the report that water had been found. We went back with him to spend the night in the place described, where we rejoiced to find that the water was plentiful. The next day the men who had discovered the river returned to report that the hills and sierras came to an end at this point, and that the river was about four leagues from our location. They were welcomed for their good news, in view of the hardships we had endured thus far, the poverty of the land, the scanty water, and the exhaustion of the horses, which was what we most regretted. For we were all in the depths of despair because of the rocky terrain on the journey in search of the long-sought Río Salado.

Twenty-five dozen horseshoes were worn out on the mountains here, since there was no way to travel save on horseback. Many horses wore out their shoes in two or three days, incredible as it may seem, and a large number of the animals became lame. So great was the hardship endured before we reached water that only those of our people who witnessed the ordeal will believe how much we suffered. If the discovery of this route were to be paid for in money, it would take an enormous sum.

The lieutenant governor expressed thanks to his companions and the fervent hope that God our Lord and his Majesty would reward them. He also assured them that in so far as might be in his power, he would grant, in the name of the king, any favor they might ask. They should not hesitate to speak, because he could never repay with money their many labors or the enthusiasm with which they had helped him; for if they were to be rewarded with cash it would require a great sum. As if with one voice, his followers replied that they would always be ready to withstand such hardships as they might have to endure, since their main interest lay precisely in doing what the lieutenant governor ordered, in the name of his Majesty. For this he thanked them and said that, by God's will and with His favor, he trusted that they would accomplish their purpose, since it was a very worthy one, and that the king would reward them as he does all who serve him. The lieutenant governor was pleased at the sturdy spirit displayed by his men, and they were no less gratified by what he told them. I cannot exaggerate nor even describe here the aforementioned hardships. In short, after finding the river we were seeking, we thought we had been through the worst of the struggle, and so we remained there in great contentment for two days.

We left that place on the twenty-fifth, and after traveling for two leagues we camped for the night. We were without water.

On the twenty-sixth we set out for the river[14] we had sought so eagerly, but could not find a way down to it except by some steep slopes which we descended with great difficulty. These hardships seemed very light to all of us in our eager desire to serve God and the king. In the descent some wagons broke down, among them one containing the coffer for the royal fifths. We all dismounted and the lieutenant governor told us to go down to the river for a rest with the [undamaged] wagons and the people, while he would remain there with some men to watch the royal coffer, which he did. The next day the wagon [holding the coffer] was made ready and taken to the river.

The following day, while we were at the river, Alonso Jaimez arrived with the men he had taken along, saying [at first] that he had followed the trail specified by the lieutenant governor, and that after three days of travel he had come upon a large number of people of the Depesguan nation, who received him cordially.[15] When he explained to them through the interpreter the purpose of the trip, the natives were highly pleased and gave him many buffalo and chamois skins, fine shoes of the type they themselves wore, and a quantity of meat. They also indicated that we might travel through their region and that they would lead us to places where there were settlements and an abundance of corn. So Alonso Jaimez turned back, very satisfied with the friendship shown him by the Indians.

After his return to the camp, Jaimez [finally] explained to the lieu-

14. The Salado.
15. The word is spelled Tepelguan in version A. These were Jumano Apaches, who inhabited the region from La Junta to the Colorado river in Texas. Forbes, loc. cit. See also his *Apache, Navaho, and Spaniard*, p. 68.

tenant governor that he had not followed the route suggested by the latter, and the governor laughed at him upon learning how widely Jaimez's route deviated from the one specified, at the same time displaying all the gratification that could be desired. Jaimez admitted that he had not brought back a single Indian [interpreter, as instructed], but he added that perhaps some of us might wish to take that same route. The lieutenant governor was satisfied that, among other things, there was a river which flowed near the settlements visited by Jaimez, emptying into the one that we had reached and were to follow. Consequently the governor said that he was going to travel upstream and that when he reached the juncture of the two rivers, he would go to visit the people described. This pleased Jaimez and the men who had accompanied him, because they very much wanted the expedition to go that way.

On the twenty-eighth we traveled upstream and found a number of newly deserted rancherías.[16] One lone Indian appeared and approached the wagons, but not a single interpreter of the many brought with us could understand him. They asked him several questions and these he managed to understand. The lieutenant governor ordered that he be given some corn and asked him to summon back the people of that vicinity, telling them not to be afraid. So he left, and we settled down for the night on some low hills by the river.

We continued our journey on the twenty-ninth and spent the night on the bank of the river itself, where we caught some fish. The thirtieth we traveled on and camped at some old rancherías swarming with flies. On the following day many horses were missing; they had strayed because of the poor grazing. While searching for them, Diego Díaz de Berlanga and Francisco de Mancha discovered some large salines with incredible amounts of very white salt. We spent the night among marshes formed by water from the river, which emptied into them in considerable volume.

The first to reach this spot were Diego de Viruega, Francisco López de Ricalde, and Andrés Pérez, secretary of government. They saw some natives who were traveling, overtook them, and brought back four persons; the rest fled and hid in the marsh. These natives had with them some dogs laden with packs, as is the custom in that region, a novelty

16. Probably along the Pecos, between Sheffield, Texas, and the present New Mexico-Texas border, in Jumano territory. Castaño's route lay east of the river, as indicated by the diarist's statement on November 26, when he said that up to that point they had always followed its left or east bank.

none of us had ever seen before.[17] The men returned to camp with the four Indians, but they did not find the lieutenant governor there, as he had turned back that day to search for some of the horses. We at once released the two Indian women with all their goods, holding the two men until the lieutenant governor arrived; when he got back and learned what had happened, he was very pleased. He saw the Indians and spoke to them, but there was no one who could understand them, so he ordered that they be given meat and corn and told them by means of signs not to be afraid. They left with all their possessions, including a dog whose load consisted of two hides tied with a rope and fitted with poitrel and harness. We were all delighted at the sight of this novelty.

On November 2 we traveled on and camped for the night at a place where the Indians attacked Juan de Vega with arrows. This happened when Diego de Viruega, Alonso Lucas, Andrés Pérez, and others who were leading the way, crossed the river upon reaching an impassable spot, at which moment they saw a group of Indian men and went toward them. We all began to talk to the group by signs, some from one side of the river and some from the other. Our men drew away from the Indians, but Juan de Vega, himself a native, lagged behind. Some of the Indians, seeing that he was alone, seized him, took some ropes away from him, threw him into the river, and shot him with three arrows. The next morning a large number of natives appeared, and the lieutenant governor tried in every way to get them to come to the camp, but to no avail.[18]

While we were at this place, where we rested for a day, the men in the camp noticed the Indians driving away some oxen. The lieutenant governor, seeing their shameless behavior, ordered Cristóbal de Heredia and five soldiers to go after the thieves. During the pursuit, Heredia and his men encountered a group of Indians, who, they said, attacked them with arrows. Our men in self-defense killed some of the assailants, apprehended four, and brought them to camp. In view of the theft of the oxen and other offenses, the lieutenant governor ordered that one of the prisoners be hanged as punishment and that the other three, since they were mere youths, be kept as interpreters for the expedition. In order that they might be taught our language quickly, he entrusted

17. The travois, or dog train, used by the Plains Indians in eastern New Mexico and western Texas. Use of dogs for carrying packs up to as much as one hundred pounds was described by the chroniclers of the Coronado and Oñate expeditions. See Hammond and Rey, *Narratives of the Coronado Expedition*, pp. 262, 293, and 311; also their *Oñate, Colonizer of New Mexico*, vol. I, p. 401; and Bolton, *Spanish Exploration in the Southwest*, p. 227.

18. These Indians were clearly Jumanos, as Castaño was now traveling through their territory.

one each to Juan Pérez de los Ríos, Pedro Flores, and Cristóbal de Heredia. Despite our extreme care, they escaped with an ox as the other Indians fled. At this same place we watered our animals by hand. We found quantities of mesquite, which the humbler members of the party ate, thus saving us some provisions; this was much appreciated, as the supplies were getting low.

On the third we set out again and camped for the night by an extensive marsh where there was abundant game. The fifth we went on and spent the night on the bank of the river. On the way we passed a newly deserted ranchería that must have had many people since it extended over a large area. It was on the same day that we found many rich salt beds.[19] On the seventh we left and marched through extensive sand dunes Then we camped near a cove of the river.

On the eighth we traveled away from the river over some fine plains. We halted for the night on one that was very extensive. That day we caught a goodly quantity of fish, which we considered a great treat, aside from the fact that the catch relieved a pressing need and supplemented our provisions, as did the abundance of mesquite we found there, which was eaten not only by the humbler members of the expedition but also by the rest of us.

The tenth we continued our trip, sleeping at various places. We passed some mesquite groves and camped for the night at a bend of the river, after driving the cattle to a little island. A child, daughter of Francisco López de Ricalde, died at this place. We caught a lot of fish; and there was so much mesquite that occasionally it spared us the need of slaughtering.

On the eleventh we started out again and traveled along a varied route. We spent the night on a fine plain. Here there were many wolves, which killed some goats that had strayed from the fold.

We resumed our journey on the thirteenth, traversing a very pleasant plain and halting for the night by the river in a canebrake. Viruega caught many more fish during the day. That night an Indian couple failed to return to camp, which grieved us, as we feared they had been killed by other Indians.

The fifteenth we continued to a bend in the river where there were many tracks of cattle. On the sixteenth we traveled over a fine road away from the river to a place where it made a big bend. There, a tame deer belonging to Catalina de Charles broke a leg.

The seventeenth, while we were traversing some hills, the axle of the

19. Forbes believes that Castaño was in the vicinity of Imperial and Grandfalls, Texas, some one hundred and twenty-five miles southeast of Carlsbad, New Mexico.

large cart broke in descending a slope, so that we spent the night away from the river. By now our provisions of corn and wheat were well-nigh depleted. Since we had plenty of fish and mesquite, the lieutenant governor ordered that each person be given only one small tortilla for each meal, but that two pounds of meat be distributed also to every individual per day. All of this caused great dissatisfaction and privation, and our hardships increased.

On the eighteenth we traveled by way of a very fine plain and camped for the night in a clearing by the river at the foot of some low mesas. The nineteenth we slept on a sandy beach where Juan de Carvajal and Juan Pérez had some sort of dispute.

On the twentieth, after leaving the sandy area, we followed a fine plain lying at a distance from the river, which made a big turn at that point. We spent the night here and rested for a day, as some of the oxen had been left behind at the previous camping place. We went in search of them, found a number, and assumed that none was missing. We also saw a column of smoke on a mountain four leagues away, which some of the men wanted to investigate; but the lieutenant governor would not allow it, apparently fearing that some harm might be done to the Indians.[20] Although he did not expressly say so, this was the interpretation given to his refusal. The men argued that he should go on to find out the cause of the fire and bring back an Indian, but he replied that the attempt would be pointless since we had no interpreter for these natives. He added that those people would not be able to furnish us with any information; that he himself was satisfied we were on the right route; and that farther on he would try to obtain an Indian, since by then we should be closer to the place we were looking for. Some of the soldiers were displeased because he did not allow them to go out immediately and get Indians to serve as guides.

We resumed our journey on the twenty-second and traveled over some hills where there was a good trail. The lieutenant governor, accompanied by his servant, Juan López, today climbed to the top of the sierra and saw another mountain farther on. We camped for the night by the river on pleasant level ground. The goats broke out of the corral during the night and the wolves killed a goodly number of them.

The twenty-third we left this place, where the river turned sharply toward the west, and we came upon a very large corral used by the In-

20. Very likely the smoke column was in the Guadalupe mountains west of Carlsbad.

dians for enclosing cattle.[21] We stopped for the night on level ground extending to the bank of the river, where the sierra came to an end.

On the twenty-fourth we set out once more, noting that the river turned northeast again. We crossed it here and pressed on to a small stream where we spent the night. Here there were many willows and grapevines, as well as a large pond where we caught some catfish [*bagres*], the best we had eaten on the entire trip.

The twenty-sixth we recrossed the river, now keeping it on our right; before, it had always been on our left. There were fine plains in this locality. Here many horses were sent back. We slept by the river, although the weather was beginning to get very cold. Midway on this stretch of the journey we found a spring, the only one we had seen from the time we left the Río Bravo.[22]

On the twenty-seventh we traveled up the river over a fine plain and camped for the night on the river bank at a place thick with reed-grass, evidently of the kind that grows in marshes. This vegetation was extremely dry, indicating that it had not rained here for a long time.

On the twenty-eighth we went on to a place where the river turned northeast and followed it upstream over very pleasant level land. That day the lieutenant governor went alone to inspect a grove two leagues away toward the west which we had seen from the place where we stopped for the night. When he returned to camp he said that it was a grove of the biggest willows he had seen anywhere in the Indies. He had also noted a great many deer on the plains, the herds being so large that he was unable to count the animals. That night we camped near some sand dunes by the river, and while Juan de Carvajal and Diego de Viruega were sleeping in a bed of rushes, the servants in the camp

21. There is a possibility that this might have been a game corral, used by the Indians in driving deer and antelope into an enclosure or restricted area where they could be killed more easily. On November 28, for example, the party had noted a great many deer. Cf. W. W. Hill, "The Agricultural and Hunting Methods of the Navaho Indians," *Yale University Publications in Anthropology,* No. 18 (1938), pp. 145-146; or, as Forbes suggests, maybe the Indians even at this early date already had "livestock," presumably horses, in his opinion. The Spanish reads *ganado,* however. Forbes, *Apache, Navaho, and Spaniard,* p. 71.

22. Before the development of irrigation and the drilling of artesian wells, there was a great deal of water in the Artesia-Roswell area. The water table was probably high, caused by the streams flowing eastward from the Sacramento mountains. Mr. T. F. Stipp, Regional Geologist of the U.S. Geological Survey at Roswell, informs us that today there is a spring, known as Major Johnson spring, on the Pecos river twelve miles northwest of Carlsbad. Farther north, there is a large spring which is the source of South Spring river in the vicinity of Roswell. (Letters of February 20 and March 11, 1963, to Hammond.) It is quite possible that one of these marks the point reached by Castaño's force at this time.

set fire to the reeds, so that the two men just missed being burned alive and were saved only by the quick help given them.

The twenty-ninth we went up the river over fine plains and came to a small stream which seemed to rise in a sierra toward the west. We crossed this stream, traversing pleasant plains, and found a water hole in the middle of a level area but near a little rise. We halted for the night at a very large cottonwood grove, where we found an olla and some fresh cornhusks, which delighted everyone.[23]

On the thirtieth we traveled over some fine level land. At this point, the river turned sharply east. While we were on the march, Pedro de Iñigo came running to the lieutenant governor and said that there was a settlement on the bank of the river, that it was inhabited, and that he thought the people were leaving it. The leader hurried ahead with some men only to find that the settlement was a very large abandoned ranchería and that the people whom Pedro de Iñigo had seen were our own, although he had not realized this because he saw them from afar. We spent the night in this ranchería in the midst of extensive plains.[24]

On December 1 we left this place. After going through beds of rushes for about half a league, we came to a river which seemed to flow from a sierra rising toward the west,[25] but we could not cross it as the water was too deep. We therefore turned east to cross the river we had previously followed, into which the other stream flowed. While we were doing so, the main wagon broke down, and Alonso Jaimez and Juan de Estrada went down with it. Not being divers, they and their horses splashed about, causing considerable merriment; and they were irked about being called divers.

Here we camped. The next morning the lieutenant governor ordered Maese de Campo Cristóbal de Heredia to choose a few men and go up the river, or in whatever direction he thought best, to search for people from whom we could obtain information about the land. According to the latitude, taken at Castaño's command, it seemed to him there should be settlements in that neighborhood. The maese de campo set out on this mission, taking along Francisco López de Ricalde, Francisco de Mancha, Juan Rodríguez Nieto, Gonzalo de Lares, Cristóbal Martín, Juan López, Domingo de Santiesteban, Diego de Viruega, Juan de

23. They were pleased presumably because this discovery might indicate the presence of Pueblo Indians, who were known to grow corn.

24. This might have been the large ranchería noted by Espejo on his return journey down the Pecos in 1583. Cf. Forbes, *op. cit.*, 71; Espejo's "Narrative," p. 229.

25. Doubtless the Hondo, which rises in the mountains of Lincoln county and flows into the Pecos near the present city of Roswell. Both the terrain and the distance traveled fit this identification.

Contreras, José Rodríguez, and Domingo Hernández. They set out together, with instructions to make every effort to find some Indians and to bring one or two back to camp, so that we could learn from the captives whether there were any settlements in the vicinity. Our men were not to enter any town even if they found one, because the governor wanted to do so himself with his wagons and his entire force united in one body.[26]

On the third we started out again and traveled upstream through swamps and reeds, camping for the night in a brushy hollow on the river bank.[27] Here we blundered, permitting the lieutenant governor to go up the river alone with no one following him, because we believed he would soon come back. Instead, he traveled so far that two hours after dark he had not yet returned. We were all greatly worried and somewhat ashamed at having let him go alone, though we had erred only through negligence, assuming that he would come back in a short while. We lighted many fires, hoping that he could find his way by their light. In view of his failure to return, and our growing concern for his safety, Juan de Carvajal, Pedro Iñigo, and Pedro Flores decided to go in search of him, carrying lighted torches so that he could see them. Thus equipped, they set out and found him a quarter of a league from the camp, making his way back. All complained because the leader had gone out alone. He replied that he had not intended to go so far, and that he had done so only to explore the route, because the present trail was sandy and very difficult. Moreover, he said, the river turned there, and he wanted to get off the bad road. This was the reason for his delay. When the people saw him, their deep distress over his delay turned into joy.

On the fourth we set out from this region of sand banks and dunes, leaving the river where it swerved and taking a short cut over some plains. That day the lieutenant governor turned back with three companions to explore a river of which he had heard, flowing from the east. They reached the stream we had been following and then came back to us because there was no such [second] river. The ones who reported seeing it were Indians who on the previous day had gone in search of some stray horses, and what they had actually seen was one and the same

26. Castaño undoubtedly had or was familiar with reports of the Chamuscado and Espejo expeditions and realized he was in the area where he might expect to find the first pueblos. These two earlier expeditions had found the first New Mexico pueblos near San Marcial, on the Río Grande, very nearly in the same latitude as Roswell, between 33° and 34°.

27. While Heredia's party hurried on ahead, the main force proceeded more slowly, encumbered by wagons, cattle, and supplies.

river. Castaño, then, turned again and at sunset rejoined the people and the wagons. We spent the night on some sand dunes away from the river.

On the sixth we left this place, closely following the river, which turned northeast. We camped for the night on the bank in a field of tall grass. Here the grassy plain caught fire, and we were fearful of losing one of the wagons—a catastrophe which would have happened if we had not made strenuous efforts to put out the flames.

The following day, while we were camped at this spot, Gonzalo de Lares and Francisco de Mancha—who had gone with the maese de campo on the mission mentioned above—returned with a note for the lieutenant governor, asking for provisions, since the supplies of Heredia's party had given out. They reported that they had not found, and could not find, any people or traces of people. In view of this report, the governor asked Juan Pérez de los Ríos for an ox, which was slaughtered. He then told Gonzalo de Lares and Francisco de Mancha to take the meat to the maese de campo and his companions, adding that in regard to corn, flour, or wheat there was none left; and so they went back with the meat. Lares and Mancha were to tell the maese de campo that he should keep on looking for Indians, as he had been in-structed; but that, if he came in sight of a pueblo, he should not enter it.

The seventh [eighth?] we started out once more, crossed the river, and spent the night in some ravines where the river flowed by extensive cottonwood groves.[28]

On the ninth we continued up the river, which turned north again. We traveled over good trails and through many groves, stopping for the night among the trees on the bank of the stream. In this area there was abundant mesquite, without which we should have suffered severely. The Lord always provides in time of greatest need; and not only the Indians, but all of us, men and women alike, ate mesquite.

On the tenth we pressed forward, away from the river, which made a big bend; but we recrossed it later toward the east, for on the other side the terrain was difficult. After we had crossed, we camped for the night.

On the eleventh we traveled northeast over some hills at a distance from the stream, since the land there was broken and also because of a

---

28. By this time the expedition would have been near Fort Sumner, famous in later days as the site of the Bosque Redondo, where the Navajos were imprisoned from 1863 to 1868. See W. A. Keleher's excellent chapters on "The Long Walk," in his *Turmoil in New Mexico, 1864-1868* (Santa Fé, 1952).

big bend made by the river. We stopped for the night on a plain, without water.

We continued our march on the twelfth over very pleasant plains, eventually coming back to the river. Upon reaching it, the lieutenant governor ordered the arrest of Alonso Jaimez. The next day, and while we were still there, Diego de Viruega, who had gone with the maese de campo, returned to tell about the route we were to follow and to say that his party had not seen any natives. He had traveled some twelve leagues up the river, and found traces of people and freshly burned plains. In the distance toward the north he had also seen a sierra. The tracks of people led in that direction, and Heredia's men were following them. This was the report brought by Diego de Viruega, who had come back alone for that purpose.[29]

The next day, after leaving this place, we again crossed the river to the west bank and traveled over fine plains away from the river, since it swerved widely at that point. We camped for the night in a grove near the river, where we found an extensive field of grass from which our people gathered large quantities of seed to be toasted and ground for food.

On the fourteenth we traveled northwest, following the river, and stopped for the night in a thick clump of trees, where Don Gaspar's wagon broke down. Here we also gathered a large amount of the grass seed previously mentioned. We had only twelve fanegas of wheat left, which the lieutenant governor had brought for planting; and consequently, in view of the great hardships, he distributed very small amounts to the persons who seemed to him to need it the most. The rest got along on meat, mesquite, and grass seed.

On the seventeenth we left the grove and camped for the night by the river, at a place where Juan Pérez's big dog was killed by a kick from an ox.

On the nineteenth we traveled approximately west for about a league, through some ravines. Later we made a sharper turn to the west on account of the difficult terrain and the river; and so we camped in a canyon where there was a small stream that flowed from the northwest to disappear in the sandy bottom of the arroyo before it could reach the river we were following.

---

29. Following modern locations, the expedition now would have been near Santa Rosa, or even beyond it, on the way to Anton Chico, which would account for the river's pronounced westward turn at this point. Forbes suggests they might have been near Fort Sumner. *Apache, Navaho, and Spaniard*, p. 72.

The twenty-first we marched over a pleasant though upward-sloping plain, about a league from the river, which bent in a wide curve. We stopped for the night in a sheltered spot at some distance from the stream. Here many expressed their conviction that we were lost. The lieutenant governor and captain general told them not to worry, for he knew that the pueblos were not more than twenty or twenty-five leagues away, upstream.[30] This satisfied some of his people; others were more dubious.

We left this place on the twenty-third and traveled east over a fine plain, since the river made a big bend. That day the lieutenant governor and Andrés Pérez, the government secretary, went ahead to explore; and from a hill they saw that some of the men who had gone with the maese de campo were on their way back, driving their pack animals. As the lieutenant governor looked at them for a long time and they did not respond with any sign of recognition, he felt very grieved, inferring that they had not found anything or had met with some disaster. Going forward, he met Juan Rodríguez Nieto, on foot, with his harquebus on his shoulder and following his exhausted, saddleless horse. When Castaño inquired why he traveled that way, the soldier was reluctant to tell what had happened. Finally, however, he said that as they marched up the river they found a footpath they followed until, from the top of a sierra, they saw a pueblo.[31] They then camped for the night and the next morning they went toward the pueblo and were forced to enter it because the weather was so bitterly cold and the land was covered with snow. The Indians of this pueblo received them in a friendly manner, giving them food for that day and some eight or ten fanegas of corn.

Early the next day, wishing to turn back, the maese de campo sent some soldiers to the pueblo to ask for more corn. They went to carry out their orders; and, with a view to reassuring the Indians and further dispelling their fears, the men carried no arms. All except Alonso Lucas and Domingo de Santiesteban, who were shelling some corn the Indians had given them, walked securely about the pueblo, relying on the goodwill of the inhabitants. All of a sudden the natives began to shout and, at the same time, to hurl stones and shoot arrows. Faced with this attack, the men fell back as best they could to the place where they had left their arms. In the meantime, some Indians had come down

30. The distance from Santa Rosa to Pecos would be about seventy-five miles, a bit more allowing for the turns in the river. This fits Castaño's estimate reasonably well.

31. This was Pecos, though the diarist nowhere actually mentions it by name. From the context, however, it could not have been any other.

from the flat roofs of their three- or four-story houses and had taken some of the arms, all except about five harquebuses; whereupon the soldiers seized these weapons and withdrew from the plaza where they had camped, leaving in the hands of the Indians five harquebuses, eleven swords, nineteen saddles, nine sets of horse armor, and a quantity of wearing apparel and bedding.

When the maese de campo realized the damage the Indians had caused, he decided to go back to meet the people and the wagons coming up the river. Three of his men were wounded—Domingo de Santiesteban, Francisco de Mancha, and Jusepe Rodríguez. They started the return journey that very day, all riding bareback, using halters for reins, deprived of cloaks and coverings, and traveling for three days without a morsel to eat. Then God willed that they should meet an Indian woman on the plain who gave them some corn flour and beans, so little that it hardly amounted to a handful for each person; but had it not been for this aid they would have perished from hunger, cold, snow, and fierce winds, for the weather was very severe. Let us all give some thought to the sufferings of these men! When they reached the lieutenant governor, he received them with great joy, in spite of what had happened, though God knows how sad we all felt on seeing those men return in such distress.

In view of these circumstances, we[32] decided not to follow any farther the route along the river by which those men had returned, for they told us it was scarcely passable, on account of the numerous gullies. We turned back about a league to a spot where the lieutenant governor ordered us to rest for a few days, which we did. Then, one day, mindful of what had happened to the maese de campo and his men and of the great damage they had suffered at the hands of the Indians, our leader called us together and spoke encouragingly to us, exhorting us not to worry over past misfortunes, although he was very sorry for the hardships suffered by the men. As for the property taken by the Indians, he would go personally to the pueblo where the event had occurred and make every possible effort to recover the arms and other goods. Everyone agreed to this, much pleased with his plans.

In order to exact submission from the Indians to our king, and disregarding the scarcity of provisions, the lieutenant governor decided to take along twenty soldiers and an equal number of servants, and to

32. That is, the main expedition, with the wagons and other equipment. The diarist's use of the word "we," "dexamos la derota," and, under date of December 26, "salimos deste parage," and the phraseology of related paragraphs, suggests that Andrés Pérez, the official secretary of the expedition, was the author of the "Memoria."

set out after only two or three days' rest so that the Indians would have less time to ruin the arms. Since for many days we had had nothing to eat except a little meat and some grass seed, though there were a few fanegas of wheat set aside for planting, he now decided, in preparation for this expedition, to keep only two fanegas for that purpose and to apportion the rest among all of us. Juan Pérez de los Ríos, realizing how important it was for the lieutenant governor to carry out the proposed expedition, came to him and suggested that he should order enough animals slaughtered to supply plenty of meat for the trip, since there was no other food to take. Thus three oxen were slaughtered, and the lieutenant governor asked the maese de campo to distribute the meat among the men who were to accompany him; and so it was done.

On the twenty-sixth [of December], Castaño de Sosa set out on his journey accompanied by the maese de campo, Francisco López de Ricalde, Pedro Flores, Martín de Salazar, Diego de Viruega, Alonso Jaimez, Juan Rodríguez Nieto, Juan Sánchez de Avalos, Juan Sánchez, Francisco de Mancha, Juan de Carvajal, Diego Díaz de Berlanga, Francisco de Bascones, Cristóbal Martín, Hernán Ponce de León, Andrés Pérez (secretary), Juan López, Blas Martín de Mederos, Domingo Hernández (a Portuguese), Juan de Estrada, and seventeen servants. We all departed on horseback and camped for the night a league away by the river.

We resumed our journey on the twenty-seventh, traveling over a fine plain, and spent the night at Urraca.[33] A freak accident befell Juan Rodríguez Nieto at this place. While he was trying to start a fire, a spark flew out from somewhere, and the large and small powder flasks hanging from his belt exploded, but without doing any damage.

On the twenty-eighth we left this camp and traveled all day. One of our men, Pedro Flores, had suffered an attack of melancholia the day before, which left him exhausted and somewhat incoherent. Before starting out, the lieutenant governor asked him to go back to the others, who were following us, with instructions from our leader to camp at Urraca and await further orders. He was sure the sick man would be able to return safely and would find the wagons, at a spot four leagues away. Pedro Flores replied that he would never go back; but some

33. This is, of course, the advance party. Urraca must have been near Ribera, about twenty-five miles from Pecos pueblo where the Santa Fé Railway now crosses the Pecos river. Here there were water and fine plains, providing food for the stock, and no Indians in the immediate vicinity. Castaño's advance party, after a major tour of much of the northern pueblo area, returned to Urraca a month later to bring the main force, wagons and all, to Santo Domingo on the Río Grande. It was there that Morlete caught up with Castaño's force and arrested and took him a captive to Mexico city.

insisted that he should be ordered to do so, for they felt he was really sick and so dangerously melancholic that he appeared in a measure to have lost his mind. The lieutenant governor felt sorry for him in his suffering and again asked him to return, saying that a soldier or servant would be sent to accompany him; but he would not consent. At this point the lieutenant governor talked of turning back on account of Pedro Flores, who felt very badly about it and said that there was no reason for such action.

Since he seemed to feel better, we continued our trip and stopped for the night at a place called Caballo, near a small water hole. This place is so named because here, after the experiences above related, the maese de campo had ordered a horse slaughtered for food when there was nothing else to eat. Shortly afterward Pedro Flores, very cheerful, came to the quarters of the lieutenant governor and said he was quite well and free from pain, but very hungry because, from the time he had left the wagons, he had not eaten a thing; nor had he slept for three nights— something unheard of, it seemed to me. The lieutenant governor rejoiced at what Pedro Flores said, as well he might, because he was very fond of the man. He therefore ordered that Flores be given some meat and three tortillas; these tortillas were a real luxury, since we had almost none. The next morning Pedro Flores was missing and the lieutenant governor ordered the maese de campo to search for him, which he did, accompanied by two other men; but they could not find him and returned to camp. Then, as they were rounding up the horses, they discovered that Pedro Flores's horse was missing, as were his saddle, harquebus, and armor, all of which he had taken with him. Believing he had gone back to the wagons that day, the lieutenant governor ordered the party to proceed, and we obeyed.

We left this place on the thirtieth and camped a short league from the pueblo,[34] after marching over a bad trail. We slept on the bank of the river.

On the thirty-first, before daybreak, the lieutenant governor ordered breakfast prepared, telling us all to eat and to feel confident that we should be well received by the Indians of the entire pueblo, because it was his firm intention to cause them no harm at all. Accordingly, he asked us not to make any move save by his orders or those of the maese de campo. Then we headed straight for the pueblo.

In order that the Indians should be aware of our approach before we came in sight, the governor asked the maese de campo to dispatch

34. This was the great pueblo of Pecos.

some men by a hidden route to see if they could find an Indian who might be sent ahead to the pueblo, so that he could explain to the natives that we were coming not to molest them but to place them under the protection and authority of his Majesty. Martín de Salazar undertook this mission, together with Cristóbal [Martín] and Diego de Viruega, while the lieutenant governor and his party continued on their way toward the pueblo, straight over the path which the other men would have to take after finding the Indian spokesman.

Going forward in this manner, his men in formation and with flag unfurled, the governor, as we came in view of the pueblo, ordered the buglers to blow their trumpets. When he reached the town, he noticed that the natives were in battle array, men as well as women standing fully prepared on the terraces and down below. Surveying the situation, he ordered the maese de campo to pitch camp at the distance of an harquebus shot from the pueblo, on the side where it seemed strongest, and this was done. Then he ordered the two bronze pieces set up, asking Juan Rodríguez Nieto to take charge of them and to keep the fuse lighted in order that everything might be in readiness in case the guns should be needed for defense against the Indians and their pueblo; or rather, in case the natives should try some shameless trick like the one played previously. He urged us to be very alert and to conduct ourselves like brave soldiers, as we were accustomed to do.

After making all these arrangements, the lieutenant governor called to the Indians in sign language, but none would leave his dwelling or come out from behind the barricades, trenches, or ramparts which the pueblo maintained for its defense at the most vital points. Although these had all been constructed earlier, we could not understand the present activities of the Indians; but later they explained to us that they were at war with other groups, and that this was the reason for the fortifications, except that the many earthen bulwarks on the terraces of their houses had been newly added to protect the pueblo against us.[35]

All this took place at about eight o'clock in the morning. The lieutenant governor then left his quarters, acompanied by the maese de campo, Martín de Salazar, Juan de Carvajal, and Blas Martínez de Mederos. On nearing the houses of the pueblo, he called to the Indians and told them he would not do them any harm or injury, but this failed to calm them. On the contrary, they hastened to pile up stones on the

---

35. A part of the Coronado expedition visited Pecos in 1540, and Castañeda, the chronicler, left an excellent account of the town. See Hammond and Rey, *Narratives of the Coronado Expedition*, pp. 256-258.

terraces. The stones were brought by the women, for the men were all armed, at their posts, and shouting lustily at us.

The lieutenant governor and his soldiers circled the entire pueblo in an effort to soothe the natives with kind words and by signs, offering gifts to placate them, but to no avail. Instead of softening, the Indians shot arrows and hurled quantities of stones by means of slings, growing more and more clamorous. These maneuvers lasted about five hours, while the governor's group marched around the pueblo several times and the main body of soldiers remained in camp, as ordered. Then the group returned to camp, where the lieutenant governor ordered us all to remain armed and to round up the horses. Taking a few more articles of the kind he had given the natives before, such as knives and other small items, they went back to the pueblo, circled it once more, and tried again to give the inhabitants some presents in an attempt to find out who was the captain of the pueblo. As a result of this attempt, our men saw and talked with the chieftain. One of the soldiers in the group on this occasion was Diego de Viruega, who dismounted and tried to climb over a crumbling corner of the fortifications in order to give presents to some Indians near there who showed signs of wanting to be friendly; yet they would not allow him to ascend.

At that moment the captain of the pueblo came up and was given a knife and some other trifles; but even this failed to pacify the natives. So the Spaniards returned to their quarters, and the lieutenant governor said to them: "These Indians do not want to be our friends. What do you gentlemen think?" Several responded by asking what he himself wanted to do with the Indians, and he replied that it was his wish to subdue them by peaceful means without injury to either side. The soldiers countered by saying that he should not waste much time in this effort, as it was useless. The lieutenant governor then summoned Andrés Pérez, the secretary, to accompany him, which Pérez did; and when they had gone back to the pueblo and marched around it, the secretary was asked to certify that Castaño had tried to communicate with the natives by signs and had spent considerable time in circling the pueblo in company with the maese de campo, Martín de Salazar, Juan de Carvajal, Blas Martínez de Mederos, and Diego de Viruega. Since he, the secretary, had witnessed the peaceable overtures made to the Indians by the lieutenant governor, both previously and in the company of the said Andrés Pérez, the latter should so certify, drawing up an affidavit to be witnessed by the others.

The governor then returned to camp and once more asked his men what should be done, since the Indians would not listen to reason; and they all answered with one accord that he ought not to waste any more time on those dogs. He replied by inquiring what course they wished to take, and the men repeated that the natives should be overcome by force, since they refused to accept the friendship we had offered in peace and goodwill. The lieutenant governor objected that he thought it was by then too late to undertake the task suggested, to which his men replied that if God wished to grant them victory, there was time enough and to spare.

It was then about two o'clock in the afternoon, and we all believed that the lieutenant governor was acting as he did in order to allow the Indians more time. In view of the unanimous opinion of the soldiers, he ordered the maese de campo to post two men on a commanding elevation back of the pueblo so that they could see if any of the inhabitants were leaving. The maese sent Juan de Carvajal and Blas Martínez de Mederos to the observation post and they departed on this mission. The governor returned to the pueblo, where he made another appeal to the Indians and attempted to soothe them; but they would not relent. Moreover, an Indian woman came out on a terrace connecting the houses (which are four or five stories) and threw some ashes at him; and as she did so the natives began to shout. He turned back, commanding all of us who bore arms to make ready for battle and mount our horses. Then he ordered Juan Rodríguez Nieto to fire one of the guns over the pueblo, which Nieto did; at the same time the harquebuses were fired in the hope that this would frighten the natives. As we drew close to the pueblo, the Indians hurled showers of stones, by hand or with slings, and shot many arrows. Still the lieutenant governor went on appealing to them, while they derided him. In the meantime the Indian women showed fierce courage and kept on bringing more stones to the terraces.

Thereupon the lieutenant governor ordered the maese de campo to attack the pueblo in earnest. For our greater protection, Castaño and the maese de campo went to an unoccupied section of the pueblo, where they ordered Diego de Viruega, Francisco de Mancha, Diego Díaz de Berlanga, and Juan Rodríguez Nieto to climb to the top with one of the artillery pieces. The men did so, although with much difficulty, because the Indians were harrying them fiercely from behind a parapet and some trenches. To facilitate the ascent, the lieutenant governor attacked the Indians at this point and forced them to withdraw. When the soldiers reached the top, he told them to fire their harquebuses from there, aiming wherever the attack would be most effective. Then he returned to the maese de campo and the other men, who were facing the main forces of the pueblo. This being the strongest point, we attacked it with a large number of guns; and the Indians, realizing the strength of our onslaught, replied in kind. None of them abandoned his section or trench; on the contrary, each one defended the post entrusted to him, without faltering in the least. Such intelligence among barbarians seemed incredible.

At the time when the Spaniards were fighting near that section, Thomas, one of the lieutenant governor's Indian servants armed with bow and arrow, began to shoot at the inhabitants; and another Indian, named Miguel, did likewise. When the natives noticed that we were shooting arrows, they became alarmed and showed more fear of those weapons than of our harquebuses. The lieutenant governor then ordered us to shoot in every direction, which we did. Thomas, the above-mentioned Indian, together with Domingo Fernández, a Portuguese, entered one of the houses, while the other men remained at their posts, firing their harquebuses. The Indians, finding themselves hard pressed, abandoned some of the dwellings; and the lieutenant governor, sensing that the place could be entered safely on that side, ordered some of the men to climb to the top of the fortified point and take it. After this was accomplished, he went to the section where Viruega, Mancha, Diego Díaz, and Juan Rodríguez were posted and asked them how things were going. They replied that two of their party were wounded, but that most of the natives were abandoning the stronghold we were trying to seize. One Indian displayed great bravery, going about among his people and bringing reinforcements to the stronghold, but Diego Díaz de Berlanga felled him with an harquebus shot—incredible though it may seem, since he was so far away. When the Indians in that section of the pueblo saw that he had fallen, the majority of them abandoned the position, which was the key point we were trying to take.

The lieutenant governor now left this section, since the men were holding their posts like brave soldiers, as they had done on all other occasions; but before leaving he told them not to fire their harquebuses any more, nor to cause any further damage there. Then he took Diego de Viruega to the point where the battle was still in progress; and here he told Captain Alonso Jaimez to climb to the top with some soldiers, while others from below protected their ascent. This was done. There did not seem to be as large a number of Indians at that spot as there were before; but the few who held their posts behind the barricades defended the terraces very bravely, so that no one could climb to the top except by the slender wooden hand ladders, which only one person at a time could ascend. There were no doors leading from one room to another, but only hatchways just large enough for a single person; and therefore our men, in order to get through them and climb to the terraces, had to ascend without sword or shield, after which they passed the weapons to one another as they climbed. The lieutenant governor, perceiving the danger to our soldiers, ordered the maese de campo and many others to train their harquebuses on the enemy, though he had previously given the order that we should not shoot to kill, because he hoped that God would enable us to defeat our foes without killing them.

In obedience to these orders, the maese de campo brought down an Indian with one harquebus shot, as did both Juan de Contreras and Juan López, a servant of the governor, with the result that the natives were forced to abandon the barricade and our men took it. The first to ascend was Diego de Viruega, followed by Francisco López de Ricalde, Juan Rodríguez de Avalos, Captain Alonso Jaimez, Juan de Estrada, Francisco de Bascones, and Cristóbal Martín. Then the lieutenant governor ordered the buglers and Juan de Contreras, standard bearer of the expedition in the absence of his brother, Francicso Salgado, to climb to the top, where the former were to blow their bugles as a sign of joy and victory. When the pueblo realized that we had occupied this block of buildings, not a soul was venturesome enough to come out on the terraces.

Thereupon the lieutenant governor and captain general entered and walked through the plazas and streets of the pueblo with a few companions, while the inhabitants all appeared on the wooden corridors extending along the streets and plazas between the houses. The natives pass from one house to the other through these corridors, and also by means of wooden bridges spanning the street from terrace to terrace. In this manner they were able to move about securely from place to place, although in any case we threatened them with no harm beyond that already described; for the lieutenant governor wanted to win by friendship rather than by war. In fact, he was very sorry that the harm done, which was necessary for the protection of our men, could not have been avoided. So strong was this sentiment that, shortly before, when we had set fire to a small wooden corridor and he saw the flames, he ordered that they be put out immediately. Diego de Viruega, with his customary zeal, rushed to do so, which pleased the lieutenant governor immensely, for he said that, as Christians, we should practice Christian conduct in all that pertained to the service of God and the king. Now, as the governor walked through the pueblo with several soldiers, not an Indian threw a stone or shot an arrow. On the contrary all tried to indicate by means of signs that they wanted our friendship. Making a cross with their hands, they cried "Friends, friends, friends," which is the method they use to express their desire for friendship.

In the course of this stroll the lieutenant governor came to a plaza where the chief of the pueblo appeared in a corridor and talked to him for awhile. One of the governor's companions on this occasion was Diego de Viruega, who climbed up to the corridor in order to talk with and cajole the chief; but when he got to the top, the Indians ran away from him. Nevertheless, one old Indian who came out remained behind where the Spaniard had entered and embraced him. Viruega then descended again. By means of signs the governor told the chieftain and many others who stood in the corridor that he had not come to harm them in the least, and that they should not be afraid. The natives understood him clearly, and they soon brought out some food which they threw down to us from the corridors, since none of them dared to descend. In fact, when one Indian tried to climb down, the others restrained him and he abandoned the attempt. The lieutenant governor asked the Indian captain for the arms, saddles, harquebuses, and other articles taken from the maese de campo and his companions. The chieftain replied that they had burned all the saddles, harquebuses, and guards for the swords, and that the clothes and bedding had been distributed among the people or taken to another pueblo. Thus he gave us to understand very clearly that there was nothing left except some blades without guards.

The lieutenant governor then instructed a number of his men to try to seize some Indians in that section of the pueblo which we had not taken and where there were so many people, in order that we might learn from them what had become of the arms and other articles. Under strict orders not to harm the natives in any way, they proceeded to carry out the task. Then the governor went back to the place where he had left the native captain and assured him that his people need not be afraid, because they would suffer no harm. The Indians understood all he said, and gave signs of wanting our friendship. The chieftain climbed up to a terrace and from there addressed his people in a loud voice. Then we saw many natives coming out into the passageways everywhere, with signs of joy and friendship, although no one would come down into the plazas or streets. The lieutenant governor again asked the captain to order his people to hand over the articles they had taken from our men; and the Indian captain repeated that there was practically nothing left, but that he would ask his people to return what there was. They then brought out two sword blades without guards, a cuish, several pieces of sack-cloth, and some trifles of little value. Since it was getting late, the governor requested the captain to have a search made in order to gather up everything left and to hand it over the next day.

Our leader then returned to his quarters to find out whether his men had been able to capture any Indians. But the men said they had failed to catch any because there were many trap doors and hatchways, and because the area was so burrowed with underground passages that it was a real labyrinth. Therefore, since night was falling, they had given up the attempt. The lieutenant governor ordered the maese de campo to post sentries in this section, including the terraces, in sufficient number to prevent the Indians from leaving, so that on the next day the natives could be persuaded to come out and see that we were not causing them any harm and did not wish to do so. The maese de campo accordingly instructed Captain Alonso Jaimez to take charge of this watch, as had been ordered by the lieutenant governor, and to select the number of sentries he considered necessary. Jaimez chose Juan de Estrada, Juan Rodríguez Nieto, Juan de Contreras, Francisco de Mancha, Diego Díaz de Berlanga, and Francisco de Bascones. The lieutenant governor also told the maese de campo to post a mounted guard around the pueblo in order to prevent the people from leaving it. This group included Martín de Salazar, Francisco López de Ricalde, Juan de Carvajal, Hernán Ponce de León, Juan Sánchez Juancho, Cristóbal Martín, Juan Rodríguez de Avalos, Blas Núñez [Martínez] de Mederos, Juan López, and Diego de Viruega. With the posting of these guards everything became quiet for the day; a watch was kept also at our guard quarters.

Early the next day[36] the lieutenant governor got his horse and rode out in full military array to tour the town and inspect the plazas and streets before the sentries were removed. He found the people calm, which pleased him greatly, since this was what he wished. He therefore ordered his men to return to their quarters, and there he addressed them, thanking them for the zeal they had displayed in discharging the duties we all owe to God our Lord and to his Majesty. He entreated them all, for the love of God, not to cause any harm to the Indians, their pueblo, or its houses. This exhortation was indeed unnecessary, for everyone, without being so instructed, was trying to show friend-

36. January 1, 1591.

ship for the Indians, inspired by the zeal of the lieutenant governor in treating them well. Then the governor told the Indian servants in his army that under no circumstances were they to leave the camp, enter any house, or trouble the Indians of the pueblo in any manner.

At this time, while all of us were together and happy to see the pueblo at peace, the lieutenant governor nevertheless sent some men back to the blockhouse where the watch had been posted, in another attempt to coax the people out, for which purpose they were to take lights with them. They entered the underground passages where the natives had hidden the day before, and they found many tunnels leading to other blockhouses and to underground estufas. After examining these places, they turned back and reported that there were no people at all in the area searched. The lieutenant ordered that everything should be left as it was, and all was calm. He then went to the pueblo, accompanied by some soldiers on horseback and on foot, in order to reassure the entire population as best he could and to see what there was in the pueblo. Many people came out and made signs of friendship, while the party looked the pueblo over carefully. The most interesting things seen were sixteen underground estufas, very large and very well white-washed, built for protection against the bitter cold. The natives light no fires inside them; instead, they bring in from the outside many braziers banked with ashes, in a manner so ingenious that I find no words to describe it.

These estufas are entered through small trap doors, large enough for only one person at a time, and the natives go down into them by means of ladders set up for that purpose.

The houses in this pueblo are built like military barracks, back to back, with doors opening out all around; and they are four or five stories high. There are no doors opening into the streets on the ground floors; the houses are entered from above by means of portable hand ladders and trap doors. Each floor of every house has three or four rooms, so that each house, as a whole, counting from top to bottom, has fifteen or sixteen rooms, very neat and well whitewashed. Every house is equipped with facilities for grinding corn, including three or four grinding stones mounted in small troughs and provided with pestles; all is whitewashed. The method of grinding is novel, the flour being passed from one grinder to another, as these Indians do not make tortilla dough, although from this flour they do make many kinds of bread, corn-flour gruel, and tamales.

This pueblo had five plazas.[37] It was also provided with such an abundant supply of corn that everyone marveled. There were those who maintained that the total must amount to more than thirty thousand fanegas, since each house had two or three rooms full of it, all of excellent quality. Moreover, there was a good supply of beans. Both corn and beans were of many colors; it seemed that some of the corn was two or three years old. In the houses, the natives also store quantities of herbs, chili, and calabashes, and many implements for working their cornfields.

As for their clothing, we noticed that most of the men, if not all, wore cotton blankets and over these a buffalo skin, since this was the cold season; some covered their privy parts with small pieces of cloth, very elegant and elaborately decorated. The women wore a blanket tied over the shoulder and left open on one side, with a sash the width of a span wrapped around the waist. Over this blanket they wear another, nicely decorated and very fancy, or a kind of robe made of turkey feathers, as well as many other novel adornments, all of which is quite remarkable for barbarians.

These Indians have a great deal of pottery, red, figured, and black, such as plates, bowls *(cajetes)*, salt containers, basins, and very beautiful cups *(jícaras)*. Some of the pottery is glazed. They also have plentiful supplies of firewood, and of lumber for building houses. Indeed, we were given to understand that whenever anyone wanted to build a house, he had the lumber for that purpose ready at hand; and, furthermore, clay for adobes was available in quantities. There are two water holes, at the ends of the pueblo, which the natives use for bathing, since they obtain their drinking water from other springs about an harquebus shot away. The Río Salado above-mentioned, which flows along the route we followed, is a quarter of a league distant, although the salt water sinks into the ground many leagues back. We spent the entire day looking at the various things in the pueblo; but not an Indian ventured outside the houses. The natives returned to us some small articles of little value that had belonged to our people. Reassured by this act, the lieutenant governor ordered the sentries removed, except at our guard quarters, which adjoined the pueblo, as has been stated. He thought that by doing so he would make the Indians feel more at ease, because they themselves had asked for the removal of the guards.

37. For recent studies of Pecos pueblo, see A. F. Bandelier, "Report on the Ruins of the Pueblo of Pecos," in *Papers of the Archaeological Institute of America*, vol. I, 1881; A. V. Kidder, *An Introduction to the Study of Southwestern Archaeology with a preliminary account of the excavation at Pecos* (New Haven, 1924); and his *Pecos, New Mexico: Archaeological Notes* (Andover, Mass., 1958).

At dawn the next day,[38] not a single inhabitant was to be found in the town, a development which distressed us all greatly when we learned of it. Nevertheless, the lieutenant governor ordered that no harm be done to the Indians, even if they had abandoned the pueblo, although he commanded that the houses be searched to see if any of our goods could be found. We did this without causing any damage, and we found some of our belongings, but they were of no use to us because they had been smashed to pieces. The lieutenant governor then ordered that we take a little corn, beans, and flour from each house, which we did, twenty-two fanegas in all, sending this to the wagons at Urraca. This load was dispatched in care of eight soldiers and eight or ten helpers, while the lieutenant governor and the rest of his men remained in the pueblo to see if the natives would come back. We stayed there for several days with that object in view; but none of the Indians came. The governor therefore decided to move his army from the pueblo so that the inhabitants might return to it. He felt sorry for them because they had abandoned their homes in the bitter cold of winter, with its strong winds and heavy snows, conduct which seemed incredible to us. Even the rivers were frozen, a point I shall dwell upon more at length farther on.

The lieutenant governor then ordered us to make ready for our departure in order to visit some other pueblos. This displeased several of the men on account of the hardships involved, and because, instead of returning to the headquarters of the expedition,[39] they would have to go on in search of a road to the said pueblos, for the route we were following could not be traveled by the wagons. Furthermore, the governor carried in his pockets some samples of minerals, and he had asked the Indians at this pueblo where similar ones could be found. They had indicated by signs that there were such ores in the other pueblos mentioned earlier; and on hearing this he had decided to look for the mines, a plan which he now proceeded to carry out.

On January 6, 1591, we left this place in search of these mines. The lieutenant governor asked the maese de campo to conceal four men with very good horses in the pueblo so that, if the Indians came back to that vicinity, some might be captured and persuaded to return to their homes. Accordingly, Juan de Carvajal, Francisco de Mancha, Juan de Contreras, and Cristóbal Martín remained behind. We had not yet left our quarters when two Indians approached from one side of the settlement. We seized them and brought them to the lieutenant gov-

38. Evidently January 2.
39. That is, at Urraca.

ernor, who was with his men at a distance of two harquebus shots from the pueblo. When he saw the Indians, he treated them kindly, gave them some small presents, and told them to go back to their homes. In their presence he ordered a large cross erected on that spot, explained its meaning to them, and told the secretary to draw up a security guaranty in the name of his Majesty and on behalf of the royal service. This document he gave to one of the Indians for delivery to his chief, and then sent him away, taking the other one along as a guide on our journey. Thus we went on, the Indian contentedly leading us.

After two leagues of travel, while we were in mountainous territory, we met on the trail another Indian who was going to the very settlements we sought. We took him prisoner, and then learned that he was the son of the cacique in the pueblo we had just left; but in spite of that discovery we kept him with us. We stopped for the night on these mountains, in a canyon with many pine trees.

On the seventh we left the canyon and marched on over the sierra guided by the two Indians. It was bitterly cold and snowing. When we emerged from the sierra we came to a river, frozen so hard that the horses crossed on the ice without breaking through. We had to cut holes in it by hand in order to water them, for there was water beneath the ice. We went on, and an hour before sunset we arrived at a small pueblo, where all the people came out to meet us.[40] As we entered, they told us by signs to establish our camp close to their houses; and they brought us plenty of firewood, which we sorely needed. We camped some twenty paces from their houses; and they, friendly and unafraid, supplied us with many tortillas, corn for our horses, and some turkeys. The next day the lieutenant governor ordered us to erect a tall cross, which we did, raising it to the sound of trumpets and harquebus shots. The Indians swore obedience in the name of the king our sovereign and the lieutenant governor, accepting their allegiance, appointed a governor, an alcalde, and an alguacil, all in the name of his Majesty.

Today, the eighth of the month, we left the above-mentioned pueblo and went on to another, a league distant, accompanied by a crowd of natives; many others came out along the way to meet us. As we approached this next pueblo, the lieutenant governor ordered the bugles

40. Castaño's advance party, guided by Pecos Indians, probably went through Glorieta pass and on toward the Santa Fé area. The frozen river was perhaps the Santa Fé. The diarist, unfortunately, does not name the pueblos at which they stopped, so we must reconstruct the route on very slim evidence and by reference to an occasional pueblo which can be indentified only with some degree of credibility.

to be sounded as a sign of friendship.[41] In the settlement there were numerous people, besides the ones who had met and accompanied us. The governor tried to find out which inhabitants belonged to the pueblo, but the natives would not tell him. Thereupon, he climbed up to the terraces, brought down some Indians, and cajoled the others with soft words. Then the chief of the pueblo appeared and called together many of his people, to whom the governor explained by signs the purpose of our coming, so that they were satisfied. He asked them to pledge obedience in the name of his Majesty; and after they did so, he appointed a governor, an alcalde, and an alguacil for the pueblo. He also ordered a large cross erected and explained its meaning to the natives, who were all pleased. After this we left the settlement, with many people accompanying us.

On the ninth, the date of the events just described, we journeyed to another pueblo a league away. In addition to the people who already accompanied us, many more came to meet us along the trail. When we arrived at the settlement, the Indians proved so stubborn that we had to climb up to their houses and terraces; then they overcame their fear and approached us. We inquired for their chief, and when he appeared, the lieutenant governor treated him well, giving him some small articles such as had been presented to the other Indians previously. With friendship established, he ordered us to erect a large cross to the sound of trumpets and the firing of harquebuses, after which he explained its meaning to the natives. They pledged obedience to the king our lord, and in his name we appointed a governor, an alcalde, and an alguacil.

We spent the night in this pueblo and the inhabitants supplied an abundance of corn, flour, beans, calabashes, tortillas, and turkeys for all who were present. Here we saw an Indian carrying a bow and arrows, and the lieutenant governor called to him, asking him to hand over his arms, which he did. The governor explained to the man that no one was allowed to carry a bow or an arrow in his presence, or in that of any Spaniard; and he then broke the bow while a multitude looked on. The spectators all assured him that he would not find such weapons again; and we later learned this to be so, for we never saw the mistake repeated among them.

On that day, the tenth of the month, we left that pueblo and went on

41. These several pueblos, visited from January 7 to 10, were perhaps Tewa, and though not named may have been Tesuque, Nambé, Cuyamungué, Pojoaque, and Jacona. See Hull, "Castaño de Sosa's Expedition to New Mexico," pp. 324-325; *Benavides' Revised Memorial*, p. 232.

to another, about a league away, accompanied by a crowd of natives. When we drew near this pueblo we saw many people leaving it. The lieutenant governor sent four men to bring them back, and when they had all returned to the pueblo, we found that it had many inhabitants. Our leader explained by signs that the Indians should not run away, because he had not come to harm them, but, on the contrary, to protect them in the name of his Majesty, and to be their friend. All this was indicated in sign language, but they understood him clearly and had no objections to offer, so that everyone became calm. We raised a tall cross and explained its meaning to the people. They pledged obedience to his Majesty; and the lieutenant governor appointed a governor, an alcalde, and an alguacil. All these acts were performed with appropriate ceremony, marked by the blowing of trumpets and the firing of harquebuses. On the same day we journeyed to yet another pueblo, a league away, where we were well received and where we spent the night. The natives furnished us with an abundance of the things we needed; and the same ceremonies were observed here as in the pueblos already visited.

All six of these settlements had canals for irrigation, which would be incredible to anyone who had not seen them with his own eyes. The inhabitants harvest large quantities of corn, beans, and other vegetables. They dress in the same fashion as the people described above. Some of the settlements are small, though densely populated. The houses are two or three stories high, and all are entered by means of trap doors and portable ladders.

The next day, the eleventh of the month, we left this place during a snowfall, because of which few people accompanied us. We traveled to another valley, two leagues away, and came to a large pueblo; before reaching it we were met by many people and thus we all entered it together.[42] The pueblo consisted of four quarters and a very large square, with entrances at every corner. This town contained many inhabitants, by whom we were well received. The houses were built of adobes, very well planned and well constructed, two or three stories high, and neatly whitewashed; each house had its estufa. In the center of the plaza there was a large round building, half underground and half above ground, spanned by beams on which the Indians had built a terrace. We marveled at the thickness of the timbers, which seemed to us to be of mesquite wood. The natives gather in this building on certain days of

42. The other valley was probably the Río Grande and the large pueblo may have been San Ildefonso.

the year to perform their idolatrous ceremonies; for they have numerous idols, a fact which I forgot to mention before. In the first pueblo where the maese de campo encountered these conditions, there were many of these idols, as there are in all the settlements.

In the pueblo that I am now describing, we followed the same practice as in the others, appointing a governor, an alcalde, and an alguacil, in the name of his Majesty, and erecting a tall cross whose meaning we explained to the people, after which they pledged obedience to his Majesty. We spent the night here, and the natives furnished us with everything we needed. This pueblo lies in a very extensive valley, all under irrigation.

The next day, the twelfth, we left this place and followed a very large river toward the north. We visited two more pueblos,[43] in which we followed the same procedure as in the settlements previously visited. We were well received, and spent the night in the second of the two pueblos.

On the thirteenth we journeyed to another settlement, five leagues from the two mentioned above, arriving there an hour before sunset.[44] This pueblo was situated in a valley between sierras, and I cannot say what it contained, because it was buried under snow a yard in depth by actual measure, such as we had never seen before; it was so deep that the horses could not travel. Consequently, when we arrived no one came out to meet us, not even the Indian we had sent ahead from one of the pueblos visited previously. The very sight of us frightened the inhabitants, especially the women, who wept a great deal. In view of this situation we circled the pueblo once, but no one appeared other than an Indian who was going from one section of the town to another; and he was very fearful when he approached us. In order to reassure them all, the lieutenant governor dismounted, embraced the Indian, and led him by the hand around that quarter of the town.

Near the limits of another section, some Indians were coming out of an estufa. Our leader walked toward them, ordering every one of us to remain mounted; then he saw a group of Indians in another place and went to meet them. They waited for him and he embraced most of them. They in turn performed the ceremony of blowing on their hands and placing them on the face of the lieutenant governor and on his clothes, after which he kissed their hands and spoke soothingly to them,

43. Which are not identified in any way.
44. Possibly San Juan at the confluence of the Chama and Río Grande. See Introduction for a discussion of this question, p. 38.

asking their people to come down; but no one heeded the request. The lieutenant governor gave them some small knives and went back to his men, accompanied by some twenty or thirty Indians.

After he rejoined the soldiers, all agreed to camp for the night at some huts a long harquebus shot from the pueblo, where there were people from other places who had come to trade with this settlement.[44a] As we approached the huts, the Indians, both men and women, began to move away. The lieutenant governor sent for them to come back, which they did, and we all lodged there in peace. About twenty men from the pueblo were present, and we asked them for corn, tortillas, and firewood; but they brought us only negligible amounts. In view of this the governor doubled the sentries around the horses and the camp for the night. In the morning no one came to us except one old Indian who pretended that he wanted to trade something. This made us feel suspicious, because, in addition to his conduct, we saw that the natives were all out on the terraces, bringing up quantities of water and stones in great haste, and assembling their children.

The pueblo was very strong in people and supplies, and the houses were seven or eight stories high. The terraces were topped by a breastwork the height of a man behind which the Indians could shield themselves. Noting all these circumstances, the lieutenant governor ordered two bronze culverins to be made ready and instructed us all to mount our horses for the purpose of proceeding to the pueblo to see what the natives would do. While these orders were being carried out, his companions told the lieutenant governor that, in their opinion, we should not go to the pueblo, since the Indians were in a bad mood and it would be better to retain the meager friendship they had shown than to approach their settlement, as he suggested, for these people had not pledged obedience as the others had done. The men added that we should remain where we were for a few days to devise the best possible means of gaining the friendship of the inhabitants. In addition, the entire land was covered with snow, forcing us to stay where we were, since the horses could not advance without danger of losing the way. When God willed a change in the weather, which had been so bitterly cold, and when the snow melted, we should be able to do what we wanted to with less effort. The lieutenant governor, heeding the opinion of his men, turned away without going to the pueblo, although he

44a. Old maps and documents show a Navajo trail from the west, following generally the Chama river to San Juan, where the Indians came to trade for pottery and other Pueblo wares.

planned to come back when the weather improved, after the season of cold and snow, to establish allegiance to his Majesty in this settlement as he had in the others.

We saw in this pueblo many turquoises, and also an Indian wearing an armband which seemed to be made of rich stones. It was suggested to the lieutenant governor that he try to seize the ornament, but he replied that it was not wise to do so at present, as the Indians might get the notion that we coveted their goods and had come to their land to steal their possessions. He had faith that God would put them in such a compliant state of mind that they would accept Him and the king; other objectives could wait for the appropriate time, which had not yet come. All the lieutenant governor tried to do was to examine the armband, and he approached the Indian in order to look at it. This Indian was also wearing a beautiful buffalo skin. When the lieutenant governor came up to him to examine the ornament (as I have said), the Indian refused to show it, and the matter rested there.

We returned to the pueblos through which we had come,[45] crossing a river frozen so solidly that the ice must have been two spans thick and we had to use pickaxes to break it.

In the settlement referred to above, there was a large population and the houses were eight or nine stories high, divided into blocks, each one of which was a veritable labyrinth of wooden frames over which the natives had built their houses; or so it seemed from the outside. They have corridors connecting all these blocks, making it possible to pass from one to the other.

On the fifteenth we marched to a pueblo situated across the large river and we stopped there a couple of hours. The natives pledged obedience to his Majesty; we named the governor, the alcalde and the alguacil for the town and erected a large cross. Then we moved on to another settlement, a league away, where we spent the night. There, too, the natives pledged obedience to the king; and we appointed a governor, an alcalde, and an alguacil for them also, erecting another large cross, all to the sound of trumpets and harquebus shots. On the sixteenth we left this pueblo and went on to another, crossing the river to the east bank. Here again the inhabitants pledged obedience to his Majesty; we named a governor, an alcalde, and an alguacil; and we set up a cross, with the same ceremonies as those mentioned above.

On the seventeenth we started out from this pueblo and traveled

45. Whether the diarist refers to the Río Grande or the Tesuque, for example, must remain a matter of conjecture.

toward another valley, where there were settlements of a different nation, known as the Quereses.[46] We camped for the night along the way in very heavy snow, and the next day we reached the said valley, where we found four pueblos within view of one another. We stayed two days among them; the natives pledged obedience to his Majesty, and we named governors and alcaldes, raising crosses in all the settlements with the same ceremonies.

On the twenty-first, leaving these pueblos behind, we traveled to another, a league distant.[47] The natives pledged obedience to his Majesty; we appointed a governor, an alcalde, and an alguacil; and we raised a large cross. The next day the lieutenant governor and some of his men went out to look for mines and brought back samples of ores that seemed very good.

On the twenty-third we went on to another pueblo, about a league away, where the natives pledged obedience to his Majesty. We named a governor, an alcalde, and an alguacil, and raised a large cross. Then we passed on to yet another settlement, a short league distant. Its inhabitants were somewhat sullen; but the governor, making use of some Indians he had for this purpose, won them over and they pledged obedience to his Majesty. We named a governor, an alcalde, and an alguacil, and erected a large cross, just as we had done in the other pueblos. Here the people gave us corn, flour, beans, and turkeys in abundance, all we needed, without our doing them any harm, for we took particular care to avoid injuring them. It seemed as if the lieutenant governor was especially endowed by God to win allegiance to his Majesty from these barbarians, so that by the divine will they might be brought to a knowledge of the Catholic faith. The governor had a cross with an image of God our Lord, and whenever he came to a pueblo he held it in his hands while he and his companions knelt reverently to kiss the crucifix, at which the barbarians marveled. Moreover, he induced the Indians in all these pueblos—men, women, and children—to do likewise. On that particular day, while we were in the settlement just mentioned, there was such a heavy snowfall that the next day the ground was entirely covered, improbable though it may seem.

On the twenty-fourth, despite the heavy snow, we set out from this

46. The present Queres towns on the Río Grande, coming from the north, are Cochití, Santo Domingo, and San Felipe; and on the Jémez river, Santa Ana and Zía.

47. Though the diary does not give the direction of the march, it would seem the men were going eastward in the Galisteo valley. It is curious, however, that the diarist does not name any pueblos, whereas on the return of the entire expedition a couple of weeks later several pueblos are mentioned by name.

pueblo in the direction of the place which we had named Urraca, where the wagons were waiting. We hoped to find a passable route for them.[48] We took two Indians from the settlement as guides, explaining to them the direction we wanted to follow; after going half a league, we released one of them, but the other continued to act as our guide. We camped for the night at a pine grove where the snow was a good yard deep; and we melted some of it to water our horses.

On the twenty-fifth we traveled east through thick pine forests, stopping for the night at a ravine with many juniper trees. We melted snow in a pan to get water for the horses and for ourselves, as there was no other way of procuring any.

On the twenty-sixth we left this ravine and crossed the Salado river, stopping for the night at the Paraje de los Elotes (Place of the Green Corn).

On the twenty-seventh we went to Urraca, where the wagons were and the expedition had its headquarters.[49] We were very well received, because it was more than thirty days since we had bade farewell to our people. There was little food left in the camp—none, to be accurate—and with the scanty amount we brought, we decided to leave that place and make our way toward the populated areas.

We started out from Urraca on the thirtieth with the entire expedition, including the wagons, and stopped for the night at Rinconada, after traveling two leagues.

On February 1 we resumed our journey and spent the night at Estero, three leagues distant. February 3 we traveled on, crossed the river, and camped for the night on its bank. On the fourth we set forth again, but it took us four days to travel a league, because many of the wagons broke down and the weather was cold and it snowed.

The eighth we left the region by the river and traveled over a plain toward the west. We stopped for the night at a ravine, without other water than what we obtained by melting snow in many pots and pans. This we used to prepare food and drink both for ourselves and for the horses.

We continued our journey on the ninth, spending the night at an

48. Here one must assume that Castaño's party was somewhere among the Galisteo pueblos where it could have continued along the base of the eastern hills directly to Lamy and Apache canyon. Or it could have gone past San Cristóbal pueblo, up Cañada Estacada, past White Lakes, and along Canyon Blanco to Urraca. Cf. also Nelson, "Pueblo Ruins of the Galisteo Basin," pp. 19-20.

49. Urraca was some twenty-five or thirty miles below the pueblo of Pecos. See p. 268, note 33.

arroyo where there was a difficult pass and where we cut down many pine trees.[50] There was no water at all. It took us two days to traverse this pass, and during that time we made up for the lack of water by melting snow. The oxen went without food. On the twelfth we left this place and camped in a ravine, without water, except for what we obtained by the same process as before.

On the thirteenth we went on and stopped for the night in a sheltered spot three leagues away. The last pueblo we had visited was a league distant.[51] We took our horses and oxen to it for water, which they sorely needed, since the oxen had gone without any for some six or seven days, slaking their thirst with snow.

On the fourteenth we started for the pueblo with the entire expedition. The cold was so intense that our people were freezing and unable to travel this one league with the wagons; and so we left the vehicles in an arroyo. The fifteenth we all entered the pueblo, named San Cristóbal, where we were well received.

On the seventeenth we went to another settlement, which we called San Lucas.[52] Here, too, we were well received by the natives. The eighteenth we journeyed to yet another pueblo named San Marcos, where mines had been discovered and where we met with a favorable reception.[53]

On the twenty-third the lieutenant governor traveled to a pueblo that we had not visited before, two leagues from San Marcos.[54] The natives pledged obedience to his Majesty; a governor, an alcalde, and an alguacil were named; and a large cross was raised to the sound of trumpets and harquebus shots.

On March 1, 1591, the governor left this pueblo of San Marcos with nineteen men and started toward the pueblo where the incident related above had befallen Cristóbal de Heredia, maese de campo.[55] We spent the night in a ravine, thickly grown with pine trees, two leagues from our destination.

50. From the number of days, after leaving Urraca, that the Spaniards spent on this trip, one might assume they went via Glorieta pass and Apache canyon. An alternative route would have taken them farther south via Canyon Blanco to White Lakes and Cañada Estacada. The fact that the first pueblo they came to was San Cristóbal, which lies at the eastern end of the Galisteo basin, would in fact make this conclusion logical.

51. The pueblo of San Cristóbal.

52. This was undoubtedly Galisteo.

53. San Marcos, just north of Galisteo creek, near the Cerrillos mountains.

54. Nelson believes this might have been San Lázaro, or, more likely, Tziguma, the present Ciénega, twelve miles southwest of Santa Fé. Nelson, "Pueblo Ruins of the Galisteo Basin," p. 24; *Benavides' Revised Memorial*, p. 270.

55. Leaving the main part of the expedition behind, probably at San Marcos, Castaño and nineteen men returned to visit Pecos, to re-establish Spanish authority. This time the Indians were friendly and gave the Spaniards a liberal supply of provisions.

On the second of the month we set out again for the pueblo in question. But the lieutenant governor feared that the inhabitants might abandon it and accordingly, before we reached the town, he sent Cristóbal de Heredia and his men to post themselves in some prominent place with a view to checking the flight of the people if they should try to escape; and Heredia carried out these instructions. The lieutenant governor then went on with the others to the pueblo, where he found the people all assured and calm; many came out to meet him, and also to receive the maese de campo, who had gone by a different route. No one left the pueblo; and when all the Indians came together we saw that there was a large population. To reassure them further and overcome all fear, we paraded through the town on horseback, with trumpets blowing, which greatly pleased the Indians—men, women, and children.

We camped next to their houses, where we were continually surrounded by many people, who brought us much corn, flour, and beans, as well as some of their trinkets. The next day the lieutenant governor assembled them all and named their governor, alcalde, and alguacil; and we raised a large cross, to the accompaniment of trumpets and harquebus shots, which pleased the whole pueblo immensely. Despite the incident previously mentioned, the natives were now so calm and contented that it was a pleasure to behold them; many women and children came down to visit us, and the lieutenant governor received them very cordially. They brought him five whole sword blades and two others broken in half, as well as some shirts, cloaks, and pieces of sackcloth. They did this with a great show of zeal, and we thought that if they had had anything else, they would have brought it. Thus all the natives were calm and obedient and treated us in a very friendly manner, furnishing us with as much corn, flour, and beans as we could carry. We stayed three days among these people.

On the seventh we set forth from San Marcos [to which Castaño's party had returned and] where the mines had been discovered, although no silver was found there despite numerous attempts to extract it. Since the discovery of another site had been reported, we started out in the direction indicated and thus came to a place and a river called Pedro de Iñigo. Several of our men were left behind that day because of a shortage of horses.

We resumed our journey on the eighth, going toward a pueblo named Santo Domingo, situated on the bank of a large river; we planned to use this settlement as a center of operations while searching for the new mines. On the way, we stopped for the night at an abandoned pueblo, a league from Santo Domingo.[56] The lieutenant governor and many of the men from the expedition went on to Santo Domingo, where he ascertained that it was possible to bring the wagons all the way to this settlement. He therefore returned to the wagons, which were with the main force of the expedition, and found some of his men already there. When he discovered this, he sent Maese de Campo Cristóbal de Heredia to the pueblo of Santo Domingo, where the governor had left many of his people, with orders to arrest a certain soldier.

The maese de campo, who was also fiscal, went on this errand and cleared up the case. The fact was that five or six soldiers from the governor's company, who had remained at the pueblo of San Mateo,[57] had discussed a plot to kill him and return to Mexico because he would not let them do what they pleased. He restrained them from annoying or plundering the natives; and this was the basis of their complaints and the reason for their plotting. When the maese de campo arrived at the pueblo to arrest the soldier, by order of the lieutenant governor, Alonso Jaimez came out from his quarters, gun in hand, and asked, "Who is calling me?" No one had done so, and accordingly he was told that no one wanted him. Then Jaimez responded, "Let each man look out for himself." In view of this threat, the maese de campo lunged at him, but he fled. The maese de campo then returned with the arrested soldier to the wagons and the camp where the lieutenant governor was waiting. As soon as the soldier was brought there, our leader commanded that he should be garroted, because the finger of suspicion pointed to this man more than to any of the others. When the execution was about to be carried out, according to orders, the whole expedition, men and women, begged the governor to pardon the prisoner, for the love of God; and so, moved by pity and the pleading of the entire force, the governor ordered the execution stopped, although he had let his people think he would carry it out so that they would be disciplined by fear. We do not give the names of the soldiers here, because this affair was handled with great charity.

On the eighth [ninth?] of the month we left the abandoned pueblo and went on to Santo Domingo, where we were accorded a very friendly reception. Here the lieutenant governor learned that Alonso Jaimez had run away. The next day, the eighth [tenth?]—after the entire expedi-

56. This deserted pueblo was probably Gipuy, or old Santo Domingo, which had been abandoned prior to Castaño's visit in 1591. It was about four miles east of the present Santo Domingo.

57. Probably an error for San Marcos.

tion with its wagons had settled in this pueblo for a few days in order that we might conduct from here our search for the mines we had heard about—all of the soldiers and other people in the expedition assembled and asked the lieutenant governor, for the love of God, to overlook certain incidents that had occurred in his camp, since he had forgiven many offenses with great clemency. They pointed out that Alonso Jaimez had absented himself from the camp because he was afraid that the lieutenant governor would certainly punish him, which was the reason why he had run away; and he was very repentant for having offended his leader in any manner. Now all the soldiers and the maese de campo in unison entreated the governor to favor them by pardoning Jaimez; and he answered that, in the name of his Majesty, moved by charity and the suffering they had all endured, he would grant a pardon to Jaimez and to all others who had transgressed the law in any way. Nevertheless, Alonso Jaimez was to be relieved of his commission as captain of the party that was to go to the city of Zacatecas, the Río Grande, and other places, on a recruiting mission. In fact, this commission was revoked publicly and without delay at the time when the governor pardoned all the culprits in the name of his Majesty. We do not record here the names of the others who erred on this occasion, since they have now been pardoned.

On the eleventh a man appeared before the lieutenant governor, asking him to grant some of the company permission to leave for Mexico. He ventured to present this request because they had heard the governor say that anyone who wanted to leave could do so. Our leader told them that the statement was true, and that he reaffirmed it. All those who wanted to leave were free to depart; and he gave them permission because he would rather remain there alone to die than give occasion for unworthy acts. In view of this concession, the group did not actually leave, because there were no longer any soldiers who wanted to go. So, even though there were several disgruntled individuals, nevertheless, when it became apparent that the lieutenant governor was right and that those who wanted to leave were wrong, all the men— the former malcontents as well as the others—remained quietly and in agreement with him. They performed such duties as arose, never alluding to the recent incidents.

While we were in this pueblo of Santo Domingo, the lieutenant governor and a party of twenty men went out to look for mines and a certain pueblo which he had not visited before. As they went along, taking possession of various settlements, they crossed some mountains where they found two pueblos that had been deserted only a few days earlier on account of wars with other pueblos which forced the inhabitants to leave their homes.[58] This was the explanation given by the Indians who accompanied us, and we ourselves could see plainly that it was true, because there were signs of many having been killed. In these towns we found an abundance of corn and beans.

From these two abandoned settlements we went back to the Río Grande where we had established a camp for our army and the wagons.[59] From what we had seen there and were told everywhere in the land, we deduced that these were the pueblos whose people had killed the friars reported to have come this way. When we reached the first of the two pueblos, there were no natives left in it.[60] While we were there, we noticed that the one across the river was being evacuated in part, and in order to prevent its complete abandonment, the lieutenant governor sent the maese de campo with some soldiers to stop the evacuation. Then the governor and all the rest of us crossed the river, although it was in full flood, and forced some of the people who were fleeing to turn back. Many, however, had remained in the pueblo. Our leader reassured the natives, giving them to understand that they were not to desert their homes, and they were very pleased. When we asked why the people of the other pueblo had fled, we were told they had done so from fear, because they had killed the friars. We explained that they need not run away, and the governor sent some Indians from this [second] pueblo to call the others back. We took possession of the pueblo in the name of his Majesty and named a governor, an alcalde, and an alguacil; then we raised a large cross with the same kind of ceremonies already described.

After this the lieutenant governor went to another pueblo, a quarter of a league away, but he found few people there, as most of them had fled in fear. We recrossed the river and spent the night in the deserted pueblo. From this point, fourteen other settlements could be seen along the river. The Indians said that most of them had been abandoned

58. Lambert, reviewing this trip of Castaño de Sosa's from Santo Domingo to visit a pueblo he had not seen, on which he passed through some mountains and found two pueblos that had been deserted "only a few days earlier," believes he might have visited Paa-ko and San Antonio, and that the devastation had been caused by Plains Indians. The chronicler wrote that the natives informed the Spaniards of what had happened to these pueblos—"é lo vimos claro ser asi, por las muestras de muchos muertos que habia señales. . . . " These two towns lay in San Pedro arroyo between the Ortiz and Sandía mountains, about twenty miles east of Bernalillo, New Mexico. Lambert, *Paa-ko, New Mexico*, pp. 6-7 and 174-177.

59. At the pueblo of Santo Domingo.

60. This was the ancient province of Tiguex, made famous by the Coronado expedition. Castaño's "Memoria," unfortunately, does not name the pueblos visited, to our great disappointment.

by the inhabitants due to fear and that they had sought refuge in the mountains or in other pueblos.

The next day, when the lieutenant governor perceived the uneasiness among the natives caused by fear of what they had done, he decided to send most of his men back to the main camp, which was five or six leagues from there.[61] He himself remained behind with Martín de Salazar, Juan de Estrada, Diego de Viruega, Juan Sánchez, Diego Díaz, Andrés Pérez de Berlanga, and Juan de Contreras, hoping that with so few soldiers in their midst the Indians would overcome their fear, acquire a sense of security, and remain in their homes. In order that these hopes might be realized, the maese de campo returned to the camp, while the lieutenant governor stayed behind with his five companions.

Traveling with them up the river, he visited four pueblos, but found them all deserted, except one which seemed to contain some fifty people. He reassured the natives with kind words, gave them some small trinkets, and asked them to go and call back all the other Indians. In the meantime, the governor crossed to the opposite side of the river where still more pueblos were situated, some of which he found fully occupied, while some contained only a few people. He treated the natives generously and reassured them so convincingly that he induced large numbers to return to their pueblos. In fact, his attitude was so kind and friendly that they felt very safe, for he gave them to understand that we would not harm them at all. As a result of this treatment, we saw large numbers of Indians returning from the fields to their homes.

We spent the night in a small pueblo located in the midst of the others, although we took the precaution of posting sentries, since we were only six men. To be sure, our scanty numbers proved effective in calming the Indians, since they could see that most of our men had departed and that the lieutenant governor had only the five companions above-mentioned.

The next day we left this pueblo and went to another one, where the lieutenant governor told the people not to be afraid, since he did not intend to stay, and that they should call back the people of the pueblos where the padres were believed to have been killed. Then we traveled on to the last pueblo on this side of the river [the east bank?], a large one with many inhabitants, who received us well. We appointed

61. From this statement it would seem that these were the Indians of Puaray who had killed Fray Agustín Rodríguez and Fray Francisco López in 1582. The diarist says this was five or six leagues from Santo Domingo, about fifteen miles, or in the vicinity of the present Bernalillo.

a governor and an alcalde for it in the name of his Majesty; and we raised a large cross. This done, we continued on our way to the main camp of the expedition. When we reached a pueblo situated a league from the camp we met an Indian captain who lived there, carrying in his bosom the bowl from a silver chalice. Here the Indians said that many other Spaniards had arrived, in addition to our own forces, which pleased us all very much. The lieutenant governor asked a soldier to watch the Indian with the chalice bowl.

Traveling on, we met Juan de Carvajal, Joseph Rodríguez, and Francisco de Mancha, who were coming to notify the lieutenant governor of the arrival of Captain Juan Morlete with fifty men. The governor asked who they were, and the three soldiers named most of them; but there were none in the group from among the many men whom he had sent to Mexico and whom he was awaiting.[62] He was puzzled by the fact that the party included none of the most important people he was expecting, although he did not show his perplexity. In the afternoon he ordered that we travel at a gallop, because he wanted to enter by day the pueblo where Captain Morlete had his entire camp. Those of us who accompanied the lieutenant governor never heard him say a word beyond what has been stated. As he advanced, he was warned not to enter the pueblo, nor even to approach it, because Captain Morlete and his men were coming to arrest him. When our leader realized the situation, he asked that not a word be said, adding that if they wanted to arrest him, they were welcome to do so, although he was serving his Majesty and had ample authorization for what he was doing. If it was the king's will to have him arrested, he would gladly submit.

Accordingly, the governor accelerated his pace in order to reach his destination before dark. When he arrived at the pueblo,[63] he went to one side of the plaza while Captain Juan Morlete was passing through the center, on his way to his quarters; and as they met they greeted each other. After dismounting, the lieutenant governor walked toward Captain Juan Morlete and his men; the captain, seeing him approach, drew near with his men closely grouped about him. They greeted each other again and embraced; and then many of the others who were friends of the governor embraced him also.

When these demonstrations were over, Captain Morlete drew from his pocket a royal decree, saying that he came by order of Viceroy Don Luis de Velasco in the name of his Majesty to carry out a royal com-

62. Such as Salgado and Mederos.
63. Of Santo Domingo.

mand, which he read to him word for word. The lieutenant governor listened to the reading of the decree, and when it was finished, the captain asked him to submit to arrest. Our leader replied that he was quite willing, if that was the wish of his Majesty, for he was entirely subject to his authority. Then all of them walked to the tents, and Captain Juan Morlete gave orders that the lieutenant governor should be shackled, to which he submitted meekly. Other orders were read to him, containing provisions that concerned him, and he replied that he would obey them all since they came from his king and lord. Whereupon he took the papers, placed them on his head, and then kissed them in the presence of Juan Morlete and the men of Morlete's force and his own. All members of both contingents were greatly pleased at the humility and submissiveness shown by the lieutenant governor; and Captain Juan Morlete, observing Gaspar Castaño's meekness, honored him and treated him in the manner due his rank and merits, which gratified the soldiers of both armies.

A report of these events was drawn up and subsequently examined by the members of the Council, November 10, 1592. LICENTIATE SANTANDRÉS [Between two rubrics]

VICEROY VILLAMANRIQUE TO HIS SUCCESSOR DON LUIS DE VELASCO, FEBRUARY 14, 1590, ON THE ARREST OF LUIS DE CARVAJAL AND CASTAÑO'S RISE TO POWER[1]

IN THE KINGDOM of New León a certain Luis de Carvajal de la Cueva formerly served as governor. It was his custom to go inland with a company of evil and unscrupulous men, who would go northward to the Río Bravo and Río de Palmas, where the Indians had never seen any Spaniards nor committed any crimes. Then, like someone hunting rabbits or deer, the soldiers would seize each time from eight hundred to a thousand Indians and sell them in Mexico. Because of this practice the Indians became angered and began to resist, even to the point of stirring up the natives here to make war. The fiscal had informed the audiencia of this crime before I came. Later, after perusing this case and many others that came before me, I declared that all the Indians who might be taken should be free, and not subject to slavery, and that generally from here on the captains would not be permitted to sell the Chichimecos Indians as slaves, and I so ordered. You will find all this in the books of the secretary, Juan de Cueva.

When I had reported the matter to his Majesty, he approved, and, in section 41 of a royal letter dated in Madrid on February 18, 1588, which will be enclosed with this document, he bade me continue my course of action. My order was the principal means of bringing the Indians into their present state of peace; and because Luis de Carvajal disobeyed it he was summoned to appear before me. While he was in my presence, I instructed him not to leave the city without my permission until his case had been investigated. Paying no attention to this prohibition, he returned again to the region in question, where he once more began his criminal seizures of Indians. Moreover, not content with this, he dispatched one of his captains, Cristóbal de Heredia, accompanied by a large band of Indians drawn from the interior, with orders to take the staff of office away from the alcalde mayor in the town of Los Valles (who at that time was Pedro de Salazar Martel), and

---

1. This account is an excerpt from Viceroy Villamanrique's report of February 14, 1590, to his successor, Don Luis de Velasco, relating to Castaño de Sosa. It is in A.G.I., *Audiencia de México*, legajo 22.

to state that he was assuming possession on behalf of the aforementioned Carvajal because the town came under his jurisdiction.

Heredia obeyed these instructions and installed justices of his own, removing from office those I had appointed in the name of his Majesty. Upon hearing of this, I commanded Captain Alonso López to set forth with twenty soldiers in order to arrest Carvajal, examine the entire region, and report on the settlements that had been established in accordance with the articles of agreement concluded with his Majesty. After traversing the whole territory and scanning it with his own eyes from Tamaolipa to Mazapil, which is the portion comprising Carvajal's jurisdiction, Captain López ascertained that it held not a single settlement, aside from the fact that whenever Carvajal came to some site which seemed to him suitable for deceiving his Majesty by claiming to have complied with the agreement, he would set up four or five houses of reeds, mud, and sticks, call them a town [*villa*], appoint a justice and councilmen, abandon the site after remaining there fifteen or twenty days, and go on to repeat the performance.

Consequently, Alonso López pursued him and succeeded in arresting him at a point fifty leagues from Mazapil, in a province called Caula, where Carvajal had set up a few houses built of wooden sticks, naming the place Villa del Almadén, "Town of the Mine." While I was holding him a prisoner in Mexico, pending the conclusion of his trial (you will find the records in the hands of the secretary, Barahona), the Inquisition asked me to hand him over, explaining that he had committed the crime of heresy, and I delivered him to them in accordance with the cedula on concord.[2]

Now I have learned that while in prison he empowered a certain Gaspar Castaño to act as his lieutenant, and named various other aides, all of whom are following in his footsteps. They are stationed in the above-mentioned locality of Almadén in Caula, with more than sixty soldiers—outlaws, criminals and murderers—who practice neither justice nor piety and are raising a rebellion in defiance of God and king. These men invade the interior, seize peaceable Indians, and sell them in Mazapil, Saltillo, Sombrerete, and indeed everywhere in that region. This last fact has just come to my notice. Your Grace will make such pro-

2. Father Ernest J. Burrus, S. J., informs us that this probably has reference to an agreement or understanding between the Holy See and the Spanish Inquisition with regard to violation of the Faith, and the policy to be pursued in such cases. The agreement was frequently a source of friction, as the officials of the Spanish Inquisition were inclined to act with much independence in these matters and with even greater severity than was the case of the mother institution in Rome.

vision as you see fit for the punishment of all these malefactors and the correction of such outrageous abuses. . . . Given at Tezcuco on the fourteenth day of the month of February, 1590.

[*Endorsed:*] General observations left by the Marquis of Villamanrique for his successor, Don Luis de Velasco, viceroy of New Spain.

PART IV

INSTRUCTIONS TO CAPTAIN JUAN MORLETE FOR AN EXPEDITION TO NEW MEXICO IN PURSUIT OF GASPAR CASTAÑO DE SOSA AND HIS COMPANIONS[1]

UPON RECEIVING my letters and orders, you will take steps to recruit up to forty soldiers, the best men, with the best equipment and horses that you can find. These men shall be given one hundred and fifty pesos each, once you are assured that they will accompany you on the expedition.

You will also try to include in the company some friar who has the qualities and qualifications that you know are required for such an expedition in order to console, instruct, and set a good example for your companions, as well as for any Indians you may take along or may meet on the way.[2]

You will try to gather together all the Indians you encounter, male or female, regardless of age, who have been sold or disposed of in that region, if they came originally in any manner whatever from the kingdom of New León, and you will take them with you. You shall follow the same course of action in regard to Indians sent you from Zacatecas or any other place. While they are with you, you are to accord them the best treatment and all the comfort possible, and you will leave them along the route at the spots they recognize as their places of origin, explaining to them and other natives of the same nations and languages that your principal object in coming was to free them and restore them to their own lands, and to punish those who had troubled and injured

1. A.G.I., *Audiencia de México,* legajo 220, expediente 30-A.

2. This friar was a Franciscan, Juan Gómez. It is interesting that we find his name mentioned only in letters of Viceroy Velasco to the king, dated February 28 and May 26, 1592, and a brief reference to him in the "Asiento y capitulaciones" of Juan Bautista de Lomas y Colmenares for the settlement of New Mexico. These are printed in Pacheco and Cárdenas, *Col. Doc. Inéd.,* vol. xv, pp. 54-80.

them. You will use such good means as you can devise, and with the help of the friar taken on the expedition, you will attempt to win these natives over to peace and friendship, making clear to them that the aim of your actions is the welfare of their souls, their conversion to our holy Catholic faith, good treatment of their persons, and their enjoyment of the favor his Majesty shows his subjects.

To better attract the Indians you may meet, since the goods you have on hand are not suitable for outright distribution as gifts among them (for you know what those people are like), it will be advisable to sell the goods, converting the proceeds into small articles of little value which you can carry with you and apportion among the natives encountered, at the times and in the manner you think best.

Since you know very well how important it is to have friendly Indians, both as members of your [military] company and as guides and interpreters, you will try to take along as many as is feasible, from those who will go voluntarily, paying them a moderate fee; and what you spend for this purpose will be refunded to you on presentation of the proper accounts, such as I trust you will keep of the whole undertaking.

You know that the main purposes of your journey are these: to put a stop to the expedition planned and undertaken by Gaspar Castaño and his men in contravention of my specific order as well as the general orders of his Majesty; to check the injuries and excesses against the poor natives which have done such great disservice to God our Lord and his Majesty; and to insure the punishment of those who perpetrated the offenses, as well as giving satisfaction to the Indians for abuses already suffered and assurance that they will not be so abused in the future but will receive only wholehearted friendship and good treatment. Therefore, you will endeavor to maintain the good order, harmony, and watchfulness you know are essential, both because of the potential danger to you from the hostile Indians disturbed by Castaño and his men and because of the dangers that might result if you yourselves trusted those natives too much and belittled them. Since, as I have said, the primary purpose of this expedition is to stop Gaspar Castaño, it is important you do not come back without him and his men, using all suitable care and taking every precaution.

Bearing in mind this aim, and the fact that the members of the other expedition have several days' advantage over you, so that you might run short of provisions and be impelled to abandon our good plans, you will take all the supplies you think necessary in order that the people who accompany you may not blame you on account of shortages.

In view of the information I have received that certain evilly disposed persons, moved by greed, aided Gaspar Castaño and his men with provisions and equipment in exchange for a guarantee of repayment in slaves, and that they followed him into the interior and are still following him in order to collect this payment, you must warn everyone you meet that you will take away from them all the slaves they have seized and will return these slaves, as you proceed to the places whence they were removed or wherever they wish to go. You will also arrest the offenders, conducting the appropriate investigations and inquests to establish their guilt and bringing them back with the rest of Caspar Castaño's men, whose conduct you will likewise investigate suitably in order to ascertain the purpose of their expedition, the identity of its promoters, the persons by whose commission and advice it was undertaken, and whatever other facts you deem pertinent to the case.

You will note in all the territory through which you travel the nature and quality of the land, its climate, the places where the Indians live, whether the soil there seems productive, what kind of food they eat, what provisions they have, their occupations, whether the natives are in communication with the people we know around here, what language is generally used among them and its special characteristics, if you understand them, whether there are farmers among the natives, whether the people are industrious or lazy like the Indians here, and also the nature of the land in regard to mining prospects, so that you will be able to report to me on everything.

When by God's favor you reach Gaspar Castaño and his people, you will use every mild and prudent means you can to persuade them to give up their expedition and return with you, since that would be the best course for them. If you do so, you will bring them back in reasonable comfort; but you must always remember that you are conducting them as prisoners whose lack of conscience and evil aims you cannot trust, and you will take away their weapons from the ones you regard as especially open to suspicion. If they refuse to take advantage of the fair and mild treatment offered them, and if it becomes necessary for you to use force and arrest them, nevertheless, by proceeding in that just and mild manner, and by basing rigorous action on legal documents and injunctions to support your case, you will have executed your commission in accordance with every requirement of both mercy and justice.

When you have completed these tasks as requested, you will return with the prisoners, maintaining the necessary good order and precaution, without stopping anywhere until you have brought them before me. Throughout the return trip, you will show all possible friendliness and good treatment to the Indians under your protection, explaining to them that this laborious and costly enterprise was undertaken for the sake of their friendship and for their benefit, so that from now on they may be able to live in complete security. If any of them should wish to come back with you and appear here before me, let the persons selected be Indians of high rank. You may bring up to a dozen, so that I may show them my affection and hospitality.

At the time when you make these arrests, you will impound all goods belonging to the prisoners; and after drawing up an inventory, you will bring everything to this capital, including all their wagons. If there are women in the company of the accused, you will see to it that they are well treated and made comfortable, and that their personal decency is respected with the honor and charity I expect from you. This same kindliness and good treatment shall be shown to any children who may be in their company. In all matters, you will proceed with such prudence and moderation as you can command, qualities which I trust you to exercise.

Done in Mexico city, October 1, 1590. DON LUIS DE VELASCO [Rubric]

DON LUIS DE VELASCO TO THE KING
FEBRUARY 23, 1591[1]

Sir:

In a letter to your Majesty on October 8, 1590, I reported in detail on the situation of Governor Luis de Carvajal, his office and his administrative conduct, as well as on the efforts of a certain Gaspar Castaño (whom he had appointed as his lieutenant), in conjunction with the vagabonds who had joined him and indeed all the riffraff left over from the war against the Chichimecas, to penetrate the interior with the purpose of exploring New Mexico, a project likewise entertained by Captain Agustín de Lesaca, although the latter was acting in opposition to Castaño. I also notified you of the harm that these persons were doing to the natives by entering their lands to seize and en-

1. A.G.I., *Audiencia de México*, legajo 22.

slave them, though the victims gave no cause and were blameless, so that the whole kingdom was in turmoil.

Luis de Carvajal died ten days ago, and so the difficulties stemming from his ambitions and official status have presumably come to an end. Since his office really does not exist, and since there has been as yet no basis for establishing such a governorship, I hope that your Majesty will be pleased to give orders for its abolition and for leaving the situation as it now stands. Whenever any reason for a change does arise, I shall so inform your Majesty, in order that you may make such provisions as seem desirable; and I shall proceed in all contingencies with respect to this matter as best befits your Majesty's royal service.

After verifying the report that Gaspar Castaño had marched inland to explore New Mexico, in defiance of my written instructions and the discussions conducted with him by Captain Juan Morlete, acting in accordance with my order and commission, and since I regarded as extremely improper and injurious the damage these men were doing in capturing and selling Indians, and was mindful of the danger involved, I decided to send Captain Juan Morlete in pursuit of the malefactors. Morlete, according to the reports that I had received of him from Rodrigo del Río and others, is considered to be a trustworthy and judicious person.

I sent him with forty well-equipped soldiers and gave him the instructions herewith enclosed,[2] in the firm hope that he would bring back the men and check their activities as unobtrusively as possible, without causing scandal or disturbance. A letter from a soldier informed me that the said captain and his men had entered the land, accompanied by a Franciscan friar; that they were proceeding in good conduct and order along Castaño's trail and close behind him;[3] and that they had met some soldiers and traders returning from his force with Indian captives. These were set free by Morlete's men, with the result that the other Indians encountered along the way were reassured, came out to greet our men amicably, and remained friendly. I am awaiting the final outcome of this affair in order to inform your Majesty of it. My purpose has been to punish the disobedient, with a view to setting a good example, so essential on this occasion, and also to prevent the disturbance and unrest aroused among the natives by their en-

---

2. For Morlete's instructions dated October 1, 1590, see pp. 298-301.

3. If taken literally, this statement would indicate that Morlete's route led up the Pecos, in Castaño's footsteps. It is the only statement bearing directly on Morlete's route that we have seen, though we find it difficult to believe that he would have followed the Pecos rather than the more logical Río Grande.

slavement, so that they may be persuaded that we desire only their well-being and conversion, without seeking anything further from them.

May our Lord preserve your Catholic Majesty. Mexico, February 23, 1591. DON LUIS DE VELASCO [Rubric]

FRAGMENT OF A LETTER FROM JUAN MORLETE TO VICEROY DON LUIS DE VELASCO, JULY 25, 1591[1]

. . . very peaceful and happy, except for several deserted pueblos. It is said that the inhabitants of these pueblos fled to the mountains when Castaño and his men came to the land, since they feared that the Spaniards would harm them in revenge for the death of the friars who were killed in this region and, according to report, by the people of these very settlements. A few articles belonging to the friars have been found, such as a piece from the stem of their chalice, a book, the rack for the chalice, and some pages of a breviary. I felt keenly the lack of interpreters who would enable me to talk with the people and reassure them, but I did what I could by means of signs. The natives here speak many different languages, and there is some warfare among them.

When I reached the place where Castaño was, I found his men divided into factions, for some wanted to withdraw and abandon him, while others wished to remain. I believe that they would all have met with disaster, if your Grace had not remedied the situation, and that those who stayed would have been slaughtered by the Indians.

Throughout this whole episode and on every other occasion when I have been permitted to serve his Majesty and your Grace, certain persons have given me outstanding assistance: Father Guardian Fray Juan Gómez; Domingo Martínez de Cearreta; his son, Don Pedro; and particularly Diego Ramírez Barrionuevo, who accompanied the expedition at his own expense and without any salary, for the sole purpose of serving you. He displayed zealous good will in every way and was the first to notify your Grace and me of the plans that Castaño and

1. A.G.I., *Patronato*, legajo 22. The first part of this letter is missing.

his men had in mind. With the advice and aid of the persons above named, I found the hardships of the journey quite easy to endure. Moreover, the good teachings of the father guardian have kept us all very tranquil and calm.

From Saltillo I reported to your Grace that Captain Agustín de Lesaca likewise served you on this expedition at his own expense and without pay; that his great diligence and zeal enabled me to assemble the men for the undertaking within such a short space of time; and that he would inform you of whatever success I might achieve. Captain Lesaca was very valuable to me in every situation that arose, lending me the support in will and deed that I always expected of him; and, to give still further proof of his devotion to your service, he has decided to ride ahead in order to report on everything that happened. I beg your Grace to accept his services and to reward him as his personal achievements and zeal deserve, thereby conferring a very great favor on me.

The men I brought have done their duty and will be carried on the payroll until we reach our destination. I beg that you will order the officials to give these men their accumulated pay if the company should be disbanded in Zacatecas, for they are all very impoverished and ragged as a result of the long journey and are truly in a pitiful condition.

My company flag was used in the review I held in Saltillo, an occasion that gave it full significance. I ask your Grace's permission to carry it unfurled, if that be appropriate, wherever I conduct my men on my way to the capital; and also to display Gaspar Castaño's flag in the same manner, since I forced him to lower it and wrested it from him in your name.

The royal coffer of the kingdom of [New] León was brought to this province by Captain Castaño, who kept two of the keys in his capacity as lieutenant governor, the other being in the possession of Melchor de Pavía, whom Castaño had appointed treasurer. It was a big wooden box, made so as to be portable. I ordered it opened and an inventory made of the contents, so that they might be carried with appropriate protection. The coffer contained neither silver nor coins, nothing but the iron brands for stamping the royal fifths and twelfths, together with various papers showing that certain individuals in Saltillo and elsewhere owed money to his Majesty, either in connection with the estates of deceased persons or for other reasons involving fines payable to the treasury. An inventory of the whole was made and I had a small box constructed, ordering that the three locks and the entire contents of the large one be transferred to it. The things were packed in the small box by the aforesaid Castaño and by Pavía, who have the keys in their possession, since I instructed them to convey both keys and box to your Grace. If it should prove necessary, before I reach the capital, to take steps regarding the sums owed to his Majesty, you will so command.

I am working on the case against Gaspar Castaño and his companions, and have been engaged in this task ever since I left Saltillo. You will see from the records that their guilt is well established. I beg your Grace to send me immediate instructions as to what I am to do. . . . Río del Norte, July 25, 1591.

[*Postscript:*] The road that I am following to reach the capital is round-about, for I could go from here by another, shorter route. In order to insure an understanding, your Grace should send me, at Mazapil, in-structions as to what I must do regarding all the matters of which I have informed you. I am keeping to this route and shall complete the journey as quickly as possible.

May our Lord preserve you and your household for many years. From the Río de las Nazas, September 16, 1591. JUAN MORLETE [Rubric]

CAPTAIN CASTAÑO DE SOSA TO THE VICEROY, JULY 27, 1591[1]

OUR LORD KNOWS what grievous sorrow afflicts my heart and what shame I feel in writing this letter to your Grace, which I am unworthy to do, since I have not succeeded in serving you as my prince and master. Of all the hardships that have fallen to my lot, none has troubled me so much as the fact that I was a source of annoyance to your Grace. You may rest assured that in my conduct there has been no intent to deceive, do harm, or make trouble. I insist, as God is my witness, that if I have indeed erred I did so in sincere reliance upon authority granted by his Majesty's order to Luis de Carvajal as governor and captain general of the kingdom of New León. It was in the exercise of this authority, acting as his lieutenant, that I did the things which must have been reported to your Grace, as indicated by certain rumors heard in these parts of alleged misdeeds which never crossed my mind nor that of any

1. A.G.I., *Audiencia de México,* legajo 22.

man in my company. Even if I am in bad repute, God knows how truly zealous I am in serving your Grace and the king our Lord. You will be able to satisfy yourself on all these points when I arrive in your city, as I am more eager to do than words can say, confident that your Grace will hear my explanations and pleas.

My decision to undertake the expedition on which Captain Juan Morlete found me arose from the belief that I was empowered to make it under the authority and assurances I had received from his Majesty. Even so, while the plan was under consideration, I sent Francisco Salgado to your city, accompanied by three other men, to present my humble respects to your Grace; for I was unable to go in person at that moment, due to conditions in the land which prevented me from leaving. I felt confident that Francisco Salgado would inform you of my plans, since that was the sole purpose of his journey aside from presenting our salutations to your Grace. He asked me to set a time limit for the trip to and from the capital, and the limit was fixed at two months. When he left, I had been on the march many days, with all the equipment required for such an expedition, and I requested him to start out immediately because my men, in view of the delay, were urging me to await him at the Río Bravo for as long a period as he might need in order to go and come back with word of your Grace's decision. He assured me that if he did not return within the time specified, I might proceed confidently on my way. Although I was satisfied that you would approve my action, I refrained from setting forth when he failed to return with your reply at the end of the allotted time, so that I could be sure of doing the right thing and enabling him to reach me with his message at the place where he had left me.

At this juncture,[2] Captain Morlete arrived and told me of the orders you had given him, and your Grace will have learned how I acted in response to his report, for I understand that a certified record was made. Thus, I decided to go back and render obedience to your Grace, as it was my duty to do, but when the inhabitants, settlers, judge, and councilmen heard of my decision, they became excited and declared that if I was going to leave the land they would follow me; and in addition they besieged me with pleas and protests, all in the presence of Captain Juan Morlete. I therefore postponed my departure, with his approval, since it seemed to me that I should do better by complying with the spirit of your Grace's command than by abandoning the land, as would be necessary if I went to the capital.

2. Late in June 1590, at Almadén. See Introduction, p. 30.

Having come to this conclusion, I arranged to send another representative to present my respects to your Grace, inform you of the state of my affairs, my decision, and the reasons which made it impossible for me to return. The person sent was Alonso Ruíz, a resident of the Mazapil mining area who had come with Captain Juan Morlete. I paid him to make the trip in order to render an adequate account on my behalf; and I gave him a letter for your Grace, although I did not include a detailed statement in the letter, since the aforesaid Ruíz was to explain matters to your satisfaction. It was with this purpose that I sent him, inasmuch as he had seen all that the land held and had witnessed all the events there.

Captain Juan Morlete and Alonso Ruíz then left, the captain telling me that he, too, would report to your Grace about everything. The reason I did not wait in that same place for an answer was because circumstances forced me to depart in order to hold my people, who were beginning to leave me, and some of the Indians, too, were running away. I went on, but with the firm intention of delaying action (as I did) during the time required for the round trip to bring your Grace's order. I spent all that time in reaching the Río Bravo, some thirty or thirty-five leagues from my point of departure, while waiting for Francisco Salgado and Alonso Ruíz; and all this was done in the belief that I understood your Grace's wishes, which had to be respected and carried out, as the people with me were told and as they themselves wished. Four months passed— in fact, more than four months, because Francisco Salgado left for the capital on May 27 and Alonso Ruíz on St. John's Day [June 24]—while I stayed here in this settlement and at the Río Bravo, waiting for them until St. Francis' Day [October 4]. Then, in view of their delay and the assurance given me by Francisco Salgado, mentioned above, I decided to go on my way as I had planned. Accordingly, I pressed forward with my entire company, despite many hardships, seeking and finding a wagon route, whereby in my judgment I rendered a very considerable service to his Majesty, and also to your Grace in his name, for the consummation of the task he had entrusted to you, according to what I saw in the instructions and messages that Captain Juan Morlete brought with him.

After all these trials, God was pleased to lead me to a region where I found many pueblos. Among these settlements I discovered some mines, which was my chief aim. Moreover, during that short time, by kindness and affection, I induced the natives to pledge obedience to the king; and they received from me the protection which was their due, in conformity with his Majesty's commands. Your Grace will have an opportunity to learn about all these things if God brings us safely to your city. Although the mines thus far discovered showed very slight traces of silver in the numerous assays I made, I regard them as a source of wealth because they are rich in lead and linked with many other mines in that region, according to reliable information which I obtained by dint of great persistence and careful investigation.

While I was occupied with the search for more mines, Captain Juan Morlete arrived at the place where I had established my headquarters,[3] but he did not find me there because I was away on business befitting the service of God and the king. My people received him courteously, but immediately afterward, on the same day, I was notified that your Grace had ordered my arrest. On being informed, I hurried back to the camp where my people were and where the captain waited with his own men to arrest me. I explained to my companions and to those who brought the warning that everything was quite all right; and that, since your Grace was sending a party to arrest me, it was proper and agreeable for me to submit.

Accordingly, accompanied by all my people, I sought out Captain Morlete. We greeted each other with due courtesy, and with no comments or expressions of sentiment on my part other than the wish to obey your Grace's command. Then, feeling sure that the captain, as a discreet and valiant officer, would conduct the affair with the propriety befitting such an arrest, I asked for proof, as I or anyone else ought to have done; whereupon he took out the order he had brought, it was examined and read, and I gave myself up as a prisoner without any resistance. Now he is taking me in chains to your city, in obedience to his instructions. Although the conditions of my imprisonment are rigorous for so long a journey—since I am traveling with much difficulty, broken in strength and health, laden with a stout pair of leg irons and a chain that is very thick and heavy—yet I must be deserving of all this and more for my grievous sins. Nevertheless, Almighty God knows my innocence and the zeal I have shown, which I retain and shall always retain, in matters pertaining to the service of the king our lord.

The reason for abandoning my former settlement [of Almadén] was sufficient in my opinion, in that the mines were unprofitable and lacking in ores. Where there were any, they did not contain enough silver to pay even for the charcoal used in smelting. Surely this explanation will be believed, since we had constructed water mills, and others run by

3. At the pueblo of Santo Domingo.

mulepower, for smelting, grinding, and refining, which we would not have abandoned without cause after everything had been done so laboriously and at, God knows, what expense. This work cost me more than fifteen thousand pesos, for most of which I am in debt, aside from the many additional sums I spent on the expedition, which must amount to twenty thousand pesos, and the anxious care which I always devote to such projects. Moreover, I had in operation a farm from which I obtained many supplies. All of these things were lost because there was [no] silver, and the land was such that we could not support ourselves there without resorting to acts which would have been in a sense wrongful. That was the principal reason for abandoning the site. In addition, the settlers and other people were leaving that region, and in order to keep them with me I decided upon the course above indicated.

As for the reports that reached your Grace about slave[4] raids into peaceful eastern areas, people may well be saying that such raids and worse things, too, occurred; for who can close off portions of the open countryside? Above all, it must be remembered that anyone holding a responsible position is invariably the object of hatred and envy. I could not please everybody. It was for such reasons that these reports, and others also, were circulated. For some of us who are in these remote regions say whatever we please and whatever strikes our fancy when those in command fail to humor our whims.

In regard to this point and the whole affair, I invoke the Lord God as the sole and true judge, cognizant of everything I have done since your Grace sent me word that I must not take slaves. The few that I did take were seized in order to punish some culprits who had slain three of my Spaniards and committed a thousand other outrages and injurious acts. Your Grace can obtain information on this matter from persons who are well acquainted with all the facts, since they have been with me throughout and have shared all the hardships that every one of us has endured in this land while attempting to accomplish something that would be of service to God and his Majesty, whereby the royal revenues and power might be increased.

Now, as the result of so much labor and my own sins, I find myself abandoned and a prisoner, whereas I must admit that I had always expected to see all my earlier achievements, and this latest expedition as well, richly rewarded by his Majesty and by your Grace, acting in

4. The word is *piezas,* euphemistically used for the taking of Indians and selling them as slaves in the settled regions of Mexico. Alessio Robles, *Coahuila y Texas en la Epoca Colonial,* p. 92.

his name. In particular, it seemed to me that in this recent journey I had rendered a service important to God and the king, as I firmly believe it will some day prove to be, God willing, even though I myself merit no reward since I failed completely in the undertaking by causing trouble for your Grace and arousing your displeasure. I humbly beseech that you will pardon that failure, for the love of the One God; and I beg and implore, with all the fervor at my command, that your Grace will examine the question of my guilt, punishing me yourself if I am indeed culpable, for I do not feel that I can suffer any harm at your hands. I shall accept willingly whatever comes to me of fortune or misfortune from your Grace, once I have found my way to your presence by God's will and make known my explanations, my innocence, and the many hardships I have endured in his Majesty's service, especially those suffered in the course of discovering the route to the provinces in question.

That discovery will greatly facilitate the execution of your Grace's plan for settlement of the land, as his Majesty has urged you to do, judging by the papers brought by Captain Juan Morlete. The many things I saw in the said land indicate that this route will prove most effective in encouraging many people to go there; for I have traveled over it with wagons, and all that was reported or seen in the past is negligible in comparison with what has now been brought to light. Your Grace will receive full information on the subject when the captain and I reach the capital. Although the time allowed me was short, I believe that I accomplished a great deal, since I am never negligent in any matter relating to his Majesty's service. I have always hastened, as a loyal vassal, to discharge the tasks allotted to me; and this I shall continue to do whenever the opportunity arises and the command is given, if God wills my release from my present captivity.

I place my fate in the hands of your Grace, and not in those of jurists or attorneys, since I have no money to pay them. Accordingly, I beg and beseech you to order that all my comrades and I be brought before you with the least possible delay, for that would be a very great favor to us. I am sadly exhausted and broken in health because of the aforementioned rigorous conditions of my captivity, and therefore I beg and implore, in the name of the One God, that your Grace will command me to be conducted to you, as befits a servant of his Majesty. People will find that I am as obedient and humble now as I have always been and shall continue to be, not at all like the person pictured in the accusations heaped against me. I have made a written record of everything, and when the documents I have drawn up are seen, if your

Grace is pleased to give orders for their examination, you will be able to satisfy yourself regarding the whole affair in the light of your truly Christian charity and your zealous kindness toward those who serve his Majesty.

In this assurance, and despite all the hardships I have mentioned, I am coming to your Grace very happily in the hope that you will show me favor; and I pray God that He will grant you the long life which I, the least of your servants, desire for you.

Written on the Río del Norte route, July 27, 1591.

Noted by the members of the Council [of the Indies] on January 10, 1592. Licentiate SAN ANDRÉS.

THE AUDIENCIA OF MEXICO TO HIS MAJESTY, NOVEMBER 11, 1591[1]

NEW MEXICO has been discovered; and your viceroy has sent someone in pursuit of a certain Juan [i.e., Gaspar] Castaño and his companions, who entered the land without viceregal order or authorization. This step was taken because serious troubles arise from such expeditions into the interior, since the ill treatment suffered by the Indians on these occasions incites them to hostility and harmful acts, not to mention many other undesirable results, of which the viceroy will report fully to your majesty. All of these conditions will be avoided if the expedition is conducted in an orderly manner and with directions from the viceroy for the punishment of any person exceeding instructions or the limits of reasonable conduct.

Captain Juan Morlete, who went in pursuit of Juan [*sic*] Castaño by the viceroy's command, is bringing him back as a prisoner, but has not yet arrived; and for this reason the present report on the matter will be brief. From accounts written by the soldiers, it seems that the land is fertile, with crops of corn, beans, and cotton, and also flocks of the "chickens" native to these parts [i.e., turkeys]. When Morlete and his prisoners arrive, information based on their testimony and the certified records they bring will be sent to your Majesty at the earliest opportunity. Mexico, November 11, 1591. DOCTOR MARCOS GUERRERO [Rubric]

1. Excerpt from a report to the king by Doctor Marcos Guerrero of the audiencia of Mexico. A.G.I., *Audiencia de México,* legajo 71.

DON LUIS DE VELASCO TO THE KING
FEBRUARY 28, 1592[1]

DON LUIS DE VELASCO TO THE KING OUR LORD IN HIS ROYAL COUNCIL OF THE INDIES CONCERNING THE ARREST OF CAPTAIN CASTAÑO AND HIS MEN AND THEIR ENTRY INTO NEW MEXICO.

IN A LETTER dated November 6 of last year, I wrote to your Majesty about the situation then existing in regard to the return of Captain Juan Morlete and the arrest of Captain Gaspar Castaño and his men, all of whom have now arrived in this city. I ordered that proceedings be instituted against them, and the order has been carried out.

Moreover, other appropriate measures have been and are still being taken, and I am sending your Majesty, with this letter, copies of some of the pertinent records, so that you may better understand the circumstances in which those men were placed. They were undoubtedly in very grave danger, all the more so because they were so few in number, divided among themselves, and most of them in revolt against Castaño and eager to leave the region. Even the Indians were not enthusiastic about keeping the men in their midst, and they had grievances against Castaño and his companions of which they complained to Captain Juan Morlete.

No real success could be expected from this state of affairs, nor could these men pacify and protect the land. On the contrary, it was certain that they would meet with disaster and death, for the natives would kill them, just as they had previously killed the friars who came with a soldier named Chamuscado. I felt, and still feel, that it was most fitting and judicious to remove Castaño and his soldiers from that region; yet I also believe it would be fitting and judicious to undertake the pacification of the natives there. The attempt might prove worth while, quite aside from the service that would be rendered to our Lord through the conversion of so many natives, because they are numerous and the land has a good climate, is fertile, and produces abundant food supplies.

I have seen the articles of agreement made by the Marquis of Villamanrique with Juan Bautista de Lomas for the exploration and conquest of this region, and I am now sending a copy of them to your

1. A.G.I., *Audiencia de México*, legajo 22.

Majesty. As the marquis said that he had informed you of the trans-action, I supposed that some royal decision in the matter might have been made and was therefore waiting for it.

With reference to the said agreement, it is readily apparent that no one will care to enter into a contract for this venture without assurance of great advantages and profit, or without the aim and prospect of encomiendas and tribute from the Indians. Since the principal objective should be conversion of these natives by proper means, whereby all the other results (which may, indeed, be materially advantageous) are to be justified; since the most important requirement for such conver-sions is the outlay for the friars and religious instruction; since that outlay is to be defrayed by your Majesty even if the expedition itself is carried on at another person's expense; and since the other expendi-tures are so slight, inasmuch as these expeditions almost never involve pay for the soldiers—in view of all these considerations—I believe that the venture might best be undertaken at your Majesty's expense.

Aside from the fact that the costs would not be very high, everything would be facilitated and justified, and the faith better implanted, under the auspices of your royal name, inasmuch as the dissemination of the faith is your Majesty's sole aim, while the material profit (though it is assured and the one effect will follow upon the other) represents merely a supplementary factor. I consider it preferable for you to grant such favors as you may choose to the persons who have served and aided you well after the gains are achieved, and in order that they may be pre-served, rather than that you should make the grants now, without know-ing what is being given away, lest the gift exceed the value of the grant due. Thus, I have decided to suspend the expedition until your Majesty has ordered an investigation of the matter and made such provisions as may suit your pleasure, for I consider this delay to be less objectionable than the many difficulties that occur to me as probable results of an at-tempt to avoid expense by extending your hand to someone who per-chance stretches out his own for purposes of self-interest but withdraws it when the purpose is the service of God and your Majesty.

Father Juan Gómez, who made the journey in the company of Captain Juan Morlete, will appear before your Majesty to present an account of it, in addition to what I have mentioned. After you have heard his account, you will be pleased to issue the appropriate instruc-tions. I myself regard this cause as a very godly undertaking and one which, according to the reports received, may prove advantageous to the royal crown.

Antonio de Castro, former secretary to the Marquis of Villamanrique and son-in-law of Juan Bautista de Lomas (with whom the marquis made the agreement for the said expedition), has asked me to support his proposal, as will be seen from his petition and papers, which he wishes to submit to your Majesty. I have deferred answering until I receive your reply, for the reasons indicated above. He has complete, attested records. My opinion is that the expedition calls for a person of high quality, of an age capable of hard work, with a deeply Christian spirit and a character commanding the respect of his followers. Your Majesty will give orders for the measures best suited to your service.

Father Fray Juan Gómez, who has come from New Mexico, will not be able to leave until this year's fleet sails. May God preserve the person of your Catholic Majesty. Mexico city, February 28, 1592. Don Luis de Velasco [Rubric]

[*Endorsed:*] Find the papers mentioned in this letter and bring it together with them. [Rubric]

[*Note:*] Deliver all these papers at once to Licentiate San Andrés so that he may report on them next Monday. [Rubric]

DON LUIS DE VELASCO TO THE KING
MAY 26, 1592[1]

Letter from Don Luis de Velasco to the King our Lord in his royal Council of the Indies, concerning the progress of the legal proceedings against Captain Gaspar Castaño and his men.

In previous letters to your Majesty, and particularly in one dated February 28 of this year which was sent with the second dispatch boat, I informed your Majesty of developments in the exploration of New Mexico, an undertaking begun in earlier years by Francisco Sánchez Chamuscado, and also of my orders for the arrest and return of Captain Castaño, with other soldier companions, because they had made an expedition into that same territory without my permission, acting solely on the captain's authority. In the aforesaid letter of February 28, I reported quite fully to your Majesty on this point, and I have nothing

---

1. A.G.I., *Audiencia de México,* legajo 22.

new to relate on the subject aside from the fact that the trial of the men above-mentioned is in process before this audiencia and has reached the stage where evidence is being presented. When the case is concluded and sentence is passed, I shall forward a transcript of proceedings, if it seems to be needed, so that your Majesty may have proof of the defendants' guilt and learn of their experiences during the expedition.

I also sent your Majesty the articles of agreement made by the Marquis of Villamanrique during his term as viceroy of New Spain with Juan Bautista de Lomas, resident and miner of the Las Nieves mines. They deal with the exploration and pacification of that same region of New Mexico, of which Lomas seeks to be appointed captain general. I have indicated my opinion in this connection and await your reply in order to proceed with the matter according to the instructions you may be pleased to issue.

[Marginal notation:] *Bring whatever answer there is on this subject.* [Rubric] *A reply has now been sent.*

In the same letter of February 28, I wrote to your Majesty that Father Fray Juan Gómez would sail with the fleet and give you an eyewitness account of the nature of the territory and its inhabitants, the said father being a Franciscan who went to that land of New Mexico with Captain Juan Morlete, to whom I had entrusted the task of arresting Captain Castaño and his comrades. It seemed best to Father Gómez's religious superiors, however, that he should not make the voyage [to Spain], and they have assigned this task to Father Fray Esteban de Alzúa, custodian of the province in question, a prudent and honorable friar who will provide you with information based on the reports he is taking with him.

Although first place should be given to members of the Franciscan order because they were the earliest preachers of the gospel in the regions concerned, I consider it advisable, if this entry of New Mexico is to be undertaken, that members of all religious orders should participate. In view of the reputedly large population of that territory, there will be work enough for all, and particularly for persons of the Jesuit order, who have a special gift and teaching method for the religious instruction and education of the young.

[Marginal notation:] *Satisfactory; and for the time being, until the land is explored further and settled, it will suffice to send members of the Franciscan order, especially barefooted Franciscans, if any of that group can be found.* [Rubric]

Thus far, those who have entered New Mexico have gone northwest, as far as thirty-seven degrees. Gutierre de Miranda, governor of Florida, writes me that the English settlement on that coast is situated in the same latitude, from east to west, as New Mexico, and that the distance between the two regions, though not actually known, is not thought to be great. Once entrance by this route has been undertaken, explorations can be attempted; if the road [from Florida to New Mexico] is not long, the route will be important for many purposes that may be achieved by this means.

[Marginal notation:] *This step will be very appropriate at the proper time.* [*Rubric*]

May God preserve the person of your Catholic Majesty. Mexico city, May 26, 1592. DON LUIS DE VELASCO [Rubric]

THE KING TO THE AUDIENCIA
OF NEW SPAIN, JANUARY 17, 1593[1]

TO THE AUDIENCIA OF NEW SPAIN, INSTRUCTING THAT BODY TO CONDUCT LEGAL PROCEEDINGS AGAINST GASPAR CASTAÑO AND OTHER CULPRITS ON CHARGES OF HAVING ENTERED NEW MEXICO AND DELIVERED CERTAIN INDIANS INTO SLAVERY WITHOUT ANY ORDER OR PERMIT TO DO SO; AND ALSO ORDERING THOSE INDIANS WHOM IT FINDS ENSLAVED TO BE SET FREE, AND PROHIBITING THE ENSLAVEMENT OF ANY OTHERS.

TO THE PRESIDENT and judges of the royal audiencia in the city of Mexico, New Spain: I have been informed that Gaspar Castaño, former lieutenant of Captain Luis de Carvajal, governor of the kingdom of New León, marched into New Mexico with a company of soldiers recruited on his own authority, without any order or permit to do so; and that when the viceroy learned about these men and their many disorderly activities, which included the delivery of certain Indians into slavery, you sent Captain Juan Morlete in pursuit of the evildoers, with the result that he entered the said land of New Mexico and brought back Captain Gaspar Castaño and his men under arrest. Since it is fitting that such disobedience and impudence be punished, I hereby

---

1. A.H.N.M., *Reales Cédulas, Duplicados*, vol. II, p. 331. Reproduced in C. W. Hackett, *Hist. Docs. relating to New Mexico* . . . , vol. I, pp. 218-219, and in V. Alessio Robles, *Francisco de Urdiñola y el Norte de la Nueva España* (1931), pp. 166-167.

command you to bring to trial the aforesaid Gaspar Castaño, with the other culprits, and to proceed against them in accordance with the law. Furthermore, you shall neither encourage nor permit the enslavement of any Indians whatsoever, and if you hear of any who have been made slaves you shall set them free, with proclamations by the town crier throughout that city and in Guadalajara, New Galicia. Dated at Madrid, January 17, 1593. I, THE KING. By order of the king our lord. JUAN BÁSQUEZ.

THE SENTENCE IMPOSED
ON CASTAÑO DE SOSA, MARCH 5, 1593[1]

I, NICOLÁS ESCOTO, notary of his Majesty's criminal court in the royal audiencia and chancellery of New Spain, hereby certify that a criminal case was brought and tried before the judges of the said royal audiencia between Licentiate Herber del Corral, formerly his Majesty's fiscal in the audiencia, on the one side, and Captain Gaspar Castaño de Sosa, with Diego de Paz as his attorney, on the other. The charges against the defendant were invasion of lands inhabited by peaceable Indians, raising troops, entry into the provinces of New Mexico, and other acts cited as cause and reason in the proceedings of the said criminal case, in regard to which the above-mentioned judges pronounced a definitive sentence as set forth below:

"In the criminal case between Herber del Corral, his Majesty's fiscal in this royal audiencia, on the one hand, and Captain Gaspar Castaño de Sosa, with Diego de Paz as his attorney, on the other, the charges against the defendant being invasion of lands inhabited by peaceable Indians, raising troops, entry into the provinces of New Mexico, and other acts cited in the suit:

"We find that, by reason of the guilt proved against the said Captain Gaspar Castaño in these proceedings, we should and do condemn him to exactly six years of exile from the jurisdiction of New Spain, during which period he shall serve his Majesty in the Philippine islands, with salary, performing such duties as may be assigned to him by the governor of the Philippines, receiving his pay from this city like the other

1. A.G.I., *Audencia de México*, legajo 113.

soldiers, and liable to the death penalty if he defaults from that service. By this definitive sentence we so rule, ordering that it be executed, with costs, and that the decision shall not be subject to appeal.

"Licentiate Saavedra Valderrama; Doctor Santiago de Vera; Licentiate Don Francisco Tello."

In the city of Mexico, on the 13th of February, 1593, the judges of the royal audiencia of New Spain pronounced, in open court, the definitive sentence set forth above. Nicolás Escoto.

On behalf of the above-mentioned Gaspar Castaño an appeal was presented, adducing certain grounds for revocation of this sentence. For the purpose of determining whether the appeal should be admitted, orders were given to provide the aforesaid fiscal with a copy of it; the fiscal submitted an answer; it was ordered that the record of proceedings be exhibited; and, after examining this record, the judges issued a decree, to which they affixed their rubrics, in the following terms:

"In the city of Mexico, on March 5, 1593, having examined the criminal proceedings and the rulings in the suit between Licentiate Herber del Corral, his Majesty's fiscal in this royal audiencia, on the one hand, and Captain Gaspar Castaño de Sosa (detained in the royal prison of the capital), with Diego de Paz as his attorney, on the other, the charges against the defendant being invasion of lands inhabited by peaceable Indians, entry into New Mexico in defiance of the pertinent prohibition, and the raising of troops, the judges of the royal audiencia of New Spain, in consideration of that clause of the fiscal's plea which requests dismissal of the appeal lodged by the aforementioned Captain Gaspar Castaño with respect to the sentence originally pronounced against him, inasmuch as the sentence in itself precluded the right of appeal and should be duly observed and executed,

"HAVE ORDERED AND DO ORDER that the said sentence be obeyed and executed, in substance and in form, and that in fulfillment thereof the said Captain Gaspar Castaño be handed over to Captain Felipe de Sámano, who shall take him away, as provided by the sentence, on the ship now ready to set sail for the Philippine islands; and they also ordered that this decision be recorded in a formal instrument."

On the said day of the said month and year the decision set forth in the foregoing instrument was handed down. NICOLÁS ESCOTO.

In order to place the matter on record, I have given this certification in accordance with the facts clearly stated above and reflected in the proceedings and judicial orders of the aforesaid suit. Done in Mexico, October 7, 1593.

The record is true and exact; its collation and correction were witnessed by Lorenzo Alvarez Ortuño and Nicolás Menéndez, residents of Mexico.

Wherefore I have affixed my rubric and signature, in witness of the truth. NICOLÁS ESCOTO.

[*Endorsed:*] There are no charges. [Rubric]

DON LUIS DE VELASCO TO THE KING
OCTOBER 4, 1593[1]

37. IN LETTERS dated November 6, 1591, and February 28 and June 15, 1592, I sent your Majesty detailed information concerning New Mexico and the quite sufficient reasons for removing Captain Castaño and his men from that region. Since then, his case has been decided, and you will find enclosed a copy of the sentence. Under its terms, he was taken to the Philippines, and thus we prevented the growth of obstacles to the exploration and pacification of New Mexico which might have resulted from his continued presence in New Galicia and the kingdom of New León.

I am engaged in preparations and negotiations designed to facilitate the undertaking in New Mexico and to lessen the drain upon the royal treasury. Nevertheless, to avoid a contract with such outrageous conditions as those asked by Juan Bautista de Lomas, some expense may be unavoidable, such as the cost of the friars who will take part in the expedition, since your Majesty invariably provides whatever is needed for them in such explorations. I am making arrangements for the speedy execution of this project with the least possible expense to the royal treasury, and I shall keep your Majesty informed of developments. Mexico, October 4, 1593. DON LUIS DE VELASCO [Rubric]

1. Paragraph 37 of Viveroy Velasco's long letter to the king, dated October 4, 1593. A.G.I., *Audiencia de México,* legajo 22.

THE AUDIENCIA OF NEW SPAIN
TO HIS MAJESTY, OCTOBER 26, 1594[1]

WE RECEIVED another royal decree from Madrid, dated January 17, 1593, whereby we were commanded to proceed against Gaspar Castaño and the rest of the culprits charged with invading the land known as New Mexico and delivering certain Indians into slavery without any order or permit; and we were also commanded to arrange for the liberation of such natives as were found to be slaves, and to prohibit the enslavement of any others.

With respect to these points, the situation is as follows: Gaspar Castaño was tried in criminal court for the abuses above-mentioned and condemned to serve your Majesty in the Philippine islands for a period of six years; the sentence was carried out and he was sent to the said islands; your decree was published and proclaimed; and we will take pains to see that it is observed and enforced in regard to the liberation of Indians found in slavery. DON LUIS DE VELASCO [Rubric]; LICENTIATE SAAVEDRA VALDERRAMA [Rubric]; LICENTIATE ANTONIO MALDONADO [Rubric]; DR. EUGENIO DE SALAZAR [Rubric]; DR. SANTIAGO DEL RIEGO [Rubric]; LICENTIATE DON FRANCISCO TELLO [Rubric]; LICENTIATE DON JUAN DE FONSECA [Rubric].

1. Excerpt from a report of the audiencia of Mexico to the king. A.G.I., *Audiencia de México*, legajo 22. The cedula referred to appears on p. 316.

PART V

ACCOUNT GIVEN BY AN INDIAN
OF THE FLIGHT OF LEYVA AND HUMAÑA
FROM NEW MEXICO[1]

AT THE PUEBLO of San Juan Bautista, New Mexico, on February 16, 1599, Don Juan de Oñate, governor and captain general, leader, colonizer, and pacifier of these kingdoms for the king our lord, said that he had received information that Jusepe, an Indian, a former servant of Antonio Gutiérrez de Humaña, had fled from his service and was now in this pueblo, and therefore he ordered the following inquiry so as to learn from him what he had seen and what places he had visited with Antonio Gutiérrez de Humaña, and also what information he had gathered, in order that all of this could be brought to the attention of the king our lord, his royal councils, and others. DON JUAN DE OÑATE. Before me, JUAN VELARDE, secretary.

Witness: At the pueblo of San Juan Bautista, New Mexico on February 16, 1599, his lordship, the governor, ordered an Indian to appear before him. With the help of Juan de Caso Barahona, interpreter on this expedition, he said that his name was Jusepe Gutiérrez and that he was a native of Culhuacán.[2] He took his oath by God our Lord and a cross in due legal manner and promised to tell the truth.

On being questioned in regard to the above inquiry, he said that approximately six years ago, a Spaniard named Antonio Gutiérrez de Humaña spoke to him at his own pueblo and took him away under an agreement whereby he was to serve him in some entradas that he was going to make. Accordingly he followed Humaña as far as the valley of Santa Bárbara, where some people were recruited. With these forces he entered this land and traveled among the pueblos for about a year, the greater part of his time being spent at the pueblo of San Ildefonso, which lies about three leagues from this pueblo. From there they went inland through the pueblos of the Pecos and Vaquero Indians where, traveling slowly and resting occasionally, they reached the buffalo in a month. Here at various places they came upon herds of buffalo, and

1. Translated from a copy in A.G.I., *Patronato*, legajo 22. The document was also included in Hammond and Rey's *Oñate, Colonizer of New Mexico*, pp. 416-419, with slight variations. This declaration of the Indian Jusepe was made at San Juan on February 16, 1599. Cf. Bolton, *Spanish Exploration in the Southwest*, pp. 200-201; and also *Oñate, Colonizer of New Mexico*, pp. 746-760, for Oñate's expedition to this same region.

2. About fifty miles north of the city of Mexico.

Indian rancherías, some of them uninhabited. Along their route they saw also many marshes, springs, and arroyos with abundant water.

Proceeding on their way in a northerly direction, the farther inland they went, the larger was the number of buffalo they saw. After traveling for fifteen days more by short marches, they reached two large rivers, and beyond them many rancherías with a large number of inhabitants. Farther on, in a plain, they came to a very large settlement[3] which must have extended for ten leagues, because they traveled through it for two days, and it must have been two leagues wide, more or less. One of the two rivers they crossed earlier flowed through this pueblo. The houses were built on frames of poles, covered with straw, like *jacales* (huts or tepees?). They were built close together, along narrow streets, like alleys. However, in some places between the houses there were fields of corn, calabashes, and beans. The natives were very numerous but received the Spaniards peacefully and furnished them abundant supplies of food. These Indians obtained their livelihood from the buffalo.

On leaving this pueblo and proceeding in a northerly direction, after three days' travel the soldiers came upon such a multitude of buffalo that the plain—which was level, for there are no mountains of any kind—was so covered with them that they were startled and amazed at the sight. Continuing farther on they could not see any more Indian rancherías, but only the usual number of buffaloes. This witness says that after they left the pueblo of Pecos they found great numbers of plum trees at five or six places and that they resembled the plum trees of Castile. They found also walnut trees with small nuts. Near a large river some ten days' travel from the said Great Pueblo there were numerous plum, walnut, and some white sapodilla trees. The climate here was more temperate. This river was about one-fourth of a league wide, deep and sluggish. They did not dare to cross it.

This deponent saw that after going three days beyond the said Great Pueblo, discord arose between Captain Leyva and Antonio Gutiérrez de Humaña. The latter remained alone in his tent an entire afternoon and morning, writing, and at the end of this time he sent a soldier named Miguel Pérez to call Captain Leyva, who came, dressed in shirt and breeches. Before he reached the tent, Antonio Gutiérrez de Humaña went out to meet him, drew a butcher knife from his pocket, unsheathed it, and stabbed Captain Leyva twice, from which he soon afterward died. He was buried at once. Then Antonio Gutiérrez de Humaña

---

3. This is clearly the same settlement that Oñate and his men reached on their expedition to Quivira in 1601, in search of rich, new kingdoms, *Oñate, Colonizer, op. cit.*, p. 752.

brought out some papers and showed them to the other men. This witness heard that because Captain Leyva had said that he was going to give Antonio Gutiérrez de Humaña a sound beating with a stick, he killed him. When some Indians who were with the soldiers saw this, five of them, together with this witness, ran away when they reached the aforesaid great river and returned to these pueblos of New Mexico. Some of them became lost on the plains of the buffalo because they got separated from one another. Only this witness and another man found their way to an Indian ranchería, where they killed his companion. This witness escaped, and in another ranchería nearer this place he was taken prisoner and remained there for a year with the Apache and Vaquero Indians. Then he fled and reached a place near a pueblo of the Pecos. There he heard that Spanish people had come to these pueblos, and so he came to this pueblo, where he now resides.

This is what happened, under his oath. He ratified his testimony when it was read to him. The general questions of the law did not apply to him other than that he had been a servant of Antonio Gutiérrez de Humaña. This fact did not prevent him from telling the truth, which he did, nor was he coached by anyone. He did not know his age, but appeared to be twenty-seven years old. He did not sign because he did not know how. This statement was signed by his lordship and the interpreter. DON JUAN DE OÑATE. JUAN DE CASSO. Before me, JUAN VELARDE, secretary.

Decree: After the aforesaid, Governor Don Juan de Oñate, having examined the account that Vicente de Zaldívar had made for him of his trip to the buffalo country in which he told of finding the stopping places of Leyva and Antonio de Humaña, ordered the sargento mayor and others who made the journey with him to declare how many camp sites of these men they had come across and how far from these headquarters they had found them.[4] So he decreed and signed. JUAN DE OÑATE. Before me, JUAN VELARDE, secretary.

Witness: Then, on February 17, 1599, his lordship, the governor, ordered to appear before him the sargento mayor, Vicente de Zaldívar, Diego de Zubia, purveyor general, the caudillo, Francisco Sánchez, and Hernando de Ynojos, all of whom took an oath by God our Lord and a cross in due legal manner and promised to tell the truth. On being questioned regarding this inquiry, they agreed unanimously that the

4. In 1598, Vicente de Zaldívar with a party of about sixty captains and soldiers, had set out from San Juan to explore the buffalo country and to capture some of these animals. On the way, they found some of the camping places of Leyva and Humaña. See *Oñate, Colonizer, op. cit.,* pp. 398-405. Bolton, *op. cit.,* pp. 223-232.

governor had sent them from these headquarters to the buffalo country in September of the preceding year, 1598; that the first campsite of the said Leyva and Antonio de Humaña which they encountered was some twenty-four leagues beyond, more or less, and that at about thirty-six leagues they came upon another known stopping place. These were thought to be the places used by Captain Leyva and Antonio de Humaña, which they learned by questioning a former servant of the latter, one who had accompanied their party as guide and interpreter, and by finding horse dung and remains of their fires.

This is what they saw and learned, under their oath. They reaffirmed their deposition, and those who knew how affixed their names. DON JUAN DE OÑATE. VICENTE DE ZALDÍVAR. DIEGO DE ZUBIA. Before me, JUAN VELARDE, secretary.

Corrected and compared with the original by order of the governor [who here signed his name]. Copied at the pueblo of San Juan Bautista, New Mexico, on February 20, 1599. Witness: ALONSO NÚÑEZ, CRISTÓBAL DE HERRERA, and CRISTÓBAL GUILLÉN. In testimony of which I affixed my name and the seal of his lordship. JUAN VELARDE, secretary.

INDEX

INDEX

Mazapil: mining area, 40, 42, 297, 301, 305, 307

Mecham, J. Lloyd: cited, 4n, 5n, 8n, 14n, 17n, 51n, 53, 121n

Mederos, Manuel: Castaño's agent, 30, 33, 42, 247, 249, 294n

Medina de la Torre: pueblo, 57, 62, 105, 114

Menéndez, Nicolás: witness, 319

Men of Fame, The Nine: 68

Mera, H. P.: cited, 9, 51, 52, 59n, 60, 81n, 102n, 175n

Mesa, La: 62, 107

Mesa Prieta: 181n

Mescalero Apaches: 35

Mesilla valley: 46

Mesquital, El: 156, 207, 208

Metate: 102

Mexicalcingo: pueblo, 62, 103, 116

Mexico, Audiencia of: to king, 311; king to audiencia, 316-317

Miguel: interpreter with Castaño, 245-246, 273

Milpa Llana, La: pueblo, 179

Milpas, Las: 46

Mines: reports of, 5, 110, 114, 124, 132, 133, 138, 143, 145, 157, 168, 170-171, 176, 184, 193-198, 215, 222, 223, 227-228, 248, 279, 289, 308-309

Miranda, Alonso de: with Espejo, 153, 177, 186, 194, 199, 201, 214, 226

Miranda, Gutierre de: 315

Mishiptonga: pueblo ruin, 188n, 192n

Mishóngnovi: Espejo at, 192n

Missionaries: with Chamuscado, 68, 69, 75, 77, 98-99; remain in New Mexico, 109, 124, 127; with Espejo, 153-154, 213, 214

Mitotes: see *Dances*

Mohino: Concho locality, 156

Mohoce (Mohose, Mojose): Hopi province, 23, 24, 178, 185, 186, 189, 226

Mojarra: a fish, 208, 209

Moluccas: Castaño killed in, 48

Monclova: 29, 245

Monterrey, Count of: 115, 120, 153, 212

Montezuma's well: 197n

Moqui: see *Mohoce*

Morlete, Juan: sent to arrest Castaño, 30, 40-45, 63, 294-295; instructions to, 298-301; expedition of, 39-48, 298-322; route of, 302, 306; letter of, to viceroy, 303-305

Mormon lake: 25, 196n

Mosquitero: on the Pecos, 207, 208

Mount Taylor: 23, 26, 182n

Moxonami: see *Mishóngnovi*

Moya de Contreras, Pedro: Inquisitor, Espejo with, 16, 27n, 67n, 240n

Mulligan gulch: 81, 102n

Muñoz de Espejo, Pedro: see *Espejo, Pedro*

Museum of New Mexico: 51, 177n

N

Nadadores river: 246

Nambé pueblo: 37, 281n

Na-mo-sse: Hopi cacique, 194

Narváez, Pánfilo de: 217

Navajo Indians: 23; identified with Querechos, 182n

Nazas river: 305

Negro: with Castaño, 255

Nelson, Nels C.: cited, 39n, 55, 60, 287n, 288n

New Almadén: see *Almadén*

New Andalusia: name applied to New Mexico, 183, 213, 232, 234

New Galicia: 4; audiencia of, 150

New León: 28, 40, 245, 298, 304

New Mexico: named, 67, 149, 174; conquest of, planned, 319

New Vizcaya: 5, 68, 221, 231

Nieves, Las: mines, 315

Nocoche: pueblo, 203

Nompe: pueblo, 104, 117

Nuestra Señora de la Concepción, Valle de: 74, 76, 77

Nueva Tlaxcala: New Mexico so called, 58, 59, 60, 106, 118, 130n, 135

Núñez, Alonso: 326

O

Oalpes (Walpi): 190n, 194

Obregón, Baltasar: cited, 8, 9, 18, 21, 53, 88n, 153n, 159n, 162n, 184n, 165n, 174n, 180n, 181n, 198n, 200n, 232n

Ojo Caliente: Zuñi village, 186n

Ojo Hediondo: Espejo camping place, 188

Ojo Triste: on Espejo's route, 195

Ojos Zarcos: pools, 91

Oklahoma: Coronado in, 11

Olalla: see *Oraibi*

Onala: Hopi cacique, 194

Oñate, Juan de: 19, 28, 47, 49, 58, 63, 323, 325, 326; Ytinerario of, 51; inscription of, on El Morro, 183n

Ontiveros, Juan de: grants permit to Espejo, 18, 214

Oraibi: 25, 192n, 193

Oroz, Fray Pedro: to king, 236